Thirteen Charges
Against Benedict Arnold

Thirteen Charges Against Benedict Arnold

*The Accusations of Colonel John Brown
Prior to the Act of Treason*

ENNIS DULING

McFarland & Company, Inc., Publishers
Jefferson, North Carolina

LIBRARY OF CONGRESS CATALOGUING-IN-PUBLICATION DATA

Names: Duling, Ennis, 1947– author.
Title: Thirteen charges against Benedict Arnold : the accusations of Colonel John Brown prior to the act of treason / Ennis Duling.
Description: Jefferson, North Carolina : McFarland & Company, Inc., Publishers, 2021 | Includes bibliographical references and index.
Identifiers: LCCN 2021030882 | ISBN 9781476684918 (paperback : acid free paper) ∞
ISBN 9781476643601 (ebook)
Subjects: LCSH: Arnold, Benedict, 1741-1801,—Trials, litigation, etc. | Courts-martial and courts of inquiry—United States—History—18th century. | United States—History—Revolution, 1775-1783—Law and legislation. | Brown, John, 1744-1780.
Classification: LCC KF7642.A77 D85 2021 | DDC 343.73/0143—dc23
LC record available at https://lccn.loc.gov/2021030882

BRITISH LIBRARY CATALOGUING DATA ARE AVAILABLE

**ISBN (print) 978-1-4766-8491-8
ISBN (ebook) 978-1-4766-4360-1**

© 2021 Ennis Duling. All rights reserved

No part of this book may be reproduced or transmitted in any form or by any means, electronic or mechanical, including photocopying or recording, or by any information storage and retrieval system, without permission in writing from the publisher.

Front cover: Colonel Benedict Arnold, March 26, 1776 (Library of Congress)

Printed in the United States of America

*McFarland & Company, Inc., Publishers
Box 611, Jefferson, North Carolina 28640
www.mcfarlandpub.com*

Table of Contents

Preface	1
Introduction: "I beg your Honour will order Brigadier-General Arnold in arrest"	3
One—"An intimate correspondence and connection"	7
Two—"An able counsellor, full of spirit and resolution"	17
Three—"He would not be second in command to any person"	28
Four—"Now, Sir, is the time to carry Canada"	38
Five—"The only field officer of any share of abilities"	45
Six—"A march not to be paralleled in history"	53
Seven—"I will have an eclaircissement with him"	67
Eight—"Mr. General Arnold & I do not agree very well"	74
Nine—"Some strange kind of conduct in General Arnold"	87
Ten—"Received much abuse from General Arnold"	100
Eleven—"I wish he may be as prudent as he is brave"	109
Twelve—"And every man of common sense"	118
Thirteen—"Sir, you are a dirty scoundrel"	128
Fourteen—"An army flushed with victory"	139
Fifteen—"The mighty army of the continent"	152
Sixteen—"The greatest conquest ever known"	161
Seventeen—"Give a thief a length of rope"	172
Eighteen—"Ah! hapless friend, permit the tender tear"	185
Conclusion: "A few gentlemen became acquainted with his true character"	193

*Appendix: John Brown's Thirteen Charges Against
  Benedict Arnold and Related Letters* 199
Chapter Notes 203
Bibliography 221
Index 231

Preface

Many years ago during a summer home from college, I first read Kenneth Roberts's historical novels *Arundel* and *Rabble in Arms*. I recall sitting on my parents' front porch in the little city where the Continental Army retreated after the defeat at Brandywine. In two thick books, Roberts makes a case that, despite his treason, Benedict Arnold was a great hero of the American Revolution. One character listed Arnold's qualities: "observation, right judgment, quickness, leadership, determination, energy, and courage."

I knew I was reading fiction, not primary source material that had somehow become a bestseller in the twentieth century, but I wanted Roberts's Benedict Arnold to be the genuine article. There is something special in believing you have inside knowledge. The historical figure everyone knows as a traitor was once a leading patriot who did as much as anyone to establish American independence. Since then, I have read biographies and histories, bursting with citations, in which Arnold the soldier ranks second only to George Washington.

Long before Arnold betrayed the American cause, he was accused of misconduct by an officer with the name of John Brown. I first heard of Brown in a biography of Arnold. I don't remember which; they all agree that Brown made wild, false charges. In this storyline, Brown and men like him pushed a patriot hero to the edge of treason.

Soon, however, I met Brown under other circumstances. My interest is in Vermont history and the history of the American Revolution on Lake Champlain and in Canada. In the primary documents I began to study, Brown appeared as a determined, but sensible man, an active politician and soldier, and someone who worked well with others. The contradictions between what I read in history books and what I learned from original documents could not have been more striking.

No book-length study has previously featured John Brown or investigated his accusations. The present work, *Thirteen Charges Against Benedict Arnold*, can be read as Brown's biography, but it is his life wrapped in a controversy. This book does not pretend to be a birth-to-death biography of Arnold—we may have too many of them already—but it digs deeper where it matters, and the results are often surprising. Far from making absurd charges, Brown raised issues that should have been investigated at the time.

The early research that became *Thirteen Charges* was done in a college library. My thanks go to the librarians at Castleton State College (now Castleton University), especially Franny Ryan, interlibrary loan librarian. Thanks also go to librarians at major universities who entrusted valuable pieces of their collection to me.

I was encouraged in my research by fellow members on the board of the Mount Independence Coalition, the friends group that supports the Vermont historic site on Lake Champlain. Special thanks go to Stephen Zeoli, Ron Morgan, and site director Elsa Gilbertson.

I wrote much of *Thirteen Charges* from 2018 into 2020 while the country was focused on the testimony of whistleblowers and whether evidence against a corrupt president should be heard. Throughout, *Thirteen Charges* raises a question that is relevant today: how did military and civilian leaders fail to understand a genuine threat, even when it was pointed out to them by a smart, assertive patriot? *Thirteen Charges* is an account of deceit and misconduct—and prominent leaders and writers who were beguiled by exciting myths.

Introduction

"I beg your Honour will order Brigadier-General Arnold in arrest"

On December 1, 1776, nearly four years before Benedict Arnold attempted to hand West Point to the British, a thirty-two-year-old officer and attorney confronted General Horatio Gates at his headquarters in Albany and demanded Arnold's arrest. The accuser was John Brown of Pittsfield, Massachusetts. The *of Pittsfield* is essential. John Brown *of Providence*, Rhode Island, was a leading merchant, slave trader, and patriot, who in 1772 instigated the burning of the British customs schooner *Gaspee*. Massachusetts Revolutionary War records list 190 soldiers and sailors named John Brown. At least twenty men with that name fought at Saratoga in the decisive battles in the north.[1] And then there is the question from people with a vague understanding of U.S. history: *Didn't he start the Civil War?*

The nineteenth-century Pittsfield town history describes John Brown as "a young lawyer of commanding talents, of noble personal appearance, well connected, and withal, a true man"—but it is the nature of local histories to say such things.[2] There is no doubt he was energetic and clever, able to tell a joke or launch a persuasive argument. He had a strong sense of justice and was not a man to be intimidated by a major general. He had worked closely with Samuel Adams and the two most famous early casualties of the war, Dr. Joseph Warren and General Richard Montgomery. He was litigious and quick to defend his honor. He could be a good friend and was remembered with affection by many.

Although Brown is unknown today, that was not the case during the Revolution. In March 1775, he represented the Province of Massachusetts in Canada. In May of that year, he helped seize Fort Ticonderoga and then carried news of the victory to the Continental Congress in Philadelphia. In the fall campaign in Canada, he gained a reputation by capturing the old French fort at Chambly and seizing eleven British vessels on the St. Lawrence River. During the winter, he led a patched-together regiment from northwestern New England at the siege of Québec. In September 1777, he raided British-held Ticonderoga, taking captives, freeing prisoners, and burning boats. Three years later, he died fighting in the Mohawk Valley.

Beginning in the spring of 1776, Brown demanded a hearing on accusations made by Benedict Arnold that he had plundered the property of captured British officers. First, he complained to his superiors in Canada, but they were faced with greater problems. In the early summer of 1776, he took his case to the Continental Congress, but was referred to Major General Philip Schuyler in Albany, who sent him to General Gates at Ticonderoga, who put the issue on hold. The forts on Lake Champlain were threatened; Arnold and a small fleet were patrolling the wide lake to the north.

Brown began his quest for vindication with a demand that he himself be court-martialed on Arnold's charges. He believed that a trial would exonerate him and reveal Arnold as dishonorable. Finally, he called for Arnold's arrest. It was a bold legal maneuver that may have been doomed from the start. Although disliked by many officers, Arnold occupied a unique place in the military of the new nation. He was viewed as the most aggressive commander in the Continental Army, and even his defeats were seen as establishing the courage of the new nation.

Gates had already expressed his view on the many charges against Arnold. "To be a man of honour, and in an exalted station, will ever excite envy in the mean and undeserving. I am confident the Congress will view whatever is whispered against General Arnold as the foul stream of that poisonous fountain, detraction."[3]

Historians have searched for an explanation of why a patriot became a traitor. Perhaps it was Arnold's greed; or he was manipulated by his young wife; or he thought the French, who had become allies, represented a greater threat to liberty than the British; or he was infuriated by the pettiness and inefficiency of the Continental Congress and the state governments. Whatever explanation historians adopt, they agree that Arnold was undermined by jealous, less capable men. Brown is high on a list of those described as self-promoters, braggarts, weaklings, drunkards, cowards, incompetents, radicals, and so on. But Arnold's life is told by writers who have not spent much time researching Brown or Arnold's many other adversaries. There is always another side to the story—and there are many stories. If all of Arnold's critics, with their human quirks and failings, are dismissed, the soul has been cut from the American Revolution in order to protect one man's reputation during the early years of the war.

The word *whistleblower* did not come into use until the 1970s, but the word applies. Twenty-first-century Americans will recognize the runaround Brown was given by military and civilian leaders and the scorn his account has received from historians. Arnold's biographers assert that Brown's charges are "nonsense," "manifestly absurd," and "a highly distorted interpretation of reality."[4] Nevertheless, some allegations are unquestionably true. Others may be open to argument, or be overly legalistic, or require more evidence. However, even those charges that upend cherished narratives cannot be rejected out of hand. Brown has been blamed for being right too soon. In a letter to a friend, Theodore Sedgwick, he listed twenty-eight witnesses for his proposed trial of Arnold. He later told Congress, "Every article in the Complaint was sacredly true, and would have been proved had a proper tribunal been obtained, of which Genl. Arnold was well apprized."[5]

In a letter he handed to Horatio Gates, Brown wrote, "I have been led an expensive dance from Generals to Congress, and from Congress to Generals, and am now referred to a Board of War, who, I will venture to say, have never yet taken cognizance of any such matter, nor do I think it, with great submission to your Honour, any part of their duty. I therefore beg your Honour will please to order Brigadier-General Arnold in arrest, for the following crimes, which I am ready to verify."[6]

None of the charges was a surprise to Gates, nor would they have been to any officer in the Northern Army. Brown's thirteen charges appear chapter by chapter in the following narrative and can be found in their entirety in the appendix. Brown claimed:

1. Arnold slandered him "in the most infamous manner."
2. He reduced his rank.
3. He libeled him in an "ungentleman-like" letter to General David Wooster.
4. He "suffered" the smallpox to spread during the siege of Québec.
5. He deprived part of the army of its allowance of food as ordered by Congress.
6. He countermanded the orders of superior officers.
7. He plundered the merchants of Montréal, breaking an agreement made by the "brave and worthy" General Montgomery to protect their property and causing "the eternal disgrace of the Continental arms."
8. He issued "unwarrantable, unjustifiable, cruel, and bloody orders, directing whole villages to be destroyed, and the inhabitants thereof put to death by fire and sword, without any distinction to friend or foe, age or sex."
9. After the surrender of the American stockade fort at the Cedars west of Montréal, he entered into an "unwarrantable" and "unjustified" agreement with the British commander.
10. He ordered smallpox inoculations at Sorel without the knowledge of General John Thomas "by which fatal consequences ensued."
11. He exercised "great misconduct" in the fall 1775 march up the Kennebec River and over the height of land to Québec.
12. In the fall of 1776, he lost the American fleet on Lake Champlain through "great misconduct."
13. His behavior in late June and early July 1775 was so disobedient, insulting, and treasonous that troops at Crown Point were prepared to fire upon his vessels and take him prisoner.[7]

Brown insisted on a promise from Gates that his accusations would be forwarded to Congress. Infuriated, Gates replied, "Since you are so importunate for an answer in writing…, I think proper to acquaint you that I shall lay your petition before Congress, who will, when they see fit, give such orders as they think necessary thereupon."[8] Brown knew better than to rely on Gates and sent a copy of the charges directly to Continental Congress president John Hancock. In a few months, Brown traveled to army headquarters in Morristown, New Jersey, to present his case before George Washington.

One

"An intimate correspondence and connection"

John Brown was born in Haverhill, Massachusetts, thirty miles north of Boston, on October 19, 1744. He was the youngest in a large family—four brothers and three sisters living—born to Daniel and Mehitable Sanford Brown. John was a child when the family moved to Sandisfield, in southern Berkshire County, Massachusetts, which was then frontier. His father owned large tracts of land and was moderator of the first town meeting, deacon, and justice of the peace.[1]

As a young man, John read law in the office of his sister Elizabeth's husband, Oliver Arnold, a Providence, Rhode Island, attorney and distant relative of Benedict Arnold. Oliver was only eight years older than Brown and became Rhode Island attorney general at age thirty, likely while Brown was his student and assistant. Brown's life prior to the Revolution has confused researchers. In some accounts, he learned to despise Benedict Arnold from his brother-in-law—in these speculations a first cousin or an uncle—reducing the animosity between Brown and Arnold to a family quarrel. Both Arnolds could trace their heritage back to the village of Ilchester in Somerset. But Benedict was descended from a Benedict Arnold (1615–1678) who had been president and then governor of Rhode Island. Oliver's branch of the family arrived in Rhode Island from Watertown, Massachusetts, slightly later. His ancestor, Richard Arnold (1643–1710), was on the council for the short-lived Dominion of New England appointed by Governor Edmund Andros.[2]

In some accounts, Brown studied law in the early 1770s *after* college, but it was the opposite. In 1767 when he was twenty-two, he enrolled in Yale. At first Brown was studying alongside fifteen year olds, although two of his classmates, who planned to be clergymen, were older than him. Perhaps his brother-in-law's influence can be seen in the decision to attend college. Oliver was a supporter of education and a contributor to Rhode Island College, today's Brown University. Oliver likely saw great abilities in his brother-in-law, but also the need for further education. Brown's letters reveal him to be intelligent, but his handwriting is often a scrawl that can border on illegible. In a letter to the governor of Connecticut, he apologized for mistakes—"my paper, ink, and eye-sight are bad."[3] At the time, spectacles were seen as a sign of weakness or old age, but Brown seems to have had little choice but to wear them.

In New Haven, Brown certainly met Benedict Arnold, who was twenty-six when Brown matriculated, but already an established merchant, ship owner and captain in the port city. Arnold had a reputation for aggressiveness. In 1766, he had bullied a

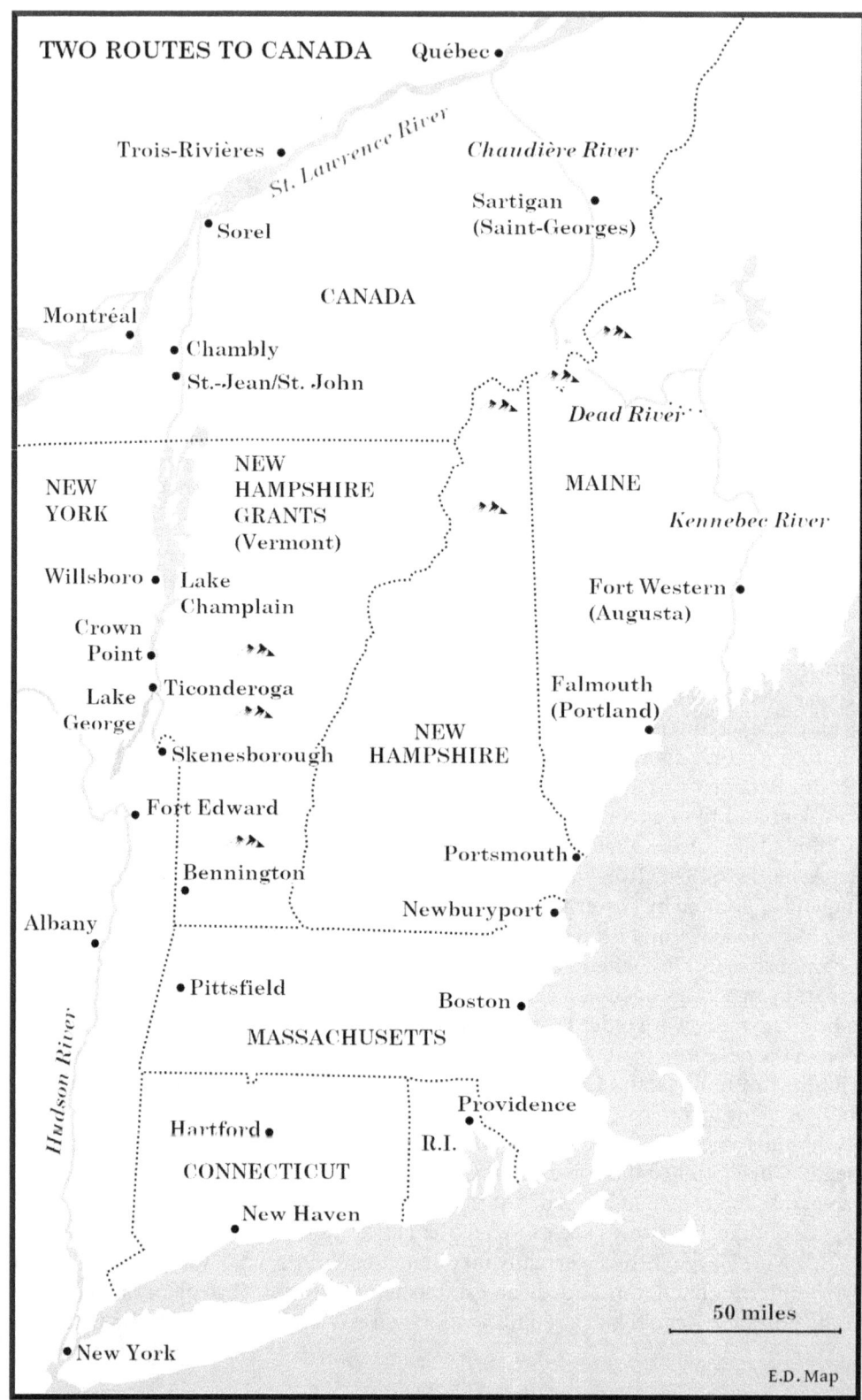

man who had informed on him for smuggling, and Arnold was brought before a justice and fined. There was talk of duels and in 1770 a rumor that Arnold had contracted syphilis while in the Caribbean. Arnold hired prominent attorney Jared Ingersoll to sue a ship captain for defamation. Brown and Arnold had some things in common, but much that was not. Both were risk-takers and quick to defend their honor. As a boy, Arnold had hoped to attend Yale himself, but his academic preparations ended when his alcoholic father was unable to provide for the family. Brown came from a close, supportive family.

Brown's brother-in-law Oliver died unexpectedly in October 1770 while Brown was in his final year at Yale. The following April, Brown wrote his widowed sister Elizabeth, telling her that he was part of a protest against the food in the dining hall, a complaint of college students through the ages. "We complained that we were oppressed in respect to commons, which was most manifestly the case. But the authority of college not being of our opinion and refusing to redress us in our way, we left college and went home." He expected an "Inquisition or Star Chamber Court" in a few weeks. "They intend to expel several, but as we have the civil authority on our side, we do not intend to be expelled." He could not visit Elizabeth until after "our tryal," but planned to attend the sale of Oliver's books.[4] Nineteen members of the Class of 1771 graduated that spring, including Brown; Joseph Barker, a future pastor and congressman; Lewis Beebe, a surgeon in the American army in Canada and later controversial preacher in Vermont; and David Humphreys, future poet and George Washington's personal secretary. Humphreys was a friend and memorialized Brown in verse.[5]

Following graduation, Brown moved to Johnstown in New York's Mohawk Valley, forty-five miles west of Albany, where he was admitted to the bar in December and became King's Attorney, the prosecutor for Tryon County. Johnstown was founded by Sir William Johnson, superintendent of Indian affairs, who owned tens of thousands of acres and lived in a mansion to the west of town. A handsome brick courthouse and a stone jail were begun in 1772; the first general court session was held in September of that year. But Brown did not remain long in New York. As a Yankee, a Congregationalist, and budding rebel, he was not at home among judges and justices who would be Loyalist leaders in the Revolution.[6]

By the end of 1773, Brown was a rising figure in Pittsfield in western Massachusetts. Established in 1761, the town was home to 828 people, 138 families, according to a 1772 census.[7] For both Johnstown and Pittsfield, it was still the age of stocks and whipping posts in the center of the village. Slaves lived in both communities, although fewer in Pittsfield. The Mohawk Valley was more diverse with a mix of English, Highland Scots, Palatine Germans, Dutch, and the Iroquois. A Mohican community remained near Pittsfield in Stockbridge. Like Johnstown, Pittsfield was a seat of the county court (a second county court alternated in Great Barrington).

Around the time Brown settled in Pittsfield, he married Huldah Kilbourne. She was born in Wethersfield in central Connecticut in 1755, but, like Brown, grew up in Sandisfield. In 1773, she was eighteen, about ten years younger than her husband. Two of their children survived to adulthood: Huldah and Henry Clinton. A third, referred to as "child of Mrs. Brown" in church records, died in 1781, months after John was killed in battle.[8] Huldah's signature can be found on an inventory list from 1782 compiled as part of probate. *Huldah* is shaped with the clarity of a child learning to write; her new last name, *Ingersoll*, is shaky and uncertain, the effort of someone who seldom held a pen.[9]

On December 16, 1773, Sons of Liberty disguised as Indians destroyed tea on board ships in Boston's harbor. About a month later, a Pittsfield town meeting appointed a committee, which included Brown, to draft instructions for the town's representative to the General Court of Massachusetts, the province's assembly. The document was written by Woodbridge Little, Pittsfield's only attorney before Brown's arrival. It balanced the views of conservatives and activists. The inhabitants of the town were "alarmed at the extraordinary conduct of a number of disguised persons" who destroyed 342 chests of tea. The action was "unnecessary and highly unwarrantable" and the perpetrators should be punished. But "we are as averse as any of the patriots in America to being subjected to a tax without our own free and voluntary consent." On one issue everyone was in agreement: if the owners of the tea sought compensation, "we have determined, at all events, never to pay or advance one farthing."[10]

Events quickly outpaced a mild statement. In March 1774, Parliament began a series of acts in response to the Boston Tea Party. First, the port of Boston was to be closed until the tea was paid for. Then on May 20, the Massachusetts charter was abrogated and self-government was severely restricted. Except for the annual town meeting, no meetings could be held without the permission of the governor. In separate acts, royal officials were to be tried outside of Massachusetts for capital crimes, and the army was allowed to requisition quarters when no barracks were available. Then in a final indignity to the seaboard colonies, the Province of Quebec was enlarged; Roman Catholics there were guaranteed the free practice of their religion; and French civil law was maintained. Together the four Coercive Acts and the Quebec Act came to be known in the colonies as the Intolerable Acts.

Sixty Berkshire County men met in Stockbridge in early July to discuss the Boston Port Act and the Massachusetts assembly's call to boycott tea and British goods. They had not yet seen the Massachusetts Government Act, which made their meeting illegal, but they believed the province's charter had been or would soon be overturned. After "animated prayer," the Berkshire representatives chose Col. John Ashley of Sheffield as chairman and Theodore Sedgwick, a twenty-eight-year-old attorney, as clerk. Sedgwick, a future speaker of the U.S. House of Representatives and U.S. Senator, was two years younger than Brown. He had attended Yale to study for the ministry but was expelled for disciplinary reasons. He read law in Great Barrington and was admitted to the bar at twenty. Brown and Sedgwick were named to a five-member committee to draft the convention's resolutions. Following the committee's report, the convention resolved unanimously, that it was the "indispensable duty of every person" to resist "these arbitrary and oppressive acts." Then the delegates signed a covenant, refusing to import, purchase, or consume British goods.[11]

On July 25, as clerk of the Pittsfield Committee of Correspondence, Brown wrote to the Boston committee, seeming to ask for advice but actually informing leaders in eastern Massachusetts what was going to happen. The Berkshire County Court was scheduled to sit in Great Barrington in mid–August. The writs to summon jurors had been issued "sooner than usual which we view as a pretence to blind our Eyes, & we are persuaded people this way will by no means submit to the New Regulations." Although Brown requested the Boston committee's "speedy sence in this Matter of so great Moment," he told them, "We expect it to get adjourned unless we should hear from you." On August 16, a crowd estimated at 1500 blocked the court from sitting.[12]

On September 1, military governor Thomas Gage called for "the representatives to the great and general court," the assembly, to meet in Salem on October 5. In Pittsfield, Brown was chosen to attend a Provincial Congress in Concord, not the governor's General Court in Salem. Finally, on September 28, as a result of "tumults and disorders," Gage canceled the General Court and discharged the delegates, who met anyway, pretended to await the arrival of the Governor and Council, and then adjourned to Concord to join the Provincial Congress.

Brown was one of seven delegates from Berkshire County. For much of the fall, his work as a legislator does not appear in provincial records. The assembly was preparing for war, while professing to be subjects of the king. Canada was a topic of discussion from the start.[13] For most of colonial history, the French in Canada had been the enemy. The Suffolk Resolves, passed in early September by Boston-area leaders and carried by Paul Revere to the First Continental Congress in Philadelphia, denounced the Quebec Act for establishing Roman Catholicism and French law in Canada, seeing it as "dangerous in an extreme degree, to the protestant religion, and to the civil rights and liberties of all America." On the other hand, Canada might share some of the concerns of the Atlantic seaboard colonies. So the Continental Congress wrote to the inhabitants of Canada, professing respect, arguing the cause of liberty, making a few threats, and hoping that "our brave Enemies would become our [best] hearty Friends." The letter was translated into French and published as an eighteen-page pamphlet.[14]

Samuel Adams, shown here in an engraving of a John Singleton Copley portrait, sent John Brown on a mission to Canada in the late winter of 1775. Library of Congress.

On December 6, the Massachusetts Congress appointed Brown to a seven-man committee to correspond with the Canadians. He was the youngest, the least distinguished, but the most enthusiastic. Brown's fellow committee members show the importance placed on the task and the impression Brown made on his fellow delegates: Samuel Adams, Continental congressman, home for the winter; John Hancock, chairman of the Provincial Congress; Dr. Joseph Warren, chair of the Suffolk Convention; Joseph Hawley, a leader in the Stamp Act crisis who had been named as a delegate to the Continental Congress, although he declined; Seth Pomeroy, a leading officer and hero in both King George's War and the

French and Indian War; and Dr. Benjamin Church, a leader of the Sons of Liberty. Hancock, Warren, and Church were on the powerful Committee of Safety.[15] Brown was now at the center of the Massachusetts resistance, linked to the leading men in the province.

※ ※ ※

When the Provincial Congress met again in February 1775, Brown represented both Pittsfield and Partridgefield, today's Peru, a small town a dozen miles to the east of Pittsfield. For nearly two weeks, nothing was done about corresponding with Canada. Then Samuel Adams and Brown spoke about the possibilities, and Adams asked Brown to consider how to establish a link with Canada, which was distant and guarded by wilderness and the frozen St. Lawrence River.

Brown suggested that a messenger follow the Hudson River and Lake Champlain as far as St. John (Saint-Jean on the Richelieu River) and Montreal while establishing contacts in Skenesborough (today's Whitehall, New York), the New Hampshire Grants, and Crown Point, the massive British fort on Lake Champlain. Apparently unknown to Brown, Crown Point had burned two years before and was no more than an outpost. He told Adams, "Should you think proper to send me to execute this Business shall exert myself to the utmost of my Power in putting your Orders into execution." He promised to "furnish you with a return before the next session of Congress."[16]

With Brown's proposal in hand, the Provincial Congress authorized the Boston Committee of Correspondence to "establish an intimate correspondence and connection" with Quebec. No mention was made of the Congress's December 6 committee for the same purpose, but Adams and Warren were in charge in any case. On behalf of the Boston committee, Adams sent Brown letters to be delivered to gentlemen in Montréal and Québec and asked that he "make the utmost Dispatch to Canada, as much depends upon it." The Provincial Congress gave him £20 for expenses.[17]

Brown left immediately for Albany where he learned that Lake George and Lake Champlain were impassable. It was between seasons: the remaining ice could not be trusted, but the lakes were not open for sailing. On the recommendation of Adams, he met with Dr. Joseph Young, a prominent Son of Liberty in the city, to make certain that the Albany and Boston committees of correspondence were linked. Young is an important figure in his own right—he was to be chief prescribing physician at the general hospital of the Continental Army in Albany—but he is better known as the younger brother of Dr. Thomas Young, a political and religious radical who had been a member of Boston's Committee of Correspondence and an organizer of the Tea Party. By spring 1775, Thomas had relocated to Philadelphia where he was already contributing to the ferment in that city. Most important for Brown's story, Thomas had been a mentor to Ethan Allen, now calling himself "Colonel-Commandant" of the Green Mountain Boys, a mob or a militia in the New Hampshire Grants (today's Vermont).[18]

While he was waiting for the lakes to open for navigation, Brown met with leaders in Bennington, the unofficial capital of the New Hampshire Grants. The territory had been in turmoil as long as Massachusetts. In Vermont tales, the contest between the Green Mountain Boys and New York authorities for control was like that of Robin Hood and his Merry Men outfoxing the Sheriff of Nottingham. For New

York title-holders west of the Green Mountains, the dispute was a time of terror in isolated clearings in the wilderness. A mob could be a dozen men dressed as Indians or wearing women's caps, or it could be a hundred—or at least feel that way to a New Yorker, surrounded in the dead of night, his farm in ruins. New York authorities issued one arrest warrant after another, finally culminating in a March 1774 law, which condemned rioters as felons deserving of death "without benefit of clergy."[19]

Fort Ticonderoga was a topic of discussion between Brown and the men in Bennington. The fort on Lake Champlain might threaten the Grants on behalf of a loyal colony of New York, or if hostilities began between the British and Americans, the fort would allow Regulars from Canada to penetrate far into the colonies. All agreed that the fort should be captured if war began. "The people on the New Hampshire Grants have engaged to do this business; and in my opinion, they are the most proper persons for the job," Brown wrote in his report on the trip.

Two Green Mountain Boys, Peleg Sunderland and Winthrop Hoyt, agreed to accompany Brown to Canada. Sunderland, Brown wrote, was "an old Indian hunter, acquainted with the St. François Indians and their language." Hoyt was "a captive many years among the Caghnawaga Indians." Both were tough, violent men, active in the resistance to New York authority. A little over a month earlier, Sunderland led a mob of thirty men to capture New York justice of the peace the Rev. Benjamin Hough, who lived in Socialborough, a New York township that overlapped the town of Rutland, established by a grant from New Hampshire. Faced with a mob, Hough ran for his weapons, but Hoyt beat him to the house, grabbed Hough's own sword and pistol, and blocked the doorway. Hough was taken forty miles south for trial. A court led by Ethan Allen found Hough guilty of favoring New York and sentenced him to two hundred lashes on his bare back. Hoyt was one of four men to carry out the sentence. Green Mountain Boy captain Robert Cochran, who was to serve in Brown's regiment in Canada, told them repeatedly "to lay on their Blows well and to strike harder."[20]

Brown did not describe his route to Canada precisely. Perhaps he rode through the New Hampshire Grants from Bennington to Skenesborough at the narrow southern end of Lake Champlain. But in his report, Brown referred to lakes, plural, so it is most likely he and his two companions followed the Hudson River north through Saratoga (today's Schuylerville), by Fort Edward, and then left the roads by the river and crossed the watershed to the southern end of Lake George. It was the route the armies took during the French and Indian War. The land was steeped in history. They saw the Bloody Pond where in 1755 the water turned red from the bodies of the slain, the charred remains of Fort William Henry, and half-built Fort George on the high ground overlooking thirty-three-mile-long Lake George. A perryauger, a schooner-rigged barge, made regular crossings of the lake in season, and there were bateaux, flat-bottomed, double-ended boats, and crews for hire. When Thomas Jefferson made the trip in May 1791, he wrote, "Lake George is without comparison the most beautiful water I ever saw."[21] Brown and his companions may not have felt that way at the end of winter with 150 miles ahead of them. The spring melt came early; most of the snow was gone and the mountains were brown except for the dark green of pine trees. At the landing at the lake's outlet, a carriage was available to take travelers and their gear over the three-mile portage to Fort Ticonderoga and Lake Champlain.

In the summer of 1776, Chaplain William Emerson, grandfather of Ralph Waldo

Emerson, wrote home that Ticonderoga's stone barracks make "as good an appearance at a distance as Harvard College." That may be the first view of Ticonderoga that Brown saw. Close up, the fort was less impressive. In May 1774, British military engineer John Montresor described Ticonderoga in a report to General Frederick Haldimand, temporary commander in chief in North America: "With respect to the Post of Ticonderoga it's [sic] ruinous situation is such, that it would require more to repair than the constructing of a new Fort." Quartered inside the collapsing walls were forty-four soldiers and twenty-four women and children.[22]

Thirteen miles north on Lake Champlain, Brown and company came to the Crown Point–Chimney Point narrows, which had been the site of fortifications on the lake since 1731. By the end of the French and Indian War, Crown Point was the largest British fort in North America with forty-foot-high earth walls surrounding a six-acre parade ground. Like Ticonderoga, it was neglected after the war. The fort's destruction came in 1773 when a chimney in one of the barracks caught fire. Nearby buildings were engulfed, the flames spread to the exterior wooden walls of the fort, which were saturated with tar, and finally the magazine exploded. Montresor found it to be "an amazing useless mass of Earth only." In the spring of 1775, there were a sergeant, eight rank and file, and ten women and children at the site.[23]

Beyond Crown Point, settlements were scarcer. Many travelers stopped at Willsboro on the western shore where the lake was four miles across. Willsboro was an enclave of civilization, farming and industry, controlled by one man, William Gilliland. If Brown stopped at Gilliland's, he found his host to be sympathetic to the struggle in Massachusetts. North of Gilliland's, the lake is ten miles wide before being divided by islands. Brown wrote, "The Lake Champlain was partly open and partly covered with dangerous ice, which breaking loose for miles in length, our crafts drove us against an island, and froze us in for two days, after which we were glad to foot it on land."

Most travelers sailed as far as St. John (Saint-Jean), which was the end of navigation on the upper Richelieu (or Sorel) River, but Brown was on foot long before the British outpost. If he was lucky, the ground was frozen much of the day. When he came north four months later as spy, he walked for three days through "a vast tract of swamp." The road from Saint-Jean to Montréal was terrible in dry weather; in March it was muck when the temperature climbed above freezing.

In Montréal Brown was welcomed by the English-speaking merchants, especially by Thomas Walker, who had lived in Boston but had been in Montréal since 1763. British authorities were aware of the visit by "the people obsessed with sham Liberty." In an intelligence report given to Governor Guy Carleton, Walker was quoted as saying, "The people of the Colonies were brave Fellows, who did not wish to be Slaves, and would defend their Liberty and Rights."[24]

Brown invited the pro–American merchants to send delegates to the Congress, which was scheduled to open on May 10, but he reported, "'no prospect' of that happening." If the English merchants refused to import English goods, the French-Canadians would take over their business, especially the Indian trade. When challenged, Brown passed himself off as wanting to purchase horses. By one account, he threatened the Canadians with an invasion of 30,000 men, who would "lay waste the whole country"; by another, it would be 50,000. He reported with eighteenth-century New England prejudice, "The French people are (as a body)

A 1762 view of Montréal from across the St. Lawrence River by Thomas Patten. Miriam and Ira D. Wallach Division of Art, Prints and Photographs: Print Collection, New York Public Library Digital Collections.

extremely ignorant and bigoted, the curates or priests having almost the entire government of their temporal, as well as spiritual affairs." In La Prairie, a village of about thirty white houses on the St. Lawrence River, he met with a group of priests and nuns. "They appeared to have no disposition unfriendly toward the Colonies, but chose rather to stand neuter," he concluded.[25]

Brown sent Sunderland and Hoyt to visit a Mohawk Indian community along the St. Lawrence about ten miles southwest of Montréal. Eighteenth-century Europeans wrote something like *Caughnawaga* with endless variations. Since 1982, the town is known in French and English as *Kahnawake* ("on the rapids" in Mohawk). Kahnawake was a Christian community. Kateri Tekakwitha (1656–1680) lived the last five years of her short life there. In 2012, she was canonized, the first North American Native to be a Roman Catholic saint.

The two Americans were welcomed to the village. Among the Mohawks were white New Englanders who had been captured, accepted into the community, and chose to stay. Hoyt had once been a captive, and although he had left, he felt affection for his Native friends. Sunderland and Hoyt learned that the British had already asked for their help "to fight Boston," but they had refused. However, they were not volunteering on the American side either. Brown concluded that the Kahnawake "are a very simple, politick people, and say that if they are obliged, for their own safety, to take up arms on either side, that they shall take part on the side of their brethren, the English in New-England." Undoubtedly they were *politick*, watching which way the wind was blowing and saying just enough not to aggravate visitors. But there was nothing simple about the calculations they were making. War was an opportunity for men to prove themselves, but if the town committed to the wrong side, they might be crushed by warring Europeans. They wrote a friendly letter to Israel Putnam, who had been an officer in Roger's Rangers in the French and Indian War, assuring him of their "peaceable disposition."

Details of Brown's trip to Canada can be found in a lengthy report to Samuel Adams and Joseph Warren written in Montréal on March 29 and entrusted to a messenger. The report is informative, but has faults. The narrative hops around; Brown's pleasure in storytelling and his Yankee prejudices get in the way. But he tried to be the voice, and the eyes and ears, of the committee of correspondence. No matter how much bluster he managed in talking to Canadians, the report is a cautious, defensive document, and it is a leap to get from it to an invasion of Canada. Brown kept his analysis of Ticonderoga until the end of his letter and emphasized that it must be "kept a profound secret." Capture the fort, he wrote, and "this will effectually curb this Province [Québec], and all the troops that may be sent here."

Brown remained in Montréal for a few more days after he sent his report. On April 4, he held a meeting with most of the English merchants at the Coffee House where, according to intelligence reports received by Governor Carleton, he "harangued" them and read Samuel Adams's letter. Although he had already told Adams and Warren that no Canadian delegates would attend the Continental Congress, a few merchants moved that the meeting establish a committee of correspondence and elect two delegates. As Carleton heard a few days later, "the Assembly broke up without anything being done that was proposed by those opposers of Government."[26]

Two

"An able counsellor, full of spirit and resolution"

The crisis in Massachusetts exploded on April 19 at Lexington and Concord, and riders galloped across New England with the news. Brown had been home only a short time when he learned that his thoughts on war, Ticonderoga, and Canada had taken on greater meaning. In New Haven on April 22, Captain Benedict Arnold of the Connecticut Footguards demanded powder and shot from the town's supplies. The New Haven selectmen asked David Wooster—Arnold's Masonic brother and commander of the militia—to calm the hot-headed young merchant, who was threatening to break down the door to the magazine. At sixty-four Wooster was so old that he could trace his military career back through the French and Indian War to King George's War and the famous expedition that seized the French fortress of Louisbourg on Nova Scotia. Few Americans had a military background to match his, but he is sometimes depicted as a laughable old man, too fond of flip, a concoction of rum, pumpkin beer, and brown sugar heated with a hot poker. In fact, he was respected, although he had no influence over Arnold. "None but Almighty God shall prevent my marching," Arnold was remembered as saying before he received the key to the magazine.[1]

Already Arnold had accurate figures on the number of soldiers at Fort Ticonderoga (fewer than fifty) and an exaggerated estimate of the artillery (eighty heavy guns, twenty brass guns, and a dozen mortars). A sloop of seventy or eighty tons sailed Lake Champlain. On the march to Boston, Arnold and his company of fifty men drafted an agreement on their beliefs. He was the first to sign this idealistic pledge. "We will conduct ourselves decently and inoffensively as we march, both to our countrymen and one another.... Drunkenness, gaming, profaneness, and every vice of that nature shall be avoided ... we engage to submit on all occasions to such decisions as shall be made and given by the majority of the Officers we have chosen." In turn, the officers would not beat their men—"a slavish practice"—but would admonish them in private.[2]

On the road to war, Arnold met Colonel Samuel Parsons of New London, Connecticut, returning from Cambridge to Hartford to recruit for the siege of Boston. Parsons was to serve in the war through Yorktown and rise to the rank of major general. He told Arnold how exposed the American lines at Cambridge were without artillery, and Arnold described Ticonderoga and the number of cannon. Their information fit together and they both resolved to seize the fort. Once in Hartford, Parsons met with members of the assembly who decided to promote an expedition against the fort. Taking £300 from the treasury—"without any consultation with the Assembly, or others," Parsons admitted—they sent two "captains" to alert Ethan Allen's brother Hemen, who lived in Salisbury, Connecticut. A day later Edward Mott, a captain in Parsons's Regiment, appeared in Hartford, and he too was thinking of Ticonderoga. Then Samuel Adams and John Hancock arrived on their triumphal journey to Philadelphia to take their seats in the Continental Congress and learned of the expedition as did Governor Jonathan Trumbull and the Council. Meanwhile in Cambridge, Arnold met with leaders of the Massachusetts Committee of Safety. He told them how many cannon were at Ticonderoga and of the fort's "ruinous condition." "The place could not hold out an hour against a vigorous onset," he wrote to Joseph Warren and the committee.[3]

The expedition from Connecticut moved north, gathering a few men here and there, but mostly officers or gentlemen who fancied being officers. Captain Mott had been advised in Hartford not to recruit until they reached the New Hampshire Grants, "lest we be discovered by having too long a march through the country." Locals must have wondered at the arrival of these strangers from larger towns who were apparently on a mission to somewhere. In Pittsfield, at James Easton's tavern, Mott took Easton and John Brown into his confidence.[4]

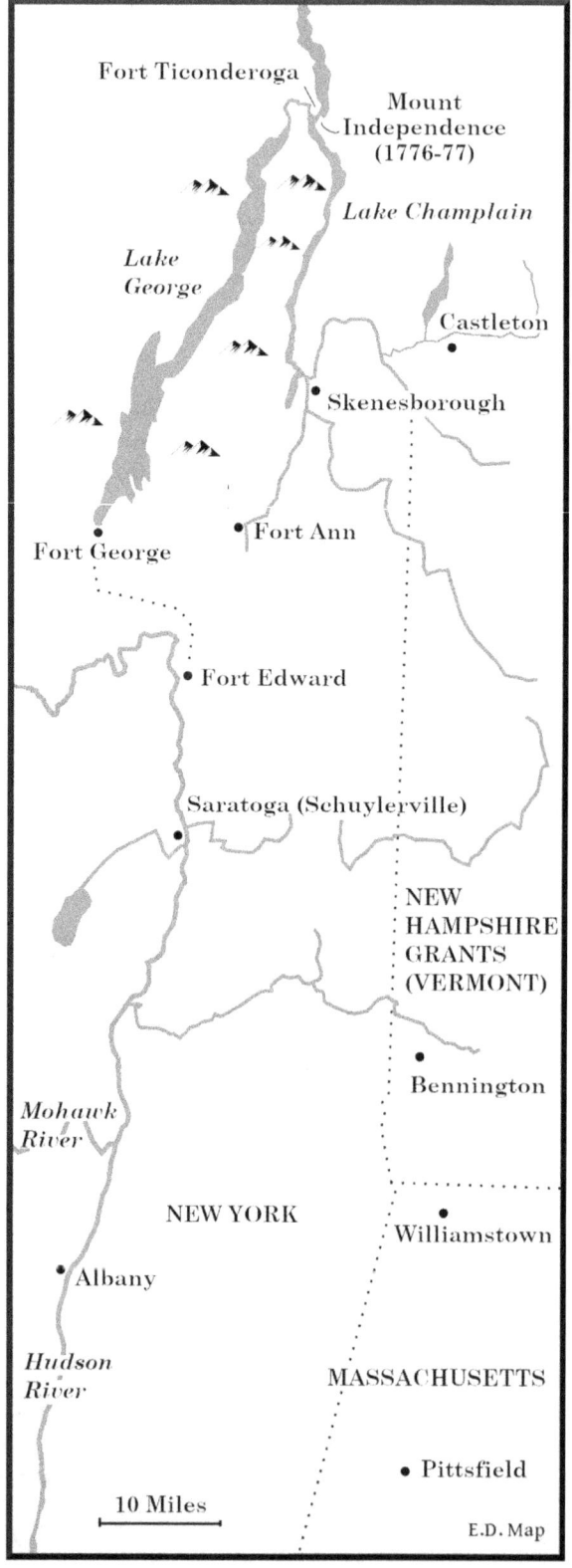

Easton, forty-six years old at the time, is a derided figure in most histories. He is the "tavern keeper," a devious braggart who makes you wonder how the young country survived such incompetence. The real Easton may have been a man with limitations. As a military leader, he needed Brown at his side. But he was church deacon, colonel of the town's militia, and former delegate to the Massachusetts House of Representatives. He was a builder, mentioned in the Pittsfield town history for constructing the first three schoolhouses as well as the stocks and the whipping post. He kept a store and is best known for the tavern, which was located at the heart of the village. Taverns were not just places to drink; they were central to the social and political life of a community. Pittsfield's nineteenth-century history contends, "His letters show sound sense well expressed, great promptness and energy of character, and a remarkable combination of zeal and judgment." Local histories can be expected to defend their favorite sons, but Easton's letters do reveal a thoughtful mind without an excess of boasting or wheedling.[5]

Easton and Brown told Mott it would be difficult to find men and provisions in the New Hampshire Grants. Then they joined the expedition themselves and helped formulate a plan. Easton and Mott were to recruit on their march north, while Brown, Hemen Allen, and Captain Epaphras Bull, whose journal tells the story, were to hurry to Bennington. In Williamstown, Massachusetts, Brown and company were stopped by twenty to thirty armed men who thought they were Tories. Then they encountered a man "directly from Ticonderoga" who insisted that the fort had been reinforced and repaired, and the garrison was ready for attack. They sent this news back to Mott and Easton and told them to stop until further orders. In Mott's account, the recommendation was that he dismiss his recruits and abandon the attempt altogether, but he questioned the reliability of the intelligence and continued north. That evening when Brown reached the Catamount Tavern in Bennington, Ethan Allen joined them. The next morning, May 3, Allen rode north, in Epaphras Bull's phrase, "to muster his Green mounting boys."[6]

On the same day in Cambridge, the Massachusetts Committee of Safety appointed Benedict Arnold "Colonel and Commander-in-Chief" of an expedition to take possession of Ticonderoga. "You are to bring back with you such of the cannon, mortars, stores &c., as you shall judge may be serviceable to the Army here, leaving behind what may be necessary to secure that post with a sufficient garrison." Orders in hand, Arnold began a hard ride of more than two hundred miles from Cambridge to Ticonderoga. At the start, he was accompanied by a few captains who were to follow with men once they had recruited some. Eventually, Arnold learned he was chasing another expedition.[7]

The men from Connecticut and western Massachusetts paused for two days in Bennington, a comfortable country town atop a hill with a welcoming tavern. The expedition itself was a New England town meeting on the move: there were officers but everyone had a say. Mott attempted to shame the men who wanted to abandon the attempt, but they still worried that the fort was now a stronghold. And who was in command? Bernard Romans, a fifty-five-year-old Dutch-born naturalist, cartographer, and self-promoter, expected to lead and was especially annoying. When he left for Albany, Mott commented, "We were all glad, as he had been a trouble to us all the time he was with us."[8]

Without a clear chain of command, sensible steps were still taken. A man was sent to spy on the fort, others for supplies, still others to block the roads so news could not reach the fort. Details of John Brown's role are missing, but in a report to the Massachusetts Provincial Congress, Mott called him "an able counsellor, and full of spirit and resolution, as well as good conduct."[9]

On May 5, the company left Bennington, rode all day, with rain soaking them in the afternoon, and stopped for the night at Smith's tavern in Rupert, thirty-some miles north of Bennington. The next morning, Ethan Allen and Captain Seth Warner joined them, and again the company heard bad news. There were eighty men at the fort, which had been repaired. "We all Seem to be in a Dilemma not knowing what Step to take," Bull noted.[10]

Brown already knew some of the leaders of the Green Mountain Boys from his trip to Canada and was to be closely identified with many of them. Captain Robert Cochran lived in Rupert to the west of the steep mountains that protected the Mettowee Valley through which they traveled north. Warner was a Bennington man who owned land in Rupert. He was second in command to Allen, but their authority grew from different sources. Allen was the charismatic outsider and a land speculator. Warner was deeply rooted in the Bennington community where he had been a road surveyor, occasional country doctor, and militia captain. Although he was outlawed for striking a New York justice with the flat of his cutlass, he was often the calm, humane voice as the Green Mountain Boys threatened New Yorkers.

As the expedition continued north, they reached settlements that had only recently been hacked from the forest. By Sunday afternoon, May 7, they were at Zadock Remington's tavern in Castleton at the edge of the frontier. At last they learned that their fears were unfounded; the fort and its garrison were unprepared. On Monday morning, the officers and gentlemen held a council of war at the tavern with Mott presiding. Forming a committee was a Yankee way of resolving the question of who was in command.

In its first action, the committee named Allen, Easton, and Warner as officers in that order "according to the number of men that each one raised," another New England answer to the question of command. Military service was a social contract between the rank and file and the officers. In the early years of the war, Yankee militiamen voted for their leaders and sometimes refused to march if they were not satisfied. The arrangement seems quaint today and no way to run an army or fight a war. It might encourage a prospective leader to value what was popular over what was necessary, but it did offer a check on ambition and militarism. The idealistic oath that Arnold and his Footguards took on the road to Cambridge grew from the same understanding of a soldier's relationship to his officers.

Next, the council ordered Samuel Herrick, a Green Mountain Boy captain from Bennington, to lead thirty men to Skenesborough (today's Whitehall, New York), twelve miles west of Castleton. The township was a small industrial center with a forge, quarry, sawmills, and lime kiln at the narrow head of Lake Champlain. The proprietor, Colonel Philip Skene, had gone to London for the winter, but Herrick could capture his son, Major Andrew Skene, and the schooner *Katherine*, which was the largest trading vessel on the lake. Boats from Skenesborough could then be rowed and sailed twenty-some miles north in order to ferry the main body of the expedition across the lake. With arrangements made, Allen, Warner, and more than a hundred men left for the lake.[11]

Two. "An able counsellor, full of spirit and resolution" 21

The plan to capture Skenesborough is a good introduction to the recurring problem of Benedict Arnold's letters and reports. Six days later he told the Massachusetts Committee of Safety that he had ordered the party to Skenesborough to seize Major Skene and the family's schooner. At first glance, the action seems to be an early example of Arnold's foresight as a commander, but he had not arrived when the decision was made.[12]

About four o'clock in the afternoon, long after the morning council, Arnold rode into Castleton and presented his commission from the Massachusetts Committee of Safety. Mott later explained to the Provincial Congress, "We could not surrender the command to him, as our people were raised on condition that they should be commanded by their own officers." But Arnold was insistent: his commission superseded any arrangements that had been made. Less than three weeks earlier, he had ignored orders from the New Haven selectmen. Now he was the one with orders from a legitimate authority. In his journal, Epaphras Bull wondered what would happen when they all met. "I Cant Say but believe the People will be a Little Averse to his taking Command." Early the next morning, Arnold rode out of Castleton in pursuit of the expedition he claimed to command.[13]

※ ※ ※

By Tuesday afternoon, May 9, a hundred fifty to two hundred men waited in Shoreham on the east side of Lake Champlain. They were about a half-mile away from the water, two miles north of Fort Ticonderoga, when Arnold and his commission caught up with Ethan Allen. The best description of Arnold's attempt to take command was written by Mott, who was behind with the supplies and not actually a witness. He blended together the arguments at Castleton and at Shoreham as if there was one long dispute, which may be close to the truth.

Arnold "strenuously contended and insisted that he had a right to command them and all their officers"; the soldiers announced that they would club their muskets and march home before serving under him. Allen and Easton intervened saying—in an argument that covers the possibilities—"he should not take the command," but if he did, "their pay would be the same." But the men said, "Damn the pay ... they would not be commanded by any others but those they engaged with."[14]

Most histories emphasize the

Pierre Eugène Du Simitière, a Swiss-born artist living in Philadelphia, drew Benedict Arnold and other leading figures around 1780. This is the only genuine portrait of Arnold. National Portrait Gallery, Smithsonian Institution.

differences between Allen, a rough frontiersman, and Arnold, an ambitious gentleman descended from a governor of Rhode Island, but the two men had more in common than either might admit. In the summer of 1757 at age twenty, Allen marched north as part of the Connecticut militia going to the relief of Fort William Henry on Lake George. When the fort fell to the French and their Native allies, the militia turned back, so that Allen was gone from home for two weeks. Arnold's military experience may have been limited to the same rescue attempt. The two might have trudged by each other. Both had planned to attend Yale College, but Allen's academic preparations ceased with the death of his father and Arnold's ended when his drunkard father could not provide for his family. In the 1770s, they organized military companies and bullied their opponents, but neither had been in battle. Both were speculators, Allen on the frontier and Arnold on the sea and in a thriving town. They were in constant fights. Allen's were the rough-and-tumble brawls of the frontier; Arnold's were sometimes, but not always, the affairs of honor of a gentleman, but just as senseless. Neither had happy marriages. Both relished the high-minded phrases of the age. Soon enough, men suspected their loyalty was open to influence. Their accounts of the capture of Fort Ticonderoga and the weeks that followed—and the accounts of their partisans down to today—seem to describe different events.

Through the intervention of other officers, surely including Brown and Warner, Allen and Arnold cobbled together a compromise. Each man interpreted the arrangement, whatever it was, to his own advantage. In a newspaper account signed "Veritas," or truth in Latin, which was certainly written by Arnold himself, the two held joint command. A British lieutenant saw it that way. Bull wrote that Arnold took the left hand of Allen, which may mean second in command. Allen biographers see Allen in charge; Arnold biographers give Arnold more credit.

※ ※ ※

The boats from Skenesborough did not appear as planned, and instead the company commandeered a scow from John Anderson, one of Philip Skene's slaves, who transported iron ore from a mine in Port Henry to Skenesborough. In the "Veritas" account, Arnold convinced forty reluctant men to embark in the midst of a storm. No one else recalled Arnold's leadership or the rain. It took two crossings by Anderson's boat and the help of a small, second boat to get eighty-three men, including Brown and Easton, on the west side of the lake before dawn. Seth Warner and the men he had recruited remained on the eastern shore.

In "Veritas," men wanted to wait for daylight and reinforcements, but Arnold declared that he would enter the fort alone "if no man had courage enough to follow him." Shamed by Arnold's bravery, the men went forward. In Allen's equally unlikely account, he gave a grand speech by the lake shore as the day began to dawn. In these remarks from his melodramatic *The Narrative of Colonel Ethan Allen* (1779), he remained true to the voluntary nature of the attack: "In as much as it is a desperate attempt, (which none but the bravest of men dare undertake) I do not urge it on any contrary to his will."[15]

The men formed three ranks with Allen front and center. In his retelling, Allen omitted Arnold entirely, a literary solution to the question of their relationship. But in most memories, they were side by side as if strapped together for a three-legged race. When the surprised sentry by the open gate snapped his musket, Allen might have been killed, but the powder was damp and the musket misfired. The sentry turned and ran, followed (according to "Veritas") by Arnold, who was first into the fort. Details of Brown's role are unknown, but Allen told the Massachusetts Congress that he was "an able counsellor, and was personally in the attack."[16]

The Americans swept onto the parade ground where they formed ranks facing the barracks and gave three shouts, "huzzas," which (wrote Allen) "greatly surprised them." When a sentry wounded one American officer with his bayonet, Allen struck with his sword, but turned the blade so that it was not a killing blow. The man surrendered and then led Allen to the steps to the commanding officer's quarters. Men remembered him yelling: "Come out of there, you damned old rat"; "you sons of British whores." He ran up the steps, shouting that he would sacrifice the entire garrison if the commander did not appear. Finally, an officer came to the door—in Allen's account he was Captain William Delaplace—holding his breeches. It was the moment in which Allen, according to Allen four years later, pronounced his own commission for seizing Ticonderoga: "In the name of the Great Jehovah and the Continental Congress."[17]

Asleep in an upstairs room, Lieutenant Jocelyn Feltham woke to "numbers of shrieks, & the words no quarter, no quarter." In his nightclothes, he knocked on Captain Delaplace's door. Then Feltham put on a waistcoat and coat, returned to the captain's room for orders, and then alone went out on to the second-floor landing. He was the man holding his breeches. "The bottom of the stairs was filled with the

Although this nineteenth-century illustration of the capture of Fort Ticonderoga is in many ways historically inaccurate, it does depict Ethan Allen's description of the event. Allen triumphs over the British commander in his nightshirt; Benedict Arnold is nowhere to be seen. The Miriam and Ira D. Wallach Division of Art, Prints and Photographs: Print Collection, The New York Public Library Digital Collections.

rioters & many were forcing their way up," Feltham wrote in a report a month later. He tried to speak to them, but the noise was too loud. Finally, "I was informed by one Ethan Allen and one Benedict Arnold that they had joint command." Allen told Feltham, "he must have immediate possession of the fort and all the effects of George the third (those were his words)." While Allen held his sword above Feltham's head, Arnold behaved "in a genteel manner." "It was owing to him that they were prevented getting into Capt Delaplace's room, after they found I did not command." At last, properly dressed for the occasion, Delaplace joined his lieutenant and surrendered Fort Ticonderoga and the 40-some soldiers of the 26th Regiment.[18]

With victory won, men turned to celebration and "tossed about the flowing bowl," as Allen put it. Arnold only saw the worst of behavior—drunkenness, plundering, and the destruction of private property. After the surrender, Warner crossed the lake and arrived during the celebration. Around eleven a.m., he was ordered to Crown Point, but that plan quickly changed. The committee worried whether their men could guard the British prisoners, now numbering about fifty after the capture of a small detachment at Lake George Landing. Arnold once again claimed to be in command, but the men refused and threatened to go home. On behalf of the committee, Mott drafted a formal commission for Allen, appointing him commander of Ticonderoga "till you have further orders from the Colony of Connecticut, or from the Continental Congress."[19]

※ ※ ※

At seven a.m., May 11, Brown set sail from Lake George Landing on his way to Philadelphia and the Continental Congress. Arnold had made an agreement with businessman John Sparding to transport men and supplies across the lake for twenty shillings a day. While the wind filled the sails on Brown's craft, British prisoners and their families boarded Sparding's schooner-rigged barge and a bateau. These two vessels left Lake George Landing at 8:45 in the morning.[20]

Brown's mission was a singular honor. After a victory commanders were expected to send their report by way of a young officer who had distinguished himself. Brown was certainly the choice of Allen, Easton, and Mott, and some historians have concluded that his selection was another slap at Arnold. But Brown was an attorney and recent member of the Massachusetts Provincial Congress. He was also close to the men who had commissioned Arnold to seize the fort and only weeks before he had been their emissary to Canada.

Meanwhile at Ticonderoga, the disputes continued. Allen wrote to the Massachusetts Provincial Congress, praising Easton and Brown and ignoring Arnold. On behalf of the committee, Mott also wrote to the Massachusetts congress, reporting on the capture and praising Allen, Easton, and Brown. But Arnold "presumed to contend for the command of the forces that we had raised," and after the fort's surrender, he "again assumed the command of the Garrison, although he had not one man there." These letters were entrusted to Easton, who was to ride through the New Hampshire Grants to Watertown, a few miles west of Boston, where the Massachusetts congress was meeting. Easton had served in the House of Representatives in spring 1774—a session in which the assembly stood up to Governor Gage and was dissolved—and would be among friends.[21]

On the same day, Arnold wrote a letter to the Massachusetts Committee of

Safety filled with complaints. His letter did not reach the Provincial Congress until May 22, five days after the congress heard a different version of events from Easton, Allen, and Mott. Arnold wrote, "There is here at present near one hundred men, who are in the greatest confusion and anarchy, destroying and plundering private property, committing every enormity, and paying no attention to publick service." Everything was "governed by whim and caprice." "Colonel Allen is a proper man to head his own wild people, but entirely unacquainted with military service." The expedition to take Crown Point is "entirely laid aside." On this point at least, Arnold was wrong. Sometime on May 11, Seth Warner captured Crown Point, which was garrisoned by nine men who were as weak as the ruined fort.[22]

Meanwhile on May 11, a race was on to take Fort George at the head of Lake George. At least four men claimed the honor, but nothing was there but another ruined fort and a handful of men. Brown might have passed through the little lakeside community as if war had not begun. Since he was riding express, he acquired a horse and exchanged it frequently. Albany was sixty miles away. Brown rode hard and arrived late on May 12, but in time for the Albany Committee of Correspondence to convene at city hall to discuss Allen's letter. Allen praised James Easton, and for perhaps the only time, he mentioned Arnold positively: "Colonel Arnold entered the fortress with me side by side." Then he called for men and provisions. "You cannot exert yourselves too much, in so glorious a cause…. Pray be quick to our relief, and send us five hundred men immediately—fail not."[23]

The committee had every reason to mistrust Allen. The members, especially chairman Abraham Yates and Albany mayor Abraham Cuyler, had struggled to keep the so-called New Hampshire Grants under New York jurisdiction. Allen was still a New York outlaw. Only three months before he flogged a New York justice of the peace. Now he claimed they were on the same side—and what had he got them into? The meeting with Brown turned contentious when he repeated Allen's demands. Men and provisions were required if they were to hold the fort and its two hundred pieces of artillery. Prisoners were on the way to Albany and needed to be guarded and fed. The committee tried to explain their reluctance, but Brown was "dissatisfied with our answer, and went away abruptly."[24]

The committee decided to send militia captain Barent Ten Eyck express to the New York Committee of Correspondence with the news and a demand for guidance. Earlier the Albany committee had written New York after receiving a request for supplies and men from the expedition against Ticonderoga, but had not yet received an answer. "As we are unacquainted with the sentiments of our Colony on this very important enterprise, we have declined interfering." But they feared that the event "will probably involve the northern parts of this Colony in the horrours of war and devastation."[25]

Brown was still in Albany the next morning when two letters from the New York committee arrived by sloop. New York wrote that the powers held by the committees of safety "are too limited to permit either Body to take an Active step in the Matters proposed, before we have the Opinion of the Provincial or Continental Congress." So when the Albany committee met with Brown again, they were firm in rejecting his demands, but did give him £13 for his trip to Philadelphia.[26] Speed on the Hudson was always dependent on wind and tide, but Brown made good time. From Newark, he took the Post Road across New Jersey. He had left Ticonderoga when there was only the beginning of springtime green; now the landscape seemed to be deep into summer. He rode through Princeton and Trenton and then south to the ferry across the Delaware River at Burlington and arrived in Philadelphia late on May 17. He had made the 350-mile journey in seven days.

News spread quickly in the city of 38,000. New England congressmen, who knew all along what might happen, were excited. Cautious delegates from other colonies disapproved of an offensive action at time when war had not spread outside of Massachusetts. George Read of Delaware—who dined regularly at City Tavern on Second Street with President Peyton Randolph, George Washington, and other congressmen—heard that evening that "one Colo. Arnold" had taken the fort. Ticonderoga, he told his wife, was "an important pass on Lake Champlain which if kept, will prevent any Army from Canada." He admitted he did not know all the facts.[27]

Arnold's sudden mention as the leader of the expedition is a surprise. Perhaps Brown now understood that many congressmen, like members of the Albany committee, opposed the fort's seizure, and he shrewdly changed the story to blame Arnold.[28] As likely, Read (or whoever told him the story) grabbed hold of a prominent detail from a confusing account. The next morning in the Pennsylvania State House, today's Independence Hall, President Randolph informed the members of the taking of Ticonderoga and called upon Brown to give a firsthand account. The congressional records do not include details of what Brown said, but an article in *Dunlap's Pennsylvania Packet* summarizes his report. Without mentioning Allen or Arnold, the article credited fifty men from Connecticut and the western part of Massachusetts, and one hundred from Bennington, said to be part of New York, and the adjacent towns for seizing the fort. "All this was performed in about ten minutes, without the loss of a life, or a drop of blood on our side, and but very little on that of the King's Troops." Brown reported on the supplies and munitions that had been seized. Crown Point had not yet been captured at the time of his departure, but "being held only by a Corporal and eight men, falls of course into our hands."[29]

The *Packet* expressed the hope that the congress would act to defend the fort "as it may be depended on that Administration means to form an army in Canada, composed of British Regulars, French, and Indians, to attack the Colonies on that side." But Congress, like the Albany committee, preferred caution. The assembly declared that seizing Ticonderoga and its stores had been a defensive action by "several inhabitants of the Northern Colonies, residing in the vicinity of Ticonderoga." The British Ministry was planning "a cruel invasion from the Province of Quebeck upon these Colonies; for the purpose of destroying our lives and liberties." Even so, the cannon and military supplies from Ticonderoga should be inventoried and taken to the southern end of Lake George so that "they may be safely returned when the restoration of the former harmony between Great Britain and these colonies, so ardently wished for by the latter" was again established.[30]

※ ※ ※

On the same day that Brown reached Philadelphia, James Easton presented Mott's and Allen's letters to the Massachusetts Provincial Congress, meeting west of Boston in Watertown, and then spoke to the assembly. Again, no record of what he said exists, but a news report appeared the next day in the *New England Chronicle*. Much of it agrees with other accounts, but the description of the surrender made

Easton the central figure. In the report, he clapped the unnamed commander of Ticonderoga on the shoulder and demanded the fort's surrender "IN THE NAME OF AMERICA." The officer sputtered, "Damn you, what … what … does all this mean?" Easton repeated that he was a prisoner. "The Officer said, that he hoped he should be treated with honour. Colonel Easton replied, he should be treated with much more Honour than our people had met with from the British Troops."[31]

The *New England Chronicle* story of Easton's dramatic words casts a long shadow. It was read the same day before the New Hampshire Provincial Congress meeting in Exeter, ten miles southwest of Portsmouth, and appeared in other papers, including *The Massachusetts Spy or, American Oracle of Liberty*, published in Worcester. It crossed the Atlantic to be reprinted in *The Remembrancer, The Scots Magazine, The Town and Country Magazine*, and even *The Lady's Magazine or Entertaining Companion for the Fair Sex*.

Easton's appearance before the Provincial Congress was a homecoming, and perhaps he got carried away in telling his friends and former colleagues of his exploits at Ticonderoga. But he was delivering letters from Allen and Mott in which he received his share of praise, but far from all the credit. More likely, the surrender scene is fiction, not from Easton, but from a journalist who wanted to enliven an article. Invented details are commonplace in Revolutionary War accounts, and a researcher should always be on guard against enjoyable, but questionable stories. False news is not a twenty-first-century invention, and it never needed the internet to go viral. Fiction or not, Easton's supposed bragging was used by Arnold to destroy his reputation. It is one of many threads that led to Brown's charges against Arnold.

Three

"He would not be second in command to any person"

The thirteenth and longest of John Brown's charges against Benedict Arnold is the earliest, based on incidents in June and early July 1775 on Lake Champlain. Brown was absent on his trip to Philadelphia during the continuing power struggle between Ethan Allen and Arnold, but he returned to the lake in time to see events spin out of control as Connecticut and Massachusetts attempted to bring order to the forces on the lake. Arnold biographers often interpret the evidence in Arnold's favor while admitting that a less proud man might have emerged from the spring campaign with a reputation for action *and* cooperation. Events are confusing, and Arnold's account contradicts that of his critics. In a letter to Governor Jonathan Trumbull of Connecticut, a Massachusetts provincial congressman sent to Lake Champlain wrote, "The particulars of it are too tedious and disagreeable for your Honour[']s attention while you have constantly business of the last importance before you."[1]

Brown charged:

> 13th. For disobedience of the orders of his superiour officers, while acting by a commission from the Provincial Congress of the Province of the Massachusetts-Bay, and for disobedience of the orders of a Committee of the same Congress, sent from that State to inspect into his conduct; and also for insulting, abusing, and imprisoning the said Committee; as also for a treasonable attempt to make his escape with the navigators then at or near Ticonderoga, to the enemy at St. John's, which obliged the then commanding officer of Ticonderoga and its dependencies to issue a positive order to the officers commanding our batteries at Crown-Point to stop or sink the vessels attempting to pass that post, and by force of arms make a prisoner of the said General Arnold (then a Colonel) which was accordingly done.[2]

Brown listed seven witnesses to the events, the most of any of his accusations. Three—Walter Spooner, James Sullivan, and Jedediah Foster—were Massachusetts provincial congressmen on a fact-finding mission. William Duer, often referred to as Judge Duer, was a landowner along the upper Hudson, who would be a Provincial and then a Continental Congressman. Green Mountain Boy Robert Cochran was by late June a captain in Major Samuel Elmore's detachment of Hinman's Regiment; Colonel Benjamin Hinman commanded a thousand men from Connecticut; and Lieutenant William Satterlee was the adjutant at Ticonderoga.[3]

※ ※ ※

Three. "He would not be second in command to any person"

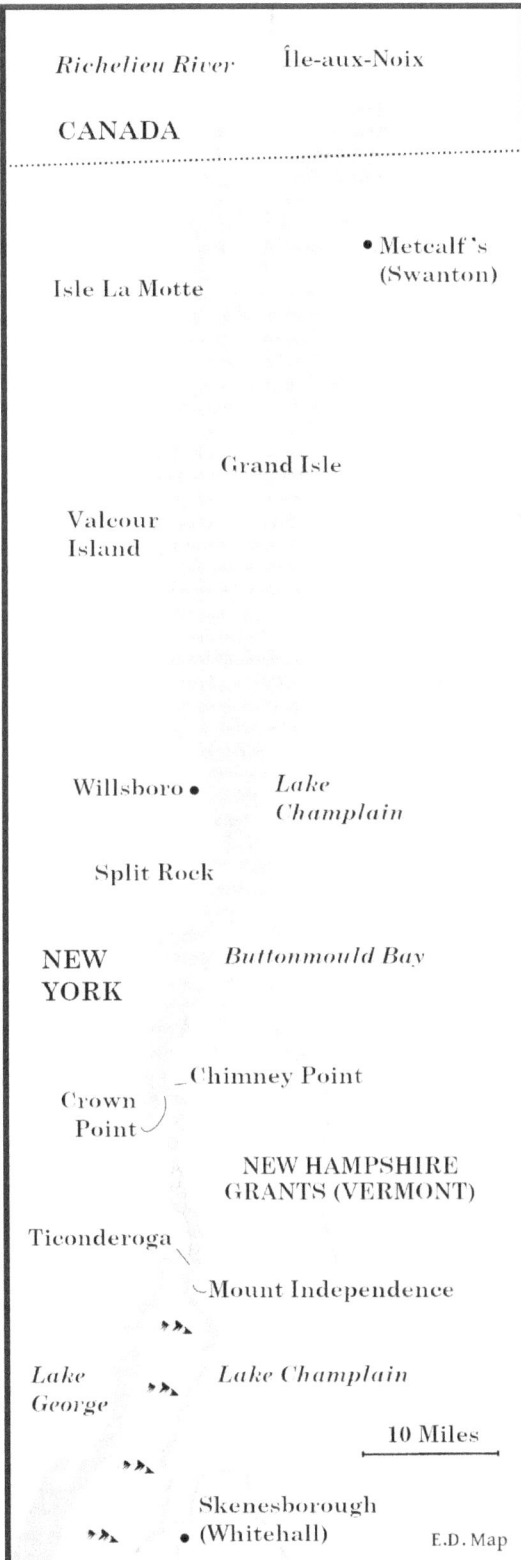

With the arrival at Ticonderoga of Philip Skene's little schooner, the *Katherine*, Arnold became a whirlwind of activity, cutting gun ports and mounting cannon and swivels guns. For the first time, he had recruits of his own. By the afternoon of May 14, the schooner, renamed the *Liberty*, and two bateaux cast off for Canada. At Crown Point Arnold went ashore to tour the massive ruin. He had already sent two reports to Massachusetts evaluating the cannon at the forts. In the second inventory, Crown Point was found to have one hundred eleven guns, sixty-eight of which were good or serviceable. Ticonderoga had eighty-six, but only fifty-seven were good and nineteen of those were swivels, the smallest gun that could be termed a cannon, and two were wall pieces, oversized muskets.[4] In the early winter, the best of the heavy guns were hauled to Boston by Henry Knox where without firing a shot, they drove the British from the city. Some of the light guns were now mounted on the *Liberty* as it sailed north.

From Ticonderoga, Ethan Allen and nearly ninety men set off in pursuit of Arnold in four bateaux. In the race to Canada, they hadn't a chance against a ship captain in a swift vessel. Early on the morning of May 18—the same day that Brown spoke to the Continental Congress—Arnold and thirty-five men took to their two bateaux at night and rowed to the British outpost at St. John. A

During the Revolution, Lake Champlain was the route to and from Canada for travelers and invading armies. "Crossing the lake" meant the length from Skenesborough or Ticonderoga into Canada.

sergeant and a dozen soldiers resisted briefly before surrendering. The Americans captured the King's sloop, as they termed it, and seven sailors. Learning that the British expected reinforcements, Arnold seized supplies and destroyed boats before sailing away.[5]

About fifteen miles south of St. John, not far from today's border with Canada, the weary Green Mountain Boys saw the *Liberty* and the King's sloop with small boats in tow. Arnold fired a cannon in salute, and Allen's men responded with a crackle of muskets before climbing aboard the vessels for refreshment. After a few toasts, Allen announced that he planned to hold the outpost St. John. Arnold later commented, "It appeared to me a wild, impractical Scheme, & provided it could be carried into execution, of no Consequence, so long as we are Masters of the Lake." But he provided his rival with provisions, Allen's men "being in a starving Condition."[6]

At St. John, Allen wrote to Montréal merchants for assistance, but he soon learned that two hundred British Regulars were on the march. When scouts reported that the enemy was near, the Americans rowed across the Richelieu River to today's Iberville and slept near the shore. They awakened to fire from three British field guns loaded with grapeshot. Under fire for the first time, Allen's men piled into their boats and manned the oars, leaving three men behind. The defeat was so humiliating that Allen omitted it entirely from his *Narrative*. Arnold commented that Allen's debacle at St. John "in least did not surprise me, as it happened as I expected."[7]

※ ※ ※

Both Massachusetts and Connecticut received disturbing reports about the state of the troops on Lake Champlain. Connecticut sent a two-man committee—Congressman Silas Deane's brother Barnabas and Colonel Charles Webb—by way of Albany where they begged for supplies. They arrived at Lake Champlain soon after Arnold's triumph and Allen's embarrassment at St. John. "We found matters in a very critical situation there, arising from the difference between Col. Arnold and Col. Allen, which had risen to great height," Barnabas Deane wrote his brother.[8]

Deane and Webb took upon themselves the "arduous task" of making peace between Arnold and Allen, and finally, according to Deane, Allen agreed "he would take no command on himself, but give it up entirely to Col. Arnold." Deane believed that Arnold deserved most of the credit: "Had it not been for him every thing here would have been in the utmost confusion and disorder; people would have been plundered of their private property, and no man's person would be safe that was not of the Green Mountain party." Arnold had been fired at twice by Green Mountain Boys and once had a musket pointed at his chest, Deane reported.

When Allen and Arnold heard of the Continental Congress's call to withdraw to the head of Lake George, they wrote similar letters from Crown Point on the strategic importance of the Lake Champlain forts. Both engaged in posturing. Arnold stressed his commission, the expedition against St. John, and the interference of "one Colonel Allen." Allen, who did not mention Arnold at all, insisted that if he had five hundred men at St. John, he could have taken Montréal. If the Congress sent an army of two or three thousand men, they could "set up the standard of liberty in the extensive Province of Quebeck." But on the main point of Lake Champlain's importance, they agreed as if they had rehearsed their arguments.[9]

William Gilliland, the most influential civilian on the northern lake, also believed that he had been the means of settling "an unhappy dispute between Mr Allen and Mr Arnold." Formerly a New York merchant, Gilliland was a pioneer and a landed gentleman with tenants, slaves, and 60,000 acres centered at Willsboro, thirty miles north of Crown Point. Gilliland's accomplishments combined the dreams of both land speculator Allen and merchant Arnold, and they might have deferred to him momentarily, as they might have to the brother of Congressman Deane.[10] Gilliland joined them in calling for a defense of the lakes, writing to Congress, "As a lover of my liberty and my country, I beg leave to offer you my warmest congratulations on the success of His Majesty's arms, under the prudent and spirited conduct of Colonel Arnold and Mr. Ethan Allen." (In congratulating "his majesty's arms," Gilliland was insisting that the American rebels were loyal to the King against the outrages of Parliament.) Although Gilliland awarded Arnold the first mention and a military rank, he praised Allen, who was "as brave as Hercules" and his men "as good marksmen as can be found in America." They were "excellent wood rangers, and particularly acquainted in the wilderness of Lake Champlain" and were worth "treble the number" of men who did not have their skills.[11]

※ ※ ※

By late May the men of the New Hampshire Grants were leaving to do their planting, and, whatever the role of Deane and Gilliland, the power shifted to Arnold, although he had only a few weeks left as commander. He worked salvaging cannon, constructing boats, and rebuilding fortifications; he armed the King's sloop and renamed it the *Enterprise*. By the end of May, Massachusetts drew up orders for his honorable discharge. Focused on the siege of Boston, Massachusetts authorities no longer wanted responsibility for a distant lake.

On Sunday, June 4, Arnold and 155 men in the *Enterprise*, the *Liberty*, and three bateaux left Crown Point to cruise the northern lake. They learned that three hundred soldiers at St. John were constructing fortifications and again had boats. The foray did not have the heroics of the earlier raid, but it put the British on notice that their enemy was alert.

On the morning of June 9, Captain Jonathan Brown, Arnold's friend and not to be confused with John Brown of Pittsfield, joined the two vessels and delivered a letter from Colonel Joseph Henshaw, who had been sent to Hartford by the Massachusetts Committee of Safety. There Henshaw learned that Connecticut planned to send a thousand men to the lake under command of Benjamin Hinman, a prominent provincial officer in the French and Indian War. Encouraged by Connecticut's plans and a promise of support from New York, Henshaw told Arnold that Hinman was "to take the command" at Ticonderoga, certainly meaning headquarters, not just the old fort. "It is expected you will continue with Colonel Allen, and put the place in the best posture of defence you are able, and guard against any surprise from the enemy till the succours arrive, and you receive further directions from the Congress."[12]

Arnold's personal notes on those days do not mention the letter. Perhaps he found it to be ambiguous. He was headquartered at Crown Point, and Samuel Herrick, who had captured Skenesborough, commanded at Ticonderoga. But it is remarkable that Arnold did not understand. Hinman, an experienced senior officer and friend of the governor with a thousand men, was not going to take orders from an amateur whose disputed command was a few hundred.

A month to the day after the capture of Ticonderoga, the *Enterprise* returned to Crown Point, and Arnold learned that Allen, James Easton, and Major Samuel Elmore of Connecticut had called a council of nearly twenty officers, including several who were supposedly in Arnold's command. Writing from his cabin on board the *Enterprise*, Arnold told them he was the only commanding officer and would not "suffer any illegal counsells, meetings, &c, as they tended to raise a mutiny." He added that he would willingly give up command when someone with proper authority arrived. In his "Regimental Memorandum Book," part personal diary, part ship captain's logbook, he recorded that this note had the "desired effect" of ending the meeting and their pretensions of command.[13]

Before adjourning, the council drafted a letter to the Continental Congress and designated Allen, Warner, and Remember Baker, another Green Mountain captain, to deliver it to Philadelphia and consult with Congress. Arnold's name does not appear in the letter. They wrote, "We are now in possession of Ticonderoga and Crown Point … our armed sloop and schooners arrived here and furnished us with intelligence.…" And just to make certain who was in charge and who deserved credit, the letter continued, garbled, "Colonel Allen has behaved, in this affair, very singularly remarkable for his courage, and must, in duty recommend him to you and the whole Continent."[14]

The next morning Arnold doubled the guard to prevent any mutiny. Soon afterwards Allen, Easton, and Warner boarded a bateau for Ticonderoga. A sentry on the *Enterprise* challenged them, and since they had no pass to leave the fort, they were taken to Arnold. We have only Arnold's word for what happened next. He was speaking to Major Elmore privately when Easton barged in and insulted him beyond what he could tolerate. "I tooke the liberty of breaking his head, and on his refusing to draw like a gentleman, he having a hanger by his side, and cases of loaded pistols in his pockets, I kicked him very heartily and ordered him from the point immediately." Easton and the others left promptly, which is what they wanted to do all along.[15]

This vivid account of Arnold's temper and Easton's cowardice comes from notes made by Arnold, and so, one might imagine, must be factual. The story reappeared a few weeks later in the "Veritas" letter, which was published in the *New-York Journal*. "Veritas" was written from the point of view of a third-person observer of the confrontation between Arnold and Easton, but was certainly Arnold's work. "I had the pleasure of seeing him heartily kicked by Colonel Arnold, to the great satisfaction of a number of gentlemen present, although he (Easton) was armed with a cutlass, and a pair of loaded pistols in his pocket." Arnold was a master—or at least thought himself a master—of what was called epistolary warfare. When his honor was offended, he bided his time and then struck with vicious accusations. Transported to the present, he would quickly understand Twitter. His memorandum book is filled with two kinds of entries: personal grievances and the exact business of conducting war. Arnold's data—time of day, numbers of soldiers, wind direction, amount of supplies—may be as accurate as anything you can find in the American Revolution, although even there questions will be raised. His descriptions of how he was wronged and how he answered back are often misleading. Easton may have been a braggart and without Brown's assistance an ineffective officer, but he was likeable and a patriot, and it is hard to imagine Allen, Warner, or Elmore standing by while Arnold made a fool of him.[16]

Two days after Allen and Warner left the lake, Arnold sent a messenger to Congress with a letter calling for an invasion of Canada. Arnold may have understood for the first time that Allen and his other American adversaries, far from being defeated, were taking their case to Philadelphia. He began his letter with the phrase "as commanding officer here" getting it on the record who really controlled the lake. As he often did in military matters, Arnold had a vision of how to proceed. Isolate the growing fortifications at St. John, he advised, and send "a Grand Division" of a thousand men to seize La Prairie and Montréal where the gates would be thrown open. Arnold would "with the smiles of Heaven answer for the success of it, provided I am supplied with men, &c., to carry it into execution without loss of time." In an attached memorandum, he listed his needs in men and equipment down to five hundred hatchets, ten crosscut saws, and six sets of house and ship carpenter's tools. He wanted "no Green Mountain Boys."[17]

Arnold's letter was too late. Allen and Warner (Remember Baker did not make the trip) arrived in Philadelphia on June 22 just as the first incomplete news of the Battle of Bunker Hill reached the city. Early the next morning, three newly appointed major generals—commander in chief George Washington, Charles Lee, and Philip Schuyler—were off to war. Later that day, Allen and Warner convinced congress that they commanded a large, organized militia, anxious to join the common cause. The congress declared that New York should enlist "those called Green Mountain Boys, under such officers as the said Green Mountain Boys shall chuse."[18]

While the competing letters and messengers were on their way to Philadelphia, Arnold enjoyed a few days as undisputed commander on Lake Champlain. Less than a week later, Colonel Benjamin Hinman arrived at Crown Point claiming to be the new commander, but Arnold refused to accept his authority, "as he produced no regular order for the same," and sent him back to Ticonderoga where Samuel Herrick was in charge.[19] By then a three man fact-finding committee from the Massachusetts Provincial Congress was making its way north with orders to become "fully acquainted with the spirit, capacity, and conduct" of Benedict Arnold and if necessary discharge him. They were also asked to report to New York, Connecticut, and the Continental Congress on the condition of the forts and their importance in defending the colonies. Brown listed these men first as his potential witnesses. For them, this was the great adventure of the war, conducted in the face of fatigue and danger.[20]

Senior member Walter Spooner from Dartmouth on Buzzard's Bay was in his mid-fifties. He had been a representative to the General Court since 1761, sat on the Governor's Council since 1770, and returned to the Council under the province's revolutionary government. He was remembered by one fellow council member as "the most clear-headed and far-seeing man he had ever known," except for Samuel Adams.[21]

Jedediah Foster, forty-eight, from North Brookfield in Worcester County, had also been a representative to General Court since 1761. He was named a Counsellor by the House of Representatives in May 1774, but was rejected by Governor Thomas Gage, which became a badge of honor. Foster took a seat in the First Provincial Congress as a delegate from Brookfield.[22]

James Sullivan, the youngest of the trio at thirty-one, six months older than John Brown, represented Biddeford in York County, now in the state of Maine. In the Provincial Congress, he was a voice for defending Falmouth (today's Portland) whose harbor was "at all seasons of the year the best in America." Many years later he was to be Massachusetts attorney general and governor.[23]

The committee rode through the New Hampshire Grants, followed the Mettowee River to Skenesborough at the southern end of the lake where they embarked for Ticonderoga. Early in the war, Ticonderoga was a shock to visitors who expected the fortress of legend. At the fort, the provincial congressmen met many officers, but the chain of command was confusing, maybe non-existent, as if there were several separate forces on the lake that cooperated haphazardly. They were impressed with Colonel Hinman, whom they found to have a "polite, generous, and manly disposition." In their report, they said nothing about Samuel Herrick, but praised adjutant William Satterlee, "a worthy man." Around that time, John Brown returned to the forts from Philadelphia. They surely knew him from the Provincial Congress.[24]

By the time Spooner, Foster, and Sullivan left Ticonderoga for Crown Point, they had heard enough about Arnold to prejudice the most open-minded of people. Arnold expected their arrival but did nothing to win them over. The committee explained to him that the Massachusetts congress recognized Hinman's commission and that he (Arnold) was no longer the commanding officer on the lake. They allowed him to read their instructions, which gave them the authority to decide his future. "He seemed greatly disconcerted, and declared he would not be second in command to any person whomsoever," Spooner reported, but "after some time contemplating upon the matter, [he] resigned the post."[25]

With the committee present, Arnold wrote a letter of resignation, stating his objections to how he was treated. "It appears to me very extraordinary that the Congress should first appoint an officer, and afterwards, when he had executed his commission, to appoint a Committee to examine if he was fit for his post." And Hinman was "a younger officer of the same rank," *younger* meaning that Arnold's commission predated his. But even this technicality, which is a staple of Arnold biographers, is not true: Hinman was appointed colonel of the provincial Fourth Connecticut Regiment by Governor Trumbull on May 1; Arnold was commissioned by the Massachusetts Committee of Safety two days later. Hinman had been a colonel in the Connecticut colonial forces since 1771.[26]

But there was no arguing with Arnold. In his "Memorandum Book," he noted, "I have resigned my commission, not being able to hold it any longer with honor." He dismissed his men and wrote to Herrick telling him to relinquish the command at Ticonderoga. The committee never learned how many men were in Arnold's regiment, but accepted his figure of between two and three hundred. Edward Mott, an Arnold adversary since the day they met on the march to Ticonderoga, sent a more alarming secondhand account to Governor Trumbull. Mott claimed that the committee had dismissed Arnold. Then when they asked to speak with his men, he refused. Arnold and his remaining supporters on the *Liberty* and the *Enterprise* cast off and dropped anchor away from shore. The committee "understood they threatened to go to St. John's and deliver the vessels to the Regulars," the British army. As the three commissioners rowed away, they were fired upon with swivel guns and small arms.[27]

Another version of the encounter appears in an 1859 biography of James Sullivan. At a dinner attended by Walter Spooner, an old man "of remarkably venerable appearance," Sullivan amused his guests with an account of their experiences on Lake Champlain. Spooner died in 1803, so the story is secondhand from long ago.

Three. "He would not be second in command to any person"

According to a dinner guest, Sullivan told how they were fired upon by Arnold's men—in the woods, not on the lake. But what the guest remembered with clarity was Sullivan's description of Spooner's response. The account gains credibility because the point of it was about Spooner and not Arnold. Sullivan reminded his listeners that they all found Spooner to be a "rigid observer ... of what was proper and decorous." Then he asked them to imagine "as they best could, that during all this encounter, he was swearing like a trooper."[28]

In the winter of 1779, Brown wrote to Joseph Reed, president of the Pennsylvania Supreme Executive Council, sending a copy of his thirteen charges. He insisted "the last charge in the impeachment, can now be fully supported." At that time, Brown was working closely with Spooner and Sullivan, who were prominent in the provincial congress's attempts to calm unrest in Berkshire County. We do not know what the men discussed about the summer of 1775, but Brown did.[29]

Brown's charges against Arnold include "a treasonable attempt to make his escape ... to the enemy at St John's." Brown claimed that the commanding officer of Ticonderoga—Hinman by then—issued "a positive order to the officers commanding our batteries at Crown-Point to stop or sink the vessels attempting to pass that post" and to make Arnold a prisoner. Were these claims about Arnold outright lies from men whose hatred of him already knew no bounds, unfair characterizations of events, or stories that had enough foundation to be prophetic?

The next day, June 24, Mott, Sullivan and William Duer—a neighbor, friend, and business associate of Major General Philip Schuyler—returned to Crown Point and tried to convince Arnold to leave the vessels. With fixed bayonets (this is again Mott's version), Arnold's men imprisoned them onboard the *Enterprise*. "We reasoned with the people on board the vessels all the while we were there," wrote Mott, "and convinced some of them of their errour, who declared they had been deceived by Colonel Arnold." Later Duer sent an incomplete account of Arnold's "late conduct at Ticonderoga" to Schuyler, the commander in New York and the Northern Department. Duer had heard rumors that Schuyler was considering appointing Arnold to be his deputy adjutant general. "I am very sensible you would not think of showing any mark of favor to any one whose unaccountable pride should lead him to sacrifice the true interests of the country," he wrote, omitting the interesting details. But Duer himself may not be a reliable source. In the 1790s, after serving as Assistant Secretary of the Treasury under Alexander Hamilton, his speculation in federal debt and bank stock, and the investors he attracted to his schemes, caused a financial bubble, followed by a panic.[30]

In Arnold's account, a few men protested their own treatment by seizing the *Enterprise* and holding *him* prisoner while they negotiated for pay they had not received. "I am reduced to great extremity, not being able to pay off the people who are in great want of necessaries, and much in debt," he wrote in the "Memorandum Book." "This gives me great trouble to pacify them and prevent disturbances." The arrival of five barrels of pork in the afternoon may have done more good than the calming words of officers and civilian leaders. That night, news arrived of the Battle of Bunker Hill. Thousands were killed on both sides, Arnold was told. So far on Lake Champlain not a single soldier had died in combat.[31]

In a final humiliation for Arnold, the Massachusetts committee appointed James Easton as second in command under Hinman. John Brown was to be the major. Once the soldiers were guaranteed their pay, most men joined Easton's Regiment willingly. Dismissed and humiliated, Arnold looked for revenge. The next day he wrote the "Veritas" letter, to counter newspaper accounts that featured Easton's heroism in the conquest of Fort Ticonderoga. Easton had been a coward, "Veritas" maintained. He was the last man to enter the fort. During the attack, he "concealed himself in an old barrack near the redoubt, under the pretence of wiping and drying his gun, which, he said had got wet in crossing the lake." Behind his back, Easton abused Arnold "in a base and cowardly manner," but Arnold "kicked him very heartily" to "the great satisfaction of a number of gentlemen present." A month later, the "Veritas" letter was strengthened with the addition of a letter from Captain William Delaplace, the British commander of Ticonderoga, who stated, "I never saw Colonel Easton at the time the fort was surprised, nor had he and I any conversation whatever relative thereto, then, or at any time since." Easton's reputation was destroyed—and it remains so.[32]

※ ※ ※

On July 10, Arnold presented himself at Philip Schuyler's mansion in Albany, up the hill from the ferry and just south of the city's common meadowland. Major General Schuyler, forty-one, commander in New York and the Northern Department, had arrived home a day earlier and been escorted by a grand procession through the city. Schuyler was an aristocrat without a title. His other home in Saratoga, present-day Schuylerville, was a mansion on the Hudson River. The village was a center of industry with sawmills, grist mills, and a flax mill, all worked by tenants and slaves. He had property in the Mohawk Valley and a fleet of sloops on the Hudson.

For much of the French and Indian War, Schuyler was deputy commissary under deputy quarter-master general John Bradstreet. Schuyler at his desk tallying barrels of salt pork may have done more than celebrated figures to achieve the British and Provincial victory over France, but it was not heroic work, nor did it prepare him to lead men in battle. "This Gentleman is the Soul of Albany County," wrote Congressman Silas Deane to his wife, "and tho' he may have foibles, he is sincere, well bred, & resolute, and I think a valuable acquaintance."[33] Deane did not elaborate on the foibles. Schuyler was prickly and exacting, a worrier, who was quick to make excuses, which often centered on his health.

This small portrait of Philip Schuyler was painted by John Trumbull, a young staff officer during the war who became the great artist of the Revolution. Yale University Art Gallery.

Arnold was a gentleman and Schuyler welcomed him to his home. Arnold brought with him a letter of thanks from "the principal inhabitants" of Lake Champlain, supposedly six hundred families. They wrote of his competency, vigilance, prudence, humanity, benevolence, valor, and good conduct. He was "a bright example of that elevation and generosity of soul, which nothing less than real magnanimity and innate virtue could inspire." Years later, William Gilliland told the Continental Congress that he wrote the address, but had learned how mistaken he had been to admire Arnold. Although Gilliland was likely involved, Arnold himself may have supplied much of the heated rhetoric. *Innate virtue inspiring a generous soul?* Whatever that means, it sounds like Arnold, who believed he could use language as boldly as he could fight.[34]

Arnold told Schuyler of the sorry situation of the army on the lakes. He had left nearly three hundred men at Crown Point and another six hundred at Ticonderoga, who had nothing to do because they had received no orders to work on the fortifications. At Fort George at the southern end of Lake George, a few of the three hundred men were building bateaux or off on scouting expeditions. "Very little provision at any of the places; none made for the sick, which are daily increasing; only five hundred weight of gunpowder at all the places, and no Engineer or Gunner at either. Great want of discipline and regularity among the troops," Arnold reported to Congress at Schuyler's request.[35]

Schuyler always mistrusted the Green Mountain Boys, but now he heard firsthand from an officer with a sense of discipline. Arnold had seen no militia, organized or irregular, only men who came and went as they pleased. Then Schuyler received a letter from Colonel Hinman, who was overwhelmed by his responsibilities. "I wait, Sir, with impatience for your arrival, as I find myself very unable to steer in this stormy situation," he wrote.[36]

Arnold's few days of comfort at Schuyler's mansion ended with the news that his wife had died, leaving their three young sons in the care of his sister. He went home to New Haven for two weeks before leaving for headquarters outside Boston where he presented Massachusetts authorities with his expenses from Lake Champlain and lobbied for an assignment that suited his ambition. His supporter Dr. Joseph Warren had been killed at Bunker Hill, and Arnold faced a skeptical committee chaired by Benjamin Church, who next to himself was the most shocking traitor of the Revolution.

Four

"Now, Sir, is the time to carry Canada"

By order of the Continental Congress, Philip Schuyler was to make an "Impression into Canada," but only if he found it "practicable and not disagreeable to the Canadians."[1] It was a formula devised by politicians that put him in an unenviable position. Ethan Allen and Benedict Arnold were certain of American success, but they were talking to the minority English-speaking merchants. Schuyler had to hope that if the American army could tiptoe into Canada as liberators, not invaders, they might be able win the support of the French *habitants* and avoid angering the northern Indians. The French landowners, the *seigneurs*, and the clergy were probably beyond reach.

On the evening of July 17, 1775, Schuyler arrived at Lake George Landing, three miles from Fort Ticonderoga. He told Washington in a letter, "With a penknife only I could have cut off both guards and then set fire to the block-house, destroyed the stores, and starved the people here." Arnold had prepared Schuyler for what he would find at Ticonderoga, but he was still shocked. "Not one earthly thing for offence or defence has been done; *the commanding officer* [Benjamin Hinman] *had no orders, he only came to re-enforce the garrison, and he expected the General!*" They did not have boats or the lumber and tools with which to construct them. Hinman's men had no tents, were crowded into the fort's barracks, and would, if nothing was done soon, be sick. Crown Point was even weaker and "an easy prey" if Guy Carleton, governor of Québec, realized his opportunity.[2]

Schuyler mistrusted Ethan Allen and the Green Mountain Boys, but they were the closest armed men to Ticonderoga—if they would enlist in great enough numbers and if Allen was dependable. Then to Schuyler's surprise, delegates to a New Hampshire Grants convention elected Seth Warner commander of the regiment by a vote of 41 to 5. Schuyler worried that a dispute between Allen and Warner would hurt recruitment, and so through August he did not commission Warner as lieutenant colonel although Warner continued to enlist men in the regiment. Finally, the New York Provincial Congress appointed Warner commander. After meeting with several officers, including Brown, Schuyler did allow Allen to remain with the army as a volunteer. Almost a year later, Brown certified that Schuyler and his second in command Richard Montgomery promised "in case Colonel *Allen* should have the misfortune to be taken prisoner, that every proper method should be taken for his redemption and exchange consistent with the rules of war in such cases."[3] Whether they actually discussed the possibility of capture or not, the point of Brown's certificate was that Allen was a real officer in the American army and not a freelance plunderer.

And to add to his other problems, in July Schuyler had no way of knowing what the British and Natives were doing. For this information, he turned to two men, Remember Baker and John Brown. Baker was another mob captain in the Green Mountain Boys and a New York outlaw. He was first cousin to both Ethan Allen and Seth Warner, although Allen and Warner were not themselves related. Baker served for five summer campaigns in the French and Indian War, finally as a sergeant. During the land dispute with New York, a justice of the peace broke down his door in the middle of the night and carried him off in a sleigh. Baker was rescued, but afterwards he was an angry man, waving his musket or an injured thumb as a commission for destroying a New York settler's cabin. Now like Warner and Allen, he was on the same side as the New Yorkers.[4]

Brown and Captain Robert Cochran left Ticonderoga for a spying mission in Canada soon after dawn on July 24. At Crown Point, they were joined by Bayze Wells and two other men, John Legger and Canadian Pierre Charlan. Wells, a thirty-one-year-old private in Hinman's Regiment, was an intelligent, inquisitive man, although the journal he kept has no punctuation, only random capitalization, and the wildest phonetic spelling. A year later he was a lieutenant on a gunboat in Benedict Arnold's Lake Champlain fleet, so he is one of few firsthand sources outside of generals and congressmen with insight into both Brown's and Arnold's stories.[5]

At ten in the morning with wind filling the sail, Brown and his four companions left Crown Point to spy on the enemy. In the afternoon, north of Basin Harbor, they encountered the sloop *Enterprise* and boarded her to learn the news. Remember Baker was returning from a scout in the north and told them of the dangers they would face. Indians were guarding the approaches to St. John and it was hard to say if Governor Carleton had issued orders to fire upon "our people" or to take captives. Baker had learned that St. John was entrenched and fortified with four hundred fifty British troops and twelve cannon. Near the Missisquoi River, he met Natives from St. Francis and Kahnawake and "was treated with great civility." They told him that seven Indian towns or nations had pledged not to fight the Yankees.[6]

By sunset on July 25, Brown and company were as far north as Cumberland Head, the peninsula that forms the bay where the city of Plattsburgh, New York, was to be built. They rowed all that night, hid their bateau in the bushes, and then, except for breakfast and a nap, marched all day. It rained that night; by 6:30 the next morning, they were hiking north again. Wells noted that it "Raind as hard as Ever I saw it about an houre ... we ware as wet as water Could make us." When they began to see signs of habitation—a horse and what looked like a footpath—they took to a swamp. Although there was plenty of water underfoot, they suffered from thirst and twice dug shallow wells and drank the muddy contents. For three days they slogged through the mire before reaching the road from Saint-Jean to La Prairie. At last they stayed in a house overnight, but had to spend the day in a chicken coop (a "hin Roost," in Wells's account).[7]

Pierre Charlan left for Chambly, further north on the Richelieu River, and returned with Captain Joseph Ménard, who led them on an all-night march back to Chambly. In addition to the small village on the Chambly Basin, there was a square, high-walled stone fort, garrisoned by a detachment of British soldiers. Wells wrote of their stay in Chambly, "we were Youused with much Kindness and Respect." Brown, who a few months earlier had found French Canadians to be "extremely ignorant and bigoted," wrote to Governor Trumbull, who was known for his opposition to Roman Catholicism, "It is impossible for me to describe the kindness received from the French, as also their distressed situation, being threatened with destruction from the King's Troops, by fire and sword, because they refuse to take up arms against the Colonies."[8]

While in Chambly, Brown met with James Livingston, a twenty-eight-year-old grain merchant and member of the influential New York family. As happened so often with Brown, the two formed a lasting relationship that benefited the American cause. Livingston gave Brown a letter to Schuyler that was received at Ticonderoga by second-in-command Brigadier General Richard Montgomery, whose wife was also a Livingston[9]

From Chambly, Brown sent Charlan and Ménard to Montréal with a letter for Thomas Walker, the merchant Brown had met during his trip in March, but they were stopped and confined. Then the four remaining spies learned that they had been discovered. They escaped out a back window and took to the woods. Friends ferried them across the Richelieu to the east side where they were safer until Cochran accidently frightened a boy who raised the alarm. To protect his men, Brown came out of hiding and spoke to the crowd. In the resulting "uprore," the party became separated, and Wells and Cochran decided to make their way home alone. Brown and Legger reached the same decision, and they all hiked southeast away from the Richelieu. At times both parties were desperate for drinking water. Once Brown shot a moose, but a single musket ball could not bring it down. On the fourth day, Cochran and Wells came to a river, the Missisquoi, and followed it west to the New York settlement controlled by Simon Metcalf, an English-born surveyor. To everyone's joy, Brown and Legger had arrived only a half hour earlier. Metcalf loaned Brown and company a canoe and they paddled for Ticonderoga. Brown was convinced that Canada was ripe for taking. He told Governor Trumbull, "Now, Sir, is the time to carry Canada. It may be done with great ease and little cost, and I have no doubt but the Canadians would join us."[10]

※ ※ ※

In early August, Remember Baker was north again and reported that the British were constructing two schooners (one was destined to be a row galley), each mounting sixteen cannon plus swivels. The news was so alarming that Captain James Stewart of the *Liberty*, on patrol, sailed south immediately, driven by gale wind. Baker's reports described British forces rapidly preparing for war. On August 22, Baker and a scouting party were again along the Richelieu River watching the approaches to St. John when Baker was killed in a skirmish with Indians. His death was news from Québec to Philadelphia and Boston. Ethan Allen's youngest brother Ira, who loved his Cousin Remember like a father, wrote from the heart, "Captain Baker was the first man killed in the northern department, and being a gentleman universally respected, his death made more noise in the country than the loss of a thousand men towards the end of the American war."[11]

※ ※ ※

With fall approaching, the American invasion of Canada was stalled at Ticonderoga. Schuyler was in Albany; many regiments, including Warner's Green Mountain Boys, had yet to appear; and second-in-command Richard Montgomery had no orders to proceed until preparations were complete.

Brown, who was far north on Lake Champlain aboard the *Liberty*, forced the issue. The day after Baker's death—although the news had not yet arrived—a spy returned to the *Liberty* with a report on the progress on the two large vessels at the St. John shipyard. Their hulls were constructed and were being blackened; masts were almost ready to be raised, and they might be able to sail in a week to ten days. "These vessels, when on the lake, will effectually command it, and the expedition is up for this year," Brown told Montgomery in a message. Brown and Captain Stewart sounded the lake north of Windmill Point, a peninsula on the east side just south of today's U.S.–Canada border, and discussed whether a battery mounted where the lake was a mile wide could stop vessels of war. Brown wrote, "If the Army are not ready to march within the time abovementioned, a plan of this kind must be executed, or we lose all, i.e. the command of the lake, which is tantamount." He apologized for "writing in a dictatorial style," but insisted that if nothing was done, the enemy "can easily sweep this lake in its present condition."[12]

Montgomery wrote immediately to Schuyler, who was still in Albany meeting with the Iroquois. "I am so of Brown's opinion that I think it absolutely necessary to move down the lake [*down* means north] with the utmost dispatch." He did not like acting without Schuyler's orders, but "if I must err I wish to be on the right side."[13] And so with encouragement from Brown, the invasion of Canada began.

※ ※ ※

On August 28, an army of 1200 men left Ticonderoga for Canada under command of Brigadier General Richard Montgomery, the son of an Anglo-Irish baronet. During the French and Indian War, Montgomery served at Ticonderoga, Crown Point, Montréal, and the Caribbean as part of the 17th Regiment of Foot. The only portrait Montgomery sat for was painted when he was

General Richard Montgomery was an early hero of the Revolution but is little remembered today. This engraving is based on a portrait by Charles Willson Peale, which followed a portrait painted while Montgomery was a young man. The Miriam and Ira D. Wallach Division of Art, Prints and Photographs: Print Collection, The New York Public Library Digital Collection.

twenty-six in Ireland, so his image is forever fixed as that of a young man. Charles Willson Peale and the engravers who followed him aged their versions of the portrait, but not successfully. Descriptions say he was tall, thin, and pock-marked. At thirty-six, he was bald on the top of his head and often depressed.[14]

In the early 1770s, Montgomery tried to purchase a major's commission, but did not have the social clout, losing out to Charles Preston, who coincidentally was to be his adversary at St. John. Instead, Montgomery chose the aristocratic version of the American Dream. He left England, writing, "As a man with little money cuts but a bad figure in this country, among peers, nabobs, etc., I have cast my eye on America, where my pride and poverty will be much more at their ease." In fact, Montgomery struggled to inspire opinionated Americans. He wrote to his wife Janet, "I am unfit to deal with mankind in the bulk.... I feel too sensibly the rascality, ignorance and selfishness among my fellow creatures."[15]

※ ※ ※

From Albany, Schuyler hurried to catch up with his army. By the time he reached Ticonderoga, he was sick with what was called bilious fever (high temperature, vomiting, and diarrhea). He rested overnight at the fort, gave orders for remaining troops to move north, and then sailed himself. On the morning of September 4, he joined Montgomery on Isle la Motte, far north in the lake. Later that day, the first Americans encamped on Île-aux-Noix, an island in the Richelieu River a dozen miles south of St. John/Saint-Jean.

In the three months since Arnold's raid on the supply depot, the British had rebuilt a fort on the site of a French fort from the last war. Two redoubts, each about 250 feet long, were connected by palisaded trenches. These earth fortifications were protected by ditches and stakes. In all, the fort stretched for more than a thousand feet along the Richelieu River and was manned by 725 troops from the 7th and 26th regiments, seventy Royal Highland Emigrants, a hundred French Canadians, and a few Natives. To the west was the marshy land that Brown and company had slogged through, nature's contribution to the defense of Canada.

Schuyler wrote a letter to the Canadians, whom he addressed as "Friends and Countrymen." He had it translated into French, and entrusted copies to Brown and Ethan Allen to carry to James Livingston and throughout the countryside. Schuyler promised to "cherish every Canadian and every friend to the cause of liberty, and sacredly to guard their property." He wrote, "Such is the confidence I have in the good disposition of my army that I do not believe I shall have reason to punish a single offense committed against you."[16]

On September 6, Schuyler ordered the first landing near St. John. In a skirmish with a party of Indians, seven Americans were killed. Then Schuyler heard from local landowner Moses Hazen that French Canadians might not rally to the American cause and that the British schooner-of-war was nearly ready to sail. At a council of war the next morning, all the officers worried the schooner would rake the low land where they were encamped, and Schuyler ordered a retreat to Île-aux-Noix. A second attempt on September 10–11 was as hapless. Men retreated from the breastwork closest to the fort and then were frightened by their own flanking parties.[17]

By September 16, Schuyler was even sicker—his bilious fever was complicated by "violent rheumatick pains." He left the army and in a heavy rain sailed south.

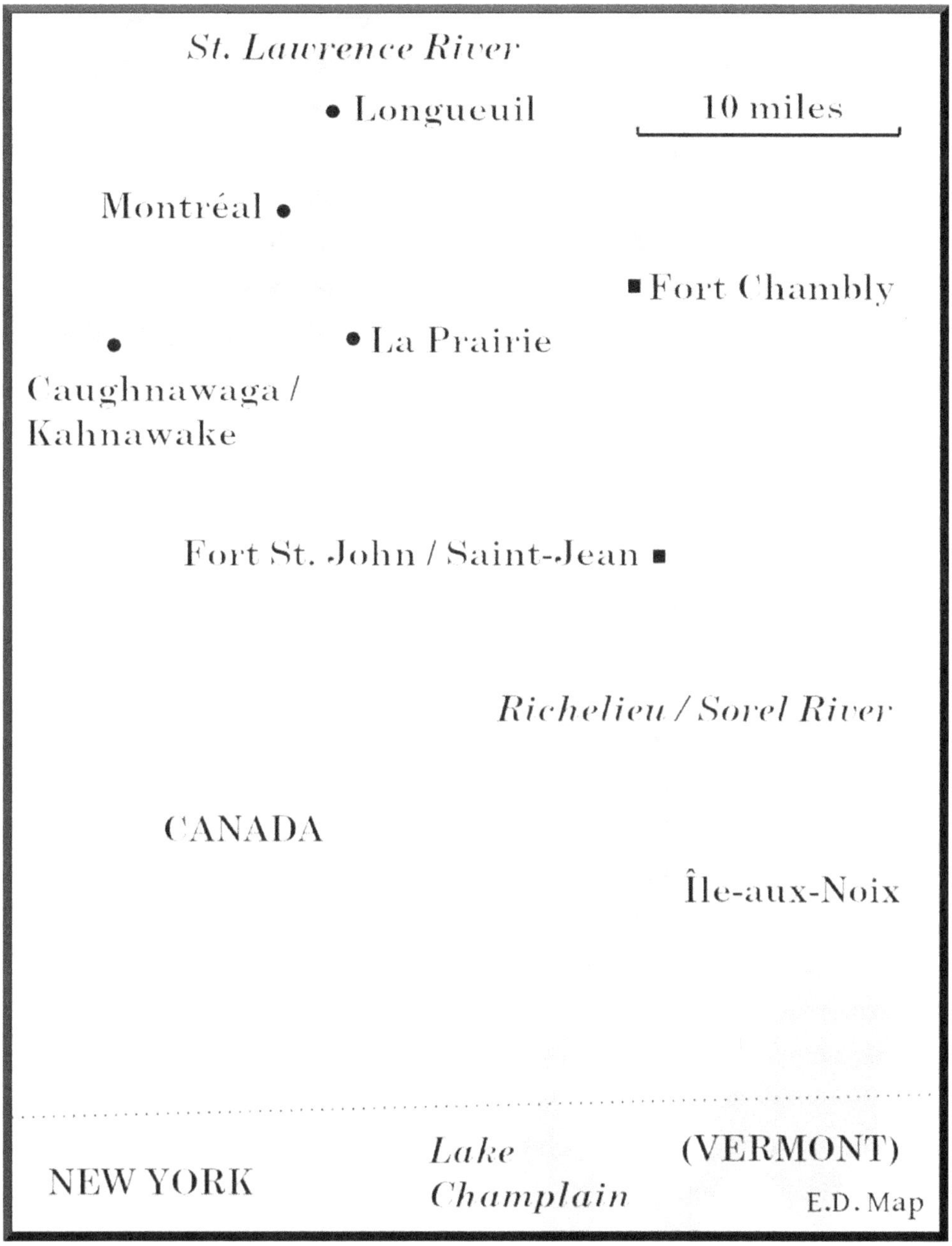

Four. "Now, Sir, is the time to carry Canada"

```
St. Lawrence River
        • Longueuil              10 miles

  Montréal •
                                ■ Fort Chambly
      •         • La Prairie
Caughnawaga /
Kahnawake


     Fort St. John / Saint-Jean ■


                        Richelieu / Sorel River


        CANADA
                                Île-aux-Noix




                        Lake        (VERMONT)
  NEW YORK            Champlain      E.D. Map
```

The American campaign in Canada in September 1775 took place along two rivers: the Richelieu (often called the Sorel), which is the outlet of Lake Champlain, and the mighty St. Lawrence.

※ ※ ※

Before departing, Schuyler ordered Brown with a hundred Americans and thirty-four Canadians towards Chambly "to keep up the Spirits of the Canadians" and recruit militia. On the night of September 17–18, Brown's contingent surprised a supply train that was bringing provisions and gun carriages to the fort and captured eight wagons. In the morning, two hundred men from the fort, supported by field guns, attacked Brown's smaller force and drove them from their camp.

In person, General Montgomery led about five hundred Yankees—Warner's newly arrived regiment, Colonel Timothy Bedel's New Hampshire Rangers, and part of Colonel Hinman's regiment—on a three-mile march through swampy land to reinforce Brown. As Montgomery's men neared, they stumbled into this skirmish. "The grape shot and Musket balls flew very thick," wrote Lieutenant John Fassett of Warner's Regiment, "but our pilots, not knowing the ground, we had not an equal chance for they all fled to St. Johns." Montgomery was disappointed as he often was. Brown had "imprudently thrown himself in [the enemy's] way." The Green Mountain Boys and the New Hampshire Rangers, the *woodsmen*, "were not so expert at forming as I expected and too many of them hung back." Still, he believed that if the thickness of forest had not made it difficult to estimate the size of the enemy, he would have captured the entire British force. Brown had hidden the captured supplies in the woods and the rum was welcome.[18]

Five

"The only field officer of any share of abilities"

Soon much of the American army was bogged down at St. John, often literally in deep mud. "We have been like half-downed rats crawling thro' the swamp," Montgomery wrote to his wife. The men suffered from dysentery, increasing cold, a lack supplies, and incessant rain. Montgomery was appalled at how undisciplined his men were and at his own powerlessness to command these "pusillanimous wretches." He wrote to his brother-in-law, Robert Livingston, the most influential Livingston, "The New England troops are the worst stuff imaginable. There is such an equality among them, that the officers have no authority.... The privates are all generals, but not soldiers." Montgomery's despair comes across in every letter and makes the siege of St. John sound like a drawn-out defeat rather than a victory.[1]

John Brown was free of all that. He and Seth Warner were sent into the countryside north of the fort to La Prairie and the St. Lawrence River. The men under their command found themselves in a foreign country, one they had been raised to fear. "I see the strangest thing that I ever see in my life," Lieutenant Fassett marveled after attending Roman Catholic Mass. "Their Ceremonies are beyond what I can express. They had six candles burning all the time." But on a trip to buy shoes for the army, he commented, "I was treated the Best I ever was in my Life with what wine I could drink and with what victuals I could eat."[2]

By September 20, Ethan Allen was giddy with his successes as a freelance hero. He was ahead of the army, negotiating with Indians, recruiting militia, and, as he put it "preaching politics." He commanded two hundred fifty Canadians, he wrote Montgomery, and "as I march, they gather fast." In three days, he planned to join the siege of St. John's with five hundred or more Canadian volunteers. In a week, he could recruit one or two thousand. "I swear by the Lord I can raise three times the number of our Army in Canada, provided you continue the siege; all depends on that," he lectured Montgomery as if the general was unsure of his duty.[3]

On the morning of September 24, Allen was on the road along the St. Lawrence from Longueuil to La Prairie when he met Brown and they decided to combine their forces and surprise Montréal. Or so Allen wrote in *The Narrative of Colonel Ethan Allen*. In the *Narrative*, Brown receives much of the blame for the disaster that followed. Allen wrote, "Brown proposed, that 'Provided I would return to Longale, and procure some canoes, so as to cross the river St. Lawrence a little north of Montreal, he would cross it a little to the south of the town, with near two hundred men, as he had boats sufficient; and that we would make ourselves masters of Montreal.'" Years later Ira Allen claimed that Seth Warner was at the meeting and agreed to cross from La Prairie with Brown.[4]

Without question, the three men did discuss the capture of Montréal, sometime, somehow. Montgomery told Schuyler, "Allen, Warner, and Brown are at La Prairie and Longueuil, with a party of their troops, and some Canadians. They all speak well of the good disposition of the Canadians. They have a project of making an attempt on Montreal."[5]

"I thought to have enrolled my name in the list of illustrious American heroes," Allen wrote to the Connecticut Assembly nearly a year later, "but it was nipped in the bud." The night was windy, and once again, as had been the case at Ticonderoga, Allen had too few boats, so that it took three crossings in canoes and most of the night to get one hundred ten men across the powerful, mile-wide river and onto the island of Montréal. In the early morning, Allen awaited three huzzas from Brown, which never came. In Ethan's account, one might suppose that Montréal was a small place where a good shout could be heard from one end of the city to the other. In fact, the walled city stretched for a mile along the St. Lawrence and contained a population of about nine thousand. La Prairie was on the south bank of a wide basin that the St. Lawrence formed between rapids. Crossings were often indirect, as much as six miles, through rapid current filled with rocks.[6]

Ira Allen wrote that Brown *and* Warner found the crossing too dangerous and did not bother to notify Ethan before going "quietly to rest." He wrote, "The conduct of Brown and Warner is hard to be accounted for, on any principles honourable to themselves. We are informed by sacred writ that *the disciples of Jesus Christ disputed among themselves who should be the greatest*."[7] But neither Montgomery, nor any other officer at the time, blamed anyone but Allen and his "imprudence" for what happened next. Some historians have taken Ethan at his word: Brown failed to do his part. Others have wondered if there was miscommunication about date and time. Or perhaps Ethan thought he saw an opportunity to show everyone, including cautious New York generals, the delegates in the New Hampshire Grants who had passed him by, and Brown and Warner—and so acted on his own. Having other officers along would only confuse the question of who deserved credit, as it had at Ticonderoga.[8]

Allen's *Narrative* is an inspiring book, but it is not reliable history. No comments from Brown survive from the time of Ethan's capture or after the publication of the *Narrative*, and Brown lived for nearly a year after the book came out in Philadelphia late in 1779. Brown was bold and persistent, and it is hard to imagine him hanging back—either in attacking Montréal or in setting the record straight. Perhaps he did not see the *Narrative* in time to respond, or see it at all. Although Allen has been called a best-selling author, we should not imagine rapid communication. By August 1780, Brown was serving along the Mohawk River and faced more serious threats than Allen's tales about what happened five years earlier.

Allen expected Canadians to welcome him as a liberator and did not know that there was less pro–American sentiment in Montréal than in the countryside. His little force faced a walled city with its gates closed. He considered re-crossing the St. Lawrence, but instead decided his men would be open to attack as they ferried back and forth in canoes. "I therefore concluded to maintain the ground, (if possible) and all to fare alike," he remembered nobly. Montréal's defenders—one hundred twenty

French Canadians, eighty British Canadians, thirty-four Regulars, and a half dozen Indians—sallied from the gates in the afternoon and rounded up Allen and his outnumbered, unprepared men. Brigadier General Richard Prescott threatened Allen with hanging and ordered him shackled aboard the schooner *Gaspé*. Gentlemen were not shackled and traitors were hanged. Warner's news of the capture was the earliest to reach Montgomery. "I have no certain knowledge, as yet, whether he is killed, taken or fled; but his defeat hath put the French people into great consternation. They are much concerned, for fear of a company coming over against us," Warner wrote.[9]

By then, Montgomery was counting on the success of an expedition led by Benedict Arnold, making its way up Maine's Kennebec River to Québec. On October 6, he wrote Schuyler, "No certain intelligence yet of Arnold's arrival, though there are flying reports to that purpose. I wish he was at Quebeck with all my heart; I believe there is nothing to oppose him." On that day, the lead bateaux on the Kennebec had reached the Great Carrying Place, the beginning of a backbreaking portage and two hundred miles from Québec.[10]

For a short time, Montgomery hoped to win the surrender of Montréal with the help of Luc de La Corne, sometimes called St. Luke La Corne. A seigneur, merchant, and friend of the Natives, La Corne was a feared man. "That arch devil incarnate," military engineer Samuel Mott, brother of Edward Mott, reminded Governor Trumbull. La Corne "has butchered hundreds, men, women, and children of our Colonies, in the late war, in the most inhuman manner." Montgomery thought he had found a crafty representative in John Brown. He told his wife, Luc de La Corne "is a great villain and as cunning as the devil, but I have sent a New Englander to negotiate with him." Yankees had a reputation for close dealing. But La Corne only toyed with joining the American cause; changed his mind entirely after Allen's capture; and sent Montgomery's letter on to Governor Guy Carleton, who burned it without reading it.[11]

Montgomery wanted to place a battery with heavy guns on a rise about four hundred yards west of Fort St. John. From there, he believed, he could approach the fort using siege techniques and demolish the nearest fortifications, making the fort open to assault. However, Brown told him that "a general dissatisfaction prevailed" in the army and that if the problem was not dealt with promptly there would be a mutiny. Montgomery was prepared to listen to Brown whom he called "the only Field officer of any share of abilities." When Montgomery called a council of war to back his plan to attack from the west, the field officers were unanimous in their opposition. They wanted to strengthen a battery on the east side of the river and destroy the schooner. Grudgingly, Montgomery agreed to the council's wishes, and a battery of two twelve-pounders sank the feared *Royal Savage*.[12]

※ ※ ※

In the dark of October 16, two boats, each holding a "nine-pound cannon," passed the guns of St. John and ran the rapids to Chambly Basin, ten miles north. A nine-pound gun got its name from the weight of the shot that it fired. In fact, a nine-pound iron gun was at least seven feet in length and weighed more than 2500 pounds. The idea for this risky venture came from James Livingston; Brown was aboard one of the boats. Near Fort Chambly, two to three hundred Canadians were joined by fifty Americans from Brown's command. Many of the French Canadians were recruited by Irish-born Jeremiah Duggan (sometimes spelled Dugan), who lived in the area. Brown promised the unpaid Canadian volunteers a share of the supplies in the fort, and was later backed by Montgomery. Duggan may have gone further in what he sanctioned.[13]

Built by the French between 1709 and 1711 on the site of earlier wooden forts, Chambly was an imposing structure with 16-foot-tall stone walls and higher bastions at the four corners. But its purpose had been to exhibit the power of the French in their conflicts with the Iroquois and not to withstand an enemy with cannon. In October 1775, the fort was occupied by seven officers and eighty-three enlisted men from the 7th Regiment of Foot, the Royal Fusiliers, and about one hundred women and children. Historian Justin Smith in his classic 1907 account of the American invasion of Canada wrote, "The 'castle' was a summer hotel rather than a fortress."[14] It was also a warehouse for provisions and military stores.

For two days, Brown and Livingston bombarded the fort with their nine-pounders. Some damage was done to the walls; a chimney was knocked over; one man was wounded; but Chambly was well-supplied and would not be easily stormed. Then surprisingly, Chambly's commander, Major Joseph Stopford, asked for terms, proposing that his men be allowed to march to Montréal "drums beating, colours flying," as if they had scarcely been defeated. Brown refused: they were "to surrender themselves prisoners of war," although they could keep their personal baggage and be accompanied by their families.[15]

Unlike the squabbles at Ticonderoga, Brown requested that Livingston sign the articles of capitulation as the man who deserved most credit, but Livingston said that he considered himself a volunteer and left that honor "to the worthy and deserving." But it was not all cooperation. The details are not clear, but Livingston thought that Montgomery had slighted him and blamed Jeremiah Duggan and a man named Maynard for a "damnable scheme" to prejudice Montgomery. Livingston called for a court-martial to clear his name or he would retire. Somehow the issues were resolved,

Fort Chambly, shown here in the early nineteenth century, was built to impress Natives with the power of the French colonists. In October 1775, John Brown and James Livingston captured the old fort and a wealth of supplies. Toronto Public Library.

and less than a month later, Montgomery appointed Livingston colonel of a regiment of Canadians. In January, Benedict Arnold named Duggan commander of a second Canadian regiment, but around the same time, Congress appointed Moses Hazen to the position. In March, Congress made Duggan a lieutenant colonel who was to command three hundred Canadian Rangers.[16]

Fort Chambly contained six tons of powder, more than 6000 musket cartridges, 134 barrels of pork, eighty barrels of flour, and other supplies and provisions. The siege of St. John took on new life. Montgomery wrote of Brown, "Upon this and all other occasions I have found him active and intelligent."[17]

※ ※ ※

The British made one last attempt to save Fort St. John. Colonel Allan MacLean advanced from Québec toward the Richelieu River with a one hundred twenty Scots, termed the Royal Highland Emigrants, sixty Regulars from the 7th Regiment of Foot, and a growing number of Canadian militia that may have reached five hundred. As young man, MacLean fought at the Battle of Culloden on the rebel Jacobite side before serving in the French and Indian War throughout the north. At fifty years old, he was experienced, determined, and loyal to the King. In Montréal, Governor-General Carleton assembled an army of nearly a thousand men to cross the St. Lawrence and relieve the fort. On October 30, they came down the river in thirty-four vessels including the armed schooner *Gaspé*, but were driven off by Seth Warner's regiment and a company from the 2nd New York. The Americans suffered almost no casualties. Along with news of the victory at Longueuil, Warner sent two prisoners to Montgomery. Negotiations for the surrender of St. John finally began. A party of officers, led by Lieutenant John André, later to be Benedict Arnold's contact as he betrayed the American cause, met with a prisoner and came away convinced the situation was hopeless. The garrison was permitted to march from the fort "with the honours of war," which they had earned through their "fortitude and perseverance." St. John had been under attack from September 6 until November 3.

The Royal Highland Emigrants and loyal Canadian recruits moved slowly up the Richelieu River, opposed by Livingston, Duggan, and Canadian rebels, who were joined by Easton and Brown's regiment. Easton had only recently returned to the army, and for the first time during the campaign, his name rather than Brown's appears in reports as commander. Brown was in an uncomfortable position: Easton was a friend—"my neighest Neighbour" he called him in one letter—but the success of the regiment and the cooperation with the Canadians had been Brown's doing. Before the rebel and Loyalist forces clashed, Maclean retreated to the St. Lawrence and sailed away. As it turned out, his retreat was fortunate for British Canada. Had he remained on the Richelieu much longer, Benedict Arnold might have strolled into the undefended city of Québec.[18]

On the night of November 6–7, Brown crossed the St. Lawrence to Berthier and patrolled the north shore. He seized the mail on its way from Montréal to Québec, which he forwarded to Montgomery, and briefly detained three men, two merchants and the local seigneur. Carleton was preparing to leave Montréal, Brown learned, and there was no need to threaten the city from the northeast. At Sorel, where the Richelieu River joins the St. Lawrence at a bend in the river, Easton and Brown mounted a battery aimed at the channel. On November 8, Brown opened fire, surprising a snow, a square-rigged ship named the *Fell*, that came within two hundred yards of their guns. "We plumed her through in many Places before she could tow off," Brown wrote to Montgomery. The *Fell* fired at Brown's battery, hit the town, and made its way to safety. "We are intirely at leasure having swept Land and Sea," Brown wrote.[19]

※ ※ ※

On November 12, Montgomery signed a capitulation with a dozen representatives of the "Citizens and Inhabitants of Montreal." He guaranteed religious freedom, free trade, no quartering of troops, the election of judges, amnesty for those who fought against the Americans, and no requirement that inhabitants take up arms against Great Britain. The first article of capitulation protected the property and was the foundation of Brown's charge that Arnold plundered the inhabitants in violation of Montgomery's solemn agreement: "That the citizens and inhabitants of Montreal, as well individuals as religious orders and communities, without any exceptions, shall be maintained in the free possession and enjoyment of their rights, goods, and effects, moveable and immoveable, of what nature soever they may be."[20]

A confusing blending of regiments took place at the end of the fall campaign. Bedel, Warner, and Brown met with Montgomery at Indian House in Montréal and received the general's permission to form a single regiment for the winter campaign. Brown was to be promoted and take command of the northwestern New England men. Bedel and Warner were to recruit reinforcements for spring. Montgomery also promised "all public Stores taken in the Vessels, to the Troops who went forward, Except Ammunition and Provisions." Easton and Brown's men were already manning the guns at Sorel, and some of Bedel's men agreed to go on. Warner's Regiment refused and returned home.[21]

※ ※ ※

The final action of the fall campaign took place at Sorel where an American battery of three 12-pounders, one nine, and two sixes guarded the narrows and awaited the flight of eleven British vessels from Montréal. Six months later, during the American retreat from Canada, Colonel Elisha Porter of Massachusetts saw the breastwork at Sorel and termed it "a shiftless thing indeed." But Carleton was a cautious man and had no way of evaluating what he faced. Twice he moved his fleet upriver away from the American guns, and then he decided that for the survival of Canada, he himself needed to reach Québec. At night in a bateau with muffled oars, he passed the battery. With Carleton gone, the command of the fleet passed to Richard Prescott, the general who had confined Ethan Allen in chains.[22]

On the morning of November 19, John Brown visited the *Gaspé* and demanded the surrender of the fleet. When Prescott doubted the strength of the American battery, Brown suggested that a British officer tour the position. The next spring Charles Carroll, a commissioner from the Continental Congress to the Canadians, wrote an imagined version of Brown's words to this gullible officer. Brown asked him to "wait a little till he saw the two 32-pounders, which were within half a mile coming from Chambly.... If you should chance to escape this battery, which is my small battery, I have a grand battery at the mouth of the Sorel, which will infallibly sink all of your vessels."[23] Based on the report of his witness, Prescott threw the fleet's powder and shot overboard and surrendered. Among a wealth of supplies, the Americans captured were 760 barrels of pork and 675 of flour. They seized Brigadier Prescott, three majors, five captains, and several lesser officers, 117 rank and file, and numerous Loyalists and officials, including the notorious St. Luc La Corne. Brown had bluffed his way to a victory.[24]

Two Canadian prisoners, Thomas Walker and Moses Hazen, were freed. Hazen, whose house was on the Richelieu opposite Fort St. John, had been mistrusted by both sides. In September, Brown had detained him north of the fort; then the British imprisoned him in Montréal. Now for the first time, he committed to the American cause. Walker's house had been burned at Prescott's orders and he had been confined in irons for more than a month. In a sworn statement given in Philadelphia in April 1776, he said he was set free "by his friend Major Brown, who delivered him from the cruel hand of tyranny and oppression and from the tools of military and arbitrary power."[25]

※ ※ ※

Two months later, Benedict Arnold wrote to General David Wooster warning him that he might hear from Brown, who stood accused of plundering and embezzling the "Public Stores and Officers baggage" taken at Sorel. A few days after that, he wrote to John Hancock that Brown and James Easton "were publickly impeached with plundering the officers' baggage taken at Sorel, contrary to articles of capitulation." Letters to Hancock in his role as president of the Continental Congress were looked upon as communications with the entire congress. In his thirteen charges, Brown denied the "unjustifiable, false, wicked, and malicious accusation" made against him and accused Arnold of "plundering the inhabitants of Montreal in direct violation of a solemn capitulation agreement entered into with them by our late brave and worthy General Montgomery." Then as now, in the thrust and parry of charges and countercharges, the objective was to reveal an opponent as a liar—better yet as a liar and hypocrite.[26]

Plundering was an elastic crime that could stretch from hungry men taking a few vegetables to wholesale stealing and the wanton destruction of property. Two articles of war covered the subject. Public stores—artillery, ammunition, clothing, or provisions—taken from the enemy became the property of the United Colonies and were not to be looted. And any officer or soldier who left his post "in time of an engagement" to search for plunder was to be court martialed. The articles left considerable room for turning a blind eye. In an attack, plundering was a useful threat: *If you don't surrender immediately, I may not be able to control my troops; I may free them to plunder*. Lifting the ban, which was never too strict, could inspire men with dreams of riches—or at least a drunken good time. Gentlemen found plundering to be a grubby, distasteful practice engaged in by Natives and the lower classes. The idealistic agreement signed by Arnold and the Connecticut Foot Guards in April mentioned plundering: "We are not mercenaries, whose views extend no farther than pay and plunder." Washington issued a stream of orders to stop "the horrid practice" with no effect. He told John Hancock, "I might almost as well attempt to remove Mount Atlas."[27]

Montgomery had his own problems stopping plundering by his cold, hungry, poorly paid men. After the surrender of St. John, the officers of the First New York Regiment and the Independent Company of New York Artillery were near mutiny when they were not permitted to seize the clothing in the garrison. Montgomery told Schuyler, "I would not have sullied my own reputation, nor disgraced the Continental arms by such a breach of capitulation, for the universe; there was no driving it into their noddles, that the clothing was really the property of the soldier, that he had paid for it."[28] Then in discussions in Montréal, going "beyond the letter of the law," he offered "all the publick stores taken in the vessels to the troops who went forward, except ammunition and provisions." The men "were half naked, and the weather was very severe," he told Schuyler.[29]

Undoubtedly, plundering took place as the Americans swarmed aboard the eleven vessels in the St. Lawrence. General Prescott claimed to have been disgracefully plundered, but as the man who had shackled Ethan Allen and Thomas Walker, he should not have expected much sympathy. In Montréal on his way to imprisonment in Philadelphia, Prescott met General Montgomery, who commented to his wife, "I have treated him with the sovereign contempt his inhumanity and barbarity merit." For a short time Prescott was confined in the common jail in Philadelphia before being given rooms at City Tavern, which offered the best lodgings in the city. In July 1776, Congress declared that "some licentious persons" had plundered Prescott's baggage and ordered General Schuyler to investigate, focusing on Timothy Bedel, by then dishonorably discharged and an easy scapegoat; Dr. Jonas Fay, a Green Mountain Boy and son of Bennington's tavern owner; and a Lieutenant House. Brown and Easton were to be included in the investigation because they were so insistent on a hearing.[30]

And someone stole a diamond ring belonging to Captain William Anstruther of the 26th Regiment of Foot. In the summer of 1776, Martin Johnson, formerly a lieutenant in the Independent Company of New York Artillery, confessed to having the ring, but claimed he did not break open Anstruther's trunk to get it. He told Congress that he "found the ring sometime after the garrison [the fleet] capitulated, and thought it to be a prize." Johnson was ordered to return it to Anstruther by way of the War Office. Johnson, by then a captain on a row-galley in the growing Lake Champlain fleet, resigned his commission in disgrace.[31]

Aside from Arnold's letters to Wooster and Hancock, no evidence exists that Brown and Easton themselves plundered or sanctioned others to do so. As the fall campaign ended Montgomery wrote to Schuyler: "Colonel Easton has shewn so much zeal & activity in the important service he has been employed upon, that I think myself obliged to speak of him in the warmest terms of acknowledgment." He admitted that Easton's "character has suffered in the public opinion by some unfortunate transactions last summer," but he wanted justice to be done for his good conduct.[32]

Six

"A march not to be paralleled in history"

Benedict Arnold's expedition up Maine's Kennebec River, across the divide between the Atlantic coast and the St. Lawrence River, and down the Chaudière River to Québec is one of the great feats of the American Revolution. At the time it was compared to Hannibal crossing the Alps and to the march of Xenophon and the 10,000 from the Tigris River to the Black Sea. Arnold's was a literate army; dozens of men left records of the trek, either written at the time, cobbled together soon afterwards with the help of other men's journals, or recorded as memoirs years later. Today parts of the route can be hiked and paddled, and there is a historical society devoted to the expedition.[1]

Arundel by Kenneth Roberts, a thick historical novel published in 1929–30, still captivates readers with Arnold's exploits. If you want a feel for what it was like to haul a 400-pound bateau up the Kennebec, read Roberts. He was a diligent researcher, and he thought about the details more thoroughly than many historians, who, in his view, assert a supposed fact from a document, cite the source, and move quickly on. The language of his first-person narrative suggests the eighteenth century while remaining that of an acerbic twentieth-century journalist. But there is another side to Roberts's career that is little mentioned. As a reporter for the

When this photograph was taken on the Maine coast in 1925, Kenneth Roberts was a writer for the *Saturday Evening Post* who was hoping for a career as a historical novelist. Library of Congress.

Saturday Evening Post, he wrote as a staunch conservative, nativist, and admirer of Mussolini. His anti-immigrant, anti–Semitic *Post* articles were published in 1922 in a book titled *Why Europe Leaves Home*. The Fascismo, he wrote in *Black Magic* (1924) "represented square-dealing, patriotism and common sense—particularly the sort of common sense that saw what needed to be done and then went ahead and did it without hedging, dodging or delaying." These were the same traits he found and admired in Arnold.[2]

Roberts's fictional Arnold was his lasting creation and has entered popular culture. "He had all the qualities of a great soldier—observation, right judgment, quickness, leadership, determination, energy, and courage—and all of them, it seemed to me, in the highest degree," wrote Roberts in the voice of fictional Steven Nason of Arundel, Maine, who makes the march to Québec. "This, too, I must add, because it's the truth, though a truth that displeases many: in none of my readings have I ever learned of anyone so persecuted and disappointed and unrewarded as this same brave and gallant gentleman."[3]

Historians have scoured the many journals and memoirs looking for comments on Arnold's role. Quoted most often is John Joseph Henry, a sixteen-year-old rifleman at the time, who a lifetime later wrote that Arnold was "beloved by the soldiery." The full quote reads, "He was brave even to temerity, was beloved by the soldiery, perhaps for that quality only; he possessed great powers of persuasion, and was complaisant [obliging], but sordidly avaricious." Henry's appraisal is a mix of what he thought at the time and what everyone was supposed to think after Arnold betrayed the American cause. At the end of the march, Arnold was kind to Henry when he was sick, finding Canadians to care for him and giving him money.[4]

In his eleventh charge, John Brown described Arnold's leadership differently:

> For great misconduct during his command, from the camp at Cambridge, in the year 1775, until he was superseded by General Montgomery, at Point-aux-Tremble, near Quebec.[5]

Brown's potential witnesses were Edward Antill, a Canadian from New Jersey; Roger Enos, second in command on the expedition, although he turned back partway; and William Goodrich, a captain from Berkshire County.[6]

Some of the outrage directed at Brown comes from his contradicting our understanding of an iconic event. Popular history is captivated by the romantic ideal of the preeminent man, Alexander the Great, Washington, Napoleon, or, recently on Broadway, Alexander Hamilton. In 1840 British historian Thomas Carlyle expressed this outlook in a series of lectures titled *Heroes, Hero-Worship, and the Heroic in History*. History was, he said, "at bottom the history of the great men who have worked here." They were the creators "of whatsoever the general mass of men contrived to do or attain."[7] In some minds, Benedict Arnold has risen to this status. But the true heroes of the Kennebec expedition may be the general mass of men (and a few women who were accompanying their husbands), choosing to continue north, triumphing against the river and the brutal portages, against hunger, cold, and flood, *and* against poor planning and inept and inexperienced leadership.

※ ※ ※

In mid–September as Philip Schuyler sickened and relinquished command to Richard Montgomery, Arnold left Cambridge with orders from George Washington

Six. "A march not to be paralleled in history"

to follow the Kennebec River to Canada. The route to Québec was based on a journal and map by John Montresor, the British military engineer who years later evaluated the forts on Lake Champlain. In the summer of 1761, Montresor and a dozen men ascended the Chaudière River from Québec, crossed the mountainous watershed, paddled and portaged through a series of streams and lakes, and rode the Kennebec to Fort Halifax in today's Winslow, Maine. It was a twenty-five-day journey by canoe. After two days at Fort Halifax, Montresor paddled north again, taking the route that Arnold later followed. In eleven days, he was at Lake Megantic/Lac-Mégantic (Chaudiere Pond in Arnold's accounts) on the Canadian side of the Height of Land.[8]

Montresor was a fine cartographer and his straight-line distances agree substantially with modern maps. But he could not draw what he did not see, nor could he represent changes in elevation, difficult terrain, or the power of the river. Although filled with hardship, his journal is at times inviting: "The land on both shores is rich and beautiful, and by the prints on the sand must be full of game." But in the version Washington and Arnold studied, details were omitted as if Montresor knew that an enemy might someday use it as a guidebook. On July 15, 1761, he noted, "Our course over the lake was [blank] our course now over the portage was [blank]. We ascended the hill, the portage conducting through the gap or breach. Its whole length cannot be less than [blank]."[9]

There were bigger problems than the omissions. Montresor did something far different than what Washington and Arnold intended. He used canoes, which were lighter and more maneuverable, rode higher in the water, and might be patched more easily when damaged. His party was small and guided by Indians who were at home in the woods. His men could extend their supplies somewhat through hunting and fishing, while an army would scare away game, eat up whatever moved or swam, and still not be satisfied. And Montresor made the trip in summer. Less gear was needed, and damp and cold did not sap a man's strength. Still, his journal records hardship, and he never forgot the hunger of the trip.[10]

When Montresor's map was spread on a table in Cambridge, an expedition to Canada through Maine looked possible. Both Washington and Arnold were enamored of the bold, unexpected stroke. While Schuyler and Montgomery threatened Montréal, Arnold would suddenly appear from nowhere and take Québec, an even greater prize.

Washington ordered Arnold to convince the Canadians "that we come at the request of many of their principal people, not as robbers, or to make war upon them, but as the friends and supporters of their liberties as well as ours." Don't allow plundering; respect Roman Catholicism; if you join with Schuyler, he is in command. Already Washington had taken some measure of Arnold: "Upon this occasion, and all others, I recommend most earnestly to avoid all contention about rank. In such a cause, every post is honourable in which a man can serve his country."[11]

At the start, Arnold had about eleven hundred men (and four women) in his command, mostly New Englanders, but joined by three companies of riflemen from Pennsylvania and Virginia under the command of Captain Daniel Morgan. Many of the officers were more experienced than Arnold as soldiers, frontiersmen, or both.

As John Brown fought the first skirmish north of St. John, the expedition embarked by ship from Newburyport, Massachusetts, for Maine. In a day, they were at the mouth of the Kennebec River, off Popham. The expedition sailed thirty miles inland before transferring to bateaux at Reuben Colburn's shipyard in Gardinerstown. Colburn, who had also made a case for the expedition to Washington, had overseen the construction of 200 of these boats out of green wood in only two weeks. Arnold asked for twenty more bateaux and these were hastily knocked together. Each boat weighed about four hundred pounds and was assigned to five men.

By the time Ethan Allen made his misguided attack on Montréal, the expedition was at Fort Western on the east side of the Kennebec in today's Augusta. Simeon Thayer, a thirty-eight-year-old captain from Rhode Island, who had bloodcurdling stories to tell about his experiences in the French & Indian War, noted that Fort Western was "formerly pretty strong ... but at present of no consequence." Still, there was a stockade fence and two blockhouses; the two-story central building was a hundred feet long and faced a large parade ground. The arrival of eleven hundred men overwhelmed the fort and the surrounding area.[12]

On the night of September 24–25, Thayer and Captain John Topham, a Rhode Island farmer, had retired to their bed in a crowded tavern near the fort when a loud argument started outside. Thayer got up to put a stop to it. The incident,

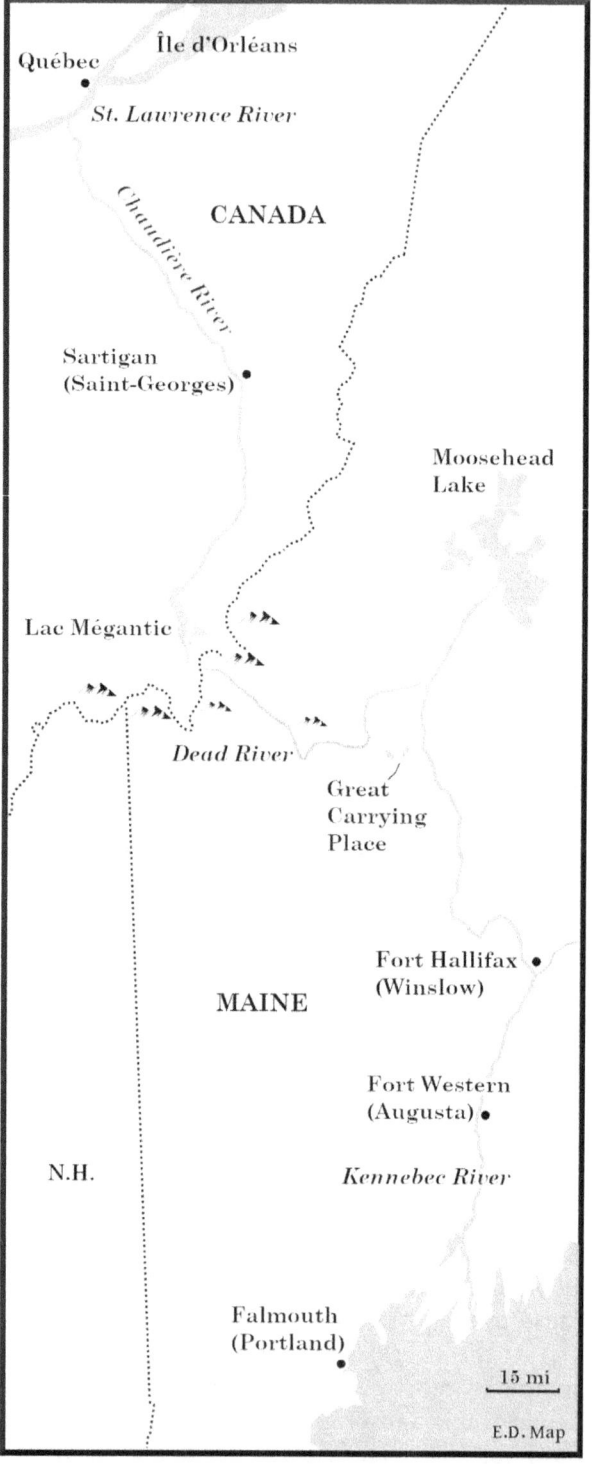

Benedict Arnold and his men ascended Maine's Kennebec River, crossed the mountainous divide to Canada, and followed the Chaudière to Québec. Arnold was to write that the trek was "longer and has been attended with a thousand difficulties I never apprehended."

Thayer and Topham's response, and the tragic result must have been fueled by alcohol. Thayer opened the door and in the dark saw the flash of a musket as the priming powder in the pan ignited but did not discharge the gun. He called for help, and by the time Topham stood in the doorway, the musket was primed again. This time the spark caught the main charge. Thayer commented that Topham "was fired at, but was miss'd." And then unaccountably, the two captains went back to bed. The active shooter—to use a present-day term that applies—reloaded, a process that might take a sober man half a minute. He opened the door and shot into the room, hitting Sergeant Reuben Bishop, who was somehow still asleep by the fireplace. In the resulting confusion, Thayer and Topham arrested the wrong man. Bleeding internally, Bishop lived for another twelve hours in terror at facing a righteous God.[13]

The next day James McCormick of William Goodrich's company was caught across the river. He was promptly tried, and although he denied the charge, he was found guilty and sentenced to be hanged. At three o'clock the following afternoon, the men of the expedition lined up to see McCormick at the gallows with a halter around his neck. A chaplain told McCormick of the "awful and never ending punishment that would await him in the eternal world if he did not repent and believe in Christ." Finally, McCormick said he did not intend to kill Bishop, but meant to shoot Captain Goodrich instead. Goodrich, who was to be one of Brown's proposed witnesses, was a tavern owner from Stockbridge, fifteen miles from Pittsfield. His militiamen had served as rangers outside Boston before getting assigned to the expedition to Québec. McCormick was from North Yarmouth, Maine, and a latecomer to the company.[14]

At the last moment, Arnold ordered McCormick back to Cambridge and George Washington. Recommending mercy, he wrote, "The criminal appears to be very simple and ignorant; and in the company he belonged to, had the character of being a peaceable fellow." Historians have seen compassion on Arnold's part, and an act of leniency that won the support of his soldiers. By exhibiting a condemned man on the gallows, he put the fear of God and their officers in the men, while he avoided the spectacle of starting the expedition with an execution. The soldiers seem to have understood that the reprieve was only a postponement. Abner Stocking, a private from Connecticut, later wrote, "I have been informed, that he died in gaol before the day of his execution arrived." At Ticonderoga, Arnold had accused the Green Mountain Boys of "committing every enormity," but as undisciplined as they were, there were no deaths under Allen's indulgent command. Discipline at Fort Western was out of control. On September 27, Arnold turned to the lash: five men were whipped for misconduct. On September 28, a sixth was given thirty-three stripes.[15]

Arnold faced another problem with his command. Captain Daniel Morgan, backed by captains Matthew Smith and William Hendricks, objected to leaving Fort Western at the same time as the New England musketmen under Lieutenant Colonel Christopher Greene, putting them under Greene's command. Washington had intended the riflemen to be separate, Morgan claimed. Arnold might well have remembered his clash with Ethan Allen and the Green Mountain Boys.

Morgan was six foot two inches and, at thirty-nine years old, five years senior to Arnold. As a young teamster in the French and Indian War, he had endured 499 lashes for striking a British officer. His farm on the Virginia frontier was near Winchester, and to reach Boston, he and his riflemen had marched six hundred miles in twenty-one days. Captain Smith had been a leader of the Paxton Boys, the

Scotch-Irish vigilantes from near today's Harrisburg, Pennsylvania, who did not hesitate to kill Indians. On December 14, 1763, they had destroyed the Christian Indian settlement of Conestoga. Smith was a captain when a mob slaughtered the surviving fourteen Natives (three couples and eight children) in Lancaster where they were held in the workhouse for their own safety. When the Paxton Boys marched on Philadelphia, he was one of two signers of a document, a "remonstrance," that called for increased security and representation for western settlements. Smith reappears in this narrative as a member of the Pennsylvania Supreme Executive Council at the time that Arnold was military governor of Philadelphia.

Avoiding conflict, Arnold sent the riflemen a day ahead of Greene to clear paths at the portages. "There is at present the greatest harmony among the officers," Arnold told Washington. In fact, Washington had not wanted a separate status for the riflemen and told Morgan so in a letter that chased him to Canada. Had Morgan really misunderstood Washington's expectations or had he, Smith, and Hendricks bluffed Arnold to get their way?[16]

With a party of Smith's riflemen scouting the path, the army moved north in four divisions, a day apart: Morgan and the riflemen first, Greene next, followed by Major Return Jonathan Meigs and finally Lieutenant Colonel Roger Enos. Each bateau held as much as a thousand pounds of provisions and gear, meaning that the men were hauling more than a hundred tons in addition to the weight of the boats.[17]

Arnold calculated that his expedition was about 180 miles or twenty days from Lac-Mégantic, the source of the river that would, he believed, take them swiftly to the St. Lawrence and Québec. The Arnold Expedition Historical Society measures the distance from Reuben Coburn's house—about ten miles south of Fort Western—to Lac-Mégantic as 171 miles, so Arnold's estimate was actually on the high side. Montresor started north from Fort Halifax and arrived at Lac-Mégantic in eleven days. An army could not go that fast, but twenty days at about nine miles a day seemed doable. It took more than a month to reach the lake—and the suffering did not end there.[18]

After a dry summer, the Kennebec River north of Fort Western was low and rocky, but still powerful. The boatmen rowed, poled, and dragged their bateaux against the current. The hastily constructed boats, which would have leaked on a calm lake, scrapped against rocks. Flour, dried peas, and salt fish were soaked and spoiled. Much of the salt beef was bad all along. It was October and the weather grew colder by the day. The portages around Ticonic Falls, Skowhegan Falls, the mile-long rapids called the Norridgewock Falls, and the steep Caratunk Falls were backbreaking. By a conservative estimate, each man needed to move more than 250 awkward pounds at each portage, in multiple trips. Strong men weakened; dysentery was rampant, the result of bad water and diet.[19]

The Continental Congress set a daily ration at a pound of beef (or three-quarters pound of pork) and a pound of flour or bread. Three pints of dried peas a week was part of the ration. Salt fish was a substitute at the start of the expedition, but was ruined quickly; then the diet was salt meat packed in barrels that could weigh 200 pounds each. It is impossible to calculate calories: the cuts of meat and fat content varied. Contractors sometimes skimped, and a "pound" might not be a pound. By the end, men were on reduced rations. Today the Appalachian Mountain Club suggests that a 185-pound man carrying a moderate to heavy load for eight hours may burn more than more than 6,300 calories. On average Arnold's men were small and

Six. "A march not to be paralleled in history" 59

A 1903 illustration from the *Century Illustrated Monthly Magazine* shows the exhausting work of portaging around the falls on the Kennebec River. "Portage at Skowhegan Falls" by Sidney Adamson, Library of Congress.

muscular by our standards. Many were used to a hard day's work, but the loads and the terrain were extreme. From the start they did not have enough food for the work they were doing. The drain on their bodies only got worse.[20]

A twelve- to thirteen-mile portage, called by the men the Great Carrying Place, was brutal. By marching west and climbing up, rowing across three ponds, which offered a little relief, the expedition rejoined a branch of the Kennebec where it was so calm that it was called the Dead River. This portage needed to be done repeatedly, in sections, perhaps five times. Five carries over the eleven miles of walking totals an additional hundred miles, half of that with heavy loads. To make this portage, men climbed repeatedly about 1,200 feet in elevation.[21]

Arnold's letters and journal remained confident, with none of the grievances that can be found in his writings from Lake Champlain. On October 13—as Montgomery called the council of war that refused to support his plan to attack St. John from the west—Arnold reported to Washington from the third pond on the Great Carrying Place. "Your Excellency may possibly think we have been tardy in our march, as we have gained too little," he wrote, "but when you consider the badness and weight of the batteaus, and large quantity of provisions, &c., we have been obliged to force up against a very rapid stream, where you would have taken the men for amphibious animals, as they were a great part of the time under water, add to this the great fatigue in portage, you will think I have pushed the men as fast as they could possibly bear." In his letter to Washington, Arnold expressed the hope that the "greatest difficulty" was "already past."[22]

Arnold told Washington the army had been reduced to 950 effective men and had provisions for twenty-five days. Two days later he gave the same estimate of remaining food to Roger Enos, commanding the rear division. Enos had heard rumors that supplies were running low. Reassured by Arnold, Enos was surprised when Greene's Division needed food and sent back ninety men to claim it. Captain Thomas Williams gave Greene's men eight barrels.[23] During the long portage, Arnold ordered a hospital to be built by Goodrich's company. He also sent orders to Fort Western to have a hundred barrels of provisions brought to the start of the long portage. These orders were not carried out.

As Arnold reached the Dead River, he believed he was 160 miles or eight to ten days from Québec. He was counting on a rapid passage down the Chaudière. They were actually about 190 miles from Québec, and the Chaudière was life threatening. It would take twenty-five days for the first men to reach the St. Lawrence River.[24]

At first the Dead River was calm and meandering. Today the riverbed is submerged under manmade Lake Flagstaff, which is dominated by Mount Bigelow, named after Major Timothy Bigelow. There were a few portages at falls. Men saw snow on the mountains. On October 19, the day Fort Chambly surrendered to Brown, it rained lightly, but then became a torrent. "A Prodigious fall of rain for 2 days past," recorded Arnold in his journal on October 21. At four a.m. the next morning, men were awakened by a flash flood, which chased them up a small hill. To continue the march, men on foot had to wade through a stream that extended a mile beyond its banks. The current was so fast that it was "almost impossible to ascend" by bateau. Then the river narrowed and the frequency of portages increased. These were only a few hundred yards in length, but the boats had to be unloaded and carried, as well as the gear and provisions, back and forth.[25]

On October 22, Arnold noted in his journal that the provisions were "almost exhausted." A day later by his count, seven boats overturned and all the food was lost. Major Meigs believed five or six boats filled with water and "several barrels of provisions, a number of guns, some clothes and cash" were lost. That evening Arnold called a council with division commanders Morgan and Meigs and other officers. Councils of war were held for a variety of reasons in the Revolution. Sometimes a commander genuinely wanted the opinions of his officers before making a tough decision. A council could be a way to share responsibility and win the support of officers or a way to avoid shouldering all the blame. Historians have imagined a scene at Camp Disaster in which Arnold tells the truth about supplies and distance, and officers are inspired to continue despite the hardships. In fact, it is unclear what was said. The journals of the officers do not mention Arnold's influence—and his actions, journal, and letters only confuse the question.[26]

The council decided to send the sickest men, twenty-six in all, south. At the same time, Captain Oliver Hanchet of Meigs's Division and a company of the strongest men were to hurry to the Canadian settlements for supplies. At thirty-four, the same age as Arnold, Hanchet, was one of the most experienced young officers on the expedition. In 1757 at age sixteen, he first served in Phineas Lyman's own company in Lyman's Regiment—the First Company of the First Connecticut Regiment. Both Lyman and Hanchet were from Suffield, Connecticut. Lyman was to become the outstanding provincial general of the French and Indian War. Hanchet served for five campaigns in the 1st Company, seeing duty from Fort Edward (originally called Fort Lyman), to lakes George and Champlain, to Montréal. By 1761 he was quartermaster sergeant of the company that listed Lyman as colonel and Roger Enos as captain.[27]

On the morning of October 24, Arnold wrote to Enos at the rear. He calculated that Morgan's and Meigs's divisions, who were in the lead, were about thirty miles from Lac-Mégantic and that supplies would last no more than twelve to fifteen days. The distance to the lake was roughly correct, although the miles were the most formidable of the trek. But Arnold's estimate of provisions was shockingly wrong. Along with his letter, Arnold sent Enos twenty-six sick and weak men and three days of provisions. Forty-nine sick men from Greene's division joined those returning south. Arnold ordered Enos, "On receipt of this you should proceed with as many of the best men of your division as you can furnish with fifteen days' provision; and that the remainder, whether sick or well, should be immediately sent back to the Commissary."[28]

The expedition was spread out over more than ten miles; communications between divisions was difficult and mistrust had grown. Men could count the few barrels of food in their own bateau and do basic arithmetic. By late in the expedition, they were grateful for half-rations. Captains and division commanders had a more complete view of an impending disaster. Although his journal suggests he realized the threat, Arnold did not share the real figures with his second in command. Was he propping up morale? Trying to convince Enos and his men they could count on provisions upstream? Not admitting to anyone, especially an older, more experienced officer, that the expedition was at the edge of failure? Is it possible he was deluding himself? *Twelve to fifteen days of food* was a matter for concern. It was enough to reach the first settlements, but if the expedition could not purchase provisions there, hungry men would commandeer what they needed to survive and the Americans would lose Canadian support. But in fact *twelve to fifteen days of food* was recklessly optimistic. The calculation raises questions about Arnold's leadership for which there are no easy answers and is routinely ignored by his biographers. Novelist Kenneth Roberts saw the problem and wrote his way around it. After imagining Arnold's inspiring remarks at the council of war, he quoted at length from the actual letter to Enos, but began *after* Arnold's claim that twelve to fifteen days of food remained.[29]

The "journal" of Private George Morison describes Arnold at this crucial moment, but Morison's account, published in 1803, is combination journal and memoir, and it is difficult to know what he thought at the time. "In order to quiet our fears of wintering in the Wilderness, as some expressed it, our gallant Colonel himself, after admonishing us to persevere as we hitherto had done, set out with a guide for the inhabitants in order to hasten the return of provisions."[30]

Aaron Burr, a nineteen-year-old volunteer in 1775, held a different opinion of Arnold—or so we are told. Burr, the future vice-president who killed Alexander Hamilton and was later tried and acquitted for treason, held contrary opinions on many issues and may not be a reputable source. His thoughts on Arnold come from an 1836 biography and are not a direct quote. Author Matthew L. Davis, who was "intimately acquainted" with Burr for forty years, wrote, "On the march through the wilderness, he was far from being satisfied with the general. Burr thought he provided too carefully for himself; and that he did not sufficiently share the fatigues and privations of the march in common with the troops."[31]

※ ※ ※

It snowed six inches overnight October 24–25, adding to the men's misery. The next evening midway between the lead and the rear divisions, colonels Enos and Greene met with nine other officers in a council to consider Arnold's orders and to decide who should turn around. Earlier in the day Greene had hoped to talk with Arnold about the food crisis, but Arnold was gone. No journal entry mentions any discussion of Arnold's *twelve to fifteen days of food.* These men knew better. No one was expecting twelve days of provisions to go forward—even twelve days of reduced rations.

All five of Enos's officers argued that the two divisions should retreat, but Enos, who was presiding at the council, cast the deciding vote to continue. Then he met with his own officers and agreed to return with the fourth division and the sick. Dr. Isaac Senter, a young surgeon from Newport, Rhode Island, believed that Enos never wanted to continue and had allowed himself to be convinced by his officers. Enos offered to share four barrels of flour and two of pork with the men going forward, but when Captain Thayer went downriver to Enos's camp to get the food, he was allowed to take only two or two-and-a-half barrels of flour. He claimed that Enos's men were "overflowing in abundance of all sorts, and far more than was necessary for their return" and called them timorous and effeminate.[32]

In a report to Washington, Enos insisted that at the time of the meeting, his division was reduced to six days of provisions. In his account, he turned over half of that to Greene's men and began down the river with only three days of food. Enos's command was made up of about 150 men in his own division, 150 sick men, and a crew of carpenters to repair the boats. In sworn testimony at his court-martial, his officers all said that they were left with provisions for only three days. Was this the truth or an agreed upon lie? Early-twentieth-century historian Justin Smith, who studied the question as closely as anyone can, concluded that Enos started his retreat with six days of flour, perhaps a similar ration of pork. But Smith was solving an equation with too many variables and the likelihood that his constants were based on lies, bias, and misunderstandings. At one point he argued, "accepting Arnold's account of the situation..." before proceeding with his calculations. But whether Enos had rations for three days or six days or some slightly higher figure, no one was prepared for twelve to fifteen days or could supply a sizable party with food and expect the remaining men to survive.[33]

Upon Enos's return to the American army outside Boston, Washington ordered a Court of Enquiry to see if charges should be brought. Major General Charles Lee presided over a panel of six officers which notably included Nathanael Greene (third cousin of Christopher Greene, who was on the expedition) and John Stark, a captain in Roger's Rangers in the French and Indian War. They decided that "Colonel Enos's misconduct (if he has been guilty of misconduct) is not of so very heinous a nature as first supposed," but a court-martial should be held to satisfy the world and Enos's own sense of honor. The court-martial was held December 1 with Brigadier General John Sullivan presiding. An attorney in civilian life, he was the older brother of James Sullivan, who had been part of the fact-finding mission to Lake Champlain that had clashed with Arnold. Five officers from Enos's division testified that they were low on supplies on the way south. Enos was acquitted with honor. Sullivan wrote, "I am convinced that had Colonel Enos, with his division, proceeded, it would have been a means of causing the whole detachment to have perished in the woods, for want of sustenance." Enos soon resigned his commission. By the end of the war, he was a general in command of the Vermont forces on the frontier at a time when Ethan and Ira Allen were holding secret negotiations with the British.[34]

※ ※ ※

Arnold, Hanchet, and fifty to sixty men crossed what came to be called the Terrible Carrying Place, the steepest climb of all, and followed the Seven Mile Stream, now the Arnold River, from the mountains. Arnold and a small party kept to the high ground to the east and reached Lac-Mégantic. Hanchet and his men marched into a swamp south of the lake and became lost. For two miles they waded through frigid water up to their waists while they tripped on slippery roots under foot. By then Arnold was on the shore of the lake writing to Washington as if he was texting the commander in chief—"I have this minute arrived here." "I have been much deceived in every account of our route, which is longer and has been attended with a thousand difficulties I never apprehended." Later in the day, the letter to Washington was sent south to Enos, who, unknown to Arnold, had left the expedition.[35]

When Arnold realized that Hanchet was not following, he sent bateaux to rescue the men who were trapped in the bog. Arnold had relied upon Hanchet, but soon there was a break between the two men. For his mistake in entering the swamp, according to one explanation, Arnold berated Hanchet in front of his men, and the captain became another in a growing list of adversaries. Perhaps Hanchet was angered that Arnold took bateaux and men away from him and deprived him of the honor of being the first into the Canadian settlements. But perhaps as a former quartermaster-sergeant, he understood what needed to be done more clearly and was proven right.[36]

The expedition faced two mortal threats: starvation and an unforgiving geography. In his letter to Washington, Arnold explained, "I am determined to set out immediately with five bateaux and about fifteen men, for Sartigan [today's Saint-Georges] … to procure a supply of provisions and forward back to the detachment." The expedition was short of food "by reason of losing a number of loaded batteaux at the falls and rapid water." The *twelve to fifteen days*, a figure that appeared in the letter to Enos *after* the loss of bateaux, was not mentioned to Washington. For the first time in a report, Arnold admitted to food shortages.[37]

The decision to lead the resupply party in person may reveal the quintessential Arnold, boldly leading from the front, taking the greatest responsibility and succeeding.[38] But the events that followed can be interpreted differently. In racing to be the first to reach Canada, he sent back directions that were unclear, carried by a guide who did not know the way. At a moment in which the expedition most needed leadership, he was gone. Arnold's party made rapid progress down the rocky Chaudière for fifteen miles before two of his four bateaux were smashed in the rapids. Everyone survived and the party continued south more cautiously. Later Arnold's canoe was destroyed against the rocks.

※ ※ ※

This section of John Montresor's 1761 map of Maine and Québec helped to mislead Arnold's expedition. The Height of Land and Lake Megantic are clearly shown, but there is no swamp above the lake and two lakes to the east do not appear. Library of Congress.

Six. "A march not to be parrelleled in history"

Before leaving Lac-Mégantic, Arnold sent back word that the men should leave the bateaux at the last pond, now known as Arnold Pond, before making the steepest climb. Morgan's men did not get the message or made their own stubborn decision to lug their boats across. Other companies carried a single bateau planning to float gear, supplies, and a few sick men to Sartigan. Arnold advised the field officers and captains that after crossing the height of land and reaching a meadow, they should keep a "north and by east course, which will escape the low swampy land.... By no means keep the brook, which will carry you into a swamp out of which it will be impossible for you to get."[39]

On the Canadian side on October 28, the expedition gathered in what men called the Beautiful Meadow (near today's village of Saint-Augustin-de-Woburn, home of Motel Arnold) and divided the remaining provisions, each man and the few women getting about five pints of flour and several ounces of salt pork. Organization had disintegrated from four divisions to three, then to companies, bateau-mates, and finally at times to every-man-for-himself. Some wolfed down their food, leaving nothing for the following days.

No matter what route men took from the meadow, they risked disaster. Historian Justin Smith called this moment "the grand crisis of the march, a crisis threatening nothing less than the complete extinction of the whole army." Four companies—Dearborn's, Goodrich's, Ward's, and Smith's riflemen—decided to continue on immediately and never learned of Arnold's directions for avoiding the swamp. Following the river, they marched into the bog and could find no way to advance. Dearborn, who found an Indian canoe, commented, "Cap" Goodrich was almost perished with the Cold, having Waded Several Miles Backwards, and forwards, Sometimes to his Arm-pits in Water & Ice, endeavouring to find some place to Cross this River, I took him into my Canoe, and Carryed him over." Men spent the night on a few sodden knolls that rose above the bog. For firewood, they chopped at trees and dragged the wood from the frigid water. "If it had rained hard," one man commented, "it would have overflown the place we were in." In the morning, with the canoe and a few bateaux, men struggled to ferry everyone to dry land near the lake.[40]

At first Morgan's men seemed to have made the right choice in carrying their bateaux, and they made an easy passage down the Seven Mile Stream to Lac-Mégantic. Along the way, they stole a stockpile of provisions left by the Dearborn/Goodrich division while those men were rescuing their comrades from the bog. After crossing the ten-mile-long lake, Morgan's men began a rapid descent of the Chaudière. At the same spot where Arnold lost two bateaux, all seven of Morgan's boats were destroyed, much of the gear and provisions was lost, and a man drowned. Like the men whose food they had stolen, they were now without provisions.

The party that attempted to follow Arnold's directions came closest to total destruction. Five companies, more than half the remaining men on the expedition, took a northeast route from the meadow and marched into the swamp above today's Lac des Joncs (Rush Lake), a body of water that did not appear on Montresor's map and was unknown to Arnold or to guide Isaac Hall. At each step, men sank "half leg deep" in the muck. "We find now that the Pilot knows no more the way than the most ignorant of us," commented Captain Thayer.[41] They attempted to circle the lake to the east, but were blocked by another unknown lake, now called Lac aux Araignées or Spider Lake. By October 30—the day Seth Warner won the decisive battle at Longueuil—the swamp was frozen to the thickness of a pane of glass. Totally lost, they followed the shore of Spider Lake, getting even further from Lac-Mégantic, until they came to the river that feeds Lac aux Araignées, which they waded where the stream was some fifty feet wide, four feet deep with ice at the edges. Hundreds of men might have perished in the woods from starvation and exposure if they hadn't encountered an Indian who guided them to Lac-Mégantic. They were still about forty-five miles from the first settlements.

Journals from all three parties mention pathetic meals—two dogs, moose-hide breeches, a squirrel head, a shot pouch, leather cartridge boxes, hair pomade, salve. Dear friends were left behind in the certainty they would die.[42]

※ ※ ※

Arnold reached the first Canadian settlements on October 30, and the next day supply parties left Sartigan with provisions and cattle. In early November, as 150 miles to the west Fort St. John finally surrendered, the survivors of the trek up the Kennebec staggered into Sartigan where the Canadians welcomed them. The Americans were bearded in an age of shaven men; their clothes were in tatters; and many were barefoot. They were still more than fifty miles from the St. Lawrence and Québec, but the greatest hardship was over. Only six hundred seventy-five men remained out of the 1080 who started the trek. Historians argue about the loss of life. Forty to fifty dead is a likely estimate, although Private George Morison thought there might have been as many as seventy to eighty "lost in the wilds." He hoped some of those made it to a settlement and recovered. But like discussions of provisions, the one tally that deserves no consideration is Arnold's. In a letter to Washington written after reaching the St. Lawrence, Arnold claimed, the men "are all happily arrived (except one man drowned and one or two sick)—and Enos's division, who, I am surprised to hear, are all gone back." Arnold was not telling half-truths; he was lying to the commander in chief to disguise how close the expedition had come to destruction. In Arnold's account, they faced temporary supply problems which he solved through decisive action.[43]

In a letter to Schuyler written two weeks later, Arnold called the expedition to Québec "a march of near six hundred miles, not to be paralleled in history." (If you start measuring from Cambridge and include the ocean voyage to the Kennebec River, the distance is close to four hundred miles.) He admitted to food shortages: "Most [of the men] had not one day's provision for a week." By then the legend of the "famine proof veterans" (Dr. Senter's memorable phrase from his journal) was already establishing itself.[44]

Seven

"I will have an eclaircissement with him"

On the night of November 13–14, five hundred men slipped through the British ships on the mile-and-a-half wide St. Lawrence west of Québec. After three crossings in canoes, they were discovered by a guard boat and left about 150 men under command of Oliver Hanchet stranded at Pointe-Lévy (Lévis), along with scaling ladders to climb the city's walls. Arnold's decision to leave Hanchet as the last man to cross may be a symptom of the animosity between the two men. At that moment, it still seemed that Québec might be taken and Arnold was denying him another opportunity. However, in a letter written two days later, Arnold blamed the weather for not sending the boats back for Hanchet and shared details of what happened next as if with a friend. Cross the river as soon as the weather permits, he ordered Hanchet gently, confidently.[1]

In hindsight, the early morning of November 14 may have been the best moment in the next six months to seize the city. By one report, Québec was asleep and unprepared, the St. John Gate to the west of the city wide open. But as in so many other cases, there are conflicting accounts. In his journal, Dr. Senter noted, "the city gates were all closed, cannon in order, &c" and an attack was "inadmissible."[2]

That afternoon after the British captured an American sentry, Arnold's army tested the city's resolve. "We paraded and marched up within half a mile of the walls," Arnold told Hanchet, "and gave them three cheers, and were in hopes of their coming out, but we were disappointed." The defenders fired cannon about fifteen times, but the twelve- and twenty-four-pound shot did no harm. It was a scene from the Middle Ages, knights daring their adversaries to leave their castle for the chivalry of battle. The defenders yelled back, jeering Arnold as a horse-jockey, the worst sort of swindler; but they were not leaving the city. In 1759, General Louis-Joseph de Montcalm, commander of the French forces in North America, had accepted battle on the Plains of Abraham outside the city and lost his life and French Canada. Private Henry, whose comment that Arnold was "beloved by the soldiery" is quoted by most biographers, thought the demonstration outside Québec was "boy's play" and "folly." Much later, he wrote, "It must be confessed that this ridiculous affair gave me a contemptible opinion of Arnold." Morgan, Major Christian Febiger, and other officers agreed, Henry remembered.[3]

In the evening, Arnold sent an officer with a white flag and a drummer toward the city carrying a note that promised to protect property if Québec surrendered. But

The walled city of Québec rises above the St. Lawrence River in this print from 1768. The high point of Cape Diamond, the Lower Town, and the Upper Town are unmistakable. The Miriam and Ira D. Wallach Division of Art, Prints and Photographs: Print Collection, The New York Public Library Digital Collections.

"if I am obliged to carry the town by storm, you may expect every severity practiced on such occasions." Addressed to Lieutenant Governor Hector T. Cramahé, the letter went unread as the defenders fired upon the emissary. The next day Arnold sent a second message in the hope that the officer and flag had been fired upon through "the ignorance of your guards." There had been no misunderstanding and a guard fired again.[4]

Tensions within the American army were increasing. The men were still on reduced rations, and Morgan and captains Smith and Hendricks confronted Arnold. "Altercation and warm language took place," Henry heard from Smith, who told some of his men "that Morgan seemed at one time on the point of striking Arnold." Rations were increased.[5]

For a few days, Arnold remained hopeful of taking the city. "Had I been ten days sooner, Quebec must inevitably have fallen into our hands, as there was not a man to oppose us," he told Washington. But Allan Maclean, who had been driven from Sorel by Brown and Easton, intercepted a message from Arnold to Montgomery and rushed to Québec, the last British stronghold in Canada. On November 18, Arnold was told that Maclean might attack with a large force backed by field guns. (The report may have been a ruse to frighten the Americans.) Facing the battle he had wanted four days earlier, Arnold ordered a "strict examination" of the army's munitions and learned that there were no more than five good cartridges for each man and that a hundred muskets were damaged. In a letter to Schuyler, he claimed "not ten rounds each for the men." Arnold told Washington that the information was "a great surprise"; the cartridges had appeared to be "very good." This inventory—*return* in the military parlance of the day—is a curious incident. You might suppose muskets and powder would have been examined *before* crossing the St. Lawrence and offering battle. Like the provisions during the trek north, the army's weakness was widely known. A soldier with an unserviceable musket was aware of the problem; sergeants and officers would have been monitoring their men's preparedness. Arnold calling the information a surprise is surprising in itself.[6]

One of Brown's three potential witnesses, Edward Antill, likely had something to say about how prepared Québec was on November 14 and during the next five days. Antill was a New Jersey–born Canadian, a graduate of King's College (Columbia), and a lawyer, who supported the thirteen colonies. After his arrival in Québec, November 19, Governor Carleton expelled "all useless, disloyal, and treacherous persons" from the city. Antill, who was far from useless, was quickly taken into the American army as an engineer. He was so respected that after the American attempt to take the city on December 31, he was sent to Montréal and then south with the news of the defeat. He served during the war as lieutenant colonel in the 2nd Canadian Regiment, including three years as a prisoner. He had no firsthand knowledge of Arnold's march to Québec or of the controversies in the American camp, but he knew the state of defenses in the city in mid–November.[7]

※ ※ ※

On November 19—the same day the British fleet surrendered to Easton and Brown—Arnold's small army retreated to Pointe-aux-Tremble (today's Neuville) about twenty miles up the river from Québec. The men took quarters in the village and nearby farmhouses. At last they were warm and had plenty of simple, nutritious food, but they talked constantly of going home. Hanchet took his men to the tavern and promised them they would leave soon. Arnold was in communication with Montgomery's army, warning them of the armed British ships on the river. By the end of November, as thickening ice confined the British ships to the city, Arnold wrote, "there will be no danger of your coming down in boats, or any kind of water craft, except that of ice."[8]

Montgomery arrived at Pointe-aux-Tremble on the evening of December 1 along with cannon and provisions. The next day Arnold ordered Oliver Hanchet to move heavy guns by boat to Sillery, a suburb of Québec. For the first time in the historical record, the break between the two men was public. Hanchet "abruptly refus'd, alleging the Danger of such an undertaking," wrote Captain Thayer, who then took the job after flipping a coin with his friend Captain Topham. When Thayer and his men carried their cargo downriver at night, they first had to cut their way through a quarter mile of ice to reach open water. Then they rowed for all they were worth to keep warm while it snowed and ice accumulated on their boats. When the bateaux ran aground on rocks, men plunged into the frigid river trying to reach shore. This near disaster was needless. Snow was already covering the frozen ground, and even the heavy guns from Sorel could have been carried by sled.[9]

It was a time of mutual admiration as the American army returned to Québec to try again. Montgomery saw a superior "style of discipline" among Arnold's men, especially the gentlemen volunteers, such as Aaron Burr. The Yankees, he was soon to discover, were as cantankerous as the men he had commanded outside Fort St. John. Although he had worried about Arnold's ambition, he found him, as he told Schuyler, "active, intelligent, and enterprising." Compare these comments with earlier ones about Brown, written after the capture of Fort Chambly: "Upon this and all other occasions I have found him active and intelligent."[10]

Brown and Arnold had not seen each other since the early summer on Lake Champlain when the committee from the Massachusetts Provincial Congress had forced Arnold from his command and appointed Easton and Brown in his place. By early December 1775, they were twin heroes. Arnold was quickly becoming the

American Hannibal, while Brown was the conqueror of Fort Chambly and the man who tricked a British fleet on the St. Lawrence into surrender.

On December 7, Arnold ordered three companies to move into the suburb of St. Roch close to the north wall of Québec. Once again, Hanchet refused, saying the position was too exposed to cannon fire. Captains Thayer, Topham, and Hubbard took the assignment and (wrote Thayer) "were expos'd for 3 weeks to the most imminent Danger." One morning several cannon balls crashed through Thayer and Topham's lodgings. "One [shot] particularly went through our bed, and pass'd midway between him and myself, without any hurt, and clear'd quite through the other end of our Room to our astonishment."[11]

For much of December, the American army outside Québec engaged in artillery duels, which they never won, and talked of going home. They could not build proper siege works in the frozen ground, and their fortifications of ice were shattered by cannon fire. Morgan's men with their long rifles shot at sentries on the city walls, an act which the British found disgraceful. "Lie in wait to shoot a sentry! A deed worthy of Yanky men of war," wrote customs official and militia captain Thomas Ainslie in his journal.[12] Smallpox appeared in camp. Many enlistments were to run out with the New Year.

Montgomery wished he might postpone an attack until spring when he was reinforced and the city's provisions were low, but he feared that by then he would have lost all Canadian support. Deeply depressed, he made plans for an attack. In Albany around Christmas, General Schuyler heard news that Montgomery was killed; Arnold was taken captive; and the army "totally defeated." The rumor was untrue but as prophetic as a ghost standing at the foot of the bed. Men who could count the days until they were free to leave whispered about a *coup-de-main* and about who was and who was not a coward. Until the day after Christmas, Montgomery thought he had support for an attack; then he learned that three of Arnold's companies were opposed. Their captains wanted to be transferred to the command of another field officer. Most historians assume Hanchet was a leader, joined by Goodrich and Jonas Hubbard. Major Timothy Bigelow was also known to have been opposed to an assault.[13]

In a letter to Schuyler, Montgomery asked that the names of the disaffected officers be erased, which Schuyler did, leaving blanks in the record that have puzzled researchers, although nearly all have seen John Brown maneuvering behind the scenes. "Captain [a blank almost certainly for *Hanchet*], who has incurred Colonel Arnold's displeasure by some misconduct, and thereby given room for harsh language, is at the bottom of it, and has made declarations which I think must draw upon him the censure of his country, if brought to trial," Montgomery wrote. A field officer "is concerned in it, who wishes, I suppose, to have the separate command of those companies, as the above-mentioned Captains have made application for that purpose." Many historians have seen Brown as the mysterious field officer, although they have also read his name into Montgomery's next comment. "I am much afraid my friend [blank] is deeply concerned in this business. I will have an *eclaircissement* [clarification] with him on the subject."[14]

Historians have been shocked at the attempt to restructure the army at Arnold's expense. Justin Smith, in his classic history of the invasion of Canada, referred to it as a "cabal," a secret scheme to overturn legitimate authority.[15] But Smith's interpretation exaggerates what we know. It was not a mutiny. The captains "made application":

they requested. And Montgomery did not want posterity to know their names, implying some respect for the men. Such a request was distasteful to him and to Schuyler, but it was a Yankee way of doing business.

Montgomery did meet with Brown late in December and told him that he would not be promoted. Was this the *eclaircissement*? Brown described his side of the meeting in a letter that is as murky as an overcast late afternoon at the start of a Canadian winter. The letter may reveal Brown at his contentious worst, but the surviving copy was certified by General Wooster, who in April promoted Brown to lieutenant colonel, despite, or perhaps because of, its contents. "You have put me under the disagreeable necessity of demanding a fulfillment of your promise made me at Montreal," Brown began. "I have justified my conduct on every point of every article of charge laid against me, except the affair of the Gondola," Brown insisted. Not a hint survives of what happened involving a gunboat or gondola, although Captain Robert Cochran reminded Brown that when he first reported the facts to the general at Pointe-aux-Tremble, Montgomery said, "You have done extremely well." Then there was the equally mysterious accusation that Brown "did not commence a civil war when at Montreal." To this charge, Brown said that if he was faced with the same circumstances, he would act in the same way. There is no knowing the situation or the actions he took.[16]

Brown's letter does not mention attempting to lure three companies away from Arnold's command or plundering officers' baggage at Sorel, a charge later made by Arnold. Brown wanted a written response stating the reasons for Montgomery's refusal to promote him, so that he could defend himself "at a higher tribunal." What actions Montgomery took in response, if any, are unknown. He may have agreed to a promotion; he may have rejected Brown's appeal outright; or he may have postponed a decision until after Québec was attacked.

※ ※ ※

The journals and letters from December contain rumors and half-told tales. Seven men were lashed on December 22, for stealing. It was said that Hanchet and Major Bigelow displayed cowardice, "Doging when a Ball came near them." Once Arnold even apologized to his officers—"I am a Passionate man"—but it is unclear which of many issues was the cause. Perhaps one of the men who had been beaten was innocent. Perhaps Arnold had promised money to Hanchet's men and did not deliver.[17]

An assault aimed at Cape Diamond, the highest point of the fortifications to the west of the city, was planned for the morning of December 28, but a snowstorm stopped at midnight, the sky cleared, and Montgomery called off the attack. Carleton knew the Americans were coming and was prepared. Still, had they been defeated before the walls of the city, they could have retreated to fight another day.

Before dawn on the snowy morning of December 31, the American army was in motion. James Livingston and his newly formed 1st Canadian Regiment were furnished with combustibles to burn St. John's Gate to the west of the Upper Town. Montgomery had appointed Livingston colonel of a Canadian regiment in November, but the regiment and his rank were not approved by the Continental Congress until January 8, so Livingston and his men were in a gray area. As part of the same feint, Captain Jacob Brown, John's older brother, was to threaten the walls at Cape Diamond with ninety-four men, whose enlistments were up with the New Year.[18]

John Brown's role in the attack is a mystery. Historian Justin Smith, who studied the issues closely, suggested it was possible that Brown played only a minor role after plotting against Arnold. But after weighing contradictory evidence, he concluded that Brown's part was a riddle he could not solve. The nineteenth-century *History of Pittsfield* claims that a detachment of Easton's Regiment accompanied Montgomery. Perhaps Brown led these men. Another possibility is that he had overall authority for attacking the walls and burning the gate: his brother was his subordinate; Livingston, whose promotion had not yet been approved by Congress, was a partner as he had been throughout the fall. Montgomery would not have excluded Brown, however their disagreement ended; Brown would not have sidelined himself; and had anything questionable taken place, there would have been rumors.[19]

Robert Cochran and Ira Allen, both officers in Brown's detachment, were ordered to set off rockets to coordinate the feints and the genuine attack.[20] Their Canadian guide led them astray and their two rockets did not fool the defenders or coordinate anything. Around 4 a.m., sentries on the walls of the city saw lights on the Plains of Abraham. In the city, bells tolled and drums beat as the garrison manned the ramparts, joined by civilians as old as seventy. At Cape Diamond, the Yankee frontiersmen fired—"heavy & hot," wrote Ainslie—from behind a rise about eighty yards from the walls. Musket flashes briefly illuminated their faces, and the defenders "briskly" returned fire. It was all sound and fury and little danger. No one recorded an attempt with scaling ladders. Ainslie had imagined such an attack: "Can these men pretend that there is a possibility of approaching our walls loaden with ladders, sinking to the

John Trumbull's *Death of General Montgomery in the Attack on Quebec, December 31, 1775* (1786) gives a sense of Richard Montgomery's importance in the early years of the United States. Yale University Art Gallery.

middle every step in snow!" At St. John's Gate, the defenders easily stopped Livingston's men from burning the gate.[21]

Montgomery, the New Yorkers, some of Brown's men (and perhaps Brown) descended from the heights to the St. Lawrence at Wolfe's Cove, west of the city, and clambered over slabs of ice pushed onto land by the river, which is tidal as far as Québec. After two miles, they came upon an undefended palisade of upright logs in the narrow strip between Cape Diamond and the river. Men with saws cut through the wall; Montgomery himself helped pull the pieces out of the way. In the uncertain light, through driving snow, they could see a two-story house blocking the way to the Lower Town. Montgomery and captains John Macpherson and Jacob Cheeseman were about forty yards away when the men inside the house opened fire with a small cannon loaded with grapeshot and a volley of muskets. Montgomery died instantly as did Macpherson and Cheeseman. The Americans abandoned the dead and ran.

※ ※ ※

Arnold was with the small advanced party coming from the northeast along the St. Charles River. At the first barricade, in the first serious resistance that he had encountered from an enemy in the Revolution, he was shot in the lower left leg—a ricochet, Dr. Senter concluded—and was helped to the hospital. With Arnold gone, men turned to Daniel Morgan, who was not the ranking officer. Lieutenant Colonel Greene, who was, agreed with the choice.[22]

Morgan led the attack of the first barricade, capturing a hundred defenders, and advancing to a second, unguarded barricade with an open gate. Perhaps victory lay beyond, but the Americans waited, hoping for Montgomery's arrival, debating whether to advance and how to guard so many prisoners. When the Americans finally moved forward, they found the barrier held by Regulars, Royal Highland Emigrants, sailors, and militia. The Americans held the Lower Town until nearly 11 a.m. The blizzard continued and by the time of the American's surrender, their muskets were so damp and fouled that few would fire.

The final word on Captain Hanchet, whose cowardice and disaffection are woven into most accounts, may be found in the imprecise casualty figures. His company, trapped between the barricades, suffered seven men killed and one wounded, second only to Morgan's company, which lost eight killed and nine wounded. It was said that in urging on his men, Hanchet yelled to one, "Walk up, Marshall; our mothers are at home praying for us, and the enemy can't hurt us." Hanchet may have rediscovered his courage before the barricades of the Lower Town, or he may have been an opinionated Yankee who saw "great misconduct," spoke his mind, avoided Arnold's plans as best he could, and then did his duty. In captivity, only two of Hanchet's men, and one of those a drummer boy, deserted, a credit to the company's steadfastness. Hanchet was not a compliant prisoner. He participated in an unsuccessful escape plot led by Thayer and artillery captain John Lamb and was once confined in the hold of a schooner. Finally paroled, he returned home to Suffield in early October 1776. Unlike Morgan and Thayer who played important roles later—Morgan at Saratoga and Cowpens and Thayer during the defense of Fort Mifflin on the Delaware River—Hanchet was largely done with war. He remained captain of the Suffield militia company and turned out for occasional alarms. On the day before Burgoyne surrendered at Saratoga, he captured a British sloop near Poughkeepsie, New York.[23]

Eight

"Mr. General Arnold & I do not agree very well"

Not long after daybreak on December 31, 1775, two men helped Benedict Arnold into the General Hospital located in the convent in St. Roch, a suburb of Québec. Dr. Isaac Senter probed the wound to Arnold's lower left leg and extracted a shattered musket ball that had torn between the tibia and fibula and lodged in muscle. Senter begged Arnold to leave the hospital for the safety of the countryside. "He would neither be removed, nor suffer a man from the Hospital to retreat," Senter wrote in his journal. "He ordered his pistols loaded, with a sword on his bed, &c., adding that he was determined to kill as many as possible if they came into the room. We were now all soldiers, even to the wounded in their beds were ordered a gun by their side."[1]

With the death of Richard Montgomery and the capture of most of the men who made the long march to Québec with Arnold, knowledge of the American army plummets. For most of January and February 1776, researchers are left to sift through Arnold's letters and a few other scattered sources. On the afternoon of January 2, Major Return Jonathan Meigs was sent from the city to retrieve the baggage of his fellow prisoners, and Arnold learned the worst, although still in round numbers: three hundred captured; somewhere between sixty and a hundred killed or wounded. Lying on his back, in "excessive pain from my wound," he sent the information to General David Wooster in Montréal. "Many officers here appear dispirited; your presence will be absolutely necessary. I don't expect to be in a capacity to act this two months."[2]

Like Arnold, Wooster was isolated as winter shut down the north. He was one hundred fifty miles from Québec, more than a week from Albany, more than two weeks from Philadelphia. To garrison Montréal, Chambly, and St. John, he had between five and six hundred men. He did not have the confidence or respect of his immediate superior, Philip Schuyler, nor that of Arnold. Wooster could not bring himself to like Canadians, and he did not grasp the importance of public relations—or if he did, he could not swallow his pride to do the job. For a few days, Arnold had self-doubts and hoped for Wooster's arrival. On January 5 from headquarters in Holland House, he wrote Wooster, "The burden lies very heavy on me, considering my present circumstances; I find myself unequal to the task." His army was "not quite" eight hundred men, including the Canadians. The enemy was threatening to attack, although he believed they did not dare an attempt. "I pray God they may not, for we are in a miserable condition to receive them."

A day later, Arnold wrote a more defiant letter, which was never delivered and

Eight. *"Mr. General Arnold & I do not agree very well"* 75

William Faden, geographer to George III, engraved this map of Québec during the American siege. Faden's atlas of Revolutionary War battles is a major source of information on the war. Library of Congress.

found its way into the city where an extract was published in *Quebec Gazette*. "I have no thoughts of leaving this proud town, until I first enter it in triumph. My wound has been exceeding painful, but is now easy, and the surgeons assure me will be well in eight weeks." The extract later appeared in the British *Remembrancer,* an annual record of events, for 1776. Was it actually disinformation that was allowed to slip into enemy hands? Few letters left the siege, and Arnold instituted examination of many that did. He wanted to mislead the enemy into thinking his army had a chance, and although he was blunt with his superiors about the lack of money and warm clothing, the number of deserters, and his need for thousands of reinforcements, he had to reassure them he was not overwhelmed.[3]

At first Arnold may have had as little idea of the size of his army as do historians who add estimates of participants in the battle and subtract estimates of losses. And how much rounding up did Arnold do in case his message was captured? Adopting Arnold's figure of eight hundred, Justin Smith believed the army "including invalids and men detached 'on command,' amounted to about six hundred, besides the timorous Canadians." (Smith had no respect for French Canadians on either side of the conflict.) In a letter to Congress on January 11, Arnold put his forces at five hundred, plus the Canadians. Brown's mixed regiment—usually referred to as a *detachment*—was about 160 to 170 men, as many as a quarter to a third of the Americans. A February 16 muster of Brown's men showed 116 present out of 156. A few were on command, meaning assigned elsewhere on the day of the muster, but many more were hospitalized. John Brown's brother Jacob, who led the December 31 feint, had died of smallpox and his company was commanded by a lieutenant.[4]

The army was led by only a few veteran officers. Most of the men from the Kennebec march were prisoners or dead. New York regimental colonels and lieutenant-colonels never had much to do with the Canada campaign. Colonel

Donald Campbell was deputy quartermaster general and not used to commanding regiments. Major Herman Zedwitz of the 1st New York had fallen on the ice during the failed attack and was too injured to be of any use. By late summer he was under arrest for treasonous communications with the enemy. James Livingston's Canadians were blamed for not doing their job, and Livingston hardly seemed to be a real colonel. That left Brown and two majors to command the army in the first weeks after Arnold was wounded.

Prussian-born New Yorker Frederick Weissenfels, taking the place of Zedwitz, was in his late forties and one of the most experienced soldiers in Canada. He had fought as a dragoon in the War of the Austrian Succession and served in the cavalry in the Netherlands. During the French and Indian War, he had seen action at Ticonderoga and Québec. Lewis Dubois, like Brown, thirty-one years old, was a Poughkeepsie, New York, carpenter in civilian life. But a researcher can find only a few mentions of these three men in the weeks that the bedridden Arnold had to rely on them. If Brown had been promoted to lieutenant colonel, he was, or should have been, the highest-ranking field officer.

On January 2, officers including Campbell, Weissenfels, gentleman major Matthias Ogden, a chaplain, and "Mr." Aaron Burr inventoried the money that General Montgomery had carried to conduct business: Continental paper; Connecticut, Massachusetts, and English shillings; wampum, Portuguese half-Johannes, Spanish dollars, and receipts for more than £5740 in New York currency. The next day Campbell, Brown, Weissenfels, and Burr moved on to Montgomery's clothes and personal items. They gave Dick, "the negro boy," a pair of woolen socks, but much of the rest they sold in an estate sale among officers. Arnold eventually bought three of seven ruffled shirts, a silk neck cloth, cashmere waistcoat and breeches, "elegant" Indian leggings, moccasins, silver table- and teaspoons, and knives and forks. Burr bought a buffalo skin robe and a clothes brush. And when he arrived in March and took a room in the headquarters in Holland House, Seth Warner, a practical man, purchased two blankets and a bedspread.[5]

Governor-General Guy Carleton rushed from Montréal to Québec. He deserves much of the credit for saving British Canada. Library and Archives Canada / Acc. No. 1997-8-1 / e011165560.

Colonel James Clinton, commander of the 3rd New York, reached Québec two weeks after the disaster. Arnold considered relinquishing command to him until his leg healed but did not. On January 19, the American burned buildings in St. Roch to deny fuel to the city. On January 23–24, the first reinforcements arrived: 160 men from Clinton's regiment. At times, it was not clear who was besieging whom. The people in the city had worries about food and fuel, but they could seize the initiative at any moment, attacking and then retreating behind secure walls. If Governor Carleton had taken the risk, the British and loyal Canadians might have swept the field. But Carleton was a cautious man and preferred allowing cold and disease to do the work for him.

At some point in January, Brown insisted that he had been promoted. When Arnold rejected his claim, Brown asked permission to send an officer to Wooster in Montréal to resolve the issue. This request was refused as well. The surviving evidence is little more than Brown's word against Arnold's with both men claiming to have the support of witnesses. All that can be said with certainty is that Brown made his claims in the open and welcomed hearings. Arnold did not.

On January 25, Arnold wrote to Wooster warning him that he might hear from Brown, who stood accused of plundering and embezzling the "Public Stores and Officers baggage" taken at Sorel. This is the first—or at least the first *recorded*—mention of the accusation. Arnold wrote that Brown was pursuing "a scheme of his to take advantage of our present distressed condition to obtain a regiment. The title of Colonel he has already assumed, and says that Genl. Montgomery promised him the commn. [commission] when at Montreal."[6]

"That the General promised him promotion is true," Arnold continued., "He told me so some time before his death, when Major Brown applied to him for his commn. which the General told me he had denied him." Then Arnold described a version of the meeting between Montgomery and Brown. "He sent for Major Brown and they were closeted some time, after which I heard no further application and believe had the General lived, there would have been none made—For the truth of my assertion I appeal to Col. Campbell and Major Weisonfels [sic] and am ready to make good the charge when public matters will admit."

Brown was not aware of this letter until spring when General Wooster took command at Québec. The first two of his thirteen charges refer to the letter as well as to the ongoing disparagement from Arnold; his third charge introduces Wooster's letter as evidence.

> 1st. For endeavouring to asperse your petitioner's character, in the most infamous manner.

Brown's proposed witnesses for this charge were Canadian officer Jeremiah Duggan, who had been promoted by Arnold in January, and Theodore Sedgwick, secretary to Major General John Thomas and Brown's associate in the early steps toward revolution in Berkshire County. Sedgwick did not reach Québec until May.[7]

A version of what Duggan might have testified survives. On August 1, 1776, he gave a statement before John Morton, justice of the Pennsylvania Supreme Court, which was signed by Benjamin Franklin, president of the Pennsylvania Convention. It is a badly degraded document but the essence is clear. On February 22 before Duggan left Québec for Philadelphia, Arnold asked him "to impeach to Congress one certain dam'd Rascal and Villian who he said was Guilty of the Worst of Crimes and aught not to be continued in the Army." Duggan offered to carry a letter from Arnold to the

Congress, but Arnold was "very loath" to mention Brown's name and said it would be better if Duggan spoke first. When Arnold finally said he was talking about Brown, Duggan said he knew of no charge of plundering against Brown. Duggan swore to Morton "that he was perfectly acquainted with Colo. Brown during the whole time he Served in Canada and that no officer Served in that Country with greater Reputation than he did."[8]

> 2d. For unwarrantably degrading and reducing the rank conferred on your petitioner by his (General Arnold's) superiour officer, and subjecting your petitioner to serve in an inferiour rank to that which he had been appointed.

Brown listed Robert Cochran and Frederick Weissenfels as possible witnesses. Cochran was a friend. Having seen the letter to Wooster, Brown was aware that Arnold had named Weissenfels as a supporter of his claims, but Brown still wanted him to testify. By the time Brown wrote his charges, Weissenfels was lieutenant colonel of 2nd New York, having served for eight months in the same rank in the 3rd New York.[9]

> 3d. For ungentleman-like conduct in his letter to General *Wooster*, of the 25th of January last, charging your petitioner with a falsehood, and in a private manner, which is justly chargeable on himself.

Brown's witnesses for his third charge were Cochran and adjutant William Satterlee. Brown offered Arnold's letter itself as proof even though it contains information that might raise questions about his own behavior.[10]

A few days after writing to Wooster, Arnold sent a similar damning letter about Brown to John Hancock, essentially informing the entire Continental Congress. In this letter Arnold added James Easton as also "impeached with plundering the officers' baggage taken at Sorel." "I believe it would give great disgust to the Army in general if those gentlemen were promoted before those matters were cleared up." Campbell and Major Dubois were witnesses. Then in a postscript, he added, "The contents of the enclosed letter I do not wish to be kept from the gentlemen mentioned therein; the publick interest is my chief motive for writing. I should despise myself were I capable of asserting a thing in prejudice of any gentlemen without sufficient reasons to make it publick."[11]

Arnold's letter to Hancock was not one of the thirteen charges, but Brown used it as an introduction to the rest of his indictment. He wrote to General Gates, "That in the month of February last, Brigadier-General Arnold transmitted to the honourable Continental Congress an unjustifiable, false, wicked, and malicious accusation against me and my character, as an officer in their service; at the time when I was under his immediate command. That had there been the least ground for such accusation, the author thereof had it in his power, indeed it was his duty, to have brought me to a fair trial by a General Court-Martial in the country where the pretended crime is said to have originated."[12]

Brown was certain that Arnold wished him dead. In March, he wrote his wife, "Mr. Gen Arnold & I do not agree very well, I expect another storm soon. *I suppose I must be a Uriah.*" In 2 Samuel, David takes Uriah's wife as a lover and when Uriah does not forget his grievance, David orders him placed "in the forefront of the hottest battle" to be abandoned and killed. Brown described a forgotten skirmish in

Eight. "Mr. General Arnold & I do not agree very well"

which Arnold ordered him to attack a detachment that had left the city. Although he believed he was outnumbered by as much as five to one, "I accordingly marched against the enemy, who had retired to the fort, too soon for me to attack them. I expect to be punished for disobedience to orders next."[13]

※ ※ ※

Meanwhile, Seth Warner recruited in Berkshire County as well as in the New Hampshire Grants. When news arrived from General Wooster of the defeat at Québec, a few companies were ready to march. After crossing the length of frozen Lake Champlain and being trapped in Montréal by a blizzard, the first of Warner's new regiment reached Québec on February 28. Although the reinforcements were fewer and slower to arrive than generals in Albany and Canada had hoped, more than 500 men marched through snow and bitter cold and now constituted nearly a quarter of the troops facing the walled city. Nathan Peirce, a Berkshire County captain, was appalled at what he found: "The smallpox was in Almost Every house & such Cold weather As I never Saw before & in a few days my men began to be Sick with the smallpox."[14]

Even for northern New Englanders, the cold of a Canadian winter was shocking. Brown's eyesight, which was never good, suffered. Afterwards, authorities questioned whether he could serve in the field or needed a "stationary post." Seth Warner's feet were damaged by frostbite. Both men remained active.[15]

Warner, still a lieutenant colonel with a New York commission dating from September, ranked high among Arnold's officers and took over command of the northwestern New England troops: his own regiment under Major Samuel Safford, Massachusetts reinforcements under Major Jeremiah Cady, and Brown's detachment. A tally from the end of March shows 373 men in Warner's own Regiment, 132 in Cady's, and 170 in Brown's.[16] The arrangements were fluid and changed as new officers and men arrived. An undated muster roll of "Brown's Detachment of Arnold's Regiment" in the New York archives lists 244 rank and file and twenty-four officers, commanded by Colonel Ethan Allen, Colonel Warner, and Major Brown. Editors of both Vermont's and New Hampshire's Revolutionary War papers were baffled by the list, but seeing names they recognized, they included it in their state volumes. The presence of Ethan Allen was an additional puzzle: he was never part of the army before Québec and had been a prisoner of war since September. There is an explanation for the list. Even though his men were New Englanders, Warner was still officially a New York officer. Allen appeared on the list so that he would be in an established regiment when it came time for prisoner exchange. Several of Warner's captains and the men in their companies were reassigned to enlarge Brown's command and to give him experienced officers.[17]

※ ※ ※

During the fall of 1775, smallpox was in the city of Québec. As the American soldiers tightened the siege in December, they too began to sicken. Americans believed that Governor Carleton sent infected Canadians from the city. As John Joseph Henry put it later, the disease was "introduced into our cantonments by the indecorous, yet fascinating arts of the enemy," meaning infected prostitutes.[18] But smallpox did not need Guy Carleton or indecorous arts to spread.

The primitive medicine of the day did have a defense against the disease, inoculation or introducing smallpox pus into a cut in a healthy person's body. Inoculated smallpox was usually less severe, the chance of death was greatly reduced, and immunity followed. However, an inoculated smallpox victim could still spread the deadly disease. Inoculation was controversial in the colonies. In Pittsfield, Massachusetts, in the spring of 1774 and again in 1775, a doctor requested permission to inoculate, but was refused by town authorities.[19] Some New Englanders saw pestilence as a punishment from God that ought to be endured by a community that had provoked His wrath. A military commander faced another problem with no easy answer. Inoculation might save individual lives and in a month result in an army that was immune, but in the meantime, it would be helpless against attack.

The British had no qualms about inoculation and so captured American officers within Québec were inoculated and fared better than their countrymen outside the walls. After the inoculated disease took hold, Henry Dearborn and his fellow captured officers, read in the morning, played cards in the afternoon, and endeavored "to make ourselves as happy as possible under our present disagreeable Circumstances."[20]

In the most puzzling of his thirteen charges, Brown accused Arnold of allowing the smallpox to spread:

> 4th. For suffering the small-pox to spread in the camp before *Quebeck*, and promoting inoculations there in the Continental Army.

His witnesses were Dr. Isaac Senter, who was an Arnold supporter and had inoculated on Christmas day 1775, Dr. John Coates, and once again Frederick Weissenfels and Robert Cochran.[21]

Arnold's record on the smallpox epidemic seems to be clear. He issued orders that the sick were to be quarantined in a hospital, although these orders were often ignored. Hospitals were seen as places of concentrated disease and death. On March 15 and again on March 26 with the arrival of more reinforcements, Arnold issued orders forbidding doctors to inoculate. Officers were to stop men from "strolling from their Quarters." Officers who inoculated were to be "immediately cashiered"; privates were to be punished "at the discretion of a Court-Martial." But Brown would not have raised an issue that could be brushed aside by reading entries from regimental orderly books.[22]

By the end of March with Arnold's time as commander about to end, the American army outside Québec numbered 2505 with another three hundred fifty just arrived. Of Warner's 373 men, Arnold claimed 271 were sick with smallpox, "by inoculation." "The publick will incur an expense of at least twenty pounds for each of those people, who will not on an average, have done ten days' service to the 15th April to which time they are engaged," Arnold told Silas Deane. One hundred thirty-two of Brown's men, or more than three-quarters of the detachment, were sick with inoculated smallpox, Arnold wrote. These precise figures about inoculated smallpox should be read with skepticism. Sickness and death stalked Warner and Brown's men as it did everyone else, and Arnold did not like Green Mountain Boys or their allies.[23]

Without question, Warner, who came from a family of country doctors, permitted, perhaps encouraged, his men to take the treatment. Josiah Sabin, a private in Major Jeremiah Cady's detachment of Warner's brigade, told of inoculating fellow soldiers. They entered his room blindfolded so that they could honestly say they did not know who had performed the procedure. None of the inoculated died, Sabin swore in his 1832 pension application, but three-quarter of those who were infected naturally succumbed, an exaggeration of the unquestionable horror. Accused of inoculating, Sabin was arrested and brought before Arnold. Warner accompanied him, and after "many sharp words" between Warner and Arnold, Sabin was set free. Is Sabin's account evidence of a policy of permitting inoculation while issuing orders against it? By spring, everyone seems to have been in on the secret of inoculation. Newly arrived troops inoculated on arrival and then quarantined in the country.[24]

In making the charge against Arnold, Brown may be accused of hypocrisy and of adhering to the deadly letter of the law. As an educated, traveled man who survived the winter siege, Brown must have been immune to the disease, likely through inoculation. His men inoculated openly and in secret—and survived. But Brown brought his case as a prosecutor before Horatio Gates, who vehemently opposed inoculation. Gates believed that in the summer of 1776 when he took command of the defeated army, he ended the smallpox epidemic through strict enforcement of the ban against inoculation and by quarantining the sick at Fort George. Men were required to swear by the "ever-living God" that they had not inoculated. "Perpetrators of so villainous an act may be instantly brought to condign punishment." Gates's measures were possible when the enemy was distant and men were not trapped indoors. Indeed, like wildfire in dry grass, smallpox had swept through the army and moved on.[25]

From prosecutor Brown's point of view, Gates might question Arnold's decisions at Québec and wonder in what other ways had he had failed to act.

※ ※ ※

Time was against the Americans. Although winter in the north can seem endless, it was too short to reinforce and supply the troops. Soon the snow and ice highways on Lake George and Lake Champlain turned soft and punky; on land, smoothed snow gave way to slop and mud. Meanwhile, Canadians lost patience with paper money and promises. Out of necessity and frustration, an army of liberation was turning into one of invasion.

On April 1, General Wooster arrived in the American camp outside Québec, and soon afterwards Brown renewed his demand for an inquiry into Arnold's charges. Wooster refused to convene a court, but he did promote Brown to lieutenant colonel and acting commander of a regiment to be raised from the "Broken Corps of the New England Troops now in Canada." Wooster knew of Arnold's accusations against Brown and had seen Brown's December 29 letter to Montgomery. The relationship between Wooster and Arnold deteriorated, and finally Arnold left Québec to take command in Montréal. "General Wooster did not think proper to consult me in any of his matters," he complained to General Schuyler. On April 17, Brown first appeared as a colonel in the regimental orderly books.[26]

※ ※ ※

On twenty-mile-long Île d'Orléans, east of Québec, the brigantine *Peggy* was being turned into a fireship, a weapon packed with combustibles that could be set ablaze and aimed at enemy ships. The *Peggy* was owned by Arnold and had sailed to Québec as a trading vessel. Captain Ainslie first wrote of the fireship on April 9: "We now guard the river every night. Our warfs are garnish'd with guns—we have cannon in some vessels in the Cul de Sac, & strong guards in the Lower Town." On April

18 as enlistments ran out, Wooster told men of the fireship. In an account that circulated in Congress during the summer, he was imagined as saying, "My lads, I find your time is almost out, and maybe some of you think on going. But surely you won't leave me now; you must stay a little longer. Don't think that I am lying here doing nothing. No, no; you shall see a fine sight soon. I am busy building a fire-ship; and soon as she is ready, will burn all their vessels up." Congressmen mocked Wooster for his indiscretion, but the enemy knew before Wooster did himself. The walls of Québec were a sieve, and there were few secrets.[27]

All winter the northern army had been awaiting an experienced major general, and finally on May 2, John Thomas reached Québec. A fifty-one-year-old Massachusetts surgeon turned soldier, Thomas knew Canada from commanding a provincial regiment in the French and Indian War, but he was new to the Northern Army. Dr. Senter wrote that Thomas was "an utter stranger in the country, and much terrified with the small-pox." He took command of nineteen hundred men, only a thousand of whom were fit for duty. The enlistments of three hundred healthy men—the last of those who marched through Maine, Montgomery's New Yorkers, and a portion of Warner's Regiment—had expired, and they demanded to go home. Others had inoculated recently and were awaiting the outbreak of the disease. The army had a reserve of only one hundred fifty pounds of powder in the magazines and enough provisions for six days.[28]

Thomas's first orders were to ban inoculation in the "most peremptory manner." But Thomas had no time to have any impact, certainly not to stop an epidemic or to coordinate the sailing of the fireship from twenty-five miles away. At high tide on the evening of May 3, the *Peggy* under full sail came from behind Île d'Orléans. The news swept through the city, and Québec's defenders stood by their guns in the moonlight. Signals were given with no answer. At some point, the crew lashed the rudder in place and abandoned ship. Governor Carleton hailed the vessel and finally gave orders to fire upon it. Moments later the brigantine burst into flame. Americans hoped that a vessel from hell would ignite the shipping in the cul-de-sac and the fire spread to the nearby warehouses while panic seized the Upper Town. Instead, the tide carried the *Peggy* away "in a fine blaze" punctuated by explosions.[29]

※ ※ ※

Four days before the failure of the fireship, the distinguished commissioners from Congress—Benjamin Franklin, Charles Carroll of Carrollton, and Samuel Chase—arrived in Montréal. They were accompanied by Carroll's cousin John, a Jesuit, who was later to be the first Roman Catholic bishop and archbishop in the United States, and by a French printer from Philadelphia and his press. The commission was an idea born in the winter when there was still hope Canada would become the fourteenth rebelling colony. Congress sent men who by their presence would flatter the Canadians and make a point about religious toleration that was not altogether true. They were instructed to tell "our Canadian brethren" that the Americans expected to defeat the "hostile machinations of Governor Carleton" and would empower the Canadians "to pursue such measures for securing their own freedom and happiness, as a generous love of liberty and sound policy shall dictate to them."[30]

Preeminent among the commissioners was seventy-year-old Dr. Franklin, the greatest American of the age, a scientist, inventor, editor, and statesman, recognized on both sides of the Atlantic. The trip north had been hard on the old man. A heavy mid–April snowstorm delayed the party at Philip Schuyler's estate in Saratoga. Bad roads had been made worse by the passage of wagons carrying baggage and supplies for the regiments that were marching north. The party needed to break ice with tent poles to find open water on Lake George. Franklin wrote Josiah Quincy, "I begin to apprehend that I have undertaken a fatigue that, at my time of life, may prove too much for me, so I sit down to write a few friends, by way of farewell."[31]

Charles Carroll of Carrollton was a wealthy Roman Catholic from Maryland, who had been educated in France. In the spring of 1776, he was a delegate to the Annapolis Convention, Maryland's revolutionary government. He was elected to the Continental Congress after his trip to Canada—in fact on July 4, 1776. He took his seat in time to be a signer of the Declaration of Independence.

Congressman Samuel Chase, exactly half Franklin's age, was a Maryland revolutionary and the son of the rector of St. Paul's (Anglican church) of Baltimore. Chase wrote John Adams from St. John on a day that twenty-four bateaux filled with men passed the fort, "I hope You will attend to every Quarter of America, and not neglect Us, for I now esteem Myself a Canadian, and not spend your precious Time in Debates about our Independancy. In my Judgment You have no alternative between Independancy and Slavery, and what American can hesitate in the Choice; but don't harrangue about it, act as if we were."[32]

Arnold greeted the dignitaries at the wharf at Montréal, saluted them with cannon fire, and escorted them to the Château Ramezay, the most prestigious residence in the city, where they were met by a crowd of ladies and gentlemen. It was said that "a number of friends to liberty spent the evening with decent mirth," although the political persuasion of those paying their compliments may not be so simple. A month earlier Moses Hazen, then in command in Montréal, estimated that "with respect to the better sort of people, both French and English, seven-eighths are Tories, who would wish to see our throats cut, and perhaps would readily assist in doing it."[33]

Arnold had landed squarely on his feet. Carroll wrote to his father, Charles Carroll *of Annapolis*, "An officer bred-up at Versailles could not have behaved with more delicacy, ease, and good breeding." And he added, "Believe me, if this war continues, and Arnold is not taken off pretty early, he will turn out a great man."[34] Soon the commissioners learned from Arnold the hard truth about Canada. Their message of May 1 to John Hancock held out little hope unless gold and silver was sent promptly. By May 6, the commissioners suggested withdrawing from Canada and fortifying "the passes on the lakes." By May 8, they were "pestered hourly with Demands great and small that they cannot answer, in a place where our Cause has a Majority of Enemies, the Garrison weak, and a greater [garrison] would, without Money, increase our difficulties."[35]

※ ※ ※

On May 5 a council of war had been held at Holland House outside Québec to discuss abandoning the siege. John Brown was among the dozen officers in camp who consulted with General Thomas and agreed unanimously that the sick should be evacuated as should the cannon across the river at Pointe-Lévy. Later that evening Thomas received "certain intelligence" that fifteen British vessels were near the city.[36]

The siege of Québec collapsed at six a.m., May 6, when the fifty-gun frigate *Surprise* appeared from behind Île d'Orléans. *Surprise* was followed by the frigate *Isis* and the sloop *Martin*. By nine o'clock, the Americans were moving artillery and baggage in the direction of Sillery and the bateaux on the St. Lawrence. By eleven o'clock, a British force came from the city. Captain Ainslie wrote of the Americans, "they left cannon, mortars, field pieces, muskets & even their cloaths behind them. As we pursued them we found the road strew'd with arms, cartridges, cloaths, bread, pork, &cc. Their confusion was so great, their panic so violent, that they left orderly books & papers, which for their own credit shou'd not have been left." It was said that at Holland House, men from the Royal Highland Emigrants ate General Thomas's dinner. Two hundred men who were too sick to move were captured.[37]

Colonel Elisha Porter and his western Massachusetts men had every reason to be confused. They had only arrived in camp ten days earlier, just in time for the change in command from Wooster to Thomas and the failure of the fireship. First Porter's men were ordered to Cap-Santé to be inoculated, and on the next day, General Thomas declared inoculation to be prohibited. Some of Porter's men were still inoculated openly; others secretly.[38]

Porter was one of the most agreeable of journalists. In a spring in which Americans and Canadians were splitting apart, he liked Canada and the people he met. He wrote, Chambly is "a fine pleasant village," which it still is. He remembered being cheered upon arriving at Trois-Rivières and again when he left. At a convent he met "one nun a pleasant sociable woman, seven or eight small girls—at school here—who behaved very prettily." In Porter's account of the retreat, there was no panic. "When the enemy were within about 80 rods [a quarter mile] of us, we had orders to retreat slowly and in good order which we did, untill we could find a convenient place to defend ourselves. We formed in the first wood we came to and remained till the rear had got up to us." They rested in the evening and started to march again before midnight. Breakfast was two loaves of bread for seventy men. During the day, they were harassed by cannon fire from British warships.[39]

Uriah Cross of Brown's detachment and regiment remembered the confusion of the retreat in an exaggerated account dictated in 1828. He was nurse to an officer who was covered with sores from the smallpox and had been quarantined six miles in the country. At the news of the retreat, Cross hired a Canadian to carry his patient with the retreating army. Then to get his own pack and musket, he passed through the retreating American army and then slipped by the British. At camp, he found his own gear and the packs and muskets belonging to Captain Seth Wheeler and Lieutenant Parmelee Allen, formerly of Brown's Detachment, now in Porter's Regiment. Burdened—in his tale at least—with three muskets, three packs, and three hundred silver dollars, he followed the retreating Americans.[40]

By the evening of May 7, the exhausted men were at Deschambault, a bluff dominating the St. Lawrence at the Falls of Richelieu (not to be confused with the Richelieu River), thirty-five miles from Québec. In December, General Montgomery wrote that Deschambault "may be defended against all the navy and all the military force of Great Britain." But the American army had no cannon, little powder and shot, and only provisions for two or three days. General Thomas called another council of war to decide if they should make a stand. Of the fifteen field officers at the council, only three voted to remain. Brown was among the majority voting to march on. The council then decided unanimously to concentrate at Sorel where Brown had built his battery in the fall.[41]

Fresh troops were rushing to Canada. The return for May showed more than eight thousand men somewhere between Albany and Sorel—and that number included only remnants of the army that had laid siege to Québec. The flood of men was so great that it overwhelmed the supply system. "A further reinforcement will only increase our distress," the commissioners wrote Schuyler on May 10. "An immediate supply of provisions from over the Lakes is absolutely necessary for the preservation of the troops already in this Province." As new men arrived, they fed the raging smallpox epidemic.[42]

From Sorel at dawn on May 15, Arnold sent a letter express to the commissioners in Montréal calling for mass inoculation. He told them, "I have no doubt we shall have more effective men in four weeks than by endeavoring to prevent the infection spreading." As educated men, they agreed. Benjamin Franklin had departed, but Poor Richard had given his opinion years before. Inoculation was "a Method discovered to Mankind by God's good Providence, whereby 99 in 100 are saved." Around noon, Chase and Carroll wrote to General Thomas, recommending "the propriety of immediately innoculating all our Troops." They advised him to protect himself by inoculating, telling him, "it will be almost impossible for you to escape catching the small pox," but he refused, honorably, foolishly, or both. By then the disease was incubating in his body.[43]

On May 16, Arnold issued general orders to inoculate. First in line was Porter's Regiment, which had almost been treated on its arrival at Québec. Arnold had a plan that he outlined to the commissioners. Immediately inoculate the scattered troops at Montréal, La Prairie, Longueuil, and the Cedars, a fort to the west of Montréal. Order soldiers in Montréal who already had the smallpox to Sorel. Send recently inoculated men to Montréal to recuperate; if not enough barracks were available, quarter them "on the inhabitants." The last is the most unsettling. The Quartering Act was one of the Coercive or Intolerable Acts passed by Parliament that changed protest into revolution. Quartering of soldiers was to appear in the Declaration of Independence as one of the "repeated injuries and usurpations" of the King.[44]

The next day General Thomas reached Sorel and reversed Arnold's order. "It should be death for any person to inoculate," noted Dr. Lewis Beebe, John Brown's classmate at Yale and Ethan Allen's brother-in-law, although Lucy Allen had died a year earlier.[45]

Brown included Arnold's brief attempt at mass inoculation in his thirteen charges:

> 10th. For ordering inoculation of the Continental Army at Sorel, without the knowledge of, and contrary to the intentions of, the General commanding that Northern Department, by which fatal consequences ensued.

His witnesses were Major Theodore Sedgwick, Colonel Samuel Brewer, and Major Joshua Thomas, all on General Thomas's staff.[46]

As with his accusation that Arnold was to blame for the spread of smallpox during the siege of Québec, Brown was appealing to Horatio Gates. Arnold had attempted to go over General Thomas's head to the commissioners. Arnold knew the commander's views, his "intentions," if not his orders. Brown claimed that "fatal consequences ensued." Undoubtedly they did, but by then the epidemic had taken hold and there were only fatal consequences.

General Thomas sickened quickly, and on May 20 he wrote his final letter to the commissioners. The army was "disheartened," "destitute of every necessity," and "(as they think) wholly neglected." He did not complain that he was face to face with death. The pox erupted that night, and in the morning, he relinquished command and traveled up the Richelieu to Chambly. He was well enough to walk a half-mile to his quarters, and for a few days, Dr. Beebe believed his symptoms were favorable.[47]

Nine

"Some strange kind of conduct in General Arnold"

Soon after taking command at Montréal in April, Arnold ordered two hundred men under Colonel Timothy Bedel to the Cedars, an isolated outpost on the St. Lawrence about thirty miles west of Montréal. By mid–May the stockade fort was garrisoned by some 390 soldiers, many of whom were in the throes of inoculated smallpox. Bedel was usually a confident, larger-than-life frontiersman, but with the infection talking hold, he was sunk in depression. He spoke of his despair to Frye Bayley, who led a company of men from the upper Connecticut River to Canada. Arnold was his personal enemy, Bedel said; the garrison at the Cedars was too small to withstand attack; and "I am so sick with the Small Pock that I fear I shall not do well."[1]

Somehow Bedel was able to visit the Kahnawake Mohawks, whose support of the American cause was part of his assignment. It was an unfortunate trip. Major Isaac Butterfield, who was left in command at the Cedars, was even sicker, and Bedel carried the smallpox to his Native friends. Bedel was at Kahnawake when he received word that a sizable force was moving toward the Cedars. "What was I then to do?" he asked in defense of his actions at his court-martial. "I must own I was myself at a loss, Rather inclined to return immediately." The Indians told him to carry the news to Montréal himself, and he accepted their offer of a canoe and two strong paddlers to maneuver it through the rapids to the city.[2]

He arrived in Montréal on the morning of May 16 to the surprise of commissioners Chase and Carroll. They and Colonel John Paterson of Massachusetts—in command since Arnold was at Sorel—ordered one hundred fifty men under Major Henry Sherburne to reinforce the Cedars. The commissioners were not worried, even though Bedel told them that the fort was "badly provided to receive the enemy, and had been four days without any other provisions than bread." They were more shocked that he had brought the news himself, but concluded, "We apprehend the report to be altogether groundless, or occasioned by some very trifling circumstance."[3] In fact, the fort was facing more than 250 men, the vast majority western Indians—all more or less under command of Captain George Forster of the 8th Regiment of Foot. American sources later put the size of Forster's little army at six hundred, an exaggeration that made the defeat slightly more bearable.[4]

Forster demanded that Major Butterfield surrender within a half hour or he might lose control of the Indians who were not "governable to any particular will." It was an old pretense: *I would treat you humanely, but these are savages!* Frightened,

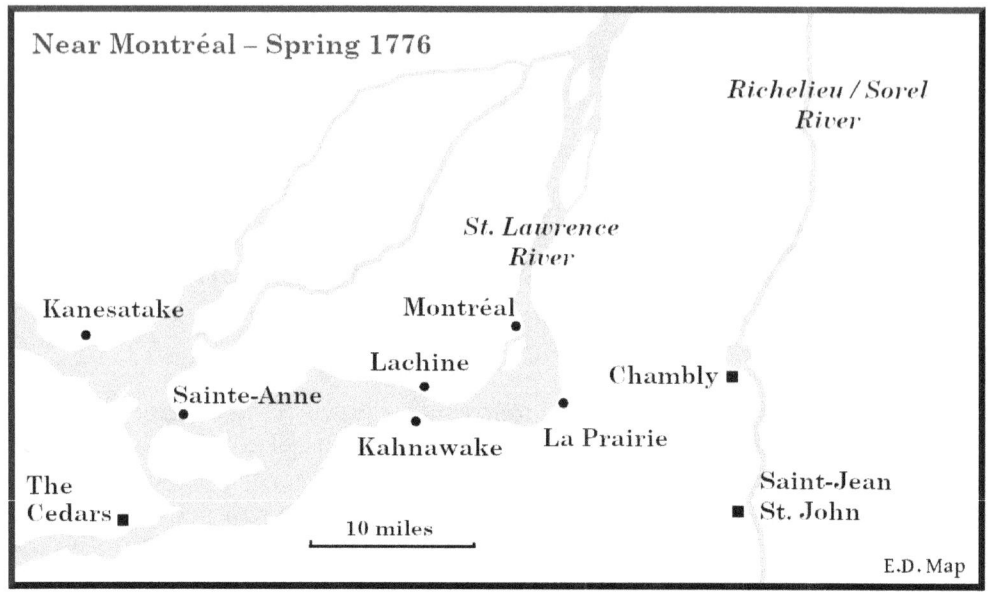

From the Cedars (Les Cèdres) west of Montréal on the St. Lawrence to the fortifications on the Richelieu River, the waterways of Canada helped to determine events in the spring of 1776.

sick, poorly supplied, in an undermanned fort, the Americans surrendered. They told their countrymen later that they were "cruelly insulted, and repeatedly stripped of almost everything, and several murdered." The British claimed that men in the fort lost "some watches and money, and perhaps a laced hat or two; but we do verily believe of nothing else, nor did they receive any other insult." In Philadelphia, John Adams took some consolation in thinking that the "Scoundrell Savages" had stripped clothes off smallpox victims and "have taken a large Dose of it."[5]

Meanwhile, reinforcements under Henry Sherburne marched west from Montréal. Bedel was with them as far as Lachine when he became too sick to continue. Sherburne had difficulty finding enough bateaux and so crossed and re-crossed the Grand (Ottawa) River. Still hoping they were coming to the relief of a besieged garrison, Sherburne's expedition advanced towards the Cedars, nine miles away. Instead, they were overwhelmed. Sherburne wrote, "I lost from my small party twenty-eight men killed in action, wounded, killed in cold blood, and carried off by the savages.... The barbarity with which we were treated by the savages, together with the sufferings for want of provisions and clothes, is beyond anything which can be imagined or described."[6]

Suddenly, the relief expedition needed help, and there were few troops to call upon. Men who had besieged Québec were waiting for their turn to cross Lake Champlain on their way home and could not be persuaded to help. The commissioners were in despair: "No duty must be expected from soldiers whose times are out, let their country stand ever so much in need of their services: witness the unfeeling flight and return, at this critical juncture, of all the soldiers, and a greater part of the officers, who are entitled to be discharged."[7] But Brown, whose mixed regiment dissolved as it reached St. John, joined a relief force under Arnold's command. Expecting attack,

Arnold and about two hundred fifty men fortified a stone building in Lachine. The Indians were so close that two men were taken prisoner, and Americans could hear drumming in the distance. By then Arnold was south of the river, hoping to gain the support of the Kahnawake. Brown was one of two officers left in command.[8]

At eight the next morning, Colonel Philip de Haas of the 1st Pennsylvania Battalion and five hundred men reached Lachine. The Americans now had the numbers on their side and moved west.[9] Brown was in the advanced guard that was first to reach Sainte-Anne (Sainte-Anne-de-Bellevue) at the western end of the island of Montréal. Kahnawake messengers carried Arnold's threat. As he told the commissioners, if the prisoners were not returned unharmed, I "would sacrifice every Indian who fell into my hands, and would follow them to their towns, and destroy them by fire and sword." The reply was equally blunt: attack and every prisoner would be killed on the spot.[10]

At five o'clock in the afternoon, the army crossed a wide bay (Baie de Vaudreuil) of the Grand River in fifteen heavily loaded bateaux and three canoes. As the Americans neared shore, the British opened fire with two field guns. The cannon balls skipped across the water. In the boats, the men rested on their oars and drifted out of range on water that was smooth as a mirror. Then in the dark they turned back to Sainte-Anne, and lit many campfires so that from a distance their numbers swelled. Arnold called a council of war, which (he told the commissioners) agreed unanimously to attack in the morning.

James Wilkinson, then a nineteen-year-old captain, later published a detailed account of the council. Wilkinson was an upper class Marylander educated in Philadelphia and able to ingratiate himself into the highest circles in the army. Unfortunately for researchers, he is a disreputable source. His *Memoirs of My Own Times*, published in three hefty volumes in 1816, is the work of a discredited man. Old Wilkinson was a major general *and* (although not known until later) a traitor to the United States, having sold his services to the Spanish in Louisiana. The latter part of his *Memoirs* is a tedious, false explanation of how he was wronged by President Madison and many others. Still,

James Wilkinson, who was nineteen in the spring of 1776, was responsible for lively stories of Benedict Arnold's heroism and misconduct. Historians struggle to know what to believe. This print is based upon a portrait painted in 1797 by Charles Willson Peale when Wilkinson was forty. The Miriam and Ira D. Wallach Division of Art, Prints and Photographs: Print Collection, The New York Public Library Digital Collections.

his stories of the Revolutionary War may be no more biased than those found in many other accounts, but they are livelier.

According to Wilkinson, Arnold proposed that they "ascend the Grand river a few miles, under cover of night, gain the rear of the enemy, and fall on them at day-break." Moses Hazen, commander of the 2nd Canadian Regiment, opposed the attack: "from his long acquaintance with the Indian character: he was satisfied their vigilance would prevent surprise, and that the moment of attack would be the signal for the massacre of their prisoners." In the French and Indian War, Hazen was a captain in Roger's Rangers in present-day New Brunswick and then a lieutenant in the 44th Regiment of Foot along the St. Lawrence. General James Murray, the first British governor of Québec, wrote that Hazen's bravery and conduct "would justly entitle him to every military reward he could ask or demand." Hazen was supported in his arguments by Philip de Haas, commander of the 1st Pennsylvania. De Haas, in his early forties, served on the Pennsylvania frontier during the French and Indian War and was part of Forbes's expedition that captured Fort Duquesne and Bouquet's expedition that ended Pontiac's War.[11]

Always the hero in his own narrative, Wilkinson claimed he took the high-minded position. The captives would "solicit the attack, at the peril of their own lives." But those who favored attacking were outvoted. Arnold was "highly irritated" and exchanged "reproachful language" with Hazen, but accepted the decision. Brown's role in the council is unknown, although he did list Hazen as a witness for two of his charges against Arnold.[12]

At two in the morning, a British lieutenant appeared under a flag of truce with an agreement between Major Sherburne and British commander Forster for an exchange of prisoners. Forster could not provide for hundreds of prisoners of war, even by the wretched standards of the day, but the men he had captured might be traded for British prisoners held elsewhere. Prisoner exchange was a practice that allowed for a glimmer of humanity amid shocking cruelty, but for much of the time, it was just another issue for opposing commanders to argue about while prisoners suffered. Arnold rejected Forster's first proposal, but finally agreed to an equal exchange. Americans held captive were "to return to their own countries" by way of St. John, but could serve again. Within two months, British prisoners in the same number and of the same rank would be released. Fighting could recommence in six days—or sooner, Arnold suggested, and the pause in hostilities was shortened to four days.

In his first letter to the commissioners explaining the agreement, often called a cartel, Arnold wrote that as soon as the prisoners were free, "I hope it will be in our power to take ample vengeance, or we will nobly fall in the attempt."[13] But where to attack? Forster's Indians would melt away if they sensed the Americans had an overwhelming force. Arnold gave orders to attack the Mohawk settlement of Canassadaga (Kanesatake), about ten miles northwest of Sainte-Anne across Lac des Deux Montagnes, the Lake of Two Mountains. Some men from Kanesatake had joined Forster's expedition, although most of the raiders were from the west. The destruction of the town would serve no purpose except revenge. It would not protect American-held Montréal and would embitter all the Mohawks. But a village was close by and the inhabitants might be surprised.

Arnold, Hazen, and Brown left Sainte-Anne for a council of war in Chambly, leaving de Haas in command. It is hard to imagine the three of them riding amiably together. David Wooster presided at the council, although the commissioners had concluded that he was "totally unfit" to command and it was his last day in Canada. The council recorded no criticism of Arnold's agreement with Forster but did call upon the commanding officer at Sainte-Anne to attack as soon as the pause in hostilities ended. In a letter to Washington, Brigadier General William Thompson, senior among the Pennsylvania officers, referred to the agreement as "the late unguarded truce and convention at the Cedars," tactful language that could not be misread.[14]

Brown wrote in his thirteen charges:

> 9th. For entering into an unwarrantable, unjustifiable, and partial agreement with Captain Foster for the exchange of prisoners taken at The Cedars, without the knowledge, advice, or consent of any officer than those present with him on the spot.

The witnesses and evidence were Moses Hazen, John Philip de Haas, and the Resolves of Congress.[15]

For the first time in his military career, Arnold had failed publicly. His settlement with the British, which seems sensible centuries later, shocked Americans in Canada and at home. Of all the disasters and defeats in the spring of 1776, the Cedars and its aftermath seemed to have no redeeming features. After Congress held hearings in July, President Hancock issued resolutions that in one breath agreed to the cartel and in the next rejected it. Arnold's agreement was "a mere sponsion," an act done for a state by an unauthorized agent. Congress would follow the agreement, provided the British in Canada turned over murderers and repaid Americans who were plundered. And since the British would not admit to murder or unrestrained plundering, Congress repudiated the cartel.[16]

After the council, Arnold repeated his orders to destroy Kanesatake and to massacre the inhabitants.[17]

Brown wrote:

> 8th. For giving unjustifiable, unwarrantable, cruel, and bloody orders, directing whole villages to be destroyed, and the inhabitants thereof put to death by fire and sword, without any distinctions to friend or foe, age or sex.

Brown's evidence was to be the orders themselves.[18]

In Sainte-Anne, de Haas called a council of war, which rejected the attack. In Arnold's account, de Haas had received a "vague and uncertain" report that the village was reinforced by seven hundred Indians, and so the council and de Haas took the cowardly way out. In Wilkinson's version of events, the young men "exulted" in Arnold's orders, but de Hass wanted to escape responsibility. Wilkinson rode through the rain to carry the dispatch to Montréal where Arnold blamed the entire detachment and declared, "None but cowards would hesitate to obey a positive order." Wilkinson answered, "Sir, you censure the detachment unjustly; several of the officers were zealous for the enterprise, and the Colonel alone is responsible."[19]

Brown's accusation stresses the inhumanity of Arnold's orders. The orders were "unjustifiable, unwarrantable, cruel, and bloody"; "the inhabitants [were to be] put to death by fire and sword, without any distinctions to friend or foe, age or sex." Historians have avoided discussing this charge or have quoted Brown as if his words are so plainly false that no additional research was needed. In fact, the charge is the most certain of all. Brown had access to a copy of the orders, which were to be presented as evidence, and we have Arnold's explanation to the commissioners that he ordered de Haas to "burn and destroy the town and inhabitants of Canassadaga."[20]

Imagine de Haas's men crossing Lac des Deux-Montagnes in the dark, landing somewhere in today's Oka—site of a 1990 dispute between Natives and the Canadian government that turned violent—and before dawn bursting upon the sleeping village of Kanesatake. Imagine Robert Roger's raid against the Abenaki at St. Francis in 1759, in which the village was burned and, according to the village's priest, ten men and twenty-two women and children were slaughtered.[21] (The raid is featured heroically in another Kenneth Roberts novel, *Northwest Passage*.) Imagine the Paxton Boys, including Matthew Smith, captain of one company of Pennsylvania riflemen on the expedition to Québec, slaughtering Conestoga Indians at home and then in Lancaster where they were being protected in the workhouse. Imagine the Gnadenhutten Massacre in Ohio in 1782. Ninety-six Lenni Lenape men, women, and children were bludgeoned and scalped. Imagine a seemingly endless list that includes Sacramento River, Sand Creek, and Wounded Knee.

The greatest mass destruction of houses and farmland during the Revolution was inflicted upon the Iroquois in 1779 by an expedition of about 4,000 men led by John Sullivan. His destructive march through upstate New York was in response to bloody raids on frontier settlements by Natives and Loyalists. Sullivan's men burned forty towns, one with 128 houses, "most large and elegant." Crops were destroyed, and orchards, including one with 1500 fruit trees, were chopped down. An officer commented when it was over, "The nests are destroyed, but the birds are still on the wing." In this cycle of revenge, in October 1780, Native and Loyalist raiders led by Sir John Johnson burned at least seven hundred buildings in Tryon County, New York, and killed nearly two hundred people including John Brown.[22]

The greatest destruction against a New England town occurred on September 6, 1781, when a force of British, Germans, and Loyalists burned New London, Connecticut, and then gave no quarter to the defenders of Fort Griswold on the Groton side of the Thames River. One hundred forty-three buildings were burned in New London. Out of Fort Griswold's 140 defenders, eighty-three were killed on the spot and thirty-six more were grievously wounded after surrender. The commander blamed an unexpected explosion and shifting winds for the spread of the fire. In his report, he ignored the massacre and praised "the coolness and bravery" of the troops. The commander was the traitor, British brigadier general Benedict Arnold, who had been born a dozen miles north in Norwich.[23]

※ ※ ※

Before leaving Canada, the Commissioners from Congress looked in on General John Thomas at Chambly. It was "a Million to a Shilling" that he would die, wrote Samuel Chase, which Thomas did early on the morning of June 2, a month to the day after he took command outside Québec.[24] With Wooster and the commissioners gone, Arnold was briefly in command in all of Canada. When Dr. Beebe heard the news, he wrote a bit of doggerel in his journal. Likely Beebe had formed his opinion of Arnold while at college in New Haven and had heard nothing to change his mind.

Nine. "Some strange kind of conduct in General Arnold"

"Thomas is dead that pious man,
Where all our hopes were laid,
Had it been one, now in Command,
My heart should not be grieved."[25]

Brigadier General John Sullivan, a thirty-six-year-old lawyer from New Hampshire, reached the Richelieu as Wooster left, and Arnold was once again second in command, although this time with a difference. For most of the previous nine months, whatever his rank or the chain of command, he had been on his own. Since April, he had been relied upon by the inexperienced commissioners and through them he often had the most authority. But his actions following the Cedars had been questioned; his friends Chase and Carroll were gone; and a newcomer to Canada with more political than military experience had taken command. Sullivan seemed almost starry-eyed in his naivety. He told Washington, "It really was affecting to see the banks of the Sorel [Richelieu] lined with men, women, and children, leaping and clapping their hands for joy to see me arrive." Sullivan was still optimistic about the invasion of Canada and believed all that was needed was a real leader such as himself. He told Washington that since his taking command more work was done in a single day on Sorel's defenses than had been since the surrender of St. John in the fall. Canadians were flocking to the American cause by the hundreds, he believed.[26]

Sullivan has been at the edge of this narrative before. His brother James was one of the delegates from the Massachusetts Provincial Congress who a year earlier had relieved Arnold of command on Lake Champlain. After Roger Enos turned back on the Dead River, John Sullivan presided at the court-martial, which found that Enos "was under a necessity of returning with the division under his command." Neither connection would have recommended him to Arnold.[27]

Before Sullivan's arrival, Arnold had established a reputation for disregarding orders from his commanders. Brown wrote:

6th. For interfering and countermanding the orders of his superiour officer.

His witnesses were to be Samuel Brewer, Theodore Sedgwick, and Moses Hazen. Brewer and Sedgwick were General Thomas's staff officers. Hazen, who had been part of the events surrounding the Cedars, was by June commander in Chambly. There is no knowing to what

Theodore Sedgwick, one of John Brown's proposed witnesses against Arnold, was a staff officer in 1776. He was later speaker of the U.S. House of Representatives and a U.S. senator. This small portrait was painted by John Trumbull in 1792 when Sedgwick was in his mid-forties. Yale University Art Gallery.

incidents Brown was referring. The evidence that Arnold interfered with Sullivan's orders is clear.[28]

※ ※ ※

The last offensive by the Americans in Canada began when William Thompson, the Irish-born commander of the Pennsylvania brigade at Sorel, learned that Allan MacLean and about eight hundred men were as far west as Trois-Rivières. Thompson ordered Colonel Arthur St. Clair's 2nd Pennsylvania Battalion to attack and wrote Arnold requesting the return of de Haas's 1st Pennsylvania. Arnold was senior to Thompson, but Pennsylvania troops were facing the greatest threat. On his arrival, Sullivan backed Thompson and ordered de Haas and Arnold to Sorel. But Arnold found reasons to stay in Montréal and to keep all the men in his command nearby. He told Sullivan that he "intended" to join the army at Sorel, but "have been much hindered by taking the goods in town. Every possible obstacle has been thrown in my way; however, I shall secure many articles much wanted by the Army." He sent off de Haas, but recalled him when he learned of a threat from the west from four to five hundred Natives and Canadians. He assured Sullivan that there was no cause to worry. "I believe the enemy below [meaning downstream on the St. Lawrence] will not advance very suddenly. I make no doubt you will have time to prepare for them, and that we shall be reinforced in time to secure this part of the country."[29]

This comforting, misleading analysis, written on June 5, is seldom quoted, for Arnold could not have believed his own words. He was making excuses for remaining in Montréal and, as he often did, leaving others to their fate. A day later, although nothing had changed, he wrote the blunt truth to Philip Schuyler, in a letter that frequently appears in histories as an example of Arnold's superior judgment. He told Schuyler that out of an army of eight thousand, only five thousand could be mustered. "Our enemies are daily increasing, and our friends deserting us. Under these discouragements and obstacles, with a powerful Army against us, well disciplined, and wanting in no one article to carry on their operations, it will be a miracle if we keep the country." He advised sending all the bateaux on the lakes north for use in a retreat.[30]

Sullivan was still optimistic that an attack on Trois-Rivières, thirty-five miles from Sorel on the north shore of the St. Lawrence, would be the first step in a triumphant return to the strongpoint of Deschambault. He told Washington that generals William Thompson and Baron Frederick William de Woedtke "have done everything in their power to assist me." But Arnold was "engaged at Montreal, upon affairs of importance" and wanted de Haas to fortify Lachine with a large force, which Sullivan could not agree to. Two days later Sullivan finally understood what Arnold was doing and told Washington, "By some strange kind of conduct in General Arnold, directly contrary to repeated orders, he has kept that detachment dancing between this [Sorel] and Montreal ever since my arrival." Sullivan wanted to take part in the attack of Trois-Rivières in person, but only after de Haas reached Sorel.[31]

On the night of June 7, General Thompson and an army of two thousand (but no de Haas) crossed the St. Lawrence from Nicolet, planning a surprise attack against a supposed three hundred men at Trois-Rivières. In the morning, Sullivan could hear cannon and small arms fire to the east. In a letter to Washington, he recorded an imagined Battle of Trois-Rivières as if he could read distant explosions like a book. "I am almost certain that victory has declared in our favor," he wrote, "as the irregular firing of the cannon for such a length of time after the small-arms ceased, shows that our men are in possession of the ground." Instead, a guide led the exhausted Americans into a swamp where they waded in knee-deep muck for hours. A British gunboat raked the slogging men with cannon fire. What Sullivan heard as a sign of victory was British target practice.[32]

Even worse for the Americans, Trois-Rivières had been reinforced by four brigades under Lieutenant Colonel Simon Fraser of the 24th Regiment of Foot. After the Pennsylvanians and William Maxwell's 2nd New Jersey Regiment emerged from the swamp, they faced a professional force of nearly equal size, but rested and supported by cannon. Colonel Anthony Wayne came close enough to the town to see the church spire, but then the Americans were driven into retreat. By one estimate, fifty or sixty Americans were killed; perhaps two hundred surrendered. General Thompson, Colonel William Irvine of the 6th Pennsylvania, several lieutenants, a doctor, and a chaplain were among the captured. The British put their own losses at twelve or thirteen killed or wounded. When asked by a captain whether to pursue a party of Americans, General Carleton said, "No, let the poor creatures go home and carry with them a tale, which will serve his majesty more effectually than their capture."[33]

※ ※ ※

In Montréal, Arnold was busy supplying the army by seizing goods. Chase and Carroll had given their permission and explained to President Hancock, "Nothing but the most urgent necessity can justify such harsh measures, but men with arms in their hands will not starve, where provisions can be obtained by force: to prevent a general plunder which might end in the Massacre of your Troops & of many of the inhabitants we have been constrained to advise the General to take this Step."[34]

By June, James Wilkinson was collecting merchandise in the city. "In case the owners should refuse the delivery, then the goods were to be seized, packed up by a guard which attended me, and conveyed to headquarters," Wilkinson remembered in his memoir. One woman gave him such a "Xantippiad" when he demanded a quarter cask of Madeira that he backed out of the establishment without the wine. Another merchant said, "These are the goods, Sir; they are in your power; I cannot deliver them but in my own wrong; you must know that your troops are about to quit this province ... and what could I do with your paper money; it would be mere chaff."[35]

Arnold ordered the seized merchandise tagged with the owner's name as if he expected a clerk in Philadelphia to record the debt of honor and see that it was repaid when the Continental treasury was full. Captain John Budd Scott of Maxwell's Regiment transported the goods to Chambly where he tried to turn them over to Moses Hazen. According to Arnold, Hazen "refused receiving or taking any care of them." So Scott left the goods near the fort on the bank of Chambly Basin. At some point Hazen placed sentries, but by then plunderers had already picked through the items. Arnold wrote to Sullivan, "It is impossible for me to distinguish each man's goods, or ever settle with the proprietors.... This is not the first or last order Colonel Hazen has disobeyed. I think him a man of too much consequence for the post he is in." Hazen promptly called for a court of inquiry or court-martial, telling Sullivan, "I am very conscious of having done my duty in every respect; but if otherwise, I am equally unworthy the honour which the Congress conferred on me, as unfit for the service of my country." The events in Chambly were to be the subject of an explosive court-martial in August 1776 and another in December.[36]

The charge that Arnold had plundered Montréal followed him for the rest of his life. No doubt he requisitioned supplies for the use of the army as sanctioned by the Commissioners from Congress. But did the seizure go beyond what would support an army? Did he profit or attempt to profit personally? In July 1776 at the Congressional hearing into the Causes of the Miscarriages in Canada, two men testified they had seen select packages labeled with Arnold's initials. "What was contained in them he does not know nor what was done with any of the goods after that," said Benjamin Thomson of Montréal, who had seen the items at Chambly. Another man claimed to have seen goods labeled "B.A." aboard a schooner on their way, he supposed, to Connecticut.[37]

Historians have reached differing conclusions about Arnold and the goods from Montréal. Jared Sparks, editor and author of many early works on the American Revolution and later president of Harvard, in the first biography of Arnold (1835) concluded that Arnold had been "too harshly judged" on the charge of seizing goods for his own profit. Sparks pointed to Arnold's letters to superiors explaining what he was doing. Biographer Isaac Arnold made the same point: "The goods were seized in accordance with orders for the use of the army." But helping the army does not preclude helping oneself. Biographer Willard Wallace wrote, "It is possible, even probable, that Arnold hoped to reap some measure of personal gain," but Wallace explained that such actions were not "necessarily considered reprehensible" at the time. At the far end of the spectrum, Edward Dean Sullivan, best-known for books on Al Capone and screenplays of gangster movies, wrote a 1932 biography with a title that describes his point of view: *Benedict Arnold: Military Racketeer*.[38]

Brown wrote:

> 7th. For plundering the inhabitants of Montreal, in direct violation of a solemn capitulation agreement entered into with them by our late brave and worthy General Montgomery, to the eternal disgrace of the Continental arms.

His proposed witnesses were to be Edward Antill, by then lieutenant colonel in the 2nd Canadian Regiment; James Colwell, a merchant; Daniel Tucker, assistant commissary officer; Major Orringh Stoddard of Colonel John Paterson's Regiment; and Captain John Patterson, adjutant in de Haas's Regiment. He hoped to have several unnamed assistant quartermasters testify.[39]

Brown's accusation is true as far as it goes—Montgomery had given his word on behalf of the United Colonies and Arnold had broken the pledge. Arnold, however, could claim military necessity and the permission of the commissioners. Montgomery's promise had been made seven months before, and by June 1776, there was no longer any hope that Canada would become the fourteenth rebelling colony. But Brown was not making a charge that could be dismissed by reading Arnold's correspondence with Chase, Carroll, and Sullivan. His accusation is a mirror of Arnold's accusation against him. Easton and Brown had permission from Montgomery to supply their men from the public stores aboard the captured vessels on the St. Lawrence, but Arnold claimed that they had done something personally dishonorable. Brown's accusation against Arnold must be read the same way. Brown was claiming that there was more to the story than that of a diligent general supplying a suffering army with provisions and supplies.

※ ※ ※

On June 12, Arnold went to St. Jean, where, by his estimate, he found nearly three thousand sick men and no work being done on the fortifications. He issued orders that the sick were to draw only half rations. Perhaps he was remembering the disaster on the upper Dead River when the expedition to Québec ran out of food. But that is not how his explanation to General Sullivan reads. His concern was that men were shirking. If they worked, they would receive a full ration; if not, they would go hungry. During the siege of Québec, food was used similarly to force sick men to the hospital: remain in quarters and receive half rations and no rum; be hospitalized and get a full ration.[40]

Dr. Beebe wrote in his journal, "The great Genl. Arnold arrived here [St. John] yesterday and began to give his inconsistent orders today & for his great pity and Concern for the sick; in the first place gave particular orders that every Sick man, together with everyone returned not fit for duty should draw but half allowance." In a letter to Sullivan the same day, Hazen enclosed a copy of the order and commented, "The officers in general think it cruel, and the soldiers murmur greatly."[41]

Brown's fifth charge refers to these orders:

> For depriving a part of the Army under his command of their usual allowance of provisions ordered by Congress.

Again, this is a legal argument based on the resolves of Congress. It does not hold up if provisions are scarce. Witnesses were to be Colonel Seth Warner and Major Jeremiah Cady.[42]

Warner and Cady were officers whose men had returned home. A brief biography of Warner written in 1795 told of his role in the retreat. He "chose the most difficult part of the business ... picking up the lame and diseased, assisting and encouraging those who were the most unable to take care of themselves.... By steadily pursuing this conduct he brought off most of the invalids; and with his corps of the infirm and diseased arrived at Ticonderoga...."[43] Brown, another officer who no longer had a command, left Canada soon after Arnold's orders to restrict provisions. Carrying the news of the defeat at Trois-Rivières, Brown reached Philadelphia around June 25.

※ ※ ※

On June 13 from Chambly, Arnold, Hazen, and Edward Antill recommended that Sullivan retreat from the St. Lawrence River and Sorel. Arnold's letter is the most memorable: "There will be more honor in making a safe retreat than hazarding a battle against such superiority which will doubtless be attended with the loss of men, artillery, &c., and the only pass to our country. These arguments are not urged by fear of my personal safety: I am content to be the last man who quits this country, and fall, so that my country rise. But let us not fall all together." Hazen and Antill, colonel and lieutenant colonel of 2nd Canadian Regiment, made the case that the American army was in a hopeless position. Remain in Sorel and the British—"the best troops in the world," wrote Hazen—would bypass the fortifications and seize Chambly and St. John, trapping the Americans in Canada. Hazen did not need to describe the geography: the St. Lawrence and the Richelieu form an acute angle, flowing at times nearly parallel. The British could ignore the Americans in Sorel, seize Montréal, and then march to the upper Richelieu.

Antill offered Sullivan an alternative. "Secure our water-carriage on Lake Champlain, and we turn the tables upon them, and I think we can meet them upon advantageous terms."[44] It is fifty miles from Chambly to Sorel, and the three eloquent letters calling for retreat may not have arrived in time to have any influence.

On the evening of June 13, Sullivan called a council of war in Sorel which made the inevitable decision. The next morning was spent calling in detachments from other villages, loading a hundred bateaux, and burning the row-galleys and schooners on the wide river. The retreat to Chambly began around noon, with the sick in bateaux and the relatively healthy marching on shore.

Meanwhile, Arnold, who had returned to Montréal, prepared to abandon the city. On the evening of June 15, the last three hundred men crowded into bateaux with their baggage and confiscated rum, molasses, and wine. Partway across the river, the sky darkened and a cold rain fell. The drops were the size of large peas, recalled teenage fifer John Greenwood, who years later was to be George Washington's dentist. The smallpox victims, a third of the force, were "huddled together like cord-wood." The retreating men burned bridges as they made their way from Longueuil to La Prairie and then rejoined the main army on the Richelieu.[45]

On June 17, the Americans burned Fort Chambly and the heavy boats on the lower Richelieu. Bateaux were portaged around the rapids, and some boats were hauled up the river by men wading in the current. St. John was abandoned altogether the next day. The fort, Moses Hazen's house across the river, and several gunboats and bateaux were burned. Once again James Wilkinson told the story that is remembered. With only one bateau remaining in St. John, he and Arnold mounted their horses and rode two miles toward Chambly. They watched the advancing British for a few minutes before galloping back. Then Arnold shot his horse and ordered Wilkinson to do the same, which he did "with reluctance." Arnold pushed the boat from the dock himself, "and thus indulged the vanity of being the last man who embarked from the shores of the enemy." Wilkinson was second-to-last, not bad for a nineteen year old.[46]

But they were far from alone. Military engineer Jeduthan Baldwin was in the bateau with Arnold, arriving at "Oil of Noix" about midnight. Elisha Porter left St. John just before dark and reached "Isle au Noir" about 1 a.m. Colonel John Stark's family believed that he and his staff were in the last boat. The next morning, slow-moving bateaux, low in the water, were still arriving at the island, which was part of Canada then and now. Today it is the location of the Fort Lennox National Historic Site, honoring later generations of British and Canadian soldiers who stood guard against an invasion from the south.[47]

Early on June 19, Arnold and Wilkinson left the suffering army, carrying a letter from Sullivan to Schuyler. Arnold used the opportunity to disparage Sullivan. From Schuyler's Albany mansion, he wrote to George Washington, claiming he had always given Sullivan good advice—to abandon Sorel, to abandon Île-aux-Noix—but Sullivan hesitated. "Genl Sullivan did not Chuse to leave the Ile aux Noix, untill he received positive Orders for that purpose, & thought it necessary for me to repair to this place & wait on Genl Schuyler."[48]

Regardless of what Sullivan wanted, he did not have enough boats to carry the sick and the healthy, and he was determined to save every man. Sullivan's defeated army made its last stand on Île-aux-Noix with a heroism that Arnold could not recognize. Dr. Beebe walked the island on the afternoon of June 17. "Scarcely a tent upon the Isle but what contains one or more in distress and continually groaning & calling for relief, but in vain! ... The most shocking of all Spectacles was to see a large barn Crowded full of men with this disorder [the smallpox], many of which could not See, Speak, or walk—one nay two had large maggots, an inch long, Crawl out of their ears, were on almost every part of the body."[49]

The sick were ordered to leave the island as soon as possible, but it was not until June 20 that the first flotilla set sail. The remaining men were trapped. When a dozen officers left the island in search of spruce beer, they were ambushed by Indians. Four were killed and six taken prisoner. Sullivan admitted to Washington that he hoped to stay on the island until he received orders, but the army sickened too quickly. He told the story that as the main guard paraded, four soldiers keeled over and "and appear like dead men." Lieutenant Colonel Joseph Vose of Greaton's Regiment reduced his daily journal entries to desperate comments: "Our Boats are not Returned from C. Point [Crown Point].... Boats not Returnd yet.... Some Part of our boats Return, for more stores ... our boats are not come, & the enemy on both sides of us.... We still Remain, & the Boats do not Return."[50]

Finally, on the evening of June 25, the army left the island. About twelve hundred men had to march on shore. Elisha Porter and Joseph Vose brought up the rear, expecting to be attacked any minute. With orders to seize cattle, Vose went into the fields with a hatchet and felled ten animals in as many minutes. The men continued to march late into a rainy night. In the morning, bateaux returned from Isle La Motte, and on June 28 the last American soldiers sailed away from Canada. For a short time, the retreat was a grand spectacle, one hundred fifty or more boats rowing into the wind on the open lake, General de Woedtke in the lead and General Sullivan in the rear. But the organization was imposed by officers who knew about marching not sailing, and soon the boats were scattered across the lake. When wind and waves grew, men were seasick and convinced their boats might swamp. But in one boat, as they pulled for home, fifer John Greenwood played a lively tune.[51]

Ten

"Received much abuse from General Arnold"

On the night of July 1–2, boats carrying more than 4,000 men reached Crown Point. John Adams described what he heard to Abigail. "Our Army at Crown Point is an Object of Wretchedness, enough to fill a humane Mind, with Horror. Disgraced, defeated, discontented, dispirited, diseased, naked, undisciplined, eaten up with Vermin—no Cloaths, Beds, Blanketts, no Medicines, no Victuals, but Salt Pork and flour." Adams's horrific details actually predated the return of the main force, but they were true for Île-aux-Noix and true enough for Crown Point for a few days. However, there was another side to the story. These men had been through hell, but they were back. Joseph Vose, who had brought up the rear on the final march, wrote, "There never was a grander Retreat made, than what we made from Sorell, to Crown Point, all the way, for I brought up the rear myself all the way, & know very well, therefore you may hear what Stories you will it is the truth what I tell you."[1]

During his time in Canada, John Sullivan had been vain and overconfident, then incapable of making a decision until events forced his hand, but he had brought the army home. On the first day back, he began making plans to defend the United Colonies, which that same day in Philadelphia declared themselves an independent nation. He issued orders to quarantine the sick—so that "the sight of such pitiful objects may not disperse the rest"—and to build row-galleys to maintain control of the lake. Sullivan hoped to continue in command, but his fate was already decided; superior officers were hurrying north. Late on July 5, major generals Philip Schuyler and Horatio Gates arrived at Crown Point, accompanied by Benedict Arnold, who had left Sullivan in Canada with a dying army and was back, attached to men with real power.[2]

At first, the soldiers at Crown Point were uncertain who was in command: some thought Schuyler, others heard Gates, and many were sorry it was not Sullivan. The temporary confusion was understandable. In mid–June, Gates, a former British officer, had been appointed commander of the army in Canada, but by the time he arrived in Albany, there was no longer an army in Canada. Schuyler insisted that by appointment and seniority he commanded the entire Northern Department, including the army on Lake Champlain, but he agreed to submit the issue to Washington and the Congress, which ruled in Schuyler's favor, although the decision was close to meaningless. Gates took command on Lake Champlain, sent reports to Schuyler, and did what he wanted. The dispute between Schuyler and Gates continued.

At forty-eight, Gates was a man of many contradictions that started with his birth.

He was the son of a housekeeper at a nobleman's estate and a Thames River boatman. Or perhaps his biological father was actually a duke and that was the reason a lowly boatman became a customs collector. Whatever Gates's birth, the patronage of aristocrats allowed him to get ahead, but he could only rise so far in a society bound by social class. He had reasons to be haughty—and he had reasons to resent the rich and powerful.[3] A portrait of Gates painted in 1782 by Charles Willson Peale shows a double chin, receding hair, and an expression that looks like a blank stare. During the campaign that ended at Saratoga, Arnold referred with contempt to Gates's "face of clay," but a German officer and prisoner thought he saw a "highly spiritual face and still a lot of vitality in his whole being." Although seemingly mild mannered, amiable, and unengaged, Gates was ruthless when it came to getting ahead. His swearing and obscenities could shock a pious New Englander. Unlike the aristocratic Schuyler, he had a way with the common man and Yankee militia.[4]

In 1776, Major General Horatio Gates supported Benedict Arnold and clashed with John Brown. By fall 1777, Gates was Arnold's adversary at Saratoga. James Peale after Charles Willson Peale, National Portrait Gallery, Smithsonian Institution; partial gift of Mr. Lawrence A. Fleischman.

※ ※ ※

The Continental Congress believed the collapse of the invasion of Canada was the fault of undisciplined soldiers and craven officers. The surrender of the Cedars, John Adams wrote, "appears to have been a most infamous Piece of Cowardice." The commander—did he mean Bedel or Butterfield?—"deserves the most infamous death."[5] Around June 25, John Brown arrived in Philadelphia with the news of the defeat at Trois-Rivières, and for the first time, Adams had a glimmer of what the Americans had endured. He told Abigail on June 26, "The Small Pox is ten times more terrible than Britons, Canadians and Indians together. This was the Cause of our precipitate Retreat from Quebec, this the Cause of our Disgraces at the Cedars. I dont mean that this was all. There has been Want, approaching to Famine, as well as Pestilence. And these Discouragements seem to have so disheartened our Officers, that none of them seem to Act with Prudence and Firmness."[6]

Brown had personal reasons to be in Philadelphia. He lobbied for the rank and back pay of a lieutenant colonel from the previous November and demanded an inquiry into Arnold's charges that he had plundered the ships at Sorel. He was also there to help his friend and former commander James Easton, who was accused of financial improprieties and was so deeply in debt that he was in prison. In April, Easton requested payment for the public stores taken at Sorel and a court of inquiry on the alleged plundering. Congress gave Easton meaningless relief: an advance of $200 and instructions that the Commissioners to Canada inquire into the plundering and give Easton a hearing in his own defense. The money was too little and Canada too far away.[7]

More sophisticated and better educated than Easton, Brown submitted a petition to Congress calling for promotion to full colonel, a settlement of financial accounts, and an inquiry into Arnold's charges against him and Easton. The petition was referred to the committee investigating "the causes of the miscarriages in Canada." He lobbied on behalf of his fellow officers in the northwest New England brigade. On July 5, at the War Board's recommendation, Congress established a new regiment to be led by Seth Warner and other officers who had served with him and Brown in Canada.[8]

The congressional hearings into the Canadian campaign began on July 1 and lasted most of the month. On July 3, the committee and David Wooster reviewed letters and reports from the campaign, and on July 4 the general gave his testimony. In Thomas Jefferson's notes on the hearings, Wooster made no excuses, presenting facts on troop strength, short enlistments, and the smallpox. The committee reported and Congress agreed that "upon the whole of the evidence that was before them, that nothing censurable or blameworthy appears against Brigadier General Wooster." Still, New England men were outraged at how he had been treated by Congress. Connecticut congressman William Williams told Joseph Trumbull, commissary general and son of Connecticut's governor, "Poor Wooster a worthy Officer is neglected. Boundless Efforts have been used to blast his Character in Congress by one of the Canada Commissioners [Samuel Chase]. He has been represented by him as a most worthless contemptible Felon & the most liberal abuse thrown out against him in Congress, such as I think totally inconsistent with their Honor & Justice to suffer, but so it is." In the end, the committee blamed the defeat in Canada on short enlistments, a lack of hard currency, and "a still greater, and more fatal source of misfortune," the smallpox. Historians have agreed.[9]

Brown and Easton were granted their day in court, but in the north, away from Philadelphia. Schuyler was ordered to sort out compensation and rewards. The issues of rank were referred to the War Board, which ruled that Brown had been a lieutenant colonel since November and that Easton was deserving of the pay of a Continental colonel from July 1775 until his discharge, which would follow at the close of the court of inquiry.[10]

※ ※ ※

On July 7, Schuyler, Gates, Arnold, Sullivan, and Baron de Woedtke met in a council of war and decided to withdraw from Crown Point and fortify a rocky, wooded peninsula across the lake from Ticonderoga that was sometimes called Rattlesnake Hill. Schuyler thought the ground "so remarkably strong as to require little labour to make it tenable against a vast superiority of force, and fully to answer the purpose of preventing the enemy from penetrating into the country south of it." Then the council resolved that "the most effectual measures be taken to secure our superiority on Lake Champlain, by a naval armament of gondolas, row-galleys, and armed batteuas, &c."[11]

Arnold quickly regained the authority he had lost at the end of the Canada campaign. In a few days, he made himself indispensable to General Gates, who established headquarters at old Fort Ticonderoga and needed an active man to oversee the fortifications on both sides of the lake, the remaining men at Crown Point, the shipyard at Skenesborough, and finally the fleet. At Crown Point, Arnold-hater Dr. Beebe did not like what he saw: "Genl. Arnold is very busy in making experiments, upon the field officers and others; within 2 days he has arrested Colo. Hazen, & Colo. Dehose [de Haas], together with 5 or 6 Captains; but for what offense I know not. I heartily wish some person would try an experiment upon him, (viz) to make the sun shine thro' his head with an ounce ball; and then see whether the rays come in a Direct or oblique direction." Hazen was arrested for neglecting the confiscated goods at Chambly, but Beebe's reference to de Haas is puzzling. De Haas clashed with Arnold about the orders to destroy Kanesatake, and Arnold might have wanted to charge him with disobedience, but de Haas was one of the elite Pennsylvanians and no recorded arrest took place.[12]

Colonel Timothy Bedel and Major Isaac Butterfield were still confined for their part in the defeat at the Cedars. Dr. Beebe had no sympathy for them: "pray that they may soon be try'd & hanged." At Crown Point, Bedel prepared a written defense. Counting his service in the French & Indian War, he wrote, "This is the Twelvth Campaign I have served, eight of which as a commissioned officer & during all of which service I never was brought to a Court martial Confined or even Repremanded before." Much of Bedel's defense rested upon questioning the actions of Arnold, "my Prosecutor." Bedel wrote that he always wanted a court of inquiry, but Arnold had prevented it. He argued that his responsibilities were broader than the fort at the Cedars, and Arnold should have been clearer in his orders if he was restricting Bedel to the fort. He had applied to Arnold for supplies, but "we were frequently living on less than half allowance of provisions." The fort was in "perfect tranquility" when he left to visit Kahnawake.[13]

Bedel's court-martial finally convened at Ticonderoga on July 16, but then recessed because of Arnold's increasing duties. No dates or details from the trial survive; the verdict was announced in the orders for August 1. Bedel was found guilty of leaving his post and was cashiered, while Butterfield was cashiered and barred from ever again holding a commission in the Continental Army.[14]

Before leaving, Bedel wrote a remarkable letter to Gates. He bragged a little—seizing the enemy shipping at Sorel was all his doing—but in an age of exaggerated honor and deep resentment, he was for the most part modest and generous. "This affair being laid to my charge, I hope your Honour will not look upon it as wilful, the fault being in my head, and not my heart; and while I live under the protection of the United States, I hope I shall ever have the esteem of my countrymen, as this was the first crime I was ever charged with. I wish the whole Army good success." Bedel's reference to the United States is significant: news of independence had reached the Lake Champlain forts less than three weeks earlier. Discharged in disgrace, Bedel returned home, but a year later volunteered as a lieutenant in the Haverhill, New Hampshire, militia company to help defeat Burgoyne. He was again commissioned as a colonel in November 1777.[15]

On July 20, Arnold was appointed commander of the four-regiment First Brigade on the peninsula opposite Ticonderoga, named Mount Independence a few days later after a reading of the Declaration of Independence. Twelve regiments, divided into three brigades, were turning a wilderness into an enormous military encampment, while on the west side of the lake, the Pennsylvania regiments, designated as the Fourth Brigade, began rebuilding the fortifications where French general Montcalm had defeated the British under General James Abercrombie in 1758. These defenses continued to be called the French Lines throughout the Revolution, although France had nothing to do with them.

Arnold's brigade was on the high ground of the Mount Independence peninsula. His men were the closest to the planned lakeside batteries and to a citadel, a horseshoe-shaped battery, on the northern height. Arnold was the only general on the east side of the lake, and in any battle he might have direct command of two-thirds of the regiments at the forts. But Arnold never showed much interest in the new fortifications, and it is likely he never slept on Mount Independence. By the time of his appointment, he was much more interested in the fleet over which he could have complete control.

※ ※ ※

Arnold wanted an immediate trial in the case of Moses Hazen and the unprotected goods at Chambly Basin, but Hazen protested, saying that the officers on the panel were not all field officers—regimental majors, lieutenant colonels, and colonels—and had been "named by his accuser." Gates told Arnold that if Hazen was correct in his claims, it was "very irregular." A newly appointed court convened on July 19, but could not take up the case because Arnold was already busy with the fleet. On July 23, Arnold arrived at the shipyard in Skenesborough. At its heart, the American navy had vessels captured in 1775: the *Liberty,* Arnold's first war vessel on the lake; the *Enterprise* captured by him at St. John; the *Royal Savage,* sunk during the siege of St. John and then raised; and the *Revenge,* also sunk and raised at St. John.[16]

In early June, the focus of construction shifted from bateaux to gondolas, flat-bottomed gunboats, as a quick way to float a navy. Schuyler sent assistant commissary general Hermanus Schuyler, a distant relative, from Lake George to Skenesborough to take charge of the carpenters, loggers, teamsters, and blacksmiths. He told Hermanus that the sawyers must work "by Night as well as by Day." When a local militia colonel ordered the men not to work on Sunday, Schuyler said to disregard him.[17]

As Gates solidified his control at Ticonderoga, he was critical of Schuyler's arrangements. "The Vessels, which should have been Constantly Arm'd as Vessels of War, have hitherto been solely employ'd as Floating Waggons," he wrote to John Hancock in a statement that was true but unfair. Before the retreat, the Americans needed transport for men and supplies. Guns, shot, and powder were required in Canada, not to cruise a secure lake.[18]

Four gunboats were complete by the time of Arnold's arrival in Skenesborough on July 23. In the stocks, he found two more gondolas and a cutter, a small and hopefully fast vessel. The gondolas would be finished in less than a week. The cutter, which Arnold termed a row-galley because it could be powered by oars, was due in eight to ten days. He hoped for an additional three gondolas in ten days and two true row-galleys following quickly. These galleys—sometimes called Spanish row-galleys after vessels on the Mediterranean and often compared to the galleys on the Delaware River defending Philadelphia—had two triangular lateen sails and could be rowed with oars. They were maneuverable and heavily armed. "In two or three weeks, I think we shall have a very formidable fleet," Arnold wrote Gates on July 24.[19]

Arnold's letter confirmed what Gates had already learned from Colonel Cornelius Wynkoop, one of the men on the spot who was overseeing the logging crews, sawmills, and carpenters under the overall command of General David Waterbury. Gates was concerned that the carpenters were too slow—"very ill-attended to, or very ignorant of their business"—but in fact the shipyard in the wilderness was constructing the first fleet in the American navy at a breakneck pace. The shipbuilders were craftsmen brought from coastal cities and paid a dollar a day and a bounty. Soldiers kept the effort going as loggers and laborers. Tools and supplies—felling axes, blacksmith's tools, blocks and cordage, deck nails, and the all-important rum—were scarce and had to be brought to Albany and then carried north.[20]

On his arrival in Skenesborough, Arnold told Cornelius Wynkoop that it was Gates's "positive orders" that he return to his regiment on Mount Independence. Wynkoop's regiment, the 4th New York, was quartered on paper at the southern end the peninsula. Wynkoop found the order relayed by Arnold "a little strange"—almost all his men were working in and around Skenesborough, not at Mount Independence—but he was ready to obey Arnold's orders until he received a letter from Gates that said nothing about a return, so he stayed in Skenesborough. "What is the reason of General Arnold's giving such orders to me I know not," he wrote Gates, "except that some of our commanders at this place see that I drive business on faster, as several have complained to General Arnold concerning me." At the end of July, the carpenters named the newest and fifth gondola the *Wynkoop* in honor of the man who had watched over its construction. "I hope you will send a good officer on board her," Wynkoop wrote Gates proudly. "I have had her made as strong as she could be made, which you will see by the work done in her." The Wynkoop name was never adopted, but this gunboat is the most famous in the fleet, the *Philadelphia*.[21]

Arnold spent four or five days in Skenesborough in July and returned for a few more days in August, although in some histories of the summer of 1776, it is as if he drove every nail himself and was the only American who realized that Lake Champlain thrust deep into New York. Gates told John Hancock, that Arnold, who was "ever active and anxious to serve his country" gave "life and spirit to our dock-yard."[22] Perhaps he did. Supplies were scarce, problems were constant, but construction struggled along before Arnold's arrival and after his departure. General Waterbury and Colonel Wynkoop continued to write to Gates. For them and the men felling and hauling the trees, sawing boards, improving the wretched road toward the Hudson, clearing Wood Creek so that timber and boards could be moved by water from Cheshire's Mill in Fort Ann, and constructing the gunboats and row-galleys, a general came and a general went and the work remained. They are the heroes of the story.

※ ※ ※

Back at the forts, Arnold was called on to settle a dispute involving Elisha Porter's regiment. Porter and most of his men arrived from Crown Point by bateaux around sunset, July 17, and pitched their tents on the Ticonderoga side of the lake. On July 20, the regiment, now assigned to Arnold's 1st Brigade, began clearing land and building huts on the east side. Porter, a lawyer in civilian life, was busy with courts-martial in the old fort, but crossed the narrow lake—"ye river," he termed it—and finally on July

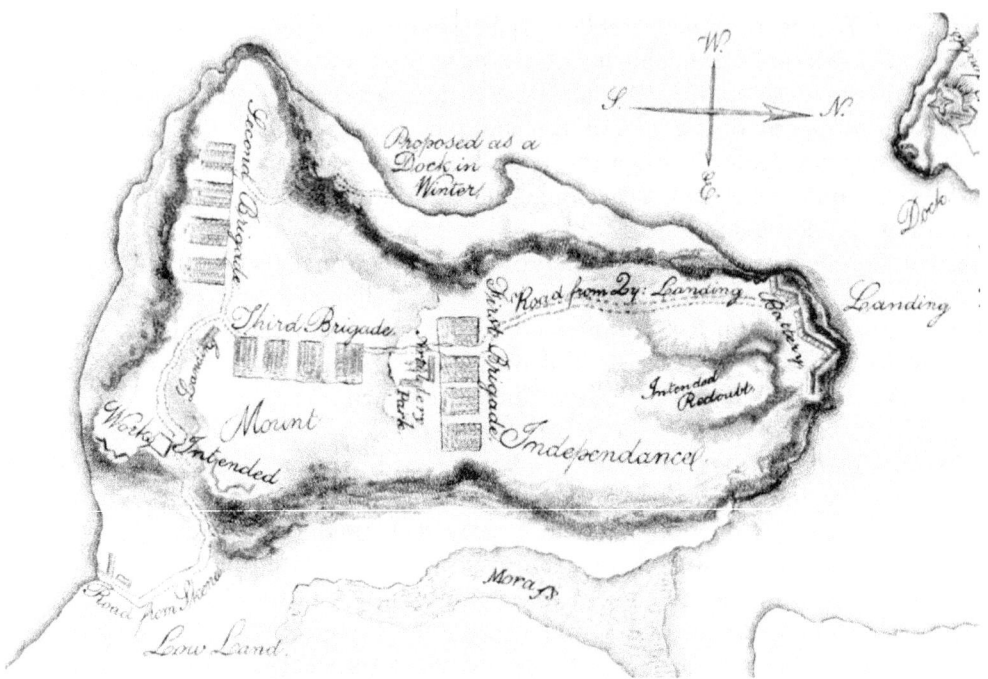

In the summer of 1776, John Trumbull sketched a map of the Lake Champlain forts, a version of which appeared in his autobiography. This portion of the map shows the encampments on Mount Independence. Benedict Arnold's First Brigade is the northern most of the three. Old Fort Ticonderoga is across the narrows of the lake. *John Trumbull, Autobiography* (1841).

26, he moved in with a captain, planning to begin building his own house the next day. In the morning, the regiment's camp was inspected by Deputy Adjutant General John Trumbull, who was barely twenty years old. (Later in life, Trumbull was the artist of the Revolution; his paintings of historical scenes are exhibited in the U.S. Capitol and major museums.) Young Trumbull did not like what he saw and, as Porter noted, he "ordered me to remove ye officers' houses, &c., and alter the front of my encampment." Camps were supposed to follow the design laid out in paces found in Humphrey Bland's *A Treatise of Military Disciple*, for fifty years and many editions the bible on best practices for the British military. Porter's men had been working for a week clearing land and building log huts—following orders, Porter believed. He noted in his journal, and told Trumbull in person, that he was "very unwilling to comply" with the changes, but he ordered work stopped for the day.[23]

When Arnold crossed the lake to hear the dispute, he said he would refer the issue to General Gates. Whatever Gates said, if anything, two days later Porter's men began moving some of their huts and changing the front of the regiment's encampment. A map of Mount Independence drawn by Trumbull later in the summer shows the brigades and regiments looking like a page ripped from Bland's *Treatise*.

※ ※ ※

On July 31, Arnold attended the reopening of Hazen's court-martial at Jones's Tavern on the Ticonderoga side of the lake. Colonel Enoch Poor, a merchant and shipbuilder from New Hampshire, presided over twelve other field officers that included Elisha Porter, still irked about having to alter his camp; William Maxwell, who had served at Québec and did not like Arnold; and de Haas, who had ignored Arnold's orders to destroy the village and inhabitants of Kanesatake. Porter and three other men were from Arnold's First Brigade. Major John Sedgwick of Burrall's Connecticut State Regiment was the brother of John Brown's potential witness Theodore Sedgwick.[24]

Historians frequently take Arnold's side in the dispute. In their view, the officers were Hazen's friends and prejudiced against Arnold. There may be some truth in the accusation that the panel did not like Arnold, but the charge remains an example of the lengths that writers have gone to avoid listening to Arnold's critics. The thirteen men represented one-third of the field officers at the forts. They were not supposed to be ignorant of Hazen, Arnold, and the events in question; they were expected to be honorable. "We had nothing but the good of our country and the discipline of the army in view," they told President Hancock afterwards. They were from five states and all four brigades. Six men commanded regiments. Colonel William Bond of the 25th Continental Infantry was to die of disease in a month and be greatly mourned. Four of them were promoted to Continental brigadier general—Poor, William Maxwell, Philip de Haas (who declined), and John Paterson—and Paterson was brevetted as a major general at the war's end. On the other hand, one man soon went over to the enemy, another was cashiered, and third, who was said to be too overweight to serve, was forced to retire.[25]

Had there been fourteen states in the new nation, Arnold's behavior at the trial of Moses Hazen might have been a fourteenth charge in Brown's indictment.

‰ ‰ ‰

The first day of Hazen's trial was businesslike, noted attorney Porter, but then decorum broke down over the role of John Budd Scott, who had brought the goods from Montréal to Chambly. Scott, an attorney in civilian life, was Arnold's principal witness against Hazen, but he was also a court official, the judge advocate. He cross-examined witnesses, but occasionally the court asked him questions. Finally, when he was called to give sworn testimony, Hazen objected and the court agreed. As Enoch Poor told Gates, the court saw in Scott a man with an "overstrained zeal to serve as Judge Advocate," who was "extremely solicitous to give evidence in the cause." Scott had already admitted that he never gave Hazen written orders from Arnold, while "divers witnesses" testified that the goods had been damaged or lost when they were Scott's responsibility. So Scott was viewed as "so far interested in the event of Colonel Hazen's trial, as to render his testimony inadmissible." The question of whether Arnold profited from the goods was always in the background. Hazen may have raised the issue himself.[26]

As testimony continued to favor Hazen, Arnold objected, saying he would enter a formal protest if Scott did not testify. From then on, the proceedings descended into chaos and comedy. It was summer, they were meeting in a tavern, and they all required refreshment. In Arnold's written protest, which was likely a shadow of his verbal one, he declared that Scott had "punctually obeyed" his orders and "of course is not the least interested in the event of Colonel Hazen's trial." He concluded, "I do solemnly protest against their proceedings and refusal as unprecedented, and I think unjust."[27]

The court found Arnold's protest "illegal, illiberal, and ungentlemanlike" and directed Colonel Poor to demand an apology. Porter commented in his daily journal entry, "Received much abuse from Genl. Arnold, which produced a spirited reprimand from ye President." In the written version, Poor told Arnold, "You have drawn upon yourself their just resentment, and that nothing but an open acknowledgment of your error will be conceived as satisfactory." The court later wrote to Gates that Arnold's protest was "couched, as we think, in indecent terms, and directly impeaching the justice of the Court." If a superior officer could "blast" a court with a protest, then the accused would always be sent "back to his room a melancholy prisoner." Poor continued, "The whole of the General's conduct during the course of the trial was marked with contempt and disrespect towards the Court."[28]

Arnold replied, "Your demand I shall not comply with." The actions of the court and its president were "ungenteel and indecent reflections on a superior officer." Although the Articles of War banned dueling, officers of the Continental Army were beginning to adopt affairs of honor as the mark of a gentleman. Arnold issued a grandiose challenge: "As your very nice and delicate honour, in your apprehension, is injured, you may depend, as soon as this disagreeable service is at an end (which God grant may soon be the case), I will by no means withhold from any gentleman of the Court the satisfaction his nice honour may require."[29]

The court had heard enough and ruled in Hazen's favor. After Gates accepted the verdict, Porter and the other members of the court dined with Hazen. Then on August 12, they ordered Arnold arrested, and Gates dissolved the court. He told John Hancock that Arnold might have crossed the "precise line of decorum," but "the United States must not be deprived of that excellent Officer's Service, at this important Moment."[30]

Eleven

"I wish he may be as prudent as he is brave"

Since April, the naval commander on Lake Champlain had been Jacobus Wynkoop of Kingston, New York, the older brother of Cornelius, who was at the Skenesborough shipyard. Jacobus was fifty-two and originally a Schuyler appointee, although his position as commodore of the fleet on the lake was approved by the New York Provincial Congress and the Continental Congress. He had served in the last two colonial wars, as he put it, "both by sea and by land, and have been in many engagements." He was honored to have served in the company that guarded the baggage of General Thomas Gage, who at the start of the Revolutionary War commanded all the British forces in North America. In one battle in which Wynkoop saw action, forty-nine men went down in a single volley—or so he told the New York Provincial Congress. "I have a good deal of experience of cannon as well as small arms," he added.[1]

Horatio Gates was not impressed. "I think the Commodore seems slow," he told Arnold, "and wish he may retain all that prowess for which he says he was so famous [in the] last war." Perhaps Wynkoop was bold in stories of the past and incompetent in the present. In most histories, he is a laughable figure to be brushed aside. Once he mistook gulls for the sails of British vessels and called a council aboard the *Royal Savage* to decide what to do.[2]

By mid–July, Gates wanted Wynkoop replaced with Arnold, and he informed Wynkoop that he was to follow Arnold's "instructions" on "what cruise he ought to make." On July 29, Gates wrote John Hancock, "General Arnold (who is perfectly skilled in maritime affairs) has most nobly undertaken to command our fleet upon the Lake. With infinite satisfaction, I have committed the whole of that department to his care." Gates's orders to Arnold, written on August 7—after the close of Hazen's trial but before the court called for Arnold's arrest—left no doubt that the fleet was under his command. Officers at Ticonderoga were aware of his expanded responsibilities. Matthias Ogden of New Jersey, who was wounded in the December 31 attack on Québec, wrote friend and stepbrother Aaron Burr, "General Arnold is taking a very active part—I mean in the command of the fleet. He will sail himself in a few days. I wish he may be as prudent as he is brave."[3]

However, it is uncertain if Arnold's promotion was communicated to Wynkoop, or, if it was, what the relationship between Arnold and the commodore was supposed to be. Perhaps Wynkoop, who was at Crown Point, should have understood he had been supplanted and was, to use a later concept, in denial. He may have been as dull and stubborn as he is often depicted. Gates's orders made no mention of him at all.[4]

The issue of command reached a crisis on Saturday, August 17, when men who were cutting wood seven or eight miles north of Crown Point believed they saw British sails in the distance and lit a warning fire. Arnold, who had arrived at Crown Point two days earlier, ordered a hundred men in bateaux and the schooners *Revenge* and *Liberty* to the rescue of the workers. Seeing vessels preparing to sail, Wynkoop ordered a swivel gun on the *Royal Savage* fired as a signal to stop. Later he told Congress that he was worried that "some design had been formed by the Captains of the said schooners or their crews to go over to the enemy." He sent his first mate to bring the captains aboard the *Royal Savage*. When he learned from Leonard Primer of the *Liberty* that Arnold had issued the orders, Wynkoop wrote a note to Arnold and signed himself *Commander of Lake Champlain*. "I know of no orders but what shall be given out by me, except sailing orders from the Commander-in-Chief," Wynkoop wrote. "If an enemy is approaching, I am to be acquainted with it, and know how to act in my station."[5]

Like Hazen's court-martial of two weeks earlier, there is a written record that reflects a spoken one. At some point, Arnold boarded the *Royal Savage* and tore into Wynkoop. He also wrote a letter, which summarizes his blistering attack. He informed Wynkoop that "some time since" he had been given the command of the

Reconstructed Fort Ticonderoga and narrow Lake Champlain can be seen from the Citadel on Mount Independence. In 1776, the view would have been bare of trees. Author photograph.

navy. "You surely must be out of your senses to say no orders shall be obeyed but yours. Do you imagine that Congress have given you a superior command over the Commander-in-Chief, or that you are not to be under his direction?" That was not what Wynkoop had written or thought. Wynkoop maintained that in the chain of command he had responsibility for the fleet and orders should come through him.[6]

Then Arnold made his final, devastating point: "If you do not suffer my orders to be immediately complied with, by sending the Captains of the schooners to obey them, I shall be under the disagreeable necessity of convincing you of your error by immediately arresting you." He signed himself Brigadier-General and Commander-in-Chief of the Fleet upon Lake Champlain, which trumped Wynkoop's Commander of Lake Champlain.[7]

According to Wynkoop, he issued orders for the two schooners to sail as soon as he understood the threat to the woodcutting party. According to Arnold, Wynkoop relented only after Arnold boarded the *Royal Savage* and forced the issue. Arnold told Gates, "I have shown him such parts of your instructions as I thought necessary, which has brought him so far to reason." As it turned out, there were no British sails in the distance. Perhaps there had been more gulls.[8]

Later in the day, Wynkoop wrote to Gates. "I have understood that General Arnold is to have the command of the Navy," meaning *I have learned*. He continued, "if that be so, he ought to have shown me his power to it; but instead of that, he sent an order for two of the schooners to get under way…. Was it not his duty to have communicated it to me, and my orders to have been given to the vessels?" Wynkoop wrote to Congress that he had not "received any intimation of being superseded in the command aforesaid."[9]

That evening the dispute was forwarded to Gates, who wrote back to Arnold, "It is my orders you instantly put Commodore Wynkoop in arrest, and send him prisoner to Head-Quarters, at Ticonderoga. You will, at the same time, acquaint officers of the fleet that such of them as do not pay an implicit obedience to your commands are instantly to be confined and sent to me for trial."[10]

Victorious in this clash with a rival commander, Arnold ordered Wynkoop to headquarters graciously—"Please let me know what time will be most agreeable"—and wrote to Gates, "If it can be done with propriety, I wish he may be permitted to return home without being cashiered." Gates agreed and told Schuyler, "He has my pass to go at liberty to Albany; but he must, on no account, be sent back here." Schuyler accepted the decision, writing that although he knew Wynkoop to be "brave and industrious," he did not know if he was up to commanding a fleet. "I have learned of General Arnold's appointment with great satisfaction, and very much approved of it."[11]

Wynkoop was never court-martialed; a trial would have turned into another embarrassment for Arnold. "A little of the dictatorial power was exerted," Gates told John Hancock in explanation, "but perhaps it never was more necessary than on that occasion."[12]

By spring 1777, Wynkoop was back with the wreckage of the fleet on lakes George and Champlain. By then Arnold and the opportunity for glory were gone.

% % %

A week after he had vanquished Jacobus Wynkoop, Arnold sailed from Crown Point to patrol the wide lake to the north. His fleet had grown to three schooners, a sloop, and six gunboats. He had with him more than 500 men, most drafted from the regiments at Mount Independence. The sun was setting, and they made only four miles before anchoring in line as if for battle. The lake was four fathoms, or twenty-four feet deep. By 10 o'clock the next morning, the fleet passed Buttonmould (today's Button) Bay on the east shore.[13]

We know fathoms, distance, and time because of the careful observations of a man who has helped to tell this story before, Bayze Wells. Almost exactly a year earlier, he had accompanied John Brown and Robert Cochran on a spying mission into Canada. Now he was a lieutenant on the gunboat or gondola *Providence*.[14] He still could not spell or punctuate, but he was an inquisitive man, a scientist and a reporter without knowing it.

After the fleet sailed through the three-quarter-mile narrows at Split Rock and the lake widened into the misty distance, Wells lowered all 240-feet of line and it did not touch bottom. Early on August 26, the fleet anchored at the mouth of the Boquet River, off Willsboro on the western side of the lake. Willsboro was the home of another man who has been important in this story before, William Gilliland, squire of an empire in the wilderness. A year before, Gilliland had recommended Arnold to the Continental Congress. When Arnold was forced from command on the lake, Gilliland played some part in the fawning letter of thanks he carried with him.

As the seaboard colonies invaded Canada, Willsboro became a stopping place. Gilliland told Congress, "From the Gen'l down to the centenel, he [Gilliland, writing in the third person] has entertained 3 or 4,000 men at his own expence—he never charged a shilling for vegetables, salmon, milk or any thing he had to spare them—has complimented them with 1,500 salmon in one season ... has lain weeks together on straw in a com'n room, that sick and wounded officers and sold'rs that were sent to or stopt at his house might be more comfortably accommodated ... had every sold'er who died in his settlement inter'd in decent coffins, with the honors of war."[15] Gilliland was prone to exaggeration, but if he did not entertain three to four thousand soldiers with 1,500 salmon, he surely fed many men with many fish. The sandy beach by the mouth of the Boquet was a good campsite; farms were a short

William Gilliland was a wealthy landowner on Lake Champlain. Early in the war, he was a supporter of Benedict Arnold. Later Arnold saw to his arrest. Gilliland's portrait was painted while he was in debtors' prison in New York. Fort Ticonderoga Museum Collection, acquired through the generous support of the Boquet Foundation in memory of Peter S. Paine.

walk from the lake; and officers and gentlemen could row up the slow-moving stream to the falls and expect to be welcomed into his home. The comfort found at Gilliland's by men fearing the rigors of Canada or shattered by the experience is a theme of Revolutionary War journals. Both Arnold and Brown may have partaken of his generosity.

Since the collapse of the invasion of Canada, Gilliland and his settlement were caught in the middle, forty miles from Ticonderoga, forty-five miles from today's border with Canada. Gilliland continued to supply the American army, but he believed he was underpaid, while some officers accused him of profiteering. And were Gilliland and his neighbors and tenants now dealing with the enemy? Thomas Hartley, in command at Crown Point, cautiously warned Gates: information "inclines me to apprehend, that the supposition that Gilliland and some others had sent down one Edward Watson and another to St. John's had some foundation."[16]

Old hands on Lake Champlain knew that Gilliland's was an American settlement. Others in Arnold's fleet believed they had crossed into British territory, and the families ashore must be Tories. Still others did not care where they were if the plunder was good. Three days before the fleet sailed, the daily orders from headquarters condemned plundering: "Marauding has become so frequent that the Genl. Expects every officer will, in a spirited manner, exert himself to prevent it & bring the perpetrators to exemplary punishment.... This Army is paid to protect, not pilfer the inhabitants."[17]

On August 25 or early on Monday, August 26, some of Arnold's men robbed houses and farms in Willsboro. Then, faced with heavy rain and gale winds, the little fleet raced back to the shelter of Buttonmould Bay on the eastern shore where they rode out the storm. On Tuesday a party from the *Providence* went ashore. Wells heard that the inhabitants "remand [remained] peaceable." The weather finally moderated on Thursday, and Arnold and his officers celebrated on the rocky point that separates the bay and the open lake. Wells was proud that his captain, Isaiah Simonds, made the best shot firing at marks. "We had a most genteel feast of a roast pig, good wine, some punch and good old cider. We drank the Congress's health, General Arnold's, and named the point by the name of Arnold's Point and then broke up." (Most of the words in Wells's journal were capitalized.)[18]

After the storm, the fleet was becalmed at Buttonmould Bay, and Arnold received the first complaints that his men had plundered nearby farms. As Wells heard the story, people claimed "their houses were rob^d of Furneture, their fields and Gardens of the fruit thereof in thare absence and suppos^d it to be done by the fleet." Arnold ordered two captains to visit the houses and fields and see that the owners were compensated. No boat could go ashore unless accompanied by an officer.[19]

The next day William Gilliland wrote to complain of plundering more than fifteen miles north on the west shore of the lake. They "wantonly and wickedly committed great destruction on several of my plantations on this settlement," Gilliland told Arnold in an angry letter, written September 1 and delivered the next day as the American fleet once again anchored off Willsboro. They "forceably raised" two fields of potatoes, destroyed an acre of peas, and ruined five or six acres of corn. Free from any discipline, they stole things that were of no use to them: two sleighs, five new windows, a bedstead, and several chairs. They acted "in the most insolent and licentious manner even before my servant's face." But Gilliland did not blame Arnold for the actions of his men and only wanted to be compensated for the damage. In a postscript, he asked for help. His cribs, the traps to catch lake salmon as they swam upstream, had been destroyed by the flood. "If your carpenters could be spared to assist me one day or two, I should very soon be able to send you some salmon."[20]

Arnold kept sailing north and did not act upon the complaint for four weeks, but then he maliciously counterattacked. "Gilliland is a most plausible and artful villain," he wrote to Gates from an anchorage off Valcour Island in the far north of the lake, sending a copy of Gilliland's letter, "not one syllable of which is true." A few men had gone ashore at Gilliland's, "but the whole stuff that was brought off, was not worth forty shillings." Arnold included a deposition filled with innuendo. Thomas Day had heard Gilliland say the "army acted like a parcel of damned robbers." With Gilliland's encouragement, a tenant had given soldiers "a mere trifle of rum" in exchange for tents, axes, and guns. And tenant John Watson told people he was not afraid of the British Regulars, because he had relatives among them.[21]

As a result of Arnold's charges, Gilliland and Watson were taken to Ticonderoga as prisoners. Even Thomas Hartley, who originally warned Gates about the two men, expressed support for them. "General Arnold doubtless will inform you the reasons that induced him to make these orders," he wrote tactfully about the commander of the fleet. "I thought that as Mr. Gilliland's family and Mr. Watson's family were in our power, there would have been no danger of either of the men, had they been inclined to act against us." Watson, whose wife was going through a difficult pregnancy, was no threat at all.[22]

Gilliland was never brought to trial on whatever charges could be made from Arnold's accusations. He spent the fall of 1776 at Ticonderoga where he befriended Jeduthan Baldwin, the chief engineer of the forts. Once Baldwin purchased a china bowl from him for three dollars, a measure of how far Gilliland's fortunes had fallen. He had lost his land and property and was to be in and out of debtors' prison. In 1777, he appealed to Congress, blaming Arnold for his misfortunes. "Bursting with pride and intoxicated with power to which he ever ought to have been a stranger, but whch he has art enough to obtain from you, he tyrannizes where he can." Arnold has "done more injury to the American cause, than all the ministerial troops," he told Congress.[23]

※ ※ ※

While Arnold's fleet rode out the storm at Buttonmould Bay, John Brown was in Albany meeting with Philip Schuyler, who found Brown's complaints disagreeable but requested more details. "Indeed there was not a day during the whole campaign but I was on fatigue, and most of the time by night as well as day," wrote Brown in a memorandum. Then Schuyler sent Brown north to Ticonderoga where there were officers and witnesses who could get to the bottom of the question, if anyone cared. Brown arrived on September 2 and the next day brought a written complaint against Arnold to General Gates. Brown claimed that on February 22 in a meeting with Jeremiah Duggan and others, Arnold accused Brown of the "worst and blackest crimes, viz: of plundering the baggage of officers taken prisoners (contrary to the articles of capitulation) and other publick stores." In May, Arnold repeated the accusation to Major General Thomas and Theodore Sedgwick and said that Brown was "a dangerous man and ought not to be continued in the army."[24]

Eleven. "I wish he may be as prudent as he is brave"

Gates was not pleased to face another potential crisis involving Arnold and postponed any hearing. The fleet was on the northern lake; the forts required constant work; and the British were coming. But if Arnold had been at Ticonderoga and the enemy a distant threat, Gates would not have acted. Nor was Schuyler genuinely interested in giving Brown a hearing. When he heard from Gates, he answered, "If Courts-Martial would severely punish officers for illiberal abuse against their superiours, such virulent and ill-founded complaints as you mention to be made by Lieutenant-Colonel Brown, against General Arnold, would soon cease. The latter gentleman will always be the subject of complaint, because his impartiality and candour will not suffer him to see impropriety of behaviour with impunity." And Gates wrote, "I am astonished at the calumnies that go to Congress against General Arnold, and more astonished they should be one moment attended to."[25]

※ ※ ※

A researcher soon discovers there were many Browns in the Revolution and that sources often do not give first names. At Ticonderoga in September 1776, there were three lieutenant-colonel Browns—Abijah, Benjamin, and John. Then there was brigade major Andrew Brown on the Ticonderoga side, a Massachusetts man from Ireland nearly always listed with no first name or rank. A Private John Brown received eighty-five lashes. From September 12 to 14, "Lt. Col. Brown" presided over a court that tried a captain for disobeying orders and neglect of duty, a civilian for selling liquor to the troops, and a private for deserting and enlisting in another company.[26] Likely the presiding officer was our John Brown, Esq., recently arrived at Ticonderoga, but it is difficult to locate him with certainty throughout the fall. On paper, he was second in command of Elmore's Connecticut State Regiment, stationed at Fort Schuyler (still often referred to by its earlier name of Fort Stanwix) in today's Rome, New York, but the editor of the *Connecticut Military Record, 1775–1848* concluded correctly that Brown did not appear to have served with the regiment.[27] He may have been in Albany in early October, but from then until the end of November, there is no mention of his whereabouts, unless he is one of the Browns without a given name in the records. Almost certainly he returned to the forts for the anticipated battle. A year later he was awarded the assignment of leading a counter-offensive, now known as "Brown's Raid," against British-held Ticonderoga, a sign that he knew the forts at the height of their strength.

At Ticonderoga and Mount Independence, Brown was among friends and fellow Massachusetts countrymen. On the Mount Independence side, four regiments were from Massachusetts. On the Ticonderoga side, Brigadier General James Brickett led a brigade of Massachusetts militia. Brown arrived around the same time as a company of Stockbridge Indians, whose home was fifteen miles from Pittsfield. They were assigned to Samuel Brewer's Massachusetts regiment and told to wear blue and red caps, so that "we may not, by mistake, kill our friends instead of our enemies." Brown and some of these men were known to each other.[28]

※ ※ ※

By mid–September 1776, the forts were beginning to emerge from a summer of sickness. In July and August, smallpox abated, to be replaced by fluxes and fevers whose horrific names disguise the fact that doctors had no idea of the cause or the treatment. Dr. Beebe listed "the dysentery, Jaundice, Putrid, intermitting, & Billious fevers" which "proved fatal in a variety of instances." On Sunday, September 8, Chaplain Ami Robbins made the rounds, but "could not pass one single tent among the soldiers wherein there were not one or more sick." But the onset of cold nights did what a regimen of bleeding, purging, and puking could not and the camps returned to what passed for health in the eighteenth century.[29]

More than ten thousand men were serving at the forts, making Ticonderoga-Mount Independence one of the largest concentrations of people in the United States. Just a few months earlier, Ticonderoga had been a neglected fort left over from the French and Indian War, guarded by rotting, overgrown fortifications to the northwest. Now the old fort was deep in a web of blockhouses, redoubts, sawmills, storehouses, tents and cabins, and defensive lines that stretched three miles from Lake George Landing to the dock where men were rowed a quarter mile to Mount Independence. In July the Mount had been wooded and known for rattlesnakes. By

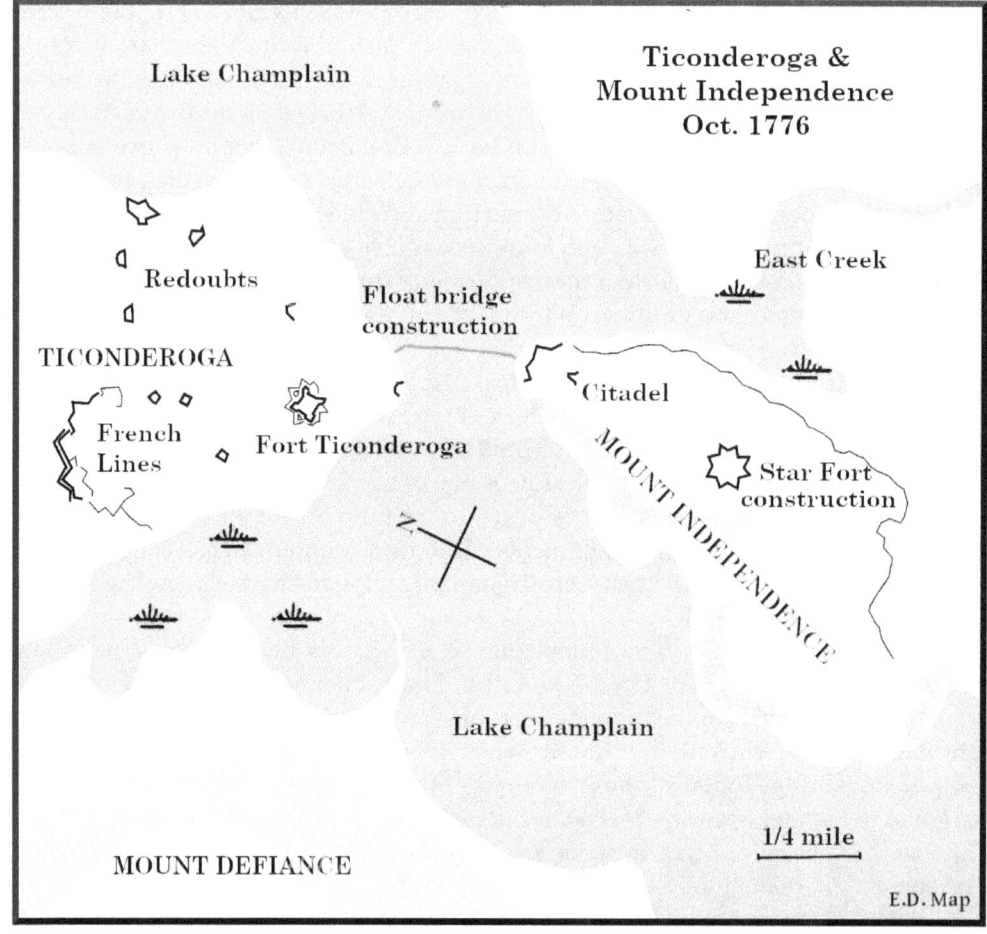

The fortifications at Ticonderoga and Mount Independence were strong in the fall of 1776. By the end of October, crews were constructing a bridge across the lake and a star-shaped fort on Mount Independence. This map is based upon one drawn by British military engineer Charles Wintersmith in 1777.

September, the rocky hill was bare of trees at the northern end and was soon to be completely clear. A grand waterside battery with twenty-eight guns dominated the lake; above it was a horseshoe-shaped citadel and the outline of a star-shaped stockade fort surrounding barracks.[30]

In late September, Brown saw his former commander, James Easton, who still hoped for reimbursement and a hearing to clear his name. After a visit to Ticonderoga, Easton wrote to Congress from Albany. While calling for a settlement of his expenses, Easton did not forget his friends. "Warner's and Cady's regiments have not got their pay, and a general murmuring ensues," he wrote. By order of Congress, Brown had applied for a hearing into Arnold's charges against him and Easton, but "it's evident General Arnold will evade the trial if possible, as there appears not the least spark of evidence against us." Easton continued, "A general complaint among officers of all ranks as well as soldiers, is heard against him, and it's hoped he will, ere long, meet the just demerits of deeds." Easton found himself in a gray area, not dismissed from the army, not encouraged to continue. But like Timothy Bedel, who had been cashiered for the defeat at the Cedars, Easton remained loyal and did not blame his country: "I don't desert this cause, nor think it a bad one, because I have been abused by General Arnold and others, but if could, shall exert myself in it, having determined never to yield until my country's liberties are secured."[31]

On October 11 in Albany, a certificate written by James Livingston was presented to Schuyler on Brown's behalf. Four other officers—Gershom Mott, Robert Cochran, William Satterlee, and Timothy Bedel—signed the document attesting that Brown "was the most active Man in the army" in Canada and "was scarcely off duty, day or night, during the campaign." Schuyler had already promised Congress that he would advise them of the "extraordinary services" that Brown had rendered in Canada, and he forwarded the certificate, along with Brown's own account of his time in Canada. The question of special recognition was referred to a committee, which reported in November that Brown had "performed many valuable services in Canada," but avoided reaching a conclusion on how to respond. They were worried about his vision: "His eyesight is so impaired by the cold weather last winter, that he will not be able to perform the duty of his office, unless it be in some stationary post." The report was ordered to lie on the table.[32]

※ ※ ※

On the morning of October 11 at Ticonderoga, General Gates called for increased vigilance. "The long stillness and seeming supineness of the enemy, strongly indicates that they are meditating some stroke of importance," read the day's orders. Unknown to Gates, that morning the British fleet, which was anchored for the night between Grand Isle and today's North Hero, sailed south to search for the Americans. On Mount Independence, engineer Baldwin began to set up the pickets for the star shaped fort. He noted in his journal, "All was well & without fear." They next day he could hear cannon fire to the north.[33]

Twelve

"And every man of common sense"

Most Americans have not heard of the Battle of Valcour Island, but even so it may be our most tangible link to the war for independence. The signed Declaration of Independence exists at the National Archives in an aluminum and titanium container filled with argon gas. Fort Ticonderoga, a stone restoration of a mostly wooden fort, is as old as a Ford Model T. Independence Hall and Faneuil Hall cannot escape being in congested cities. Williamsburg is beguiling, but can seem like an amusement park for adults. No matter what the thermometer reads, Valley Forge, Morristown, and Mount Independence will never be as cold as they were for the men who wintered there.

But then there is the gondola *Philadelphia*, sunk at Valcour and on permanent exhibit in the Smithsonian Museum of American History. It's around the corner from the Presidents and First Ladies. Depending on the direction you're walking, the *Philadelphia* is either a beginning or a culmination of the Price of Freedom, the exhibit of artifacts from America's wars. It is fifty-three feet long, fifteen feet wide, large for a museum, shockingly small and frail for battle against the British Navy. Forty-four men were crowded aboard. The massive gun at the bow is a twelve-pounder weighing more than a ton-and-a-half. The side guns are nines, well over a ton each. The *Philadelphia* was raised from Lake Champlain in 1935. In the mid–1960s, it was located in the future museum, and the building was completed around it. Today conservators monitor the gunboat as it continues to age. In 2019, the museum began a multiyear preservation project.[1]

Early historians did not know what to make of the Battle of Valcour Island, but by the end of the nineteenth century it had become the next-best-thing to a great victory, a position it continues to hold today. Benedict Arnold appears at his best, carrying the battle to the enemy, exercising shrewd tactics, and fighting defiantly in defeat. Novelist Kenneth Roberts, who portrayed a heroic Arnold in *Arundel*, continued the story in *Rabble in Arms* (1933), which centers on Arnold's deeds on Lake Champlain. But as he had in his evaluation of the march to Québec, Brown claimed that Arnold engaged in "great misconduct." This charge alone may be enough to explain why historians have dismissed his accusations. Once again there is another side to the story.[2]

※ ※ ※

"It is a defensive War we are carrying on," Horatio Gates wrote to Arnold ten days before the dispute with the hapless Commodore Wynkoop, "therefore, no wanton

Twelve. *"And every man of common sense"*   119

The gunboat *Philadelphia* is on permanent display in the Smithsonian's National Museum of American History. It was raised from Lake Champlain in 1935 and placed in the museum while the building was being constructed. Division of Political and Military History, National Museum of American History, Smithsonian Institution.

risque, or unnecessary Display of the Power of the Fleet, is at any Time, to influence your Conduct." However, if the enemy should "attempt to force their Way through the Pass you are stationed to defend in that Case you will act with such cool determined Valour, as will give them Reason to repent their Temerity." Gates ordered Arnold to defend either of two narrows: Île-aux-Têtes in the far north or Split Rock at the south of the broad lake. Gates wrote as a soldier and began one sentence, "As I am entirely unacquainted with maritime Affairs...."[3]

Although never much more than eighty miles from Ticonderoga, Arnold must have felt himself to be as far from the constraints of headquarters as an explorer lost on the South Sea. The fleet sailed as far as today's border with Canada, skirmished with the enemy, and was battered by gale winds and heavy seas. Simonds, captain of the *Providence*, suffered from the periodic fevers of the ague (malaria); Bayze Wells had the itch and three times bathed in brimstone tallow and tar. When Ansel Fox slept on his watch, he was canned a dozen strokes on his naked buttocks. Arnold had nothing but contempt for the "wretched motley Crew" of his fleet: they "are not equal to half their Number of good men," he told Gates. The marines were "the Refuse of every Regiment"; few of the sailors had ever been "wet with salt Water."[4]

Finally, on September 24, the fleet anchored between rocky Valcour Island and the western shore of the lake. It was a sheltered harbor, about three-quarters of a mile wide, opening to the south. Arnold had been promoting the location in his letters to Gates. "There is a Good Harbour and if the Enemy venture up the Lake it will be

In this watercolor by Charles Randle, Arnold's fleet is anchored off Valcour Island. The *Royal Savage* is center. The row-galley *Washington* is second from the left; the *Philadelphia* is third. Library and Archives Canada, Acc. No. 1996-82-2.

impossible for them to take advantage of our Situation, if we should succeed on our Attack on them it will be impossible for any of them to Escape, if we are worsted our Retreat is open and Free," he told Gates from Isle La Motte. In another letter, Arnold continued his praise of Valcour: we are "moored … as near together as possible. & in such a form that few Vessels can attack us at the same Time, & then will be exposed to the fire of the whole fleet." Arnold saw the advantages of Valcour clearly, but he misled Gates—perhaps he misled himself, as he could do when an idea took hold. With care, it was possible to sail north around Valcour Island, but that would bring the fleet into the open lake where the British would hold every advantage. Essentially the Americans were in a cul-de-sac; retreat was far from "open and free"; and the fleet could be bottled up and destroyed at leisure. Gates had been clear: "Remember how exceedingly you ought to Guard against the possibility of the Enemy's possessing any Narrow Pass in your Rear [meaning between the fleet and the American forts]; a Caution, which you so-much approved, in the Orders, & Instructions you received."[5]

The day after arriving at Valcour, Arnold hosted the officers for a picnic on the island. "A most agreable Entertainment," noted Wells, although around noon they heard British cannon in the distance. The first of the row-galleys, the *Trumbull*, reached Valcour on the last day of September and saluted the fleet by firing an impressive seven guns. The captain of the *Trumbull* was another man named Seth Warner, a sailor from Haddam, Connecticut, who had been recruited by Arnold. Six days later the galleys *Washington* and *Congress* appeared. By then, Wells's journal, usually rich in detail, was about rum, cider brandy, and the weather, which was cloudy—he spelled it *clouda*—for days on end.[6]

At eight in the morning, October 11, a clear day with snow visible on the mountains, the British fleet appeared off the peninsula called Cumberland Head. An American guard boat fired a warning. From Cumberland Head to the southern tip of Valcour Island is slightly more than six miles, no distance at all with a strong breeze. General David Waterbury, in command of the galley *Washington* and second in command of the fleet, met with Arnold. Waterbury, a fifty-four-year-old brigadier from Stamford, Connecticut, had been in Skenesborough most of the summer overseeing the construction of the fleet. Gates had appointed him second in command because he believed that he and Arnold were "upon the best terms." Gates told Schuyler, "I am satisfied no Dispute about command, or want of Confidence in each other will retard the public service." Arnold had known for weeks that he wanted to fight at Valcour, but apparently he had never informed his officers of his plans. Waterbury told John Hancock, "I gave it as my opinion that the fleet ought immediately to come to sail, and fight them on a retreat in the main Lake, as they were so much superiour to us in number and strength, and we being in such a disadvantageous harbour to fight a number so much superior." Brown was to list Waterbury as a witness against Arnold.[7]

The Americans had been watching the British in St. John and realized they were outgunned without knowing the specifics. In fact, British superiority was overwhelming. On open water, the *Inflexible*, a square rigged ship carrying eighteen twelve-pounders, might alone have destroyed the American fleet, as could the radeau *Thunderer*, in the unlikely event that some of the clumsy vessel's six 24-pounders and six twelves could be brought to bear. The schooners *Maria* and *Carleton* outgunned the two schooners in Arnold's fleet. In addition, the British had a large gondola and twenty (perhaps twenty-four) gunboats. In a single round the British could fire more than a thousand pounds of shot to the Americans' six hundred forty-five. The calculation of flying metal does not take into account the greater skill of the British gunners or their larger reserves of shot and powder.[8]

Arnold was insistent that the fleet remain at Valcour, and he ordered the three row-galleys and the *Royal Savage* into the main lake to meet the British. Soon it was clear they faced as many as thirty vessels, and the galleys and schooner were recalled. Unable to maneuver into the wind and return to the American line in the bay—"by some bad Management," Arnold explained to Gates—the *Royal Savage* was crippled by British fire and run aground off the tip of Valcour Island.[9]

As Arnold had predicted, because of the wind from the north and the narrowness of the bay, the British could not bring the destructive weight of their fleet into range and so relied on their gunboats to approach the anchored Americans. Arnold's maneuverable galleys could row forward from the line, fire a few rounds, and then slip back into place. A powder magazine on one British gunboat exploded. The British schooner *Carleton* worked its way close enough for its six-pounders to be effective, but then it faced fire from five American vessels and was disabled. On board the row-galley *Congress*, Arnold aimed many of the guns—"which I believe did good execution," he told Gates. "The Battle Lasted Eight hours Very hot," Wells recorded. At sunset, the British set the *Royal Savage* afire, so that it burned in the darkness at the mouth of the bay.[10]

The British triumph was near total. According to Arnold, some sixty Americans were wounded or dead (out of more than seven hundred). Wells heard 50 killed. The *Congress*'s hull was badly damaged and her main mast was splintered in two places. The *Washington* was shot through the hull and the mast needed replacement. Three-quarters of the American gunpowder was gone. The *Philadelphia* had been hit so many times that she sank. The British needed only to wait until morning to destroy what was left of the American fleet. Instead, during the night, the thirteen remaining vessels led by the row-galley *Trumbull* slipped south, keeping close to the New York shore. Colonel Edward Wigglesworth, another of Brown's potential witnesses, was in command of the *Trumbull*; Seth Warner of Haddam, Connecticut, was shipmaster. "The enemy did not attempt to molest us," Arnold told Gates as if the British had second thoughts about fighting. The Americans escaped as a result of the "extreme Obscurity of the Night," explained Captain Pringle, commander of the British fleet.

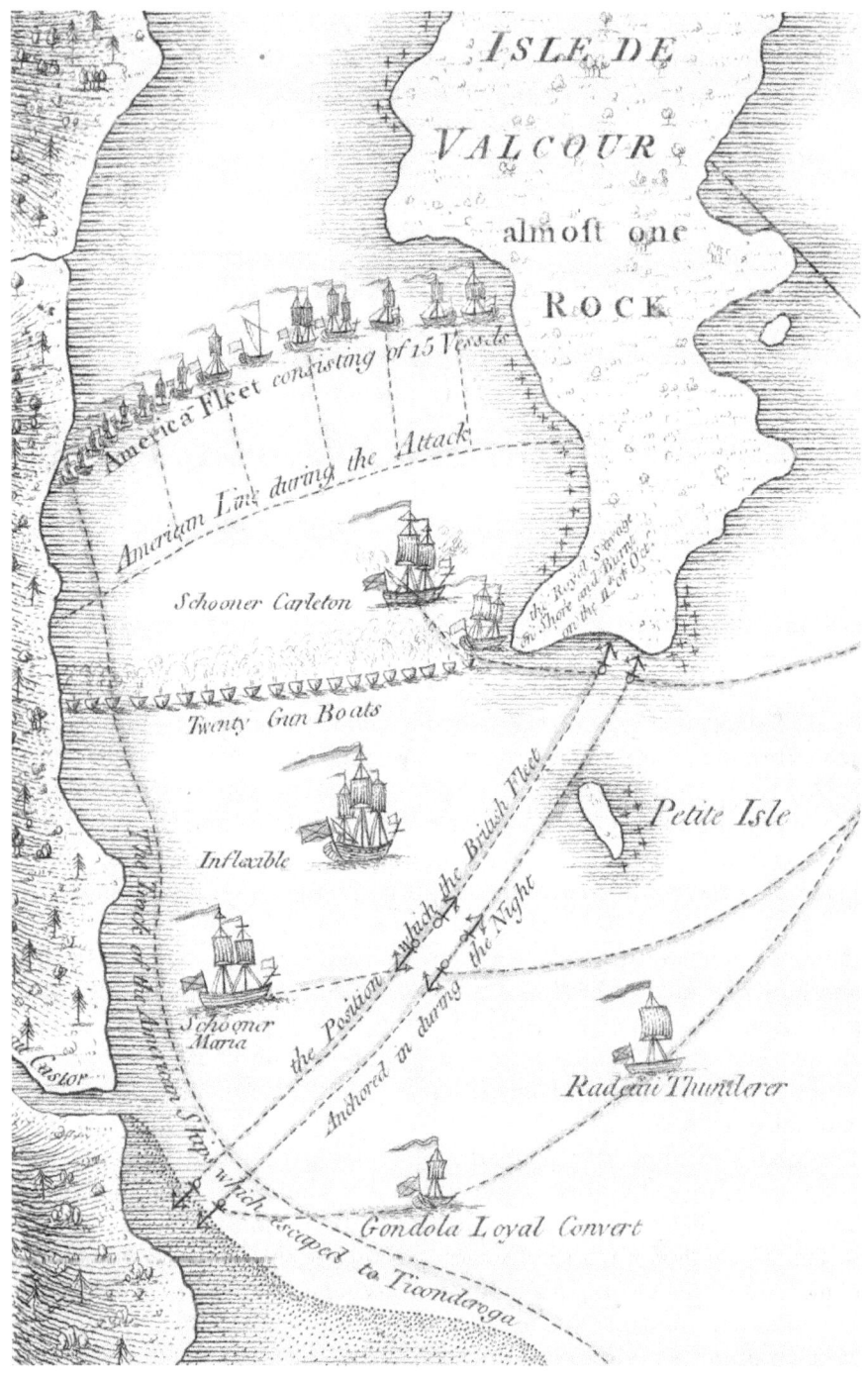

A portion of a British map engraved by William Faden soon after the battle shows the strengths and weaknesses of the American position at Valcour Island. Arnold's fleet was drawn up in a line and could concentrate its fire. However, escape to the south appeared to be nearly impossible. At night, the fleet slipped between the British and the shore. Newberry Library Collection / Norman B. Leaventhal Map & Education Center at the Boston Public Library Digital Collections.

Not so, answered the captains of the *Inflexible*, the *Maria*, and the *Loyal Convert* in an open letter to Pringle written eight months after the battle. "The rear of the British line was at least one mile from the western shore, and the van beyond the small island at the Southern end of Valcour. From this disposition Sir, and not from the extreme obscurity of the night as you are pleased to say, the rebels escaped."[11]

Some of the American fleet came together at Schuylers Island, about eight miles from Valcour. The wind was from the south, holding them there while they made repairs to the leaking vessels. Briefly the British were baffled by the escape, but then began their pursuit, beating into the wind. At Schuylers Island, Arnold wrote an optimistic report to Gates, concluding, "On the whole I think we have had a Very fortunate escape, & have great reason to return, our humble, & hearty thanks to Allmighty God for preserving. & delivering so many of us from, our more than Savage Enemies."[12]

Deliverance did not last. Bayze Wells described the events in one confusing, forceful run-on sentence: "the Enemy Came hard against us So we ware Oblig^d to Leve three Gondolas and make the best of our way with boats two of which we distroy^d and one of them the Enemies made A Prise off the Rest made thare Escape this Day by Rowing all night...."[13]

By the next morning, October 13, Arnold was off Willsboro—"28 miles from Crown Point," he noted. The American vessels were spread over seven miles with the row-galley *Washington*, commanded by Waterbury, last in line. The *Washington* was "much damaged and [had] a great deal of water in [her] & was a dull sailer," Waterbury wrote. He sent his boat to Arnold, two miles ahead, to ask permission to beach the galley and blow it up. "I received for answer, by no means to run her ashore, but to push forward to Split Rock, where he would draw the fleet in line, and engage them again." But by the time the *Washington* reached the narrows, "the whole fleet was making their escape as fast as they could, and left me in the rear, to fall into the enemy's hands," Waterbury told President Hancock. Alone, the *Washington* faced the mighty *Inflexible* and the schooner *Maria* and quickly surrendered.[14]

Now the *Congress* was last in line, trying to shepherd four gondolas and facing the *Inflexible*, the *Maria*, and the *Carleton*. Arnold described the scene to Philip Schuyler: "They kept up an incessant Fire on us for about five Glasses [two-and-half hours, beginning around noon] with Round and Grape Shot, which we returned as briskly—The Sails Rigging and Hull of the *Congress* was shattered and torn in Peices, the first Lieutenant and 3 Men killed...." A mile-and-a-half south of Buttonmould Bay with seven British vessels swarming after them, Arnold ordered the *Congress* and the four remaining gondolas into Ferris Bay, today's Arnold Bay, on the east shore. With flags still flying, they burned the row-galley and the gunboats and made their way on foot to Chimney Point.[15]

At eleven-thirty, Colonel Hartley at Crown Point sent news on to Gates at Ticonderoga. "The enemy are approaching. The wind is very favourable to them. They have been firing, for two hours past, a few heavy guns. I know not whether our fleet will be able to effect a retreat to this place or not." Panic spread quickly. The Americans burned the buildings and defenses at Crown Point and destroyed nearby farms. The remains of the American fleet reached the safety of Ticonderoga around three o'clock in the afternoon. They were followed by settlers from both sides of the lake. Some ran five, seven, or eight miles "in the woods with women and Children in the greatest distress," engineer Jeduthan Baldwin noted from Mount Independence. They had left their houses and all their possessions "to the enemy, or to the flames."[16]

※ ※ ※

The debate on the impact of Valcour and the retreat on the lake began immediately. At Ticonderoga, General Gates was quick to express the official view. He had little choice: he had trusted Arnold and given him free rein, and any criticism would lower the morale of the troops at Ticonderoga and Mount Independence. Orders for October 14 read, "[the General] "Returns his thanks to General Arnold and the Officers, Seamen, & Marines of the Fleet for the Gallant Defense they made against the Great Superiority of the Enemy Force. Such Magnanimous Behavior will establish the Fame of American Arms throughout the Globe."[17]

But the soldiers at the forts knew they had been dealt a crushing defeat. Colonel William Maxwell wrote to the governor of New Jersey, William Livingston, "You must have heard that a few days ago we had a fine fleet and tolerably good army, but General Arnold, our evil genius to the north, has with a good deal of industry, got us clear of all our fleet, only five of the most indifferent of them, one row-galley excepted; and he has managed his point so well with the old man, the General, that he has got his thanks for his good services." But Maxwell believed—or professed to believe—incorrectly that the American fleet "by all impartial accounts, was much the strongest." Maxwell's inaccurate description of the sizes of the fleets has been used to dismiss all his observations. Perhaps "Scotch Willie" was one of the jealous, less competent men who supposedly made Arnold's life miserable.[18] In fact, Maxwell might have been jealous, but he was far from incompetent. He oversaw the gathering of the Durham boats for Washington's surprise crossing of the Delaware River, and in the winter of 1777 fought a brilliant campaign harassing the British in New Jersey. David Hackett Fischer in his Pulitzer Prize–winning *Washington's Crossing* (2004) termed Maxwell "an extraordinary character and a combat leader of true genius."[19]

Maxwell concluded his letter to Governor Livingston with an accurate prediction: "If they do come and attack us, as is generally thought, we have no more opinion of his abilities by land than water. I am something of opinion they will not come, but be contented for this time, as they have done more than they had any reason to expect."[20]

At first Congress heard about the valor of Arnold and the fleet, but within a few weeks, influenced by David Waterbury's account, the tone changed. In early November, Congressman Richard Henry Lee described Arnold as "fiery, hot and impetuous, but without discretion." He "never thought of informing himself how the enemy went on, and he had no idea of retiring when he saw them coming, tho so much superior to his force!"[21]

In his thirteen charges, Brown wrote,

> 12th. For great misconduct in his command of the Continental fleet in *Lake Champlain*, which occasioned the loss thereof.

Witnesses: General David Waterbury, second in command; Colonel Edward Wigglesworth, third in command; Captain Allin; "& Every Man of common Sense."[22]

Waterbury was paroled after the surrender of the *Washington* and allowed to go home to Stamford, Connecticut, to await exchange. At Ticonderoga, he met with

Arnold and other officers in Gates's house. Brown must have learned of Waterbury's thoughts about the battle in the short time he was at Ticonderoga. The men from the *Washington* were not allowed to land, so that their defeat would not discourage the forts' defenders.

Waterbury came to be criticized for surrendering the *Washington*, especially when his actions were compared to Arnold's defiant gesture. "I think it was taking a Great advantage of a man's character behind his Back," Waterbury wrote Gates a few months later. Waterbury had wanted to beach and destroy his row-galley, but "I was kept from that privilege by his [Arnold's] orders."[23]

If we can trust Brown's spelling, the witness he called Captain Allin is likely Captain John-Baptiste Allin of Livingston's First Canadian Regiment. Allin returned to Canada as a spy and provided Americans with intelligence on the progress being made by the British. However, relying on Brown's spelling is risky. Once he referred to "Ebr. Allin," meaning Captain Ebenezer Allen, a Vermont ranger who had served in Canada and had knowledge of the islands in northern Lake Champlain. And there are many other Allens. So Captain Allin or possibly Allen is not certain. Whoever he was, he may have had knowledge of what Arnold should have known—or knew and ignored.[24]

Most dramatically in his letter to Theodore Sedgwick, Brown added to his list of witnesses this statement: "& Every Man of common Sense." The assertion is a challenge to historians who think the Battle of Valcour Island is nothing but the story of Arnold's foresight and tenacity.

Early historians of the Revolution William Gordon (1788), David Ramsay (1789), and Mercy Otis Warren (1805) recognized Arnold's bravery on Lake Champlain, but disagreed about the meaning of the battle. Gordon quoted a letter written from the forts: "The fleet was strong, but our posts are much stronger." It is a point seldom made by Arnold-partisans. Arnold could sacrifice the fleet because thousands of men had worked through the summer, and were now healthy and reinforced as they awaited attack. Ramsay praised Arnold's "great judgment and ability" in making the nighttime escape from Valcour, but credited the "delays contrived by general Gates" for slowing the British advance until winter made retreat necessary. Warren's chronology was confused, but she stressed the bravery of Arnold in the retreat from Canada and at Valcour. In her account, Ticonderoga was weak: "The garrison there had been reinforced by some militia from the eastern states, but they were in no condition to meet general Carleton...." She continued, "They had nothing to hope—an immediate surrender to mercy was their only resource."[25]

In his 1816 *Memoirs of My Own Times*, James Wilkinson discussed Valcour at length. Like the march through the wilderness of Maine, he wrote, the Battle of Valcour Island "eventuated in heavy expense, and the loss of many valuable lives, without a solitary ray of solid advantage to the public service." It did nothing but "exalt his [Arnold's] character for animal courage, on the blood of men equally brave" but it did "procure for him all the credit which could have been attached to a splendid victory."[26]

Arnold's reputation for courage at Valcour continued to grow throughout the nineteenth century. "Search the naval history of our English ancestors, from Frobisher to Nelson and our own, from Paul Jones to Perry and Decatur down to Farragut, and there is no instance of more desperate valor," wrote Isaac Arnold in his

1880 biography.[27] Although the battle was seen as an inspiration to Americans and a lesson to the British that their adversaries were willing to fight, it was seldom seen as having any strategic value. Then in 1898 naval historian Captain (and later Rear Admiral) Alfred Thayer Mahan wrote an article in *Scribner's* magazine titled "The Naval Campaign of 1776 on Lake Champlain." Mahan was known internationally for *The Influence of Sea Power Upon History, 1660–1783*, published in 1890. His theories were being turned into warships by the major powers in an arms race that is one of the threads leading to World War I. Within months of Mahan's article on Valcour, a modern American navy destroyed two antique Spanish fleets while suffering the lightest casualties.

Mahan argued that Arnold's "indomitable energy" and "indomitable courage" had preserved the American cause for a year, setting the stage for the victory at Saratoga, the turning point of the Revolution. "The little American navy on Lake Champlain was wiped out, but never had any force, big or small, lived to better purpose or died more gloriously; for it had saved the lake for that year," he wrote. Mahan examined the disputes about the battle and decided, "Arnold's behavior was excellent throughout." With only minor revisions, Mahan included the article in *The Major Operations of the Navies in the War of American Independence* (1913).[28]

Mahan's view has been widely adopted by writers, but it has flaws. He made no mention of the more than ten thousand men at Ticonderoga and Mount Independence, or the fact that the Americans on the lake were far stronger in the fall of 1776 than they were in the early summer of 1777. In Mahan's history, Arnold stands alone against the might of Great Britain. And Mahan finessed the key question: Was it the presence of the Americans on the lake or Arnold's desire to fight that delayed the British? A cautious cruise under uninspiring Commodore Wynkoop might have had the same result as Arnold's glorious battle—and preserved the fleet.

In three days, Arnold's navy was swept from Lake Champlain, and British power extended uncontested from St. John to Crown Point. "This success cannot be deemed less than a compleat victory," Carleton wrote to General John Burgoyne, who was in command of the army but chafing in a secondary role. From the *Maria*, anchored at Crown Point, Carleton

Alfred Mahan, the influential naval historian and strategist, argued that Benedict Arnold's actions at Valcour Island saved the American cause for a year, leading to the decisive victory at Saratoga. This photograph of Mahan was taken in 1904. Library of Congress.

also wrote to Lord George Germain, the British Secretary of State for the American Department: "The season is so far advanced that I cannot yet pretend to inform your Lordship whether anything further can be done this year." The convoluted sentence gives it away—there was little thought of continuing. Having endured the siege of Québec, Carleton knew far better than his critics then and now what winter warfare meant.[29]

※ ※ ※

The defeat of the American navy on Lake Champlain changed the perspective of the men at the forts. "The near approach of the enemy, has as it were reanimated our officers, and put new life and vigor into our Soldiers," noted Dr. Beebe, whose journal for once was free of any criticism of Arnold. "Every one exerts himself to the utmost, for an approaching battle—our works go on day and night without cessation." Express messengers hurried south calling for men and supplies.[30]

If an attack was imminent, Brigadier General Arthur St. Clair, a western Pennsylvanian from Scotland, who had served in the British army, was to command at the French Lines, the extensive fortifications that were originally built by the French. Militia brigadier James Brickett was assigned old Fort Ticonderoga, behind any initial fighting. Arnold was commander in the three-quarter-mile-wide flats between the French Lines and the lake. His assignment was the most difficult and dangerous. The flats were protected by four or five small forts or redoubts, built under the direction of Jeduthan Baldwin, who was a model of Yankee ingenuity but did not always understand military theory in locating and constructing his works. A successful attack on one redoubt could snowball, expose the rear of the French Lines, and open the old fort to attack. On the Mount Independence side, three brigade colonels shared responsibility.[31]

At about nine o'clock on October 28, an alarm was fired from the Jersey Redoubt and answered by a gun at the French Lines and then finally by one in the Citadel on Mount Independence. Taking advantage of wind from the north, three or four British gunboats approached the American fortifications. With drums beating, the entire garrison occupied the defenses. At eleven o'clock one gunboat came under fire from the heavy guns in the Jersey Redoubt by the lake and from the row-galleys *Trumbull* and *Gates*, stationed to defend the boom, the floating logs that crossed the lake to stop navigation. Men counted about fifteen bateaux filled with soldiers in the distance.

A lifetime later, artist John Trumbull described the scene. "The whole summit of cleared land, on both sides of the lake, was crowned with redoubts and batteries, all manned with a splendid show of artillery and flags. The number of our troops under arms that day (principally however militia) exceeded thirteen thousand."[32] An hour before sunset, the British boats retreated north, and although the Americans did not know it for a few days, the invasion from Canada was over for the year.

The militia left Lake Champlain almost immediately, and the regular forces demanded to go home. The British had been stopped and winter was coming. In their excitement to be gone, men damaged their huts and barracks, and Gates ordered them to be "careful to preserve everything that can in the least degree be useful to those who remain here." Gates, Arnold, and Brickett left together on November 18. Three days later, they met with Schuyler in Albany and decided that most of the troops at Ticonderoga and Mount Independence should be sent home to recruit. By December, Albany was the center of a shrinking northern army.[33]

Thirteen

"Sir, you are a dirty scoundrel"

Albany was the Northern Army's storehouse, its ship chandlery, and headquarters for General Schuyler, whose mansion overlooked the Hudson, a half-mile south of the city. Since the start of the war, regiments passed through Albany on their way to the lakes and Canada or to the Mohawk River to the west. Although 150 miles inland, it was a port city. At the top of the hill, Fort Albany, also called Fort Frederick, was another leftover from earlier wars. The Albany Committee of Safety, a more revolutionary version of the committee Brown met with in May 1775, struggled to govern during wartime. In November 1776, as men left Ticonderoga and Mount Independence, the committee resolved not to pay local militiamen who returned too soon without "proper Leave." They learned that cannonballs were lying in the street in front of the Continental storehouse, and there was "great Waste committed by Children and others." Glass was needed for the barracks, and wells and pumps in the city required repair. On November 27, Deputy Quartermaster General Morgan Lewis met with the committee for help in finding vessels to carry the troops to join George Washington, wherever he might be in his headlong retreat across New Jersey. They explained that so late in the season, this would be an expensive undertaking. Good sailors would be hard to find, and the sloops themselves might have to be impressed.[1]

Thousands of defenders from Ticonderoga and Mount Independence overwhelmed Albany's resources. With cold weather upon the North Country, the men took every bed and open space on the floor of the barracks and public houses, and wanted to be gone as soon as possible. Some New Englanders crossed the river and walked home for the winter or for good; others awaited the river sloops. Perhaps General Horatio Gates stayed at Cartwright's Inn at the corner of Green and Beaver, not far from the docks. The tavern had been known as the King's Arms until six months earlier when a mob tore down the sign and burned it. It still provided Albany's finest accommodations.

Gates had a lot on his mind, some of it the challenges of leadership during a crisis, some of it undoubtedly how to advance his own career. On December 1, the remnants of three regiments—still called Porter's, Greaton's, and Bond's—were boarding sloops to sail south, but not too far, for the British and Hessians controlled eastern New Jersey. Elisha Porter was sick and at home; John Greaton had been hospitalized and then named commander of another regiment; and William Bond was dead. Joseph Vose, who had taken such pride in the retreat from Canada, commanded the force of about five hundred men. Gates was preparing to sail the next day with another four regiments.

Washington had botched the campaign around New York, and for the first time since the start of the war, there might be an opening at the top of the Continental Army. Charles Lee, an idiosyncratic former British officer who was considered to be a brilliant soldier, would be first in line if Washington fell. Gates was allied with Lee and, if he played his cards right, would be a step behind. He knew he was hurrying toward an unfolding disaster. Within weeks, he might rescue Washington—or Gates and his army might be engulfed by the commander in chief's defeat. And then there was Arnold. Historians search for the moment when Gates's opinion of Arnold changed. When did he go from being a reliable subordinate whose actions enhanced Gates's reputation to being a rival and a threat? Recently Moses Hazen had brought a charge against Arnold for libeling him while the controversial goods from Montréal were at Chambly. An inquiry was scheduled for December 2.

John Brown might have been encouraged by Hazen's success in gaining a hearing, although he may have lost all perspective in his outrage. Once again his timing was wrong. In the fall, the Northern Army and Arnold's fleet were facing invasion; now the entire American cause was threatened with collapse. "These are the times that try men's souls," Thomas Paine wrote in *The Crisis*, dated three weeks later. How could Brown think that events would pause for a trial that would bring together dozens of witnesses who had more important duties? How could he think that Gates would sideline Arnold, no matter what he had done? And how did he think Gates could justify such an action to Washington, the Congress, and the general public for whom Arnold was a hero? Historians who see Brown as unbalanced have a point. But when was the right time? Did they need to wait until Arnold did something so damaging that it could not be glossed over? *This is the wrong time* is always a bulwark of authority.

Sometime in the late fall, Brown renewed his call for an inquiry, and Gates told him to take his complaint to Congress's War Board in Philadelphia. A revision of the Articles of War, which passed Congress on September 20, 1776, included the board as a possible tribunal. Gates may not have explained the change to Brown, or he may not have noticed it himself and only wanted Brown to be gone. On December 1, Brown was back with a letter and the long indictment at the heart of this narrative. "I have been led an expensive dance from Generals to Congress, and from Congress to Generals, and am now referred to a Board of War, who, I will venture to say, have never yet taken cognizance of any such matter, nor do I think it, with great submission to your Honour, any part of their duty," Brown wrote and likely said. "I therefore beg your Honour will please to order Brigadier General Arnold in arrest for the following crimes, which I am ready to verify."[2]

Unlike Hazen, whose hearing was the next day, Brown was questioning Arnold's behavior as an officer and a gentleman throughout the war. Gates knew that once witnesses started complaining, a flood would follow. Testimony on Arnold's actions on Lake Champlain was the most troubling, for if Arnold had been guilty of great misconduct, then Gates might be seen as failing to control a subordinate. Over the next day, Gates and Brown exchanged angry words and then letters for the record. When Gates refused to act upon the petition, Brown demanded to know the reasons, asked that his accusations be forwarded to Congress, and insisted on a written promise. Infuriated, Gates told him to put this final demand in writing, and Gates replied, "Since you are so importunate for an answer in writing to your petition of yesterday,

I think proper to acquaint you that I shall lay your petition before Congress, who will, when they see fit, give such orders as they think necessary thereupon." Gates must have been glad to board a sloop and be rid of Albany, Brown, and perhaps even Arnold.[3]

※ ※ ※

Writers have been uniform in their judgment on Brown's charges. Jared Sparks, in the first Arnold biography, wrote that Brown exhibited a "warmth that indicated too great a degree of excited feeling." But Sparks did wonder why Arnold did not request a court of inquiry to silence his enemies. Isaac Arnold, a distant relative whose 1880 biography of Benedict is still informative, concluded that although "it is now difficult, if not impossible, to determine the exact merit of the quarrel," it is remembered principally because of Arnold's treason. The judgment of so many officers and politicians in ignoring Brown's accusations settled the issue. Carl Van Doren, whose 1941 *Secret History of the American Revolution* remains the most detailed account of the steps to treason, found several of Brown's charges "preposterous [and] none of them proved." Mid-twentieth-century Arnold biographer Willard Wallace agreed. One could sympathize with Brown, he wrote, "but for his vindictiveness and the speciousness of his allegations." Clare Brandt, whose portrait of Arnold in *The Man in the Mirror* (1994) is perceptive, still found Brown's charges "outlandish," "breathtaking," and "nonsense." Arnold's foremost scholarly biographer (at least through 1777), James Kirby Martin, called the accusations "a highly distorted interpretation of reality" and suggested that by the late fall of 1776 "Brown's dogged vendetta against Arnold had become too consuming, perhaps to the point of mental instability." And Arnold's most recent biographer, Stephen Brumwell, refers to Brown's "long list of far-fetched allegations."[4]

One trouble with the unanimous verdict of history is that none of these writers pursued Brown's accusations. They have repeated each other's opinions—it is repetition all the way down. They have not made the acquaintance of Brown's potential witnesses and have dismissed any critic as jealous, indecisive, or incompetent. Brown's charges are not proven—or for that matter disproven—because authorities and historians refused to investigate them.

※ ※ ※

Arnold planned to sail from Albany on December 1, but delayed his departure to attend the new inquiry involving the stores at Chambly. Hazen claimed that Arnold had accused him of selling the army's rum to a tavern-keeper. General Brickett, who had traveled from Ticonderoga in Gates and Arnold's company, presided over a panel that included Colonel Edward Wigglesworth, third in command of the Lake Champlain fleet, and Colonel Philip Van Cortlandt, the new commander of the 2nd New York.

Hazen produced a receipt for a load of army rum upon which Arnold had written, "Colonel Hazen can best tell how much he sold." Arnold countered with a witness who had seen eight or ten kegs of rum in a cart leaving the fort on its way to a tavern owned by a French Canadian. Both Hazen and Arnold examined witnesses, but tempers stayed under control—or at least the brief record of the proceedings did not note the outbursts. The court found Arnold's comment to be "an aspersion of

Colonel Hazen's character, and therefore think the complaint just." No penalty was assessed. Hazen had scored by convincing the board that he had been wronged. Had Brown limited his complaint to Arnold's libels, he might have gained a similar victory. Instead, he drew a more complete portrait of his adversary, which was harder to deal with.[5]

※ ※ ※

Morgan Lewis, deputy quarter-master general in the Revolution, governor of New York from 1804 to 1807, and a major general in the War of 1812, told a tale about those same days in Albany. Or perhaps someone attached it to Lewis's name because we would be inclined to believe such a prominent man. Careful historians dismiss the story, but it may have the kind of truth found in a *Saturday Night Live* sketch: not a word is factual, but it comes closer to the heart of the matter than the thoroughly sourced lead story in the *New York Times*.[6]

In the tale, when Arnold heard of Brown's accusations against him, he "applied a variety of epithets coarse and harsh to Col. Brown" and said that he would kick Brown "wheresoever and whensoever he should meet him." Morgan Lewis asked if Arnold had any objection to his repeating the remarks to Brown. "Certainly not," he replied.

That evening, Lewis spoke with Brown, "a mild and amiable man, and he made no remark of particular harshness or bitterness in respect to Arnold." Finally, Brown said, "Well, Lewis, I wish you would invite me to dine with your mess to-morrow."

The next day Brown entered the room where sixteen, maybe eighteen, officers sat at a long table. Arnold stood at the far end with his back to the fire. Brown walked "with deliberate step" through the room and then spoke so that everyone could hear. "I understand, sir, that you have said you would kick me: I now present myself to give you an opportunity to put your threat into execution!" When Arnold did not answer, Brown said, "Sir, you are a dirty scoundrel." Arnold "was still silent as the sphinx." Brown apologized to the officers for interrupting their dinner and left.

The real Arnold would not have endured such public humiliation. The real Brown would have got a good laugh out of the tale.

※ ※ ※

On December 2, a cold and windy day, four small regiments from Lake Champlain, five hundred men in all, were packed aboard river sloops for the trip south. The men enjoyed a few days in Kingston, New York, before marching sixty miles southwest over the watershed to the Delaware River. They were without tents; their clothing was thin; their shoes were so worn that many men wrapped their feet in rags to keep them from the frozen ground.[7] On December 11, in northwest New Jersey in the valley between the Kittatinny and Walpack ridges, they were caught by a snowstorm and found shelter as the best they could in a sparsely settled area. From Isaac Van Campen's Inn on the Delaware River, Horatio Gates wrote to George Washington and sent aide James Wilkinson to find the commander in chief, wherever he was.

Learning that Washington had crossed to Pennsylvania, Wilkinson rode toward Morristown, New Jersey, headquarters for Major General Charles Lee. He found Lee before dawn in a tavern in Basking Ridge, about four miles away from his troops. Lee had snide things to say about Washington and then wrote a letter to Gates: "*Entre nous* [between ourselves], a certain great man is most damnably deficient. In short unless something which I do not expect turns up we are lost. Our counsels have been weak to the last degree." Lee hoped patriots would burn Philadelphia, which was the only hope. At that moment, British dragoons surrounded the tavern. Wilkinson grabbed the letter and ran, expecting to fight for his life. Instead, the British were glad to seize Lee and get quickly away. The letter concluded with ambiguous advice, friend to friend: "As to what relates to yourself, if you think you can be in time to aid the General, I would have you by all means go; you will at least save your army." *Save the army, not Washington?*[8]

Gates sent his four regiments ahead under command of Benedict Arnold. They crossed the Delaware River at Easton and moved into Bethlehem, Pennsylvania. Accompanied by a small guard, Gates made his way by a separate route. In Bethlehem, he received a letter from Washington that did not improve his assessment of the general's chances. "Before this comes to hand, you will have heard of the melancholy situation of our Affairs," Washington began and then told of having been "pushed through the Jerseys without being able to make the smallest opposition." He had not yet heard of Lee's capture and was expecting Lee's army to arrive on the New Jersey side of the Delaware, not far from Easton. "If we can draw our Forces together I trust under the smiles of Providence, we may yet effect an important stroke, or at least prevent Genl Howe from executing his Plan." Gates replied that he was ill and asked permission to go to Philadelphia. In a letter that was tactful but can hardly be misread, Washington answered that he would "not object," but wished that Gates would remain with the army for two or three days.[9]

Meanwhile, ten British warships and eighty transports had been seen on Long Island Sound, off New London, Connecticut, and by letter Washington ordered Arnold to southern New England. He was to work with Major General Joseph Spencer, at sixty-two another of the old soldiers. Washington and Arnold met briefly before Arnold's departure. By then, the British had taken Newport, Rhode Island, and with the damage already done, there was less reason for Arnold to hurry away. However, Washington did not ask him to stay several days as he had with Gates. Arnold was at his best working with a superior who leaned heavily on his abilities; he was at his worst when called upon to cooperate with other officers. In the dreams of some Arnold-partisans, Arnold deserves some credit for Washington crossing the Delaware and surprising the Hessians at Trenton. An 1835 history of England is an extreme example: Arnold "suggested a daring manoeuvre, Washington readily gave into the scheme, and adopted a plan for putting it into execution." Other writers have imagined Arnold strengthening Washington's resolve.[10] But Washington's plans were well underway, and they did not include Arnold. At the last moment, Washington learned they also could not include Gates, who had followed Congress to Baltimore. Gates told James Wilkinson that the enemy would cross the Delaware and take Philadelphia before Washington realized what was happening.[11]

Among the first to cross the Delaware was John Greenwood, the teenage fifer who played a merry tune while the defeated army rowed south on Lake Champlain. While Greenwood waited on the New Jersey side for the army to march, drizzle turned to hail and snow. Men tore down rail fences to feed the fires, and Greenwood turned round and round to avoid being cooked in front and frozen behind. "None but the first officers knew where we were going or what we were going about, for it was a secret expedition, and we, the bulk of the men coming from Canada, knew not the disposition of the army we were then in, nor anything about the country," he wrote more than thirty years later.[12]

John Sullivan, who had led the retreat from Canada, had command of the right wing. Since leaving Lake Champlain in July, he had attempted to resign, was promoted to major general, taken prisoner at the Battle of Long Island, and then exchanged for General Richard Prescott, who had been captured on the St. Lawrence by Brown and Easton. Under Sullivan, Arthur St. Clair commanded the four Lake Champlain regiments, which made up about 20 percent of the men who crossed the Delaware.

In Birmingham (today's West Trenton) about five miles into their nighttime march, the two divisions, Sullivan's and Nathanael Greene's, split. Men realized that their muskets were so wet as to be useless. From Birmingham to Trenton, another four or five miles, the men struggled to dry their muskets by squibbing or firing priming powder, which makes a hiss, not a telling bang. John Stark's men were in the lead and most of them had bayonets. They encountered Hessian pickets first and pushed them back. Wilkinson, who had left Gates and attached himself to St. Clair, recalled that Stark "dealt death wherever he found resistance, and broke down all opposition before him."[13]

For teenage John Greenwood, the Battle of Trenton began when a nearby artillery horse was struck in its belly by a cannon ball, a six-pounder, he supposed. The animal was knocked onto its back and lay kicking in agony while the men moved forward. Soon through the mist and gloom of early morning, Greenwood saw several hundred Hessians drawn up in battle lines. At the orders of Major Henry Sherburne, who in May was captured while attempting to relieve the Cedars, Greenwood left his pack, never to see it again. He always remembered the "beautiful suit of blue clothes, turned up with white and silver laced."[14]

The order came to "charge bayonets and rush on!" Only one in five men near him had a bayonet, Greenwood recalled, and by then none of their muskets would fire, but "rush on we did." They faced a Hessian volley at pistol-shot range that hit no one. Then the enemy broke "and ran like so many frightened devils into the town, which was at a short distance, we after them pell-mell." Following the battle, the American army paraded through town, marched passed Hessian prisoners in a field, and then wheeled to the right, which brought them face to face with the Germans. They did it in a grand style, Greenwood remembered: "Yes, and as regular as a Prussian troop."[15]

Sullivan told Meschech Weare, president of the New Hampshire Council, "General Washington made no scruple to say publicly that the remains of the Eastern Regiments were the strength of his army, though then their numbers were comparatively speaking small.... Believe me, Sir, the Yankees took Trenton before the other Troops knew anything of the matter more than there was an engagement."[16]

※ ※ ※

While the New England regiments made their way south to the Delaware River, John Brown remained in Albany. On December 6, he sent a copy of his charges against Arnold to Theodore Sedgwick "for your amusement." In the margin he listed twenty-eight different witnesses, including Sedgwick himself, three times.[17] Then on December 10, he wrote directly to John Hancock, sending a copy of his original petition to Gates, the thirteen charges, and the exchange of outraged letters. Brown had Gates's promise to forward his petition to Congress, but he doubted if that would happen. The version that can be found in the Papers of the Continental Congress is the one Brown sent himself.[18]

Brown apologized for "the necessity of troubling you on a subject which ought to have been considered and determined by a different tribunal, agreeable to the rules of war." He requested trials for himself on Arnold's charge of plundering and for Arnold on the thirteen charges. "I must also request that proper provision be made for summoning, and compelling if need should be, such witnesses to attend the trial as shall be thought necessary." On December 26, the letter was read before Congress in Baltimore.[19]

As of January 11, Brown was listed as furloughed to Pittsfield by Schuyler. In the past two years, he may have stopped at home briefly between journeys, but this was his longest visit since the start of the war. In early February, he was back in Albany, again asking Schuyler to call an inquiry into Arnold's charges against him. Schuyler gave him permission to take the issue to George Washington.[20] In the third week of February, Brown arrived at the winter encampment in Morristown, only about thirty miles from British-held New York City but screened by the Watchung Mountains and the Great Swamp. By then, many men were sick with inoculated smallpox in the first compulsory, mass inoculation in American history. Washington had been reluctant to order inoculation, but the disease was spreading on its own among soldiers and civilians, and doctors urged him to act.[21]

Washington surely greeted Brown with respect and courtesy, what the eighteenth century praised as *condescension*. As their conversation turned from news of Ticonderoga and Albany to Brown's personal concerns, it might have become frosty. Washington was known for great calmness and bursts of anger. The suggestion that he should recall Arnold to settle an issue from the fall of 1775 must have taxed his self-control. If Brown brought up his thirteen charges, he might have provoked the hidden wrath. Washington told Schuyler simply, "I have spoke to Lt Colo. Brown about the Enquiry he prays. General Arnold being at Rhode Island & not a single Witness here, It cannot be made. he has received an Answer upon the Subject."[22]

Brown did not take Washington's *no* for the final word. He may have continued to Baltimore where Congress was meeting and made his plea to John Hancock in person. On February 22, he sent or handed Hancock another petition and scrawled a note that was abrupt and at places nearly illegible. It reads like something delivered in person, another of those hurried pieces of writing that reflect angry words. "You will oblige me in a Singular Manner to present the enclosed Petition, and let me know the State of it as soon as may be. for as to serving any longer I am determined I will not—but Shall put myself in a Situation to do myself satisfaction another Way."[23] A more eloquent resignation letter appears in a lecture on Brown given by attorney and writer Henry Cruger Van Schaack in 1857, but cannot be found in the Papers of the Continental Congress. Van Schaack, whose wealthy uncle lived in Pittsfield after the war, gathered an extensive collection of Revolutionary era documents, including Brown papers that are now lost. In the resignation letter quoted by Van Schaack, Brown asserted, "That no power on earth shall force me to serve with an officer who is impeached of treason & everything else, unless he is brought to justice." Possibly these words are Brown's summary of his resignation found in some other document. *I told the Congress* "that no power on earth…." His resignation was approved by Congress on March 15.[24]

Home in Pittsfield, Brown commissioned the printing of a handbill with his charges against Arnold and saw that it was widely circulated. The handbill has not survived. A portion appears in Van Schaack's lecture and was copied into the Pittsfield town history. The handbill listed charges against Arnold, and Brown added, "I appeal to every person of common understanding, whether in a military character or not, that, if Gen. Arnold did not know himself guilty of the charges laid against him, he would not [would he not?] have endeavored to bring himself to a trial, to clear up his character, which, had he been able to do, he certainly might have called his impeachers to account for false and malicious charges, and put the saddle upon the other horse; but, very far from this, he has used every possible art to prevent a trial, as if his character was not worth a sixpence." The rambling statement—even the confusing negatives, if they were Brown's fault—is Brown at his angriest. But it remains a good question: if the charges were nonsense, why didn't Arnold face Brown in a court?[25]

In many histories, the handbill ended with the prophetic words "Money is this man's God; and, to get enough of it, he would sacrifice his country." The statement was first published in 1838 as part of the Morgan Lewis story about Brown confronting Arnold in the officers' mess in Albany. Only later did writers claim it came from the Pittsfield handbill—and perhaps it did. But the thirteen charges were never primarily about treason and greed. Brown accused Arnold of ungentlemanly and dishonorable behavior, misconduct, disobedience, and cruelty.[26]

※ ※ ※

By February 1777, Arnold and Major General Joseph Spencer had decided on a plan to retake Newport that seemed to combine the December and May attempts at Québec. A total of eight thousand men would attack from two directions with a small feint and two fireships adding to the confusion. "We Are making every Necessary preparation of Boats, Artillery &c. which will be compleat in Two, or three, weeks, nothing will be wanting but Men, we have at Present only four Thousand," Arnold told Washington. In mid–February, Arnold traveled to Boston where he was received as a hero. Soon he was wooing a sixteen-year-old Tory beauty, "the heavenly Miss De Blois," as he called her in a letter asking for assistance from Lucy Knox, wife of Henry Knox, the chief artillery officer of the Continental Army.[27]

While Arnold was in Boston, Congress in Baltimore took up the naming of new major generals. "The debates were perplexed, inconclusive, & irksome," noted North Carolina congressman Thomas Burke. In their notes and letters, the delegates did not record what they really thought of candidates, if they knew anything about them at all. David Wooster and Benedict Arnold, number one and two in seniority among brigadiers, were mentioned for major general, but were rejected. It was said that Connecticut had more generals than the proportion of troops. The delegates feared the power of the military and wanted to make certain that the army was under civilian control. John Adams insisted that he had no fear that an officer passed over for promotion might resign. "If they have virtue they will continue with us. If not, their resignation will not hurt us." Was this a philosophical principle or did he mean Benedict Arnold? And what did the delegates say about Arnold when they were taking their refreshment or strolling about the small, muddy city? Was Arnold the hero of Valcour Island or the man who needlessly threw away the fleet? Before voting, the delegates resolved, "A due regard shall be had to the line of succession [seniority], the merit of the person proposed, and the quota of troops raised, and to be raised, by each State."[28]

Five men were chosen for major general: William Alexander, who insisted on being called Lord Stirling; Thomas Mifflin of Pennsylvania; Arthur St. Clair, the only new major general who had served in Canada or on Lake Champlain, although his actions at Trenton and Princeton may have been more to the point; Adam Stephen of Virginia; and Benjamin Lincoln of Massachusetts. The new major generals were listed in the order that they became Continental brigadiers, preserving their seniority. Lincoln, who had only been a state militia major general, was listed last. He had been clerk of the First Massachusetts Provincial Congress in the fall of 1774 when Brown was a delegate.

Two days later Congress elected ten brigadiers. Included on the list were three men who had served on Lake Champlain: Enoch Poor, John Philip de Haas, who declined, and Anthony Wayne, who was still in command at Ticonderoga. John Stark, who might seem to be an obvious choice, was omitted. When Stark learned of Congress's action, he immediately resigned his commission.[29]

In Morristown, Washington learned of the promotions from a newspaper and wrote to Arnold asking that he "not take any hasty steps" as a result. By then Arnold recognized that the attack on Newport had no chance of success and that he was now second in command in a place of no significance. "Their promoting Junior Officers to the Rank of Major Generals, I view as a very Civil way of requesting my resignation, as unqualified for the Office I hold," he wrote to Washington. He ended the letter by calling for a court of inquiry. Soon afterwards, he received bad news of another kind—Betsy Deblois was not interested in his advances. Arnold's bitterness grew letter by letter. In writing to General Gates, he blamed a villain who "has been busy with my Fame and basely slandered me." He vowed "a Brave Revenge for Injured honor." By then he was close to resigning and told Gates that he would not draw his sword until his reputation, which is "dearer than life," was cleared.[30]

Washington hoped to convince Arnold to ignore the failure of Congress to promote him. He was "not overlooked for want of Merit," Washington assured him. However, an investigation was unlikely "as no particular charge is alledged against you."[31]

※ ※ ※

Arnold left Rhode Island in April, bound for home, then Philadelphia and the resignation of his commission. He was in New Haven on April 26 when word arrived that a large British force under William Tryon, the last Royal governor of New York, had landed thirty miles to the west and marched inland toward the supply depot in Danbury, Connecticut. David Wooster, out of favor since the Canada campaign, was home in New Haven as well. The two rival brigadier generals, both of whom had been passed over for promotion, rallied the local militia and then rode west on the Post Road to Fairfield and then north to Redding where they joined General Gold Silliman and the militia. That night the sky was red as houses and supplies burned in Danbury.

In the morning, having destroyed four thousand barrels of meat, a thousand barrels of flour, five thousand pairs of shoes and stockings, and more than a thousand tents, the British marched west and then toward Long Island Sound and their transport ships. Wooster, the senior of the three generals, divided his small army. He sent Arnold and Silliman and about five hundred men cross country to intercept the

British at Ridgefield. With two hundred men, Wooster entered Danbury and then pursued the retreating enemy. He surprised the rearguard at breakfast and took prisoners. But by the time of his second attack around eleven o'clock, the British were prepared with field guns and grapeshot. It was said that Wooster turned in his saddle and yelled, "Come on, my boys! Never mind such random shots." A musket ball shattered his spine and entered his stomach; he lingered for five days.[32]

In the afternoon at Ridgefield, Arnold blocked the British retreat. His horse was shot—nine times, said the farmer who skinned the animal. He was nearly pinned underneath the fallen horse and escaped by shooting a British soldier with a pistol. The next morning, a second horse was shot from under him. Arnold, Wooster, and Silliman and their hastily mustered, poorly trained militia had surprised the raiders with the strength of their opposition. The British claimed victory, but in the end they were grateful to make it back to Long Island Sound with only (by one scholar's weighing of questionable claims from both sides) twenty-five dead, one hundred seventeen wounded, twenty-nine missing or captured, which was nearly 10 percent of the force. Still, Arnold complained about "the behaviour of the Connecticut Militia, and of the supineness of the country which suffered such an insult without resistance or proper revenge." Wisely, Congress chose to bury Arnold's criticism of his men. "You will easily perceive that publishing such things would have no good effect," wrote one Congressman.[33]

On the same day as Wooster's death, Congress promoted Arnold to major general for (in John Adams words) "his Vigilance, Activity, and Bravery." Adams toyed with the idea of having a medal struck in honor of his deeds, showing him on one side rising from under a fallen horse and on the other again mounted and receiving a "Discharge of Musquetry." Adams told Nathanael Greene, "This Picture alone, which as I am informed is true History, if Arnold did not unfortunately belong to Connecticutt, would be sufficient to make his Fortune for Life. I believe there have been few such Scenes in the world."[34]

But Congress did not restore Arnold's seniority over the five major generals promoted in February, so that whatever glowing words delegates said, he was not satisfied. By the time he arrived in Morristown on May 12, he had a copy of Brown's handbill and was prepared to use it in a masterful counterstroke. Beginning with George Washington, a series of important men were shocked by the document's contents. The outrage was genuine, but any surprise required selective memory. For more than a year, Brown had been trying to gain a hearing for himself and then attempting to provoke Arnold into demanding an inquiry. Now Arnold had the upper hand. Washington told Congress, "If any such aspersions lie against him, it is but reasonable, that he should have an Opportunity of vindicating himself, and evincing his innocence.... It is universally known, that he had always distinguished himself, as a judicious—brave Officer—of great Activity—enterprize & perseverance."[35]

Arnold made a stir upon arrival in the city. A hero already, he brought an exaggerated report that the British lost six hundred men in the Danbury raid, 30 percent of the raiders, making his resistance an extraordinary victory. He immediately demanded an inquiry from Congress. "I am publicly impeached (in particular by Lt.-Colonel Brown) of a catalogue of crimes, which, if true, ought to subject me to disgrace, infamy, and the just resentment of my country." Congress acted quickly, sending Brown's accusations to the Board of War and awarding Arnold a "properly caparisoned" horse—a mount with the finest saddle, reins, and trappings—for his gallant conduct during the Danbury Raid.[36]

Arnold spent the evening of May 21 with the War Board. In making his case, he had the support of his friend Charles Carroll, former commissioner to Canada and a member of the board, and whatever copies of letters he had gathered from his time on Lake Champlain. But this was not an inquiry with two sides, witnesses, and cross-examination. Even before the board met with Arnold, Congressman Richard Henry Lee told Thomas Jefferson: "One plan, now in frequent use, is, to assassinate the Characters of the friends of America in every place, and by every means. At this moment, they are now reading in Congress, an audacious attempt of this kind against the brave General Arnold."[37]

"He has been basely slandered and libelled," board member John Adams wrote to Abigail before dawn on the morning after the hearing. "The Regulars say, 'he fought like Julius Caesar.'" The next day a one-sided report was read before Congress. The board was entirely satisfied "concerning the general's character and conduct, so cruelly and groundlessly aspersed in the publication." In his letter to Abigail, Adams added, "I am wearied to Death with the Wrangles between military officers, high and low. They Quarrell like Cats and Dogs. They worry one another like Mastiffs. Scrambling for Rank and Pay like Apes for Nutts."[38]

Fourteen

"An army flushed with victory"

Ticonderoga and Mount Independence were safe from attack until spring, but they were weaker than ever before. In December 1776, cold besieged the garrison of 2,500 men, which shrank to fewer than 1,200 by the end of January 1777. Plans for the winter called for men to build more blockhouses, strengthen the old fort and the boom that stretched across the lake to block ships, build a hundred gun platforms and a thousand handbarrows (a barrow without a wheel to be carried by two men), and repair shovels, picks, spades, and axes. Instead, it was enough to chop and haul wood to avoid freezing to death. Sometimes men burned the abandoned huts from summer and the tangle of branches in front of their fortifications. Disease stalked the camps. Once men from New Jersey fought Pennsylvanians for possession of two freshly dug graves. There is no record of how many died or where they were buried.[1]

As the season turned toward spring, reinforcements straggled in, but they were poorly equipped. Some were without muskets and were issued spears as if they were Renaissance pikemen. Others had to borrow shoes before going on patrol. General Anthony Wayne pleaded with Philip Schuyler for help. "I must beg, sir, that you would once more endeavor to rouse the public officers in those [New England] States from their shameful lethargy before it be too late. I do assure you there is not one moment to spare in bringing in troops and necessary supplies."[2]

But too many generals and politicians believed their own propaganda that raw courage, not preparation, had turned back the British invasion in 1776—and that what had happened once would happen again. Meanwhile, Horatio Gates and Philip Schuyler feuded over command of the Northern Army, and no one prioritized the overwhelming number of construction projects. Distant leaders agreed that the forts were secure. When John Hancock ordered Arthur St. Clair north in April, he told him what he'd learned from Washington: "No serious attempt would be made upon Ticonderoga; at most it would be a diversion only." The British would shift much of their army from Canada as soon as the St. Lawrence opened for navigation, Washington believed.[3]

On June 13, the day that St. Clair took command, two captives were brought to Ticonderoga. Questioned, they claimed that the enemy under General John Burgoyne would be at the forts in force in two weeks. A second British army would advance from the west on the Mohawk River. In all, ten thousand men were aimed at Albany. This news was accurate: Burgoyne intended to seize Albany from two directions and, with the cooperation of a large army under General William Howe coming up

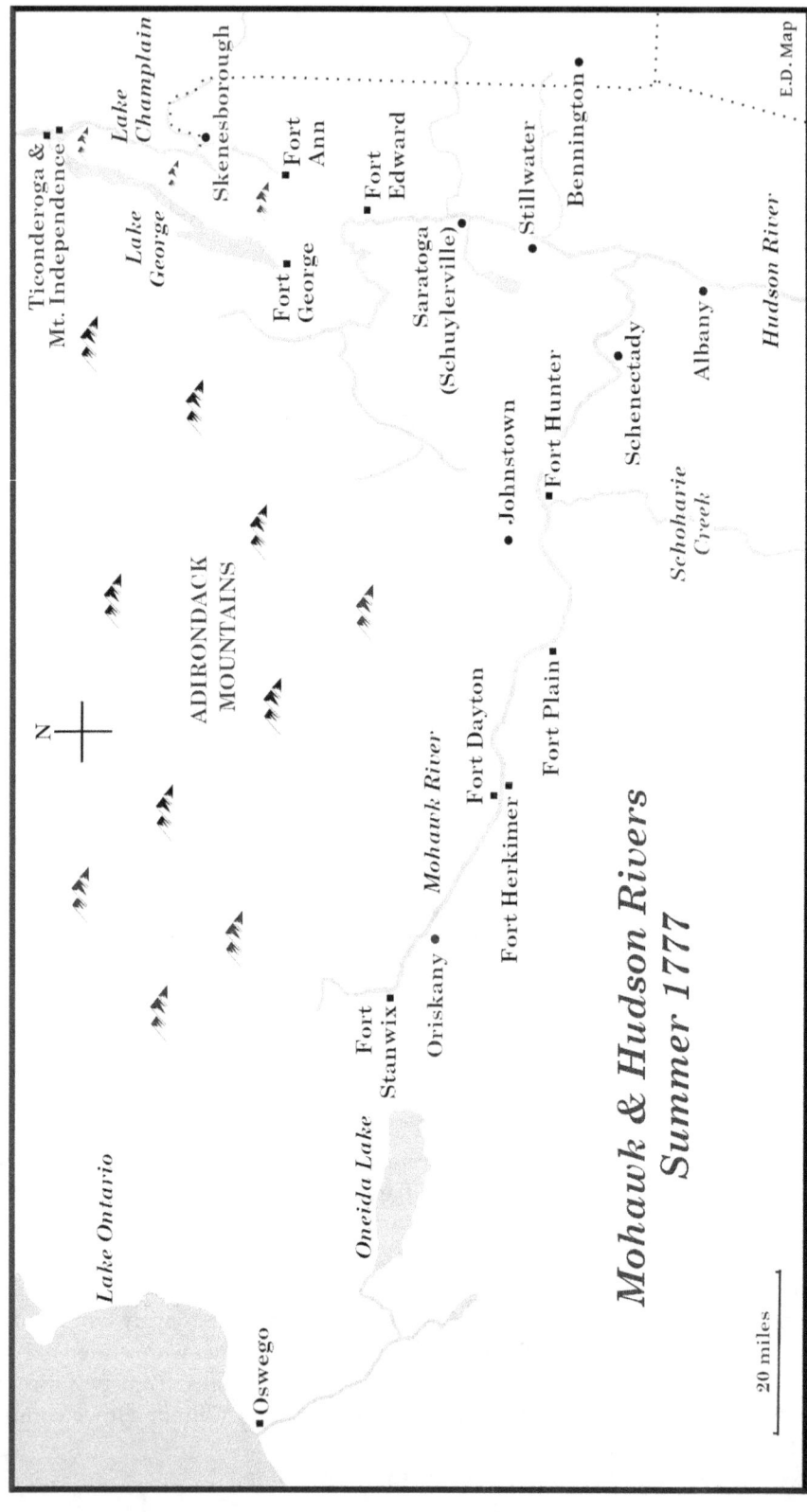

the Hudson River, divide the mid–Atlantic states from New England—and end the war. But the threat on Lake Champlain seemed farfetched to St. Clair and then to Schuyler. When Washington heard the intelligence, he dismissed it as well: "I cannot conceive that it will be in the power of the Enemy to carry it into execution." He was convinced the garrison at Ticonderoga was "sufficient to hold it against any Attack."[4]

On June 23, a scout reported that the British and many Indians were at William Gilliland's settlement of Willsboro. Even this intelligence lagged behind events; the next day the Regulars were at Crown Point. Another two days and the news was that a party of five hundred Indians and Tories had been sent up Otter River to Middlebury and into the heart of the territory that would soon be called Vermont. Still, St. Clair hoped that it was all a feint. "From their manner of beginning the campaign, I conclude they are either in full force or very weak, and hope, by letting loose the Indians, to intimidate us. I incline to believe the last." Finally, he learned the hard truth: he was facing a massive, well-prepared invasion that was quickly bearing down on the forts.

Major General Arthur St. Clair arrived at Ticonderoga thinking the fort was safe for the summer. In three weeks, his army was in retreat. Sketch by John Trumbull—William Henry Smith, *The St. Clair Papers* (1882).

On July 1, enemy bateaux could be seen at Three-Mile Point, named for its distance from the old fort. A day later, St. Clair ordered everything at Lake George Landing carried away or burned, and the forts lost their main connection to supplies and reinforcements from the south. On the same day, the British seized the outpost on Mount Hope, a mile-and-a-half northwest of the old fort, and the armies skirmished at the French Lines. Meanwhile, British gunners prepared batteries facing the fortifications on the Ticonderoga side. Germans from Braunschweig (Brunswick in English) worked their way south along the east shore, opposite Mount Independence. It would only be time before they cut off the retreat from Mount Independence on a rough military road into the Green Mountain territory. On July 4, the British mounted two 12-pounders on to the heights of Mount Defiance, sometimes called the Sugar Loaf or Sugar Hill, southwest of the American fortifications, opening the American camps and fortifications to crossfire. Years later, St. Clair described the state of his garrison: "Had every man I had, been disposed in single file on the different works and along the lines of defence, they would have been scarcely within the reach of each other's voices."[5] He was exaggerating only slightly. On July 5, he called a council of war which agreed unanimously to abandon the forts that night.

On the same day, John Brown and the Berkshire County militia were marching north to reinforce Ticonderoga. Arnold was in Philadelphia preparing to resign from the Continental Army.

※ ※ ※

Early on the morning of July 7, General Schuyler left Albany to take command on Lake Champlain. Each letter from St. Clair had been more discouraging; Indians were raiding the Mohawk frontier and no troops could be moved from there to Ticonderoga. Twenty miles north of Albany, an express messenger brought word from Brigadier General Ebenezer Learned stationed at Fort Edward that the army at Ticonderoga had retreated. A detachment that sailed south on the narrow lake had been routed in Skenesborough. Schuyler sent the news immediately to Washington with his own pessimistic conclusions. Within hours, his worst fears were confirmed. Everything had been lost; St. Clair's whereabouts were unknown; and Schuyler had no idea what route the enemy might take. He told Washington in his second letter of the day, "My prospect of preventing them from penetrating is not much—They have an Army flushed with Victory, plentifully provided with provisions Cannon and every Warlike Store—Our Army, if it should once more collect is weak in Numbers, dispirited, naked, in a Manner, destitute of provisions; without Camp Equipage with little Ammunition, and not a single piece of Cannon."[6]

Schuyler gathered his small force in Fort Edward, a village located as far north as small boats could go on the Hudson before encountering rapids and falls. He wished for news of St. Clair and the army, but he knew only that they had marched into the Green Mountain territory. When Samuel Adams heard a report of Schuyler's ignorance, he commented, "There is something droll enough in a Generals [sic] not knowing where to find the main Body of his army." He wanted Schuyler replaced by Gates.[7]

Brown and the Third Regiment of the Berkshire County militia were already in Fort Edward under command of General John Fellows of Sheffield, Massachusetts. Fellows had been a delegate to the fall 1774 provincial congress. Referred to in the records as *Major* Fellows, he was given committee work on the province's preparedness for war. By spring he was a colonel in the Massachusetts forces. He led a regiment at the Battle of Bunker Hill and then served with Washington outside Boston. The Berkshire militia had been called up when it was clear Ticonderoga was threatened. Had Burgoyne been slower, they might have reinforced the forts.[8]

It is possible to imagine what Brown was thinking. Men who had come through the retreat from Canada and then stopped Carleton in October 1776 were shocked. All that they had struggled for was lost without a fight. The Rev. Thomas Allen, a pastor from Pittsfield, was a chaplain at the forts and wrote in the *Connecticut Courant* that most of the garrison was filled with "astonishment, grief, and indignation" at the surprise retreat. Some men "vented their grief by tears and lamentation, and others by execrations and bitter reproaches." Patrick Cogan, the quartermaster in Cilley's New Hampshire regiment, wrote to his former commander, John Stark, now a civilian, telling him, "Such a retreat was never heard of since the Creation of the world." It was needless and chaotic, Cogan maintained—and no field officers were consulted. "Surely we were fifty thousand times better off than General Sullivan was in Canada last year; our men was in high spirits, and determined to a man to stick by the lines till they lost their lives, rather than quit so advantageous a Post." And when Washington received the news, he commented, "The Evacuation of Tyconderoga and Mount

Independance is an Event of Chagrine & Surprize not apprehended, nor within the Compass of my reasoning."[9]

Historians have been much kinder, seeing in the retreat the seeds of Burgoyne's defeat at Saratoga three months later. Had St. Clair remained, the argument goes, the forts would have been surrounded and cut off from supplies and reinforcements. The surrender of the entire garrison was the likely outcome. As it was, Burgoyne, who was prepared for a lengthy siege, not a quick pursuit, became overconfident and marched south away from his supplies, deep into enemy territory. But that is hindsight. In July 1777, with the forts on Lake Champlain captured in a few days, Schuyler did not have the men or resources to stop the invasion from reaching the Hudson and Albany.

On July 7, Seth Warner blocked the British and German pursuit at settlement called Hubbardton, high in the hills of Vermont. By eighteenth-century standards, the battle was an American defeat, but Warner protected St. Clair's retreating army. Another battle was fought in Fort Ann, New York, on July 8. The British claimed the field and victory, but withdrew to Skenesborough.

In Fort Edward, Schuyler ordered the Berkshire County militia toward Fort Ann to fell trees, destroy bridges, and seize cattle and wagons. In the fall of 1776, when the 3rd New Jersey Regiment marched north to reinforce the forts, one man called the route to Fort Ann "the worst and most disagreeable swampy road that ever was." Skenesborough is only eleven miles from Fort Ann, but the road passed through a narrow marshy valley that followed twisting Wood Creek. During the summer of 1776, the road was used to supply and reinforce the shipyard in Skenesborough, and Wood Creek was opened as much as possible so that lumber from a sawmill in Fort Ann could reach the yard. But this was a losing battle, and by fall the creek was clogged with logs.[10]

At Schuyler's orders, men with axes made the roads even worse and the creek impassable. It was dangerous work. Indian scouts might be hidden in the forest. Falling trees and overhanging branches could surprise a man no matter how skilled he was with an ax. One soldier in Brown's regiment, Josiah Ball of Stockbridge, suffered a broken arm and a broken leg and was "greatly disabled." In 1780, the Massachusetts Congress awarded him one-third of his pay as compensation, backdated to January 1779.[11]

The road from Skenesborough to Fort Ann and south to Fort Edward posed a dilemma for Burgoyne. Critics then and now have argued that he made the wrong decision and lost the advantages gained at Ticonderoga. Perhaps he should have returned to the forts with his entire force and taken the traditional water route to Fort George and the good road to Fort Edward. His cannon needed to go that way in any case. Or perhaps he should have maintained a force in Fort Ann, continually strengthening it, even if he was open to attack from Schuyler. Instead, his army remained in Skenesborough, and the only risk he took was being too cautious.

Schuyler's delaying action played a part in slowing Burgoyne, but how much? Burgoyne wrote on July 11 from Skenesborough, "I am indispensably obliged to wait some time in this position to clear roads and make bridges." But he was also waiting for all his provisions and tents to catch up, so although the British army was put to "incredible toil" (as Sergeant Roger Lamb put it), clearing the road and constructing some forty bridges, they did so "with a spirit and alacrity which could not be exceeded." Two years later, deputy quarter-master general Captain John Money

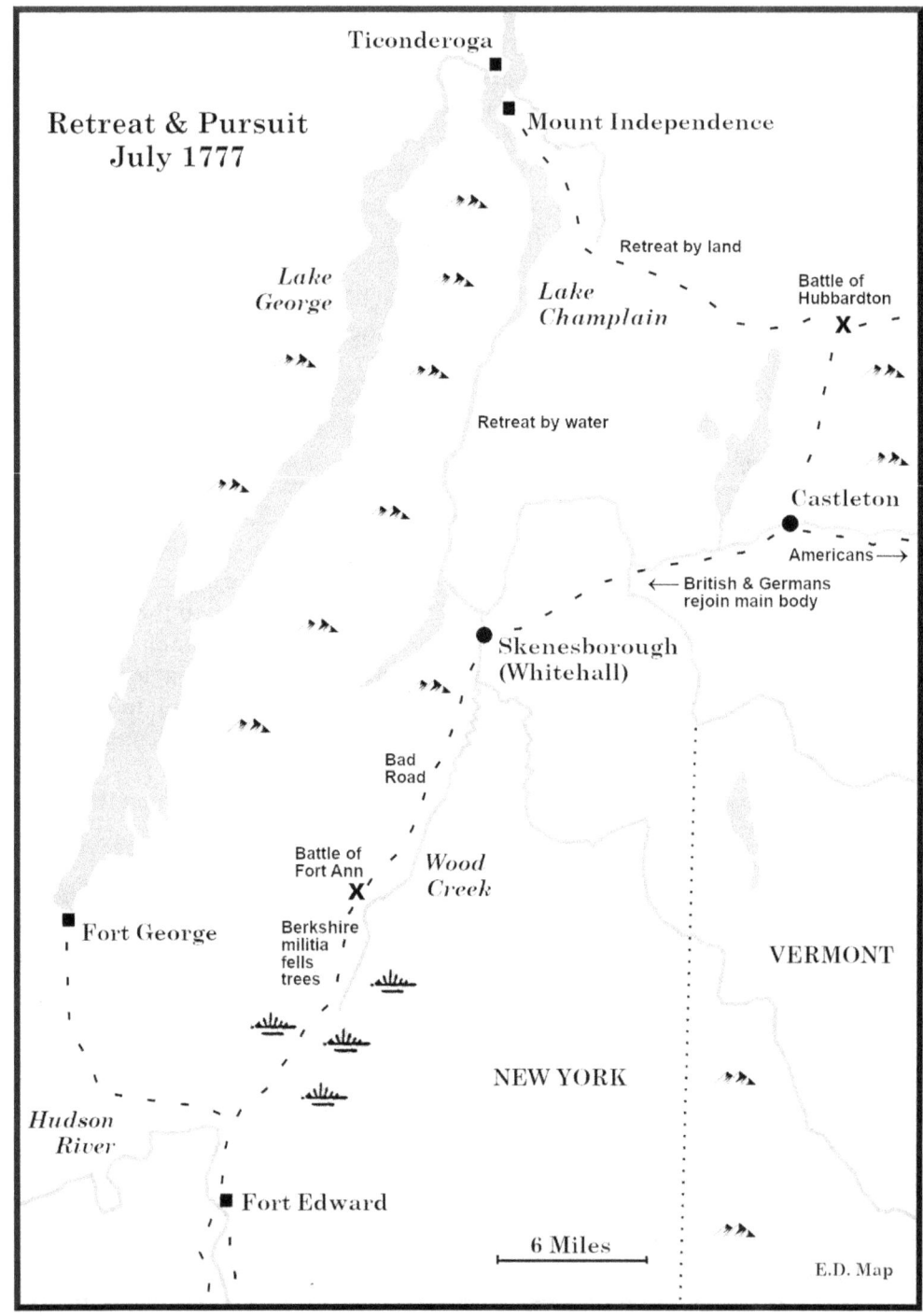

The American retreat from Ticonderoga and Mount Independence began on the night of July 5–6, 1777. After battles at Hubbardton and Fort Ann, Burgoyne consolidated his army at Skenesborough. To slow his advance, John Brown and the Berkshire County militia felled trees along the bad road from Skenesborough to Fort Ann and Fort Edward.

testified before the House of Commons that it took six or seven days to build the roads from Skenesborough through Fort Ann to Fort Edward, but obstructions were not the problem. "The rebels had cut down some few trees which took the provincials in our army some few hours to clear." Of course, that is what you might expect a British officer who was loyal to his commander to say under the circumstances.[12]

The Berkshire militia did not stay in the north long. By July 23, Schuyler told Washington, "about three hundred remain and I am morally sure most of these will run off." In Half Moon, just north of the Mohawk River, General Fellows learned from a friend that couriers between Burgoyne and General Howe in New York City exchanged dispatches on Sundays about halfway between the two armies. Fellows believed his source—"a person of real Dependence," he told Washington—and sent John Brown back to Fort Edward with the information he had learned. According to Fellows's source, Burgoyne would move from Fort Ann in a few days as soon as his train of artillery had arrived from Lake George. Fort Schuyler/Stanwix was threatened from the west by a large force that "had no Doubt of carrying the Place with little Difficulty."[13] And "General [William] Howe was to make a Diversion on the Eastern Coast with part of his Force and with the Remainder to come up the Hudson's River as far as Peekskill to divide our Force."[14]

The surviving details about the British messenger, Fellows, Brown, and Schuyler are confusing and may have more to say about the relationship between Schuyler and New Englanders than they do about what actually happened. Schuyler was outraged that Fellows had not somehow seized the courier and the dispatches, and instead had sent Brown thirty-six miles to Fort Edward "to know what was proper to be done." Schuyler's annoyance was constant in his dealings with Yankees and should not be taken as evidence that Fellows and Brown were neglectful. But whatever Brown said in explanation and whatever Schuyler heard, Schuyler ordered Brown and a small party of men to find the courier.

Somehow Brown managed to seize a Mr. Arthur (the first mention of a name in these bewildering accounts) and to turn him over to a cavalry captain coming north from Washington's army. To Brown's embarrassment—"mortification," he told Schuyler from Kinderhook, New York, in a description that could come from an eighteenth-century novel—Arthur got away. "About Midnight thro' a small window in a Bedroom in the Chamber—He went out headlong & fell on the Roof of a Stoop from whence he rolled into the mud & so escaped." Brown had warned the captain to guard the prisoners closely. "I take the Liberty to give You this particular Account as I wash my hands of any neglect whatever," Brown wrote before leaving for Pittsfield, twenty-five miles away.[15]

Schuyler was once again disgusted. Brown's letter contained no useful information and left it unclear whether Arthur was the actual courier. By then, August 1, Schuyler knew that Howe had sailed into the Atlantic, but he suspected the purpose was to draw Washington toward Philadelphia before turning the British fleet up the Hudson.[16]

※ ※ ※

During the summer of 1777, every important officer seemed to have a grievance. On July 1, Nathanael Greene, Henry Knox, and John Sullivan all threatened to resign over the rumored appointment of Philippe Charles Tronson du Coudray, another self-important foreigner, as a major general and commander of the artillery. Congress responded by telling Washington to reprimand the generals. Their letters were "an invasion of the liberties of the people ... indicating a want of confidence in the justice of Congress" and if they did not wish to serve under the authority of Congress, "they shall be at liberty to resign their commissions and retire." They didn't resign, but the issue was not entirely resolved until September when Coudray's frightened horse fell from a ferry on the Schuykill River and the general drowned.[17]

On July 11, Benedict Arnold did resign. He had never given up on having his promotion to major general backdated so that he would once again outrank the five men appointed in February. His anger grew as he had to deal with *Major General* Thomas Mifflin in Philadelphia and saw *Major General* St. Clair gain command at Ticonderoga. His resignation, he told Congress, did not come "from a Spirit of Resentment tho' my Feelings are deeply wounded." His highest ambition was "that of being a free citizen of America." By then Washington had received Schuyler's first letter of July 7, with the account of the retreat from Ticonderoga. Knowing Schuyler's pessimism, Washington suspected that the news was "premature and groundless," but he recognized the need for a response and suggested to John Hancock that Arnold be sent north to command the militia.[18]

Without acknowledging his resignation, Congress ordered Arnold to headquarters in Morristown. In his response, Arnold made the nicest point of honor. He would follow Washington's orders regarding the militia "with whom I shall be happy as a private citizen to render my country every service in my power." Late on July 17, Arnold reached Washington's headquarters, now near the New York–New Jersey border. Washington told Schuyler, "Altho' he conceives himself, had his promotion been regular, superior in Command to General St. Clair, yet he generously, upon this Occasion, lays aside his Claim, and will create no dispute should the good of the Service require him to act in Concert."[19]

By the evening of July 22, Arnold was back with the Northern Army, which was preparing to retreat from Fort Edward in the morning. Schuyler worried that he might be accused of abandoning another post. "It was once a regular Fortification," he told Washington, "but there is nothing but the ruins of it left, and they are so totally defenceless that I have frequently galloped my Horse in on one Side and out of the other." And even if the old fort by the river was in repair, it was dominated by a hill on which the British could place cannon.[20]

Schuyler welcomed Arnold's return and gave him command of the division on the west side of the Hudson, putting the river between him and Arthur St. Clair, the other major general in his command. Within days, Arnold provoked St. Clair, who knew all along that his reputation might not recover from the abandonment of Ticonderoga and Mount Independence. St. Clair told Washington in an aggrieved letter, "Both at Albany on his way up, and here before he could possibly be properly informed to enable him to make any judgement at all, [Arnold] publicly condemned the retreat from Tyconderoga, and declared that some person must be sacrificed to an injured Country." St. Clair spoke to Arnold—"gently remonstrated," he explained to Washington—but Arnold said that he did not remember saying anything like that. "If he had said any thing, it was only repeating the Sentiments of the Army & Country, or a few questions he had jestingly put to General Paterson."[21]

At the direction of Congress, St. Clair was soon recalled and then court-martialed for abandoning the forts. Although acquitted "with the highest honour," he never again received a battlefield command in the Revolution. He was the next-to-last president of the Continental Congress and governor of the Northwest Territory. In 1791, he fought a confederation of Natives in a battle that is sometimes called simply "St. Clair's Defeat." His losses were greater than Custer's at the Little Bighorn.[22]

As he faced Burgoyne on the Hudson, Schuyler saw himself as continually betrayed and put upon. "It is a melancholy consideration that while our Force is daily diminishing the Enemy increase theirs by a continued Requisition of Tories in very considerable Numbers," he wrote John Hancock on August 4. Schuyler estimated he had four thousand troops: "If Men, one third of which are Negroes, Boys, and Men too aged for Field or indeed any other Service can with Propriety be called Troops." He blamed "the States from whence these Troops are come," meaning New England.[23] On the same day in Philadelphia, Congress named Horatio Gates as Schuyler's replacement.

Schuyler's racist remarks on Black soldiers cannot be allowed to pass without comment. Blacks served in New England town militia companies and enlisted in northwestern New England regiments. Sometimes these men can be identified by their names—a Roman name such as Caesar or Pompey—or by a note in a muster roll that the man was a "negro." Pittsfield soldiers included Jaffry, who fought at the Battle of Bennington; Titus, who died in the service in 1780; and Prince, who was part of the crews that felled trees near Fort Ann to slow Burgoyne's advance. Most Black soldiers in New England were free; others were still enslaved, serving as substitutes in the promise of freedom; some were escaped slaves starting their lives over. They were privates, servants, and laborers, but in a world of inequality, the army might still be a step up. In the fall of 1776, Captain Persifor Frazer of Anthony Wayne's Fourth Pennsylvania Battalion was as shocked as Schuyler at the New England troops. He told his wife, "The miserable appearance and what is worse the miserable behaviour of the Yankees is sufficient to make one sick of the service ... among them there is the strangest mixture of Negroes, Indians and Whites with Old Men and mere children." When he discovered that his escaped slave, Jacob Down, was enlisted in a Massachusetts regiment at Mount Independence, Frazer seized the man. Down's captain paid fifty-one dollars for his freedom.[24]

※ ※ ※

Schuyler still did not know William Howe's intentions, although he found it hard to believe Howe would not cooperate with Burgoyne, for it was the worst nightmare of the American leaders. Although Washington received a report of the British fleet of 228 sails off Cape May, New Jersey, he still believed that Howe was "practicing a deep feint" and his object all along was the North River, the Hudson. The more Washington thought about the mystery, the more ways he saw that Howe might help Burgoyne. He might land in Connecticut, Massachusetts, or even Rhode Island and divert American forces from the Hudson River. Schuyler shared Washington's worries, but the news upon which he based his concerns was older.[25]

On August 7, Schuyler learned of the Battle of Oriskany, fought near the Mohawk River, ninety miles west of Albany. The Tryon County militia going to the relief of Fort Schuyler was "entirely cut to Pieces" and most of the field officers killed. Schuyler first heard that General Nicholas Herkimer was among the dead; in fact, he survived the battle to die ten days later when an unskilled surgeon attempted to amputate his leg. Two days after the news from Oriskany, the resolution from Congress relieving Schuyler of command reached him in Albany where he had been negotiating with Indians and worrying about the threat to the Mohawk Valley.[26]

Through depression, pessimism, illness, and a belief that everyone was against him, Schuyler carried on. "I return to the Army immediately, shall surrender the Command and obey the Order of Congress without delay," he told John Hancock. Then he made two crucial decisions. He approved a plan proposed by Benjamin Lincoln, John Stark, who was back as a New Hampshire brigadier, and Seth Warner to harass the enemy's rear from the east side of the Hudson. Militia regiments were ordered to Bennington, which now claimed to be in the independent state of Vermont. They had gathered there when Germans attempted to raid the town and a Continental supply depot. And he sent Brigadier General Ebenezer Learned's brigade of eight to nine hundred men to relieve Fort Schuyler.[27]

Learned is a man whose name appears in any narrative of the campaign that ended at Saratoga, but never with enough details to make him come alive, so he fights his battles in the shadow of better-known leaders. From Oxford, Massachusetts, he was forty-nine in summer of 1777, one of the old men, and in poor health. Colonel John Brooks, a young lieutenant colonel at twenty-five, recalled that Learned was "a weak man," and the description has stuck. But James Wilkinson, usually a cynic, referred to him as "a brave old soldier." Like John Brown, Learned was a delegate to the Massachusetts Provincial Congress before he was swept into the war.[28]

The story of Learned's relief expedition is encrusted with legend, and has become another of Arnold's great triumphs. Dates, distances, and documents suggest there is a richer story, but it is easier to focus on one man we have all heard about. In the traditional account of the beginnings of the expedition, Schuyler called together his officers in Stillwater on August 12, proposed a relief expedition, and asked for a brigadier to volunteer. Accounts of the meeting appear in Benson Lossing's *Life and Times of Philip Schuyler* (1860) and then in Isaac Arnold's biography of Arnold (1880). The gist can be found in recent histories as well. In the tale, Schuyler's officers were opposed to a plan to divide the army in the face of the enemy. One commented, "He means to weaken the army." Schuyler was so exasperated that he bit down and snapped his clay pipe. But the "brave and impulsive Arnold, ever ready for deeds of daring" volunteered, even though he was a major general, not a brigadier. The next morning, they drummed up eight hundred more volunteers and set off to rescue Fort Schuyler.[29]

The facts are not as melodramatic. On August 11, a day before the purported meeting with officers, Schuyler ordered Learned's brigade to march from Van Schaick Island at the mouth of the Mohawk River. On the day of the alleged meeting, he wrote Herkimer, who had four days to live, that Learned's brigade was on the way. Arnold received his orders in Stillwater on August 13. Schuyler thanked him for having "offered" to take command on the Mohawk. But the Continental troops he commanded were already two days into their hundred-mile march to Fort Schuyler. Arnold did not catch the expedition until August 20 at Fort Dayton in today's Herkimer, about twenty-five miles from Fort Schuyler.[30]

Arnold was at Fort Dayton when he received a letter from Horatio Gates. Schuyler had been relieved of command; Gates was soon to be in charge; and Congress had once again refused to restore Arnold's seniority. Arnold wrote a bold reply, promising,

Fourteen. "An army flushed with victory"

"You will hear of my being victorious, or no more; and as soon as the safety of this part of the country will permit, I will fly to your assistance." Then he called a council of war, which resolved that "it would be imprudent and putting too much to the hazard to attempt the march to the relief of Fort Schuyler, until the army is reinforced." It is unclear if Arnold favored the decision or believed he had no choice but to go along with timid officers. He was angry that he received so little support from Tryon County. "No Dependence can be placed on the Militia of this County, Notwithstanding my most earnest Intreaties, I have not been able to Collect one hundred," he told Gates after the council.[31]

So instead of marching toward Fort Schuyler, Arnold attempted a trick suggested by John Brooks of the 8th Massachusetts Regiment. Hon Yost Schuyler, a Loyalist who had been sentenced to be hanged as a spy, was freed to carry an exaggerated description of Arnold's force to the Natives besieging Fort Schuyler. In traditional accounts, Hon Yost was mad but cunning, and Indians held him in respect because of his bizarre and prophetic behavior. The story was summed up in the title of a 1956 article in *American Heritage*: "How a Madman Helped Save the Colonies: Fort Stanwix was doomed—until the Iroquois heard the ravings of Hon Yost Schuyler."[32]

In too many histories, when the Natives learned from Hon Yost Schuyler that "Dark Eagle" or "Heap Fighting Chief" was advancing with more men than the leaves on the trees, they ran in panic. They were simple-minded enough to be fooled by Hon Yost's exaggerations, but wiser than the Continental Congress in recognizing Arnold's abilities. These "Indian names" for Arnold are fake. Arnold was first called Dark Eagle by an Indian character in an 1847 gothic romance titled *Washington and his Generals: or, Legends of the Revolution*, written by George Lippard. Although little known today, Lippard may have been "the most read writer in the United States" from 1844 to his death at the age of thirty-one in 1854.[33] He was a close friend of Edgar Allan Poe and supported him when Poe was down and out in Philadelphia. In the spectrum of historical writing from academic to bodice-ripper, Lippard's work was at the low end, appealing to a popular audience at the dawn of the era of mass communication. Still, in the introduction to *Washington and his Generals*, C. Chauncey Burr, another Poe friend, who somehow became a

George Lippard may have been the most popular writer in the United States when he created the name "Dark Eagle" for Benedict Arnold and helped to make him a romantic hero. Library of Congress.

reverend, called Lippard a genius and compared him to Byron, Shakespeare, Burns, and Keats. He wrote, "Altogether we take this to be the best book that has been written on this portion of our history. In the dull popular idea of history, this book is not merely history. It is something more. It is a series of battle pictures; with all the truth of history in them, where the heroes are made living, present and visible to our senses."[34]

In the "Third Book" of *Washington and his Generals*, which features Arnold, the Indian Natanis offers a prophecy during the march to Québec: "The wilderness will yield to the Dark-Eagle, but the Rock will defy him. The Dark-Eagle will soar aloft to the sun. Nations will behold him, and shout his praises. Yet when he soars highest, his fall is more certain. When his wing brushes the sky, the arrow will pierce his heart!"[35] *Dark Eagle* is so evocative of a certain image of Arnold that is the title of books and chapters in books and appears in many histories as if Natives actually used the name.[36]

Heap Fighting Chief, which historians now avoid as racist, comes from a 1903 biography of Arnold that imagined how Natives talked, but the name wasn't even in quotes. It next appeared in a 1917 novel written as if it was Arnold's memoir. It can be found in a respected biography from 1953, which was reprinted by an academic press as late as the 1990s.[37]

By now careful writers go along with the substance of tale: Arnold won a victory with no bloodshed because his name alone was worth several regiments. Learned's actual regiments, and the men who stubbornly held Fort Schuyler, get less credit.

The real reason the Natives fled and the Tryon County militia did not turn out quickly in numbers that satisfied Arnold: neither side wanted a repeat of the carnage at Oriskany. Before Hon Yost ran into camp with his news, British commander Lieutenant Colonel Barry St. Leger concluded, "The same zeal no longer animated the Indians; they complained of our thinness of troops, and their former losses." Through Hon Yost and Indian scouts also carrying misinformation, St. Leger learned first that Arnold was advancing rapidly with two thousand men, then three thousand. St. Leger suspected treason and cowardice, but could not restrain his Indian allies. Major Robert Cochran, former Green Mountain Boy and Brown's friend, led a party out of the fort and discovered that the siege was broken and the enemy gone.[38]

Arnold joined Gates on Van Schaick Island on August 30 as the army was preparing to move north.

※ ※ ※

An argument can be made that Gates arrived at dawn and took credit for the sunrise. In his memoir, James Wilkinson wrote, "I loved Gates, but I loved justice better; and my heart bled for Schuyler, when he was obliged to resign the fruits of his labours, and sorrowfully laid down his command." If Schuyler had remained, the army would have soon moved north once again (as Schuyler told Washington), "taking such Ground, where they [the enemy] must attack to a Disadvantage, should our Force be inadequate to face them in the Field." The elements of an American victory along the Hudson River were nearly all in place.[39]

But for many men, the return of Gates marked the turning point. Henry Dearborn, who had made the march to Québec with Arnold, noted in his journal for August 19, "Genrl Gates takes Command of the Northern army this Day which I think will Put a New face on our affairs." From the 6th Massachusetts Regiment, the colonel and three lieutenant colonels told Gates, "Gladness appear'd in every Countenance, Joy circulated thro the Camp."[40]

On September 7, Gates issued orders that the army would advance north the next day. "Marched in the Front with the Carpenters & pioneers," engineer Jeduthan Baldwin wrote in his daily journal. The advanced party, which included Daniel Morgan's riflemen, reached Stillwater about noon. Two hours later Baldwin's men began to construct a float bridge across the Hudson. Meanwhile, the army moved another three miles north to Bemis Heights and began digging and felling trees for fortifications. Students of the Saratoga Campaign have always enjoyed arguing about who selected the ground that the Americans occupied. Perhaps farmer John Neilson suggested the position. Maybe Schuyler first recognized this ground where the enemy "must attack to a Disadvantage." Historians who are certain of Arnold's military genius see his hand in choosing the location. James Wilkinson gave himself a sizable share of the credit. Biographers of Thaddeus Kosciuszko are certain the young Polish engineer first saw the potential of this high ground. John Armstrong, who was an aide to Gates, recalled sixty years later that when Dr. Benjamin Rush was overly "lavish" in his praise of Gates, the general replied, "Stop, Doctor, stop, … the great tacticians of the campaign, were *hills* and *forests*, which a young Polish engineer was skillful enough to select for my encampment."[41]

Under Kosciuszko's direction, Bemis Heights became a formidable position that could block Burgoyne's advance and force him to attack whether he wanted to or not. At the eastern redoubts, American guns on a one-hundred-foot bluff could dominate the flats and the road to Albany that paralleled the river. Kosciuszko's entrenchments stretched three-quarters of a mile to the west, climbing into the hills. At first seven thousand men began digging and hauling logs, and the number swelled daily as more militia arrived. In mid–September, Burgoyne's army crossed to the west side of the Hudson at Saratoga on a bridge built upon bateaux. Afterwards the bridge was broken up, committing the army to reaching Albany and making a battle inevitable.

Fifteen

"The mighty army of the continent"

After the Berkshire County militia felled trees to slow Burgoyne's advance, John Brown rode to Boston to rally the state government and so missed the Battle of Bennington. In his absence, the Pittsfield men marched under command of Lieutenant Colonel David Rossiter, although many writers have preferred telling amusing stories about Pittsfield's militant pastor, Thomas Allen. In the best known, the Reverend Allen arrived at the height of a rainstorm on August 15 and demanded that General Stark lead the men into battle. In this charming tale, John Stark replied, "If the lord should once more give us sunshine, and I do not give you fighting enough, I will never ask you to come again." The next day western Massachusetts militia attacked a redoubt built by Loyalists and drove them across the Walloomsac River. Vermont and New Hampshire men surprised a German hilltop fortification from the north and west while the bulk of the New Hampshire militia seized the key bridge across the river. Militia from three states could take credit; Seth Warner's Continentals arrived in time to defeat German reinforcements.[1]

By early September, Massachusetts militia reached Bennington in great numbers and were ordered north by Benjamin Lincoln. The operation was a version of Schuyler's Lincoln-Stark-Warner expedition that had been interrupted by the Battle of Bennington, but with differences. Stark and the New Hampshiremen were out of the picture. Many of them were suffering from measles and were already counting the days until their enlistments were up. Stark himself had been sick since the battle; he was cantankerous and already had his moment of glory. Rather than march through Cambridge and White Creek (today's Salem), New York, where Loyalists could easily report their movements to Burgoyne, the Massachusetts expedition followed the Mettowee Valley to the stronghold of Pawlet, forty miles north of Bennington. At Pawlet, there is a confusion of hills and mountains where the Mettowee River turns northwest, winding towards Skenesborough. "Not unlike *my ideas* of the strength of Thermopylae," Lincoln wrote a few years later, referring to the narrow pass where the Spartans fought a massive Persian army in 480 BCE. The new expedition had the goals of freeing prisoners and destroying supplies and boats at Ticonderoga. Richard Varick, a Schuyler supporter, called it an "airy Scheme" that would keep Lincoln and the men under his command away from the real action.[2]

Most often the expedition is called "Brown's Raid," although some historians have maintained that the name is a misnomer. Perhaps it should be the "Pawlet Expedition," as a more complete description of three simultaneous movements against Burgoyne's army. Lincoln had overall authority, but he was in the north for less than two weeks, never participated in the actual raid, and was ordered south by Gates while the outcome was still to be decided. Lincoln was a heavy man, not used to wilderness marching, and he did not know the lake or its forts. Although he had ties of class and background to the Massachusetts militia officers, he had never commanded them. In fact, he had never commanded a field operation, let alone one in the wilderness.

Lincoln gave Massachusetts militia brigadier Jonathan Warner of Worcester County "general direction" of the expedition, and told the Council of Massachusetts that he had "the greatest confidence in [Warner's] prudence, fortitude, and zeal."[3] But General Warner was commander on paper only. He was late to arrive, and Brown did not hesitate to point out his faults or to issue orders that were only slightly disguised as requests. Brown himself might seem to be a surprising choice. His poor eyesight had led a congressional committee to wonder if he was any longer fit for a field command. He had spent the past year quarreling with important men, including Washington, Schuyler, Gates, and Hancock. But he was known and trusted by the civilian and military leaders of Massachusetts and he had close ties to the Vermonters, especially Colonel Seth Warner. Gates may have taken satisfaction in knowing that Brown's role would annoy Arnold.

On the afternoon of September 12, the raiders marched north from Pawlet. Colonel Benjamin Ruggles Woodbridge of the Hampshire County militia, accompanied by Seth Warner and a detachment of Warner's regiment, was to seize Skenesborough, send bateaux north, and then march south to Fort Ann and perhaps Fort Edward, cutting off Burgoyne from the road back to the lake. Colonel Samuel Johnson of the Essex County militia, commanding Massachusetts and Vermont militia and another detachment of Warner's Continentals, was to attack Mount Independence from the east. And John Brown, accompanied by Berkshire militia, Vermont rangers under Samuel Herrick, and another contingent from Warner's Regiment, was to attack Lake George Landing and then old Fort Ticonderoga itself.

A guide led Brown's detachment toward narrow Lake Champlain. The land was forested and there were no blazes to follow. Once a man was ordered to climb a tree to look for the lake, but the ribbon of water was sunk deep in a narrow valley. Finally, at three in the morning, they reached the heights above the lake at a spot known as Cold Spring, some fifteen miles south of Ticonderoga. Officers clambered down to the shore where they hid when they saw a bateau on the lake and captured five British soldiers who came ashore for water. In the early morning, boats arrived from Skenesborough to ferry the expedition the few hundred yards across the lake. By nine o'clock, Brown's expedition was on the west side of the lake in today's Dresden, New York. Ordered to be quiet, the detachment moved away from the lake where it might be discovered and (in the words of Lemuel Roberts, whose memoir was published in 1809) hiked toward Ticonderoga through "an uncultivated wilderness seldom exceeded for its roughness." The land was thickly wooded, and rose and fell as if storm-tossed. Exhausted from the previous night's march, the men built crude shelters of branches and slept by a stream.[4]

By the afternoon of September 17, scouts could see cleared Mount Independence on the east shore, British vessels of war at anchor, and in the distance the old fort. They were less than two miles from Lake George, but a high ridge stood in the way. The men rested and waited for nightfall. Brown asked two men to swim across

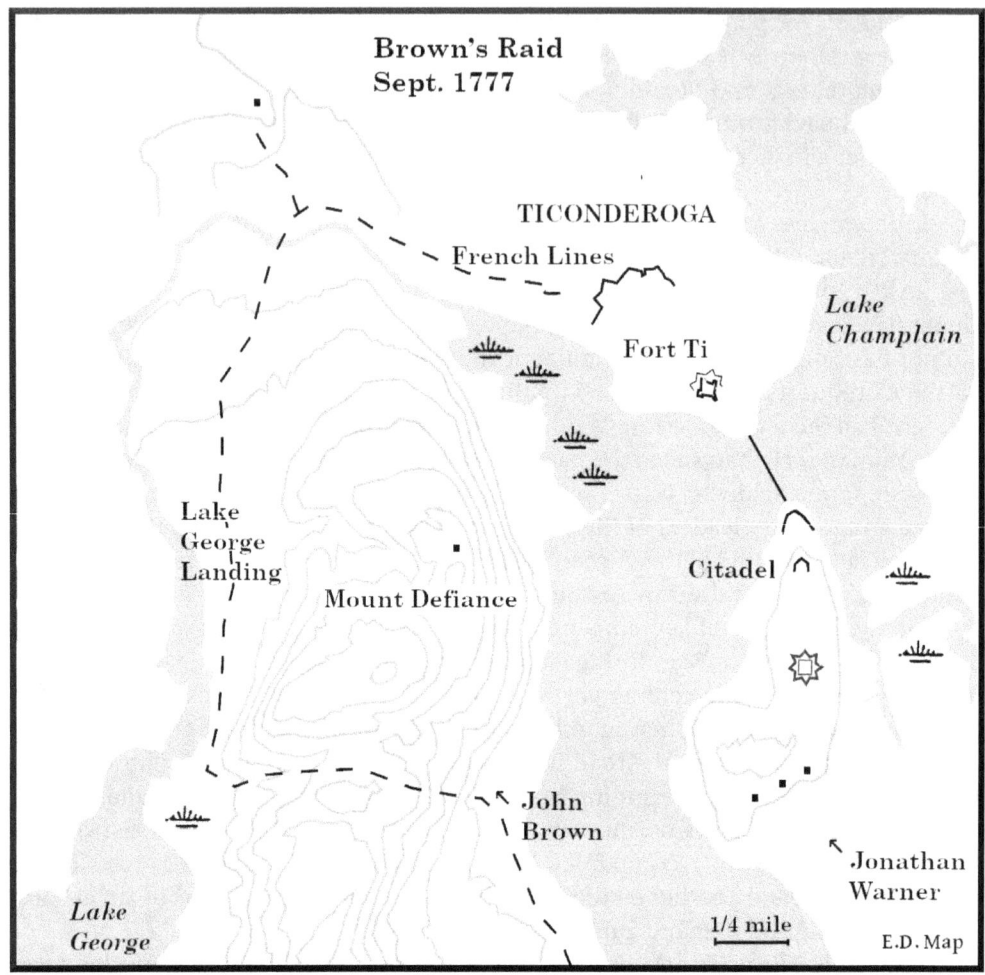

John Brown and his men crossed a mountain from Lake Champlain to Lake George and surprised a sleeping British garrison. Captain Ebenezer Allen climbed Mount Defiance. On Mount Independence side of the lake, General Jonathan Warner approached Mount Independence from the east.

the lake to deliver a message to the detachment under Colonel Johnson, who should have by then arrived near Mount Independence. Richard Wallace of Herrick's Vermont Rangers remembered, "With deep anxiety for the event, we undressed, bound our clothes upon our backs, drank a little ginger and water, and entered the cold waters of the lake, here about a mile in width." (Actually it's closer to a half mile, but that correction hardly diminishes the cold or the swimmers' fatigue.) "When we got into the middle of the lake, the wind blew and dashed the water onto our bundles of clothes and wet them and made them very heavy." Several times Wallace despaired of reaching shore. Once his companion, Samuel Webster, cried, "For God's sake, Wallace, help me, for I am adrowning!" Reaching shore first, Wallace dragged Webster to safety. Now they were lost on the Vermont side of the lake. After stumbling through the woods in the dark, they found a sentry, but they didn't know the countersign and couldn't tell if the American voice belonged to a Patriot or a Loyalist. At this dangerous moment, Wallace asked if there were another sentry nearby. There was, and "to my great joy, I knew the man." The swimmers delivered their message, and still cold and wet they slept in blankets borrowed from the commissary.[5]

That night, Brown's men crossed the saddle between Mount Defiance and the ridge to the south (South Mountain). When they became scattered, they hooted like owls, and were "frequently saluted with the jingly of rattle snakes." As day was breaking, Brown and Herrick's men paused to drink at another Cold Spring, a stream that tumbles down Mount Defiance into Lake George. Briefly, the leaders argued about precedence. Brown insisted upon leading the attack with Herrick's Rangers part of his party. Herrick answered he should command his own men whatever their assignment. Brown agreed, and Herrick took a longer route to seal off escape. Through the woods, Brown advanced toward the sleeping British camp at the landing. A sentry issued a challenge. "Surrender or you are a dead man," was the reply. Without firing, the sentry ran to an officer's marquee. A dozen British soldiers struggled from their tents, but soon surrendered.[6]

Meanwhile, forty men commanded by Vermont ranger captain Ebenezer Allen bushwhacked toward the summit of Mount Defiance, which is so steep that once Allen had to climb upon a man's back to scramble up a cliff. At the top, Allen led the way, and as he told the story, "his men came after him like a stream of hornets to the charge." The fight was over in minutes. Prisoners were sent down a cleared road, and Allen turned his attention to the cannon. Although he had never fired a great gun before, after a few shots from one of the twelve-pounders, a British vessel prudently moved its position.[7]

From Lake George Landing, Brown's and Herrick's men rushed through the morning fog to seize British outposts and to free American prisoners taken at the Battle of Hubbardton. "They had been confined, fatigued and dejected to such a degree that one could scarcely conjecture what they were," Brown wrote. "They came out of their Holes and Cells with Wonder and Amazement, indeed the Transition was almost too much for them."[8]

The Americans took British prisoners so fast that they could not guard them all. More than a mile-and-a-half from Lake George Landing, they forced the company in a blockhouse to surrender after confronting them with a captured field gun. The French Lines, which faced north and served no purpose in the current British defenses, fell easily, and from there the Americans fired field guns at the old fort. The British replied with the heavy guns from the Citadel on Mount Independence, a mile-and-a-quarter away. Brown's guns were too light to do much damage; the Citadel's guns were too far away.

Brown sent a sprightly note to the British commander, Henry Watson Powell: "On reception of this, you will at once surrender the Garrisons of Ticonderoga & mt. Independence, as it will very soon [be] out of your power to stop the Mighty Army of the Continent surrounding you on every side." Powell was cut off more completely than St. Clair had been two months earlier, but less threatened. He replied in the best eighteenth-century style: "The Garrison intrusted to my charge I shall defend to the last."[9]

On September 18, Brown captured 293 of the enemy and freed 118 American prisoners of war. He seized 150 bateaux on the Lake Champlain side of the portage and fifty bateaux, seventeen gunboats, and one armed sloop on the Lake George side.

Only three or four Americans were killed and five wounded in the attack. More boats were gathered in as they arrived at Lake George Landing. Brown wanted to seize the old fort and was hopeful the British might abandon it. He kept firing all night with his captured guns, but he did not have heavy guns to batter the walls and his men were mostly militia. At 6 a.m. the next morning, he wrote Lincoln in Pawlet, "It is most certainly out of my Power to cast the Enemy from that place, should they chuse to keep it, without too great loss of Men." He considered crossing the lake and joining the other detachment in an assault on Mount Independence.[10]

※ ※ ※

In the middle of the night of September 17–18, while Brown's men were crossing the ridge to Lake George, General Jonathan Warner caught up with Johnson's detachment and called a council of war, which resolved not to attack until reinforced. Lincoln's orders gave the commanders on the east side some leeway: "If upon inquiring you find that an attempt might be made on that Post [Mount Independence] without risking too much you will do it." In a letter to Gates, Lincoln made it clear that the threat to Mount Independence was to be a diversion only.[11]

Mount Independence rises steeply from the low land between East Creek and the lake. Germans from the Prinz Friedrich Regiment had inherited the fortifications to the southeast constructed by the Americans. British and German engineers built three new blockhouses facing east; the forest was cleared further back; and at the foot of the hill there was the tangle of branches, known to eighteenth-century soldiers as abatis. The British schooners *Maria* and *Carleton* were anchored where they could fire across the low neck of land.

The action on the Vermont side of the lake became the butt of jokes. "It is an undenyable truth that the Mount was never attacked by the Rebels otherwise than by paper," wrote Lieutenant John Starke, captain of the *Maria*, mocking the American enemy. "The only living creature (except the paper messengers) who approached it after Sept. 18th was a poor strayed cow, that in the night of the 21st being thick fog, caused a general alarm." Brown could not tolerate General Warner's inactivity: "Still believe had you attacked at the time I proposed you had carried the Mount," he wrote. As the days went on, Brown was more worried about counterattack than ways to subdue Ticonderoga. Finally, he requested—although *ordered* is closer to the truth—that the army retreat.[12]

On the afternoon of September 22 in a heavy rain, the Americans on the east side of the lake pulled back. Although they were worried that the Germans might attack, by ten o'clock that night they had all rowed or marched away. On the west side, Brown's men burned carriages, boats, and supplies, and slaughtered some horses and cattle, but drove many others into the woods. By four p.m., four hundred twenty men embarked at Lake George Landing in a fleet consisting of a sloop, two gunboats, and seventeen bateaux. The plan was to surprise a British garrison on Diamond Island, a heavily fortified speck of land in the lake about five miles from Fort George.

But one of Brown's captives, who was supplying potatoes to Ticonderoga, broke his word of honor and during the rainy night, sailed away, warning the troops on Diamond Island. When Brown's men began their attack around nine a.m., they learned quickly that the British were prepared. In an exchange of fire that lasted nearly two hours, the hull of the sloop was badly damaged—"between Wind & Water," as Brown

The Southeast Battery on Mount Independence was built by the Americans. At the time of John Brown's Raid it was occupied by German troops. A line of fortifications overlooking the low land to the east made capturing Mount Independence nearly impossible. Author photograph.

put it—and had to be towed away. One gunboat began to sink and was abandoned. Four men were killed and several others so badly wounded that Brown left them to the care of the enemy. On the island, not a single British soldier was killed or injured. The Americans sailed into a nearby bay, burned boats and extra baggage, and marched twenty miles to Skenesborough with their load of plunder.[13]

※ ※ ※

Horatio Gates had been Benedict Arnold's patron through the campaign of 1776, but now the two were on a collision course. Perhaps Gates suspected Arnold of being on Schuyler's side in the dispute over command. He might have viewed Arnold as a new rival. Certainly Arnold was offended when a few regiments were shifted from his command. Perhaps it all came down to how personality influenced decisions. Arnold was aggressive, although not most recently on the Mohawk; Gates was cautious and defensive. In the fall of 1776, Gates had reminded Arnold, "It is a defensive War we are carrying on," and Arnold had invited battle at Valcour Island. Both men were devious and self-promoting, but Gates was better at the machinations of advancement, while Arnold's temper put him at a disadvantage. Quickly, they perceived slights perpetrated by the other. Their young staff officers—James Wilkinson, twenty; Richard Varick, twenty-four; Henry Brockholst Livingston, son of the governor of New Jersey, nineteen—darted about, making matters worse with gossip and youthful outrage. Gates may have coolly provoked Arnold, but then Arnold's arrogance would have tried the patience of a far more generous commander.[14]

On September 19, Burgoyne sent a force of 3,500 men under generals Simon Fraser and James Inglis Hamilton west away from the Hudson, posing the question for the Americans, *should they remain in their fortifications or meet the enemy on the field?* From Arnold's left wing of the army, Daniel Morgan's corps tested the British, and the fighting grew at a farm owned by Loyalist John Freeman. The battle—Freeman's Farm or First Saratoga—is often seen through the lens of the Gates-Arnold dispute. Varick wrote to Schuyler, who was following events closely from Albany, "Arnold has all the credit of the action on the 19th, for he was ordering our troops to it, while the other [Gates] was in Dr. [Jonathan] Potts' tent backbiting his neighbors." Was this an insider's astute observation or a young man's misunderstanding of leadership, which can be calm and patient as well as energetic and aggressive?[15]

Some writers have depicted Arnold leading his regiments on the battlefield, but two days later, Wilkinson wrote to Arthur St. Clair with glee, underlining the key sentence, "General Arnold was not out of camp during the whole action." Was this a fact or a lie told to cheer up St. Clair, now with Washington's army but without a command? Wilkinson continued, "General Gates despises a certain pompous little fellow as much as you can, and tells me confidentially, that nothing could give him so much satisfaction as your presence here." Admirers of Arnold's military genius put themselves in a bind over the Battle of Freeman's Farm. Arnold must always be the man who barreled down the Chaudière River to find food for his starving men, who personally aimed the guns on the row-galley *Congress* at Valcour Island, who had two horses shot from under him during the Danbury Raid. If he was within the fortifications, he was little better than Gates, even if he was gathering information and issuing vital orders. Biographer Isaac Arnold countered claims that Benedict was not on the field with pages of inconclusive evidence and the assertion, "If so, this was the first time he was ever near a battlefield and not at the head of his troops." A memory that was not published until a century after the battle (but was "vouched for" by a reverend at a theological seminary) captured the Arnold of legend. On September 19 "nothing could exceed the bravery of Arnold on this day; he seemed the very genius of war, infuriated by the conflict, and maddened by Gates' refusal to send reinforcements, which he repeatedly called for, and knowing he was meeting the brunt of the battle, he seemed inspired with the fury of a demon."[16]

In his memoir, Wilkinson recounted reactions at Bemis Heights late in the day. Gates and Arnold stood at the front of the fortifications listening to the "peel of small arms" a mile-and-a-half away. When Morgan Lewis returned from the field with news that the battle was still undecided, Arnold said, "By God I will soon put an end to it," mounted his horse, and galloped off. Lewis spoke to Gates, "You had better order him back. The action is going well. He may by some rash act do mischief." Gates sent Wilkinson after Arnold, and he somehow managed to "remand" him to camp.[17]

Whatever Arnold's role, the Americans came close to a decisive victory, but low on ammunition, they retreated when the Germans arrived with two six-pounders firing grapeshot. Burgoyne claimed victory, but he had won nothing but a farm field. It rained for much of the next week, adding damp and depression to the anxiety of not knowing what was going to happen next. Burgoyne considered attacking again on

September 20; Arnold wanted to do the same had he been able to influence Gates; but neither side moved. The British kept the ground at Freeman's farm, buried their dead, and began entrenchments.

Two days after the battle, an express arrived with news of Brown's success at Ticonderoga. Thirteen cannon were fired in celebration and there was what engineer Jeduthan Baldwin called "a genl. Whooray throo all our camp." When Brown reached headquarters, Baldwin recorded the details of the raid: 315 British taken prisoner; two hundred bateaux, seventeen gunboats, and one sloop destroyed; £10,000 of plunder taken.[18]

On September 22, Gates wrote his official report to Congress on the events of September 19. "I was informed by my reconnoitering parties…. I immediately detached Colonel Morgan's corps … hearing from prisoners that the whole British force and a division of foreigners, had engaged our party, I reinforced with four more regiments." Except for two men who had the misfortune to be killed, no officers were singled out for praise. "They all deserve the honour and applause of Congress," Gates wrote, which sounds generous, but leaves Arnold and his division out of the picture. Gates included letters about Brown's Raid from Benjamin Lincoln, who had been promoted over Arnold's head in February, and from Brown himself, who for more than a year had been demanding Arnold's court-martial.[19]

Brown continued to receive far more praise than Arnold as the news of the triumphs in the north reached other civilian and military leaders. On September 28, Washington ordered a four o'clock celebration to include a gill of rum for each man and a salute of thirteen cannon. The battle on September 19 took place between "Genl Burgoyne's army and the left wing of ours under Genl Gates." After the details about Freeman's Farm that omitted Arnold, Washington's General Orders turned to the raid on Ticonderoga: "The Commander in Chief has further occasion to congratulate the troops on the success of a detachment from the northern army under Col. Browne, who attacked and carried several of the enemy's posts, & have got possession of the old french lines at Ticonderoga."[20] The orders included Brown's figures on prisoners taken, Americans freed, and boats seized. There was no mention of Benjamin Lincoln or of his choice for overall commander, Jonathan Warner.

When Congress's Committee for Foreign Affairs wrote to the American Commissioners in France on October 6, they had disturbing news about Philadelphia, which had fallen to the British. (Three days later, they added reports about the defeat at Germantown.) But there was good news from the north—the defense of Fort Stanwix, the Battle of Bennington, the September 19 battle at Saratoga, and "our successes in the rear of the enemy on the Lakes George and Champlain by Col. Brown." Arnold was mentioned for his relief of Fort Stanwix, but not for Saratoga. Lincoln received credit for sending Brown to Ticonderoga and for being in Burgoyne's rear with "a strong body of troops." The committee promised, "We hope e'er long to be able to give you information of definitive success over the british army in that quarter."[21]

※ ※ ※

The blows to Arnold's pride accumulated. Since coming north, he had not had to work closely with the major generals promoted above him in February. With Lincoln's arrival on Bemis Heights, September 22, Arnold could no longer ignore the affront to his honor. On the same day, Gates assigned Morgan's riflemen to headquarters, taking them away from Arnold. "Colonel Morgan's corps not being attached to any brigade or division of the army..." began the orders.[22]

Arnold immediately confronted Gates. "High words and gross language ensued," noted Wilkinson. "Both were warm—the latter [Gates] rather passionate and very assuming," wrote Henry Brockholst Livingston, who heard the account from Arnold. Gates said that he did not know that Arnold was a major general or had any command in the army at all. Arnold had left himself open to this retort when in accepting the assignment in the north, he claimed to do so as a private citizen.[23]

Arnold returned to his tent to write a more dignified version of what he had said to Gates. Militia regiments had been shuffled about, placing him "in the ridiculous light of presuming to give orders I had no right to do." His division, which had carried the fight on September 19, had been ignored in the report to Congress. No attention had been paid to his proposals, and "I have been received with the greatest coolness at head quarters." Then Arnold requested a pass to go to Philadelphia to join Washington where I "may possibly have it in my power to serve my country, tho I am thought of no consequence in this Department."[24]

More letters flew back and forth in the camp on Bemis Heights and then off to Schuyler in Albany as Gates and Arnold argued about the etiquette of a formal pass. Livingston was dismayed that Arnold was determined to leave. "He is the life and soul of the troops," he told Schuyler. "Believe me, Sir, to him and to him alone is due the honor of our late victory. Whatever share his superiors may claim they are entitled to none. He enjoys the confidence and affection of officers and soldiers. They would, to a man, follow him to conquest or death. His absence will dishearten them to such a degree as to render them but of little service."[25] Livingston's opinion has always been the bedrock of discussions on the Gates-Arnold feud, but it may be little more than the imaginings of one young man swept up by Arnold's emotions. One careful student of the battle found that outside of Varick's and Livingston's complaints, journals and memoirs pay little attention to the dispute and show no evidence of a loss of morale. Jeduthan Baldwin recorded skirmishes, but ignored the major generals and their disagreements. Henry Dearborn, whose light infantry was in the thick of the fighting on September 19, did not mention Arnold in his journal entry on "one of the Greatest Battles that Ever was fought in America." In the days that followed, he recorded nothing on the dispute. Like Baldwin, he looked forward to the next engagement.[26]

Enoch Poor, who had called for Arnold's arrest after the Moses Hazen court-martial in August 1776, led an attempt at reconciliation. Regimental colonels signed an address thanking Arnold for his actions on September 19 and asking him to stay. Some officers pointed to Henry Brockholst Livingston as a troublemaker. When Arnold heard the accusation, he said (this is Livingston's account), "His judgment had never been influenced by any man, and ... he would not *sacrifice a friend to* please the 'Face of Clay.'" By then Livingston was out of control. "I can no longer submit to the command of a man whom I abhor from my very soul," he wrote a few days before leaving camp.[27]

Bitter and angry, with no authority, and ignored by Gates, Arnold remained on Bemis Heights.

Sixteen

"The greatest conquest ever known"

On October 7, as Horatio Gates dined with his staff at headquarters, they heard musket fire to the north. Or at least that's one account, told by John Brooks, the officer who had proposed the Hon Yost Schuyler ruse. The story comes from a curious document published in 1858, said to be an interview conducted on horseback in 1816 on the way to Brooks's inauguration as governor of Massachusetts. Gates was eating ox heart, Brooks remembered precisely. Arnold was at this meal. It is news that they could tolerate each other's company. Not a word of the stilted dialogue may be accurate, but given blunter words and flushed faces, the substance may be true.[1]

"Shall I go out, and see what is the matter?" asked Arnold.

"I am afraid to trust you, Arnold," Gates answered.

"Pray let me go," Arnold said. "I will be careful; and if our advance does not need support, I will promise not to commit you."

Fifty-eight years after the battle to the day, Ebenezer Mattoon described the same moments in a letter to a grandson of General Schuyler, also a Philip Schuyler. Mattoon had been twenty-two at the time and not at a dinner at headquarters. He heard two signal guns, and the troops were drummed to the lines on Bemis Heights. Lincoln and Arnold galloped away; there was musket fire from pickets closer to the Hudson. When the generals returned, Gates stood in the doorway of his cabin, while officers crowded around to hear the news. Lincoln reported that the threat was not at the river but at the American left where a large force was moving to seize a low ridge. "That point must be defended or your camp is in danger," Lincoln said. Gates ordered out Daniel Morgan's riflemen and Henry Dearborn's light infantry.

"That is nothing; you must send a strong force," Arnold objected.

Gates answered, "General Arnold, I have nothing for you to do; you have no business here." Mattoon recalled, "Arnold's reply was reproachful and severe."[2]

In James Wilkinson's boastful account, he went forward to a wheat field—the Barber Wheatfield, about a mile from the American lines—and observed the enemy for fifteen minutes before reporting to Gates. "They are foraging, and endeavoring to reconnoitre your left; and I think, Sir, they offer battle," he said.

"What is the nature of the ground, and what your opinion?" Gates asked.

"Their front is open, and their flanks rest on woods, under cover of which they may be attacked; their right is skirted by a lofty height. I would indulge them," answered Wilkinson.

"Well, then, order on Morgan to begin the game," Gates said, not influenced by Arnold or Lincoln, who are absent from Wilkinson's account of the battle's beginning.[3]

And then there is a recently discovered letter from adjutant Nathaniel Bacheller of Colonel Abraham Drake's Regiment of New Hampshire militia, written to his wife two days after the battle. The letter appeared on eBay early in 2016, sold for $2,925, and then vanished again, leaving a digital image to study. Contradicting every other source, Bacheller describes a cooperative meeting between Arnold and Gates at the front lines near Arnold's headquarters in the Neilson House: "General Arnol [sic] says to General Gates it is Late in the Day but Let me have men & we will have some Fun with them Before Sun Set."[4] Could we actually be hearing Arnold's voice across the centuries or is this just an obscure adjutant in an obscure militia regiment imagining what a cocky Continental major general would say? Gates's presence at the Neilson House is in itself noteworthy. In other accounts, he stayed at his headquarters, even further from the fighting. Wilkinson described Gates at the end of the battle debating the merits of the Revolution with captured and mortally wounded Sir Francis Clerke, Burgoyne's aid-de-camp. Gates was more interested in besting "so impudent a son of a bitch," as he called him, than he was in news from the battlefield.[5]

Along with the engagement on September 19, the battle on October 7—Bemis Heights, Second Freeman's Farm, Second Saratoga—was the turning point of the American Revolution and a deciding event in world history, but it is remarkable how much is uncertain. Too often what comes down to us are the memories of old men, most of them doing their honest best to tell the truth across decades, but occasionally exaggerating their youths, settling old scores, repeating what they read as if it was original with them, or saying what they thought posterity wanted to hear. The old men were joined by nineteenth-century historians, who, freed from a body of hard facts, engaged in storytelling. Sometimes the Battle of Saratoga seems to be all smoke and mirrors. Bacheller's letter may represent a breakthrough—it is the earliest source and uninfluenced by Arnold's later treason. But it is also the most recent source, plucked from the internet, untested by bickering historians.

※ ※ ※

Around three p.m. the Americans advanced upon the Barber Farm in three columns, Daniel Morgan to the left, Ebenezer Learned in the center, Enoch Poor and the New Hampshiremen on right. The Americans were later reinforced by the Albany County militia, commanded by Brigadier General Abraham Ten Broeck, provincial congressman, chair of the New York congress's Committee of Safety, and Philip Schuyler's lifelong friend. Ten Broeck had been a member of the Albany Committee of Correspondence in May 1775 when Brown brought Ethan Allen's letter from Ticonderoga demanding men and supplies. The Albany County militia at more than 1800 men outnumbered the troops Burgoyne had committed to battle. The American army had grown to more than thirteen thousand, while Burgoyne's entire force stood at slightly more than seven thousand.[6]

In traditional accounts, Arnold did not stay out of the fight for long. Biographer Isaac Arnold has him saying, "No man shall keep me in my tent to-day. If I am without command, I will fight in the ranks; but the soldiers, God bless them, will follow my lead." Isaac Arnold is usually a reliable, if opinionated writer, but he gives no source for the quote, which may be a piece of pleasing fiction. In the most dramatic of

Sixteen. "The greatest conquest ever known"

contradictory stories, Arnold (according to Wilkinson) "rode about the camp betraying great agitation and wrath" and was "observed to drink freely." According to a doctor who was treating the wounded near a cask of rum, Arnold downed a full dipper before riding off to battle. The observation appeared in a local town history in 1878, and there is no knowing when or to whom Dr. Edmund Chadwick told his tale. The local history found a moral: "Like other traitors, it appears that Arnold was a brave devotee of King Alcohol." On the assumption the story is accurate, writers argued about the alcoholic content of a dipperful of rum and whether Arnold was drunk.[7]

Constructing a smooth narrative out of Saratoga has always been a challenge. Some writers blast inconvenient sources out of the way and fill gaps with speculation. Others quote sources extensively and let them take the blame for the contradictions. Writers have little choice but to pick and choose among Wilkinson's entertaining, self-serving, spiteful stories. Perhaps his account of Arnold's drunkenness and "exceedingly rash and intemperate" behavior was no more than malice—one traitor showing his contempt for another. But Wilkinson is also the foundation for the account of Arnold's greatest heroism on October 7. "I would not offer injustice even to a traitor," he wrote, no doubt with a feeling of smugness.

Gates sent aide John Armstrong to order Arnold back, much as he dispatched Wilkinson on September 19, but this time Arnold was gone, galloping on a black stallion or a brown mare, borrowed from Morgan Lewis or Leonard Chester.[8] He was raging drunk in Wilkinson's telling, so lost to reason that by accident he struck one of Morgan's officers with his sword and did not realize it at the time. On a visit to Saratoga on the fiftieth anniversary of the battle, Samuel Woodruff claimed that Arnold "behaved (as I then thought), more like a madman than a cool and discreet officer. Mounted on a brown horse, he moved incessantly at a full gallop back and forth...." But then Woodruff could have been repeating what he read in Wilkinson, not what he saw at the time.

At the centenary of the battle, one old man, former U.S. Senator Lafayette Foster, related what he heard of the battle from his father. "Arnold came dashing along the line, the speed at which he rode leaving his aid far behind him." When Arnold asked what regiment was near him, Captain Foster told him it was Latimer's Connecticut militia. Arnold answered, "Ah! My old Norwich and New London friends. God bless you! I am glad to see you. Now come on, boys; if the day is long enough, we'll have them all in hell before night."[9] The incident appears in many histories as if it's reliable testimony and not an old man's memory of an old man's memory. Still, the point contradicts many other tales. Arnold appears as a self-possessed leader, knowing how to inspire men to face shot and bayonet.

Arnold took command of Ebenezer Learned's brigade as if it was still his own, which it had been during the relief of Fort Schuyler, and then he issued orders to Daniel Morgan. "That officer upon a grey horse is of himself a host and must be disposed of. Direct the attention of some of the sharp-shooters among your riflemen to him." A few minutes later, Simon Fraser, victor at the Battle of Hubbardton and Burgoyne's right hand, was struck in the gut. He died the next morning after a night of agony. One history from 1845 claimed the shooter was Tim Murphy, a frontiersman from Schoharie County, New York, although there is reason to be cautious. History buffs have enjoyed debating the question whether Murphy was the shooter or an unnamed old man with a long hunting gun (as Ebenezer Mattoon contended), or someone else altogether. What seems to matter most to some writers is that Arnold issued the orders. Fraser was brought down not by a random shot or by a sharpshooter who picked his own target, but through Arnold's agency. It was Achilles and Hector, one Great Man in battle with another.[10]

After the British were driven from the wheatfield, the Americans charged a redoubt commanded by the Earl of Balcarres, but the fortification was too strong. Colonel Philip Van Cortlandt, commanding the 2nd New York Regiment in Poor's Brigade, recalled Arnold issuing orders that made taking the redoubt less likely. Van Cortlandt did not blame Arnold—his paragraph on the charge is chaotic like the event. Arnold's order "arrested our progress"; then Arnold "rode as fast as he could to counteract his own orders."[11]

John Brooks described Arnold to the Rev. William Gordon, who published the first history of the American Revolution in 1788. These are Gordon's words with Brooks cited as the source: "Gen. Arnold was next to military mad. He appeared, in the heat of the engagement, so beside himself as scarce to know what he did. He struck several of the officers with his sword, without any apparent reason; and when they told him of it the next day, meaning to remonstrate and require satisfaction, he declared he recollected nothing at all of it, and was sorry if it was so. Some of his orders were exceedingly rash and injudicious, and argued thoughtlessness rather than courage."[12]

By the time the Americans charged the Balcarres Redoubt, the battle was won, although incompletely and it was late in the day. In some accounts, Arnold

Benedict Arnold on his black horse charges across the Saratoga Battlefield in this textbook illustration from the 1890s. Josiah H. Shinn, *History of the American People* **(1899).**

single-handedly turned the American effort northwest toward the enemy right and a German redoubt commanded by Lieutenant Colonel Heinrich von Breymann. Arnold's heroics at that moment grew over the next two centuries. James Wilkinson described the scene briefly in his memoir: Arnold "dashed to the left through the fire of the two lines and escaped unhurt; he then turned the right of the enemy."[13]

The most lasting chapter of George Lippard's romantic, fictionalized history *Washington and his Generals* was "The Black Horse and his Rider; or 'Who Was the Hero of Saratoga?'" Into the twentieth century, textbooks on public speaking included abridged versions of "The Black Horse and his Rider." Delivered with dramatic gestures and intonation, the oration carried an audience into the October 7 battle alongside a mysterious horse and rider. "Is it not a magnificent sight, to see that nameless soldier, and that noble Black Steed, dashing like a meteor through the long columns of battle." And later: "The soldiers in every part of the field seemed to know that Rider, for they hailed him with shouts, they obeyed his commands, they rushed after him, over yonder cannon, through yonder line of bayonets." And finally (to be "uttered with the utmost power, joyfulness and clearness of tone"): "Who was the rider of that black horse? Do you not guess his name? Then bend down and gaze on that shattered limb, and you will see that it bears the mark of a former wound—a hideous wound it must have been. Now, do you not guess his name. That wound was received at the Storming of Quebec. That rider of the Black Horse was Benedict Arnold."[14]

※ ※ ※

In Ebenezer Mattoon's account, Arnold convinced John Brooks to attack the Breymann Redoubt. But that is not exactly how Brooks told the story. He remembered how his regiment emerged from the woods to face the redoubt. Although he acknowledged that Arnold's "energy gave spirit to the whole action," no lone galloping horseman, no discussion with Arnold, inspired a reckless charge by Brooks's regiment. Instead, when a volley from the redoubt appeared to cut down an entire company, Brooks and Captain James Bancroft rushed to the position to find that the men had dropped to the ground safely. Both officers were shaken by the experience, and Brooks pointlessly accused Bancroft of leaving his place in the regimental line. "I am ready to obey your orders, colonel," Bancroft snapped, and Brooks gave orders to take the redoubt. Angry and embarrassed, Bancroft led the way, crying, "Come on, my boys, and enter the fort."[15]

Arnold and the American right swept aside a Canadian outpost and entered the German fortification from behind. At the moment that victory was certain, Arnold was shot in the left leg and his horse went down on him, shattering the bone. In a tale collected in 1848, Arnold gallantly spared the life of the German who shot him. "He's a fine fellow—don't hurt him," he called out. In 1815 in a letter to Wilkinson, Henry Dearborn described how he had helped to remove the horse from Arnold's body. The young Dearborn kept a journal during the war. The entry for October 7, 1777, is detailed, but does not mention Dearborn's moment with the fallen Arnold. In the War of 1812, both Dearborn and Wilkinson were incompetent generals, but they could still insist that they had always been at the center of events. Dearborn told Wilkinson that he asked Arnold if he was badly hurt. Thinking of his wound at Québec, Arnold said it was the same leg, and "wished the ball had passed his heart." The quote seems to open a window on Arnold's tortured soul and has appeared in many histories.[16]

Learned took command and called for a council, hoping it would decide to withdraw. Men were still arguing when orders arrived from Gates to remain where they were "at all hazards."[17]

※ ※ ※

In 1887, John Watts de Peyster, a New York aristocrat, militia brevet major general and military theoretician and historian, erected a monument to Arnold on the Saratoga Battlefield near where he was wounded in the attack upon the Breymann Redoubt. It remains a not-to-be-missed stop on a tour of the Saratoga National Historical Park. The carved stone depicts a boot, topped by an epaulet and sprig of leaves, hanging from an upright cannon. Viewing the monument for the first time is like one of those chilling moments in the Harry Potter books in which some frightened character whispers about "He Who Must Not Be Named." With no mention of Arnold at all, the monument is dedicated to the memory of the "most brilliant soldier of the Continental Army," who won "for his countrymen the Decisive Battle of the American Revolution."

※ ※ ※

On the morning after the battle, Brigadier General John Fellows and thirteen hundred Berkshire County militia forded the Hudson at Saratoga, today's Schuylerville, and occupied the hill above the river. Fellows had with him "the Whole of the men under my Command," so it is possible that Brown was part of the surprise move. By the middle of October there were twelve brigadier generals, forty-four colonels, and forty-five lieutenant colonels near Saratoga, so that it is not remarkable that Brown is lost in a crowd. Fellows's men worked all day constructing fortifications above the road and the Fishkill (Fish Creek). From the barracks in the village, Fellows wrote to General Lincoln that

The Boot Monument at the Saratoga National Historical Park was dedicated to the "most brilliant soldier" in the Continental Army. Benedict Arnold's name does not appear. Americasroof, Wikimedia Commons.

he needed four thousand men to hold the post. By then Benjamin Lincoln had been shot in the leg while reconnoitering between the two armies and was in no condition to take the message. He may have been emulating Arnold's bravado—another major general proving his courage by riding recklessly into danger.[18]

That evening Burgoyne's army began a retreat through heavy rain toward Saratoga, eight miles away. Thoroughly wet and miserable, they stopped before dawn in Dovecote, just south of the village. Had they continued, the destruction of Fellows's Brigade might be an incident in Burgoyne's miraculous escape. Staff officer James Wilkinson, in the name of "the General," sent express couriers on both sides of the river to warn Fellows of Burgoyne's "rapid retreat" and the "possibility of your being overpowered by numbers." In the morning Fellows's men abandoned their fortifications and forded the Hudson by way of an island and then continued retreating nearly five miles to the east before regrouping and returning to the river. It rained more that afternoon, and the evening was dark and damp. Around nine p.m., British bateaux reached Saratoga, and a little-known skirmish began as Americans tried to seize the bateaux while British soldiers attempted to drive the attackers away from the river.[19]

Frye Bayley, who appeared in this narrative previously at the Cedars, told how his company from the upper Connecticut River, captured eleven boats and two scows. He later heard that 150 boats had been stopped. Bayley's company spent the remainder of the night carrying captured provisions and equipment to a depot in the woods. But they were "plundered in turn, of all our best and most valuable articles, by Col Brown's Regiment, as we supposed, of Rangers." Included in the stolen loot were several chests of gold-laced hats, which Brown's men sold to the Continentals. But the battle of the boats was about more than plunder. If the British could get enough bateaux north of the village, their engineers could construct a float bridge, and the army could cross the river quickly and sweep any Americans from their path as they retreated to the safety of Lake Champlain. Instead, the British and Germans continued Fellows's work of fortifying the heights above Saratoga.

Fellows was in command on the east bank, but the organization was haphazard. At one point, Fellows, Jacob Bayley of northeastern Vermont, and William Whipple of New Hampshire compared the dates on their commissions to learn who was the senior officer and able to decide an issue. John Stark was east of the Hudson as well, but it is hard to imagine him comparing the July 18, 1777, date on his New Hampshire brigadier's commission with anyone. On October 4, Congress named Stark a Continental brigadier for his victory at Bennington, but in an era of communication on horseback, he remained a state militia general with a recent commission. But General Gates, who had questioned if Benedict Arnold was still a major general, treated Stark as one of his favorite brigadiers.

Sometime before October 10, a few hundred men under the command of Major Robert Cochran, who was on leave from the 3rd New York, entered the village of Fort Edward. Cochran served as a courier between General Gates and the leaders of Vermont and volunteered as an officer in Seth Warner's brigade of militia, rangers, and Continentals. The ruined fort was no prize, but the location was. It had always been a place to cross the river. Earlier there had been a bridge. Even in October, desperate men might ford the Hudson south of the village.[20]

On October 10, Burgoyne sent Lieutenant Colonel Nicholas Sutherland with his 47th Regiment, marksmen, Loyalists, Canadians, and engineers to scout the road on the west bank of the Hudson. The only obstacle to a retreat by that route was the Snook Kill, which runs deep where it enters the Hudson about three miles south of Fort Edward. While engineers worked to rebuild a bridge, scouts went forward and observed a few hundred men near the fort. Sutherland thought he had found an escape for the army: push forward and seize the Hudson crossing and the road north to Fort Ann, and the army could slog back to Lake Champlain.

But in a cascade of cause and effect, Gates and Burgoyne were making bad decisions. When Fellows's men reported that they had observed a large British column marching north on the west side of the Hudson, Gates assumed Burgoyne was escaping and ordered an attack for the early morning of October 11. When Burgoyne learned that the enemy had taken the heights above the Fishkill River in "great force," he recognized that the Americans were "making a disposition to pass and give us battle," and he recalled Sutherland to reinforce the lines at Saratoga. Surprised and annoyed, Sutherland left the working party with Loyalists as guards at the half-built bridge across the Snook Kill. Not long afterwards, they were attacked by a company of Americans under the command of Robert Cochran. The guards fled, leaving, as Burgoyne explained, "the artificers [the construction crew] to escape as they could, without possibility of their performing any work."[21]

That night scouts returned to Burgoyne with word that the Americans were entrenched at the ford south of Fort Edward and there were fires on the heights north of the old fort. If the Americans lost the ford, they still held the high ground, protected by a breastwork and supported by cannon. But the Americans might have been looking over their shoulders as they built defenses facing south. A scouting party sent out by Vermont ranger Samuel Herrick had captured a German sergeant major near Mount Independence. The prisoner told them that Ticonderoga had been reinforced and that a detachment of six hundred men was planning to make a forced march to Burgoyne's aid. In fact, reinforcements were not coming, and Brown's Raid deserves credit. Five days after Brown's raiders retreated, Barry St. Leger, who had been besieging Fort Schuyler, reached Ticonderoga after a 450-mile trek from the Mohawk Valley to Lake Ontario, down the St. Lawrence, and up Lake Champlain. Defeat was in the air: the boats to cross Lake George were destroyed; Ticonderoga was isolated and short of supplies; and it was hard to imagine that Burgoyne's army was in worse shape or could be helped by St. Leger's reinforcements.[22]

※ ※ ※

In the early morning fog on October 11, Daniel Morgan's men crossed the Fishkill on rafts of logs a mile upstream from its mouth. Ebenezer Learned was to Morgan's right, while John Nixon's and John Glover's brigades moved across the fields near the smoldering remains of Philip Schuyler's house to ford the creek closer to where it joined the Hudson. For few minutes, the Americans advanced toward what might have been the Third Battle of Saratoga, a defeat that allowed for Burgoyne's escape or a bloody victory that eclipsed in historical memory the battles of September 19 and October 7. Before the fog lifted and the scattered firing became a general battle, a British scouting party was captured and the Americans learned that they were facing fortifications that were fully manned. By then more than twelve hundred of Nixon's and Glover's men were across the creek. As the fog lifted, they saw (wrote Wilkinson) "the British army under arms; their park in our front, and our left exposed to the centre." The British lines erupted in cannon and musket fire and the American retreated "in great disorder."

Wilkinson, who is once again the star of the drama, rode hard to the west to where Learned was preparing to attack the grenadiers and light infantry entrenched on the top of a hill. Wilkinson begged Learned to stop, but he resisted the advice of this presumptuous twenty-year-old aide. On October 7, Learned wanted to retreat at the end of the fighting and was opposed; now he wanted to attack and was told he was wrong again. Wilkinson argued that Nixon and Glover were in retreat and the firing from the east was all from the British lines. He said, "Although I have no orders for your retreat, I pledge my life for the General's approbation." Several officers including John Brooks joined the argument and convinced Learned to pull back.[23]

※ ※ ※

On the afternoon of October 12, Burgoyne called a council of war and presented the hard facts. The enemy on the west of the Hudson numbered fourteen thousand, he believed; the size of the force to the east was unknown, but one corps was estimated at fifteen hundred. Burgoyne's army no longer had any bateaux to build a bridge. Provisions might last until October 20, but there was no rum or beer. Burgoyne did report one hopeful piece of news brought by American deserters and Loyalists: the British army in New York had at last moved north and taken Fort Montgomery on the Hudson, forty miles from the city. Maybe this expedition under the command of Sir Henry Clinton was by then closer to Albany. Burgoyne asked for opinions. Should they wait where they were? Should they attack now—or later if the Americans concentrated on their left? Should they retreat with artillery and baggage, and seize the ford near Fort Edward? Or should they retreat that night without artillery and baggage, ford the river north of Fort Edward, and march around Lake George to Ticonderoga? If it was the latter, Burgoyne's army faced a trek through the wilderness, because all the boats had been destroyed—another contribution by Brown to the British surrender. "It must be remembered that this route was never used by any one except small parties of Indians," Burgoyne cautioned. Even so, the council decided on the long march. Six days of provisions were to be distributed, and patrols were sent north to determine if they could escape without being detected. *Impossible* was the report and the retreat was postponed.[24]

On the night of October 12–13, Stark's and Warner's men crossed the Hudson. By the morning, the brigade had seized and fortified a narrow pass about a mile north of the British lines. On the Americans' left was marshy ground near the river; on their right was a steep hill called Stark's Knob today. Burgoyne could order his seven thousand men north, but geography would funnel them down to an exposed few, a forlorn hope, facing an entrenched enemy and cannon loaded with grapeshot. An attack never came. As a local historian put it succinctly, Stark "corked the bottle."[25]

※ ※ ※

On the morning of October 17, James Wilkinson rode with General Burgoyne to the site of Fort Hardy, a French and Indian War fort on the flats near the Hudson River to the north of the Fishkill. The two men had met as part of the negotiations leading to surrender. In Wilkinson's account, he—"a youth in a plain blue frock, without other military insignia than a cockade and sword"—had stood up to senior European officers and helped to force a settlement when Burgoyne nearly reneged.[26] In the end, Burgoyne received favorable terms. General Gates held virtually every card of value—men, morale, provisions, position—but he worried about Sir Henry Clinton's expedition on the Hudson and the possibility of being trapped between two British armies. And so, Gates gave Burgoyne favorable terms. In a fine point of eighteenth-century honor, Burgoyne was not even capitulating, but agreeing to a convention. Burgoyne and Wilkinson paused by the river and Burgoyne gazed across. *Was it fordable?* he asked. They were close to where Fellows's men waded in panic eight days earlier. "Certainly, Sir," Wilkinson replied, "but do you not observe the people on the opposite shore?" "Yes, I have seen them too long," Burgoyne answered.[27]

Then Burgoyne, his staff and senior officers rode south across the Fishkill, past the charred remains of Philip Schuyler's house, to a marquee that served as the surrender site. Gates held Burgoyne's sword briefly before returning it. After introductions and handshakes, commanders and staff moved into the marquee for toasts and a dinner of ham, goose, beef, and mutton in which officers from both armies pretended that victory and defeat were matters of little consequence among gentlemen. No one kept a list of who was in the marquee tent around the plank tables of refreshments. Lieutenant Anton Adolph Heinrich Du Roi of Johann Specht's Brigade recorded the important men he met at the surrender dinner: Philip Schuyler, brigadier generals John Glover and Francis Marquis de Malmedy, and colonels Frederick Weissenfels (a Prussian by birth, he noted approvingly) and Seth Warner. Warner, Weissenfels, Brown, and Cochran had been part of the winter 1776 siege of Québec. Perhaps there was a reunion of the frostbitten.[28]

※ ※ ※

Burgoyne's troops started out of their lines on the heights above the river at about 10:30 a.m., fifes and drums playing. In a field by the ruin of Fort Hardy, officers ordered them to pile their firearms, discard their cartridges, and abandon the field pieces. Historians have always had difficulty getting the timing right, for there were more than five thousand dejected men converging on the site.[29] Some splintered the butts of their muskets or smashed drums rather than turn them over to the rebels. Then they waited while their commanders dined and made small talk. Finally, they dressed their ranks and at about two in the afternoon, they began to follow James Wilkinson, Morgan Lewis, and a company of dragoons across the Fishkill into the American army.

Three thousand British soldiers came first followed by twenty-four hundred Germans, and at the rear nearly three hundred women. According to the convention agreed to by Gates and Burgoyne, the British and Germans were on their way to Boston, a march of 200 miles. Once at the port, they would board ships for England, and although pledged not to fight in North America again, they could free up other men for that duty. It did not happen that way. The Continental Congress, while proclaiming Gates's brilliance, soon wanted to evade the easy terms to which he had agreed. Much as they had after Arnold's cartel at the Cedars, they found justifications.[30] The Convention Army spent the rest of the war as prisoners, neglected and marched about the country, Massachusetts to Virginia, and then back to Pennsylvania. But on the road south from Saratoga, the armies watched each other with respect and wonder. "A grand sight as was ever beheld by the eye of man in America," wrote Ralph

Cross, whose Essex County regiment had been part of Brown's Raid and suffered heavy losses on October 7. "Supposed to be 7,000 men in arms, their extent three deep, as upon their march, was supposed to be seven miles, including baggage etc." And in this journal, Henry Dearborn called it "the greatest Conquest Ever known."[31]

※ ※ ※

The American commissioners to France—Benjamin Franklin, Silas Deane, and Arthur Lee—had already won friends and clandestine aid for the American cause. By the summer of 1777, French arms were beginning to have an impact. But although France gladly caused trouble in ways that could be denied, the government was not going to recognize the United States as an independent nation, enter the war as an ally, or openly supply the arms needed for victory. That changed with the surrender at Saratoga.

On December 4, anticipating news from America, the commissioners met with playwright and arms supplier Pierre-Augustin Caron de Beaumarchais at Franklin's house in Passy, then on the outskirts of Paris. When a messenger, Jonathan Loring Austin, who was a young merchant from Kittery, Maine, rode into the courtyard, Franklin demanded, "Is Philadelphia taken?" Hearing that the city had indeed fallen, Franklin turned away. "But sir, I have greater news than that. General Burgoyne and his whole army are prisoners of war!" Austin called.[32]

Austin had crossed the Atlantic in four weeks from Boston to Nantes with news of Burgoyne's surrender and the letter from the Committee for Foreign Affairs, written in York, Pennsylvania, in early October. The commissioners wrote immediately to Foreign Minister Comte de Vergennes, making the most of Saratoga and downplaying the defeats at Brandywine and Germantown and the loss of Philadelphia. Washington and Gates were cooperating, and William Howe, "it was hoped … would soon be reduced to submit to the same Terms with Burgoyne." They included a tally of "Prisoners &c." totaling 9203. By adding British losses and freed Americans, they were able to announce that 413 men were "Kill'd & taken at Ticonderoga by Brown." Washington, Gates, and Brown were the only officers mentioned in the electrifying report to the French government.[33]

An alliance with France was signed on February 6, 1778. The armies, fleets, and supplies that followed changed a colonial rebellion into a world war and led to the American and French victory at Yorktown.

Seventeen

"Give a thief a length of rope"

In November 1777, John Brown visited the Continental Congress in York, eighty miles west of British-held Philadelphia. He was likely renewing his campaign against Arnold and hoping for compensation for the raid on Ticonderoga. He had never been notified whether his resignation from the Continental Army had been accepted by Congress (it had), and so he might claim to have attacked the fort as a Continental officer. While in York, he met with Charles Thomson, secretary of the Congress, and learned for the first time about Arnold's meeting with the War Board in May to settle Brown's charges.[1]

Early in 1778, Brown resigned his commission as colonel of the Third Regiment of the Berkshire County militia, and in May he returned to the Massachusetts House of Representatives. He was an active delegate, dealing with petitions from veterans and their widows, and with issues arising from unrest in Berkshire County. He had been away from the assembly for three years and much had changed. Earlier, he had been a radical voice; now he found himself in the uncomfortable middle. Before the Revolution, western Massachusetts was the conservative part of the colony, but now, led by Pittsfield's pastor Thomas Allen, Berkshire County opposed the new Massachusetts government and its courts and demanded a constitution that gave towns the right to elect judges, justices of the peace, and militia officers. In 1776, while Brown watched the smallpox spread outside Québec, the Reverend Allen blocked the Court of Quarter Sessions from meeting in Pittsfield. In rallying support, he read to the county committees of correspondence from Thomas

The Rev. Thomas Allen, Pittsfield's fighting pastor, favored a more democratic constitution with a bill of rights. John Brown was caught between the Constitutionalists and his conservative friends and colleagues. As found in Joseph E.A. Smith, *History of Pittsfield* (1869).

Seventeen. "Give a thief a length of rope"

Paine's *Common Sense*. Soon the Constitutionalists, as Allen's party called themselves, made the inclusion of a bill of rights their issue. The Berkshire Constitutionalists were opposed by Theodore Sedgwick, Brown's friend and potential witness against Arnold, who called his party the "Friends of Order."[2]

In August 1778, Berkshire County again petitioned the Council and House of Representatives, contending that four-fifths of the inhabitants were against the courts until they were established under a constitution ratified by the people. As a result, a committee was sent to Berkshire to hear "all Complaints of Difficulties, and Grievances of every political kind, or Nature" from all the towns in the county. On behalf of Pittsfield and six other towns, the Reverend Allen wrote a lengthy statement on the nature of liberty, arguing for a constitution, and justifying keeping the courts closed. The document ended with an attempt at reconciliation. The county delegates were "willing to forego our own opinions" and submit to the imposed court system—"if it shall be thought best by our Constituents."[3]

The fact-finding committee concluded that if civil officers were appointed, the "Clamours about the Executive Courts ... would very soon subside." Meanwhile, in January 1779, there was more unrest in Hancock, west of Pittsfield. The committee's report was referred to yet another joint committee which included Walter Spooner and James Sullivan, who had clashed with Benedict Arnold on Lake Champlain in the summer of 1775. This committee recommended a pardon for rioters and that the courts be reopened. Brown, Sullivan, and Robert Treat Paine, a signer of the Declaration of Independence, formed yet another committee to draft bills relating to Berkshire County.[4]

Brown and three others were appointed judges on Berkshire's Inferior Court of Common Pleas, which was to adjudicate civil cases exceeding forty shillings. Ten days later the pardon written by Brown, Sullivan, and Paine became law. For a short time, it seemed as if the trouble in western Massachusetts had been calmed with Brown playing a prominent role. Then in May, a mob of three hundred men blocked the Superior Court from meeting in Great Barrington. No state-sanctioned courts sat in the county until 1781, so Brown's appointment as a judge was meaningless. Pittsfield did not reelect him to the House of Representatives. The new delegates were told to work to repeal the act of amnesty, which was "fraught with reproach, discrimination, and such severe reflection upon the county as they utterly disdain." The instructions were written by the Reverend Allen. James Easton was a signatory.[5]

※ ※ ※

John Brown's life at home can be imagined through an inventory of his property made after his death. We might see him at work on his seventy acres wearing an old green beaver hat or at leisure among ladies and gentlemen in his flowered silk jacket. He owned striped woolen breeches, a calico jacket, a dimity jacket, silk and linen stockings. He left behind a pair of boots. (His best boots were stripped from his body at his death.) The estate included one grenadier cap, a red silk sash, and a gold lace hat band, all prizes of war. We might imagine the Browns at dinner. They owned—legally only John, although the estate provided a division of property for Huldah—six large and six small silver spoons, eight knives and four forks, fourteen "earthen" plates, and four candlesticks. The tablecloth was damask, a patterned weave. The curtains were blue and white. They slept in a feather bed. (Their son John Henry was conceived in the summer of 1778.) There were two looking glasses. And so on—three pages of John and Huldah's life together enumerated precisely in pounds, shillings, and pence. They were not wealthy, but comfortable, although by then in debt. By 1782, two years after John's death, livestock included a mare and yearling colt. Brown's favorite horse undoubtedly went down with him when he died fighting in the Mohawk Valley. There were two grown cows, a heifer, and a calf. Brown had a good library for the time and place. It included a volume of lyric poetry by the hymnist Isaac Watt, a theological text in Latin, the epic poem *The Shipwreck* by William Falconer, half of a dictionary, half of a book of medical advice, and a Bible. He owned nineteen law books and one on surveying. His most valuable possession, except for real estate, was Mathew Bacon's five-volume *A New Abridgment of the Law*, listed at £15. This set and other books may have come from the library of his brother-in-law, Rhode Island attorney general Oliver Arnold.[6]

The Browns had at least one servant, a Black named Thomas Brown. Although *servant* was sometimes a euphemism for *slave*, Thomas was not enslaved—had he been, he would have appeared as property in probate. By 1780, slavery was dying in Massachusetts. One of the final blows against slavery was struck by Brown's conservative friend Theodore Sedgwick when he sued on behalf of Mumbet, who became Elizabeth Freeman and was beloved by the Sedgwick family. Thomas's family name suggests there is an interesting story to be found, but what it is remains a mystery. In the summer and fall of 1780, Thomas was a waiter to an unnamed chaplain in Captain William White's Company of Brown's Regiment. In being assigned to a pastor, Thomas must have been a promising young man.[7]

At the time of his death, Brown owned real estate appraised at £1200—but in fact in the 1780s worth much less—and other property valued at £500. He owed twenty-six men, many of them prominent citizens of Pittsfield, a total of more than £700. Burdened with interest that could never be paid, his estate was declared insolvent in 1802.[8]

※ ※ ※

After Saratoga, Congress restored Arnold's seniority in an opaque resolution that would baffle anyone who was not following the dispute closely. Washington was ordered to "regulate" Arnold's rank and that of two other men. The commander in chief took his time, congratulated Arnold, and worried about Benjamin Lincoln, also wounded at Saratoga, who had now lost his seniority.[9]

Arnold did not leave the hospital in Albany until the late winter or early spring of 1778. After a visit home, he traveled to Valley Forge. When the British evacuated Philadelphia on June 18, he entered the city as military governor. Washington told him to "preserve tranquillity and order in the city, and give security to individuals of every class and description."[10] Philadelphia had been ravaged by a nine-month occupation, and a military governor with tact and integrity would have been challenged by the assignment. Quickly, Arnold and civilian authorities loathed each other.

In December 1779, Joseph Reed became president of the Pennsylvania Supreme Executive Council. Reed had been prosecuting Loyalists, most notably two older Quakers who were hanged for treason. Reed remains a controversial figure. A list of his positions—secretary to George Washington, adjutant general, Continental congressman, Pennsylvania president—would seem to make him a major figure in the American

Revolution, but few writers outside of his own grandson, who wrote a flattering two-volume biography, have warmed to him. Major nineteenth-century historian George Bancroft could not find a good word to say. Reed was "shuffling, pusillanimous, and irresolute," "tainted by duplicity," and a "vacillating trimmer," who was disloyal to Washington and considered defecting. Scholarly biographer John F. Roche, writing in the 1950s, argued that Reed's "misgivings, shaken confidence, and signs of hopelessness" were twisted by foes to be signs of treason. He concluded that Reed was a "moderate man caught up in the turbulence of revolution." He was "too perceptive and too cosmopolitan to adopt the doctrinaire outlook of the extremist." But Roche's view has not been widely adopted. Nathaniel Philbrick, who writes carefully researched popular histories, put it this way in *Valiant Ambition: George Washington, Benedict Arnold, and the Fate of the American Revolution* (2016): "Arnold eventually became a traitor of the highest order, and ultimately he alone was responsible for what he did. However, one cannot help but wonder whether he would have betrayed his country without the merciless witch hunt conducted by Reed and his Supreme Executive Council." The phrase *witch hunt* has taken on additional baggage since Philbrick wrote, but it has always meant unjust harassment.[11]

Joseph Reed, president of the Pennsylvania Supreme Executive Council, was Benedict Arnold's adversary in Philadelphia. Reed's historical reputation has suffered. This engraving is based on a portrait by Pierre Eugène Du Simitière. National Portrait Gallery, Smithsonian Institution.

Reed had a flair for eighteenth-century rhetoric. In the summer of 1778, when he was offered a bribe of £10,000 to influence fellow congressmen toward reconciliation with Britain, he told Congress of the affair. As the account appears in the *Journal of the Continental Congress*, "He (Mr. Reed) replied, 'He was not worth purchasing, but such as he was, the king of Great Britain was not rich enough to do it.'"[12] Reed may have exaggerated the incident—he may have been measuring how he could benefit from it—but even so Arnold biographers stay as far away as they can. Less than a year later, Arnold was negotiating for £10,000.

Early in the winter of 1778–79, the Pennsylvania council moved to bring charges against Arnold. At first there were eight, then a Congressional committee reduced the number to two, and then Congress sent four to George Washington. Most were for profiteering. It was charged that Arnold gave permission for vessels owned by people of suspect loyalty to bring goods into patriot held ports. After shutting shops and stores in the city, he "privately made considerable purchases for his own benefit." He made militiamen perform "menial offices" and justified his actions. He involved himself in a dispute about prize money for a captured vessel in order to profit. He used Pennsylvania government wagons to transport cargo captured by a privateer from the New Jersey coast to Philadelphia, again to profit. He refused to explain his use of the wagons. He gave permission for persons to go through enemy lines into New York. He favored Tories.[13]

Unlike Brown's thirteen charges, Pennsylvania's eight charges have been thoroughly studied, although many details remain murky. Wishing for more facts and figures, most researchers conclude that, yes, Arnold was using his office to enrich himself—but corruption was rampant and he may have been no worse than many others. For all the outrage from Pennsylvania authorities, there was not much solid evidence to support the charges in a court of law. Historian Carl Van Doren commented, "It was less like impartial justice closing inexorably in on a distinguished malefactor than like furious vigilantes pouncing on a hated suspect." And even William Reed, Joseph's grandson, wrote, "It is impossible to withhold the expression of surprise, that the State authorities were able to accomplish his conviction on any one of the charges preferred."[14]

The heart of the dispute between Pennsylvania leaders and Arnold was not in the legal issues. A seemingly silly incident in which Arnold's aide David Franks ordered a militiaman to fetch a barber and Arnold refused to reprimand Franks represented the gulf between the powdered, coiffed or bewigged upper class and people of simple dress and presumably honest virtue. "Freemen will be hardly brought to submit to such indignities," wrote the militiaman's father, secretary of the Pennsylvania council Timothy Matlack. Arnold left himself open to such accusations. In a city that was in the forefront of the Revolution, he adopted an extravagant lifestyle as if he were a British commander or one of the wealthy Loyalists who thrived during the occupation. He took up residence in the Penn Mansion, just vacated by General William Howe, and rode about the city in a carriage. He appeared to treat Loyalists with great sympathy and he socialized with families that supporters of the Pennsylvania government judged to be little better than the enemy. Soon he was courting eighteen-year-old Margaret (Peggy) Shippen, daughter of Judge Edward Shippen, a man who kept his distance from the Revolution. In March 1779, just before he married Peggy, Arnold purchased Mount Pleasant, a mansion overlooking the Schuykill River.

In one of his ardent letters to Peggy, Arnold recycled much of what he had written to Betsy Deblois not six months earlier in a last effort to win her affection. "Dear Peggy [or Betsy, as the case may be], suffer that heavenly bosom (which cannot know itself the cause of pain without a sympathetic pang) to expand with a sensation more soft, more tender than friendship [or *to expand with friendship at least, and let me know my fate*]." Among Arnold biographers, Clare Brandt recognized that these repetitious letters offered insight into Arnold's character. She commented, "Peggy Shippen deserved better, although nobody, including herself, suspected that yet."[15]

Some writers have blamed teenage Peggy for enchanting Arnold and leading a patriot astray. She was Eve with the apple. Aaron Burr—or at least Burr's first biographer—claimed on authority that she was "privy to, if not the negotiator" of the treason. But starting with Arnold's aide-de-camp David Franks, Peggy had defenders. Isaac Arnold devoted six pages to arguing that she knew nothing of the plans, and a recent biographer, Joyce Lee Malcolm, concluded "they have damned an innocent woman. As George Washington, Alexander Hamilton, Peggy's family, those who knew her believed, she was not guilty." Poor Peggy, she can be everything from a conniving temptress to a loving wife and mother to a hysterical nitwit. In any case, she charms men with her grace and beauty.[16]

The turmoil in Philadelphia divides historians—and present-day political progressives and conservatives. Some see Pennsylvania's Constitution of 1776 as a step toward democratic government. Pennsylvania expanded the right to vote, limited the influence of the upper class, restricted the power of the president or governor, and protected religious freedom. In 1780, Pennsylvania became the first of the thirteen states to begin the abolition of slavery. Others see Joseph Reed's conservative opponents, including Arnold, as resisting mob rule and advocating for responsible government such as could be found a decade later in the U.S. Constitution with its emphasis on checks and balances. Even the vocabulary becomes a hurdle. Reed and council secretary Matlack are often described as radical or extreme Whigs as if Pennsylvania invited Robespierre to a civilized revolution. In turn, Reed's opponents, the anti–Constitutionalists or Republicans, are called moderate Whigs, moderation being a good thing. Reed liked the terms "real Whigs" and "designing Whigs." Resolving these disputes is far beyond this narrative, except when Reed's and Matlack's excesses are used to imply that Arnold's selfish tenure was somehow principled.[17]

※ ※ ※

After the Pennsylvania council brought its charges, Arnold counterattacked in the *Pennsylvania Packet* for February 9, 1779: "Conscious of having served my country faithfully for near four years, without once having my public conduct impeach'd, I little expected at this time to be charged with crimes of which I believe few who know me would have suspected me."[18]

In the February 27 issue of the *Packet*, Timothy Matlack replied to Arnold's letter, signing himself as T.G. for the Roman tribune and reformer Tiberius Gracchus. Matlack's life may reveal as much about the Revolutionary generation as that of more celebrated founders on their pedestals. Disowned by the Society of Friends, he helped establish the Free Quakers, a group of two hundred Friends who supported the Revolution. (Today Betsy Ross is the

Timothy Matlack, a fighting Quaker and secretary of the Pennsylvania Supreme Executive Council, battled Benedict Arnold in a series of letters published in *Dunlap's Pennsylvania Packet*. This 1802 portrait is attributed to Rembrandt Peale. Andrew W. Mellon Collection, National Gallery of Art.

best-known member.) A brewer and beer bottler by trade, Matlack liked horse racing, cock fighting, and the company of lower class men. Along with Benjamin Franklin, he was on the six-man committee that drafted the Pennsylvania constitution. As a colonel, he commanded militia in the winter campaign of 1776–1777. He had a quick temper and was combative. He opposed slavery, favored good and just relations with Natives, and was accustomed to listening to the thoughts of women in a Quaker meeting house. When he explored the rivers of northwest Pennsylvania in the 1790s, he met with Seneca women to hear their formal address. He is also the answer to a trick trivia question: Who wrote the Declaration of Independence? Matlack penned—*engrossed* is the technical term—the version of the document signed by delegates and found in the National Archives. At the time, he was assistant to the secretary of the Continental Congress, Charles Thomson.[19]

"The General's memory seems to have failed him," Matlack responded in the *Packet* and then published Brown's thirteen charges. Likely Matlack received a copy from Thomson, another Pennsylvanian. Two sections were italicized for emphasis: "plundering the inhabitants of Montreal" and Brown's lengthy description of Arnold's orders to destroy "whole villages" and to slaughter the inhabitants "without any distinction to friend or foe, age or sex." "How far these charges can *all of them* be supported it is unnecessary to say," Matlack wrote, "but it is certain that they were published to the world with Lieutenant Colonel John Brown's name thereto; and he pledged himself to support them before a Court-Martial, where his evidence could be heard, which Court-Martial he demanded."[20]

In the next week's issue, Arnold parried that his accusers were not inventive enough "to frame new slanders" so they called upon "the feeble aid of old calumnies, however groundless, and however well refutable." Arnold included the findings of the War Board that his "character and conduct" had been "cruelly and groundlessly aspersed."[21]

Around the same time, a letter from President Reed reached Brown in Pittsfield. He was home from the legislature, having worked unsuccessfully with Walter Spooner and James Sullivan in the attempt to calm Berkshire County. In reply, Brown sent another copy of the thirteen charges. In the accompanying letter, dated March 7, 1779, he suggested that "the last charge in the impeachment, can now be fully supported, which tho' trifling, connected with Genl Arnold's character, yet might affect that of a better man." Brown's thirteenth charge was that in the early summer of 1775 Arnold threatened the committee sent by the Massachusetts Provincial Congress and may have considered going over to the enemy. Historians have always found the accusation improbable, even granted that an infuriated Arnold may have acted in ways a gentleman should not. But Brown claimed to have solid evidence. We do not know what Spooner and Sullivan's testimony might have been—Brown did. The other charges could still be brought, he wrote, but "the evidence is now much dissipated."[22]

After writing, Brown received a letter from Matlack with enclosures about Pennsylvania's case against Arnold. In a postscript to the letter he had just written, Brown thanked Matlack and commented, "Can assure your hon^r that I am extremely happy to hear, that so great a villian is at last detected, or the old proverb verified 'give a Thief [a] length of rope, and he will hang himself.'"[23]

In the battle of letters-to-the-editor, Arnold's counterattack had been too hasty. Brown told Reed and Matlack of Arnold's "sham trial in congress" in May 1777, but the Pennsylvanians already knew. Matlack wrote in the *Packet*, "It will require that some faith be exercised by the next generation, before they can believe that Congress really acquitted you of those charges upon hearing such evidence as you could produce *in your own favor*, and without hearing *the evidence against you*. Indeed, General, this looks very like *jockeying*." Matlack allowed that Congress may have based its decision on "the improbability that any one man was ever so guilty of so many crimes, and of so black a dye." His rhetoric ended with a deadly thrust: "When I meet your carriage in the street, and think of the splendour in which you live and revel, of the settlement which it is said you have proposed in a certain case, and compare these things with the decent frugality necessarily used by other officers in the army, it is impossible to avoid the question: From whence have these riches flowed if you did not plunder Montreal?"[24]

※ ※ ※

In April, Brown wrote to Samuel Adams on behalf of James Easton, calling for the trial that had been promised to vindicate Easton's honor and to allow Easton and his men to benefit from the plunder taken on the St. Lawrence. Brown mentioned that he himself was "exactly on a footing with Easton" regarding the trial, but he kept his personal complaints to a minimum, realizing that he had made enemies in Congress. In a decision that could be slipped into *Catch-22*, Congress ruled that "it was the duty of Colonel Easton long since to have procured such court to sit." He "has contentedly drawn his pay to this time," the War Board concluded, before dismissing him from the service. Easton tried again unsuccessfully in 1786 and 1791. He appears in most histories as a buffoon.[25]

On June 6, Brown wrote a bitter memorial and remonstrance to Congress, which reads as if it could have been written a few days after his visit to York, Pennsylvania, a year and a half earlier. By June 1779, Brown's political and military careers had unraveled, and he may have been looking back in frustration. He wrote that he was outraged by the "extraordinary trial of Gen. Arnold" before the War Board. Arnold's meeting with the board was "ex parte, unconstitutional, and illegal on every principle." There was not a single witness "who ever had it in his power to know any thing of his own knowledge respecting one of the charges laid in the complaint." Congress had found Brown guilty of publishing "false and groundless assertions and complaints" when in fact "every article in the impeachment was sacredly true and could have been proved so could a proper trial have been obtained, of which Gen. Arnold was well apprised, or he would have been as fond of his trial in the army as his impeachers were." Brown's memorial was read before Congress and "ordered to lie on the table" where it remained.[26]

※ ※ ※

The court-martial of Benedict Arnold on Pennsylvania's charges convened in Middlebrook, New Jersey, on June 1, 1779. Major General Robert Howe of North Carolina, who had served almost entirely in the South, was to preside over thirteen other officers. Before they were sworn in, Arnold objected to three men on the panel: Brigadier General William Irvine, Colonel Richard Butler, and Lieutenant Colonel Josiah Harmar. Arnold expressed "great respect for them" and did not wish to give reasons for his objection. They were the only Pennsylvanians among the officers and that alone may be explanation enough. However, we may again see the shadow of Brown's charges. Irvine had been captured at the Battle of Trois-Rivières after Arnold dodged orders from General Sullivan to support the attack. Butler was commander of the 9th Pennsylvania. His second in command had been Matthew Smith, captain on the march to Québec and now a member of the Pennsylvania Supreme Executive Council. And in May 1776, Josiah Harmar had been a captain under Colonel John Philip de Haas when de Haas clashed with Arnold about whether to destroy the village and inhabitants of Kanesatake. But before a decision on the objection could be reached, word arrived that a British force was moving up the Hudson and the trial was adjourned.

In the meantime, Arnold and John André—a friend of Arnold's young wife and an aide to Henry Clinton, the British commander in New York—began to correspond through intermediaries, using ciphers and code names. In mid–June, Clinton suggested through André what actions Arnold might take in betraying the American cause: "Join the army, accept a command, be surprised, be cut off: these things may happen in the course of manoeuvre, nor you be censured or suspect." For the surrender of five or six thousand men, he would receive twice the number of guineas (a gold coin valued at one pound, one shilling). But Arnold expected £10,000 for his services no matter what happened as well as compensation for financial losses. As proof of his sincerity he sent intelligence on John Sullivan's planned expedition against the Iroquois in western New York and on the movements of Washington's army on the Hudson.[27]

Events in Philadelphia spun out of control as prices rose and food and necessities became scarce. On October 4, a mob menaced prosperous citizens and then attacked the home of James Wilson—lawyer, a leader of the Republican Society, a moderate (or "designing") Whig—in what had become a raw class struggle. Shots were exchanged: one man in the house died; perhaps five in the crowd were killed and fourteen wounded. Reed, who had been home sick, rode with the City Light Cavalry, to break up what came to be called the Fort Wilson Riot. When Arnold arrived on the scene in his carriage, he spoke of Reed with contempt: "Your President has raised a mob and now he cannot quell it." Historians see the riot as a turning point in Pennsylvania history as people began to reject the more democratic provisions of the Constitution of 1776. On October 13, Arnold broke off negotiations with the British.[28]

※ ※ ※

Arnold's court-martial finally opened in Norris's Tavern in Morristown, on December 23, 1779, with Robert Howe still presiding. Pennsylvanians Irvine, Butler, and Harmar had been excused. Briefly Moses Hazen, who had been defendant and then plaintiff in the earlier trials involving Arnold, was mentioned as a possible member of the board, but he was replaced without a challenge being recorded. Five officers, including William Maxwell and Frederick Weissenfels, had been part of Sullivan's Expedition against the Iroquois and had been betrayed by Arnold. But then he had passed on information about "Gen. W's whole Army" as well.[29]

Acting in his own defense, Arnold was calm, seemingly factual, and at times eloquent. His rhetoric from the trial could be mined by a biographer to depict a patriotic officer and gentleman persecuted by lesser men—except he had spent much of the last eight months negotiating with the enemy. He introduced into the record commendations from George Washington and Congress. "If these testimonials have any foundation in truth ... is it probable that after having acquired some little reputation, and after having gained the favourable opinion of those, whose favourable opinion it is an honour to gain, I should all at once sink into a course equally unworthy of the patriot and soldier?" he asked. Historians have been wrestling with this question ever since.[30]

Arnold was indignant—"the presses of Philadelphia have groaned under libels against me"—but, if a reader can judge from the *Proceedings* published by order of Congress, his temper was under control. He answered the accusations against him at length, and he expanded his defense to include charges that Congress had decided not to send to court-martial. He was helped by a prosecution led by Timothy Matlack that did not have solid evidence. Of the charge that he had taken advantage of the closed shops of the city to purchase goods, the Supreme Executive Council could only claim, "as is alledged and believed." Arnold replied with sarcasm: "I am not conversant in the study of jurisprudence; but I have always understood, that *public* charges ought to have some other foundation to rest upon, than mere unsupported '*allegation*' and '*belief*.'"[31]

And so it went: weak evidence confidently refuted. Knowing his audience, he worked in the rumors that Joseph Reed, the "chief" of his prosecutors, "in the hour of *danger*" considered betraying the cause. "I can say I never basked in the sunshine of my general's favour, and courted him to his face, when I was at the same time treating him with the greatest disrespect, and vilifying his character when absent. This is more than a ruling member of the council of the state of Pennsylvania can say, '*as it is alleged and believed*.'"[32]

Arnold ended his defense with a stirring appeal: "I have looked forward with pleasing anxiety to the present day, when, by the judgment of my fellow soldiers, I shall (I doubt not) stand honourably acquitted of all the charges brought against me, and again share with them the glory and danger of this just war."[33]

A reader of the court-martial proceedings who is innocent of any background might conclude that Arnold was sharp in his dealings and indiscreet for someone in such an important position, but not criminal. The officers on the panel were far from uninformed about Arnold. They may have all suspected that he ruined lives and reputations, that he could not be entirely trusted, and that he certainly looked out for his own self-interest. But the charges were being brought by civilians, and, whatever Arnold's faults, he was one of their own and his exploits were a credit to the Continental Army. The verdict was a balancing act. Arnold was justified in closing the shops; the charge that he profited as a result was not supported by evidence. The officers did not even bother to describe the incident of young Matlack being sent for a barber, and simply acquitted Arnold of the "third charge." But the panel found him guilty of giving a pass to the *Charming Nancy*, against the rules and articles of war. His request to use government wagons for private purposes was "imprudent and improper" given "the delicacy attending the high station in which the general acted." He was sentenced to receive a reprimand from General Washington. The verdict, which was then approved by Congress, can be seen as coming close to vindication. Arnold was so satisfied with the results that he asked Silas Deane to have the court-martial proceedings translated into French and published at Arnold's expense.[34]

Some writers have been fooled by a version of Washington's reprimand that appeared in the first full-length study of Arnold's treason, published in 1816 by François Barbé-Marbois, who had been secretary of the French legation to the United States during the war and later negotiated the Louisiana Purchase. In the English translation of the supposed French translation of the letter, Washington was said to write, "I reprimand you for having forgotten, that, in proportion as you had rendered yourself formidable to our enemies, you should have been guarded and temperate in deportment towards your fellow citizen: exhibit anew those noble qualities which have placed you on the list of our most valued commanders." Washington closed by promising Arnold the chance to redeem himself. Biographer Isaac Arnold found the letter to be a "eulogy, such as has rarely been bestowed upon a public officer, and its warm commendation and generous ... sympathy were intended to, and did, express Washington's confidence and respect." But it is a false document.[35]

Washington's genuine reprimand was issued in the General Orders for April 6, 1780, and published in newspapers. The history of court-martial was repeated at length, including all four charges in their entirety and the complete findings of the court. Washington's personal comments followed: "The Commander in Chief would have been much happier in an occasion of bestowing commendations on an officer who has rendered such distinguished services to his Country as Major General Arnold; but in the present case a sense of duty and regard to candor oblige him to declare, that he considers his conduct in the instance of the permit as peculiarly reprehensible, both in a civil and military view, and in the affair of the waggons as 'imprudent and improper.'" The words of censure—*peculiarly reprehensible* (which did not come from the findings of the court), *imprudent*, and *improper*—were set in a harsh, public context.[36]

Three weeks later Congress's Board of Treasury made its report on Arnold's claims for financial reimbursement. The findings were impenetrable then and now. Any evaluation quickly becomes lost in a wilderness of exchange rates, depreciating currency, and missing receipts. The study had been going on for a year, and a congressional committee had admitted to failure. Throughout its report, the treasury board was skeptical of Arnold's claims, finding no proof for many and comparing others unfavorably to the expenses of other generals. In the end, the board computed that rather than deserving reimbursement, Arnold owed the treasury $2,328 in specie, not depreciated Continental currency.

The nineteenth-century account of treason often relied upon Arnold's greed. "Money is this man's God; and, to get enough of it, he would sacrifice his country," John Brown is supposed to have written. But other writers have sympathized with how much Arnold lost by neglecting his business, how expensive it was to be a major general and governor in Philadelphia, and how cheap authorities from the Massachusetts Provincial Congress in 1775 to Continental Congress in 1779 were in reimbursing him for legitimate expenses. Indeed, Congress and state governments often did treat the officers and men who served in the Continental army and the state militias disgracefully, and many, like James Easton and John Brown, were deeply in debt. It was not a problem unique to Arnold. The new nation was built on the backs of men who suffered financially and persevered.

At his death in 1784 after a long illness, Seth Warner owed money to sixteen men and one woman, and his property was sold to cover his debts. Vermont leaders appealed to Congress, writing that the circumstances in which the family found

Seventeen. "Give a thief a length of rope"

itself are "quite necessitous." Nothing came of the petition. An anecdote about debt involves Brown's friend Robert Cochran, who served from the taking of Ticonderoga to the end of the war. As the army was being disbanded, he spoke to Inspector General Baron Von Steuben, who faced his own financial problems. "For myself I care not. But my wife and daughters are in the garret of that wretched tavern, and I have nowhere to carry them, nor even money to remove them." Steuben visited the family and gave them all the money he could afford. Unlike Warner, Cochran had his health. After the war he settled in Ticonderoga and then Sandy Hill (today's Hudson Falls, New York), a short distance from Fort Edward where he is buried.[37]

※ ※ ※

Sometime in May 1780, through handler Joseph Stansbury, Arnold "declared were it not for his Family, he would without ceremony have thrown himself into the protection of the King[']s Army."[38]

On August 5, Arnold took command at West Point, the fortress that guarded a bend in the Hudson River and kept the British to the south. If he had wanted to defend the fortifications, he had one great advantage. He was working with able officers who had served with him and admired him—although less every day. In hindsight, John Lamb, Richard Varick, David Franks, and others had indications what was happening, but they made allowances for decisions that weakened defenses, for his greed in the personal use of public supplies, for his sympathy toward men of questionable patriotism, and for his vile temper. Arnold had escaped responsibility so many times before that he acted as if he was untouchable.

Arnold continued to correspond with friends as if he was not standing on a cliff—or for that matter, had long ago jumped. When news arrived that an army commanded by Horatio Gates was routed by a smaller force under Lord Cornwallis near Camden, South Carolina, and afterwards Gates rode hard away from his defeated army, Arnold wrote to Nathanael Greene. "It is an unfortunate piece of business to that hero and may possibly blot his escutcheon with indelible infamy. It may not be right to censure characters at a distance, but I cannot avoid remarking that his conduct on this occasion has in no wise disappointed my expectations or predictions on frequent occasions." The comment was similar to what he wrote after Ethan

The importance of West Point in stopping British vessels and armies on the Hudson River is evident in this print based on a drawing by military engineer Pierre Charles L'Enfant. The Miriam and Ira D. Wallach Division of Art, Prints and Photographs: Print Collection, The New York Public Library Digital Collections.

Allen embarrassed himself at St. Jean. It "did not surprise me, as it happened as I expected."[39]

Arnold's plot to hand West Point to the British might have succeeded if it had not been for James Livingston, who five years earlier ran the Richelieu rapids and with John Brown captured Fort Chambly. Since the invasion of Canada had failed, Livingston's 1st Canadian Regiment scraped by, recruiting where it could. The return for September 1780 showed only 122 men, and the regiment was scheduled to be dissolved at the end of the year.[40] From their station on the east side of the Hudson River, the 1st Canadians could do nothing about the British sloop-of-war *Vulture*, which sometimes hovered in the river's Haverstraw Bay. Wanting to surprise the sloop, Livingston requested ammunition from John Lamb at West Point. The two had known each other since Lamb led an artillery company at the siege of St. John and was grievously wounded in the attack on Québec. Lamb was skeptical that light cannon could do much damage, but he did as Livingston asked.

On September 22, the 1st Canadians opened fire upon the *Vulture* from Teller's Point, the peninsula that divides Haverstraw Bay and the Tappan Zee. They did not know that the *Vulture* had delivered John André to a nighttime meeting with Arnold and was waiting to take him back to the city. The *Vulture* endured cannon fire for two hours before leaving its station and stranding André behind enemy lines. Dressed in civilian clothes, he attempted to make his way back to New York. He was captured with evidence in his boot that implicated Arnold.

Arnold's treason was a near miss. Had he been more cautious in his planning, had he been—as Matthias Ogden put it about the Lake Champlain fleet—prudent as well as brave, the British might have taken West Point. Had Arnold been lucky in his timing, they might have also gathered in George Washington and his senior generals. The capture of West Point would have been a blow to the American cause; the loss of Washington might have ended the war.

When Arnold's plans came crashing down on September 25, he had himself rowed to the *Vulture* and began a career as a cruel but ineffective British general.

Eighteen

"Ah! hapless friend, permit the tender tear"

While Arnold's betrayal played itself out along the Hudson River, British, Loyalists, and their Native allies moved toward the Mohawk and Lake Champlain frontiers. Although there is no documentary evidence that the attacks were planned to coordinate with the fall of West Point, Americans in New York believed that they were Arnold's victims. Still, even if Arnold had never contemplated treason, New York west of Albany would have been in flames in 1780. The Iroquois, whose homeland had been destroyed by Sullivan's Expedition, wanted revenge as did the Mohawk Valley Loyalists, who had lost their homes.[1]

The raiders used the same general routes as in 1777, threatening Albany from the north and the west at the same time. In 1780, the goal was destruction and terror, not conquest, and the combined armies were about a fifth the size of Burgoyne's and St. Leger's. The Americans had been surprised in 1777, although they shouldn't have been; now they were hardly surprised but were even less prepared.

On September 20, one day before Arnold and André met to make their final plans, Sir John Johnson reached Oswego, on Lake Ontario. He was joined by Mohawk leader Joseph Brant, Seneca war chief Cornplanter, and 265 Iroquois. The raiding party included Butler's Loyalist Rangers, British Regulars, and a few German Jaegers for a total of about 950 men.[2] On September 28, Major Christopher Carleton, Guy Carleton's nephew, and nearly a thousand men sailed from St. Jean to Île-aux-Noix.

※ ※ ※

John Brown was already stationed on the Mohawk River. He returned to the army as a result of the struggle for a Massachusetts constitution. In 1779, as a member of the legislature, he had worked for a constitution, but the effort failed and he lost his seat in the assembly. A constitution, drafted largely by John Adams, was approved in June 1780. There were property qualifications for voting. A Senate was elected by the wealthy. The governor was chosen by the General Court after local input and could veto legislation, although the veto could be overridden by a two-thirds vote. But one aspect of this conservative document appealed to the Constitutionalists like the Rev. Thomas Allen: militiamen chose their captains and lieutenants, who in turn elected the colonel. And so on July 14, 1780, through an election, Brown once again commanded the middle Berkshire County Regiment. He named James Easton's son, also James, adjutant.[3]

That summer when Berkshire levies—short term soldiers in the Continental service—were called up, John Ashley, Jr., of Sheffield, senior colonel in the county and commander of the southern Berkshire regiment, was ordered to the Mohawk Valley. The Berkshire men were as far as Albany when Ashley fell ill. Brown was already in the city on business and agreed to take command.

He borrowed two pistols from Ashley, giving him a receipt. The tale of the borrowed pistols is among several peculiar stories generated by Brown's death. According to *The History of Pittsfield*, Ashley died not long after Brown, and when the executors of Ashley's estate found the receipt, they insisted on payment. In fact, Ashley lived until 1799 and made the petty demand himself. Brown's estate paid £6 s7.[4]

It was said that on his way to the Mohawk, Brown visited Mother Ann Lee, the Shaker prophet, in the celibate sect's first home, seven miles northwest of Albany. This much of the story is unquestionably true: western Massachusetts and the New York towns on the border were already swept up in a religious revival, and in May of 1780 several pastors met with Mother Ann and spread word of the sect's beliefs. Although the Shakers were far from the national curiosity they were to be become in the nineteenth century, people in Berkshire County were intrigued. In a story that may have started as one of Brown's jokes—if there is any truth to it at all—he told Mother Ann that after his service on the Mohawk, he and his wife would join the Shakers. In the tale, following his death, two Shaker sisters arrived at Huldah's house in Pittsfield and told her of her husband's promise. But "she was not to be duped, and bade them begone."[5]

In fact, on April 28, 1782, Huldah—"widow Brown," in the church records—then 29, married Jared Ingersoll of Pittsfield. Her second husband had served in the militia in the Revolution, at least once in Brown's regiment, and finally in the Continental Army. Known as *Captain* Ingersoll, he kept a popular tavern, which was firmly under Huldah's control in his absence. Jared took the side of the rebels in Shay's Rebellion and was imprisoned in Northampton, but returned to Pittsfield as a respected citizen. His graceful handwriting indicates a good education. Huldah strove to improve her own literacy. In 1782 her signature was shaky; by 1794 she signed a legal document with confidence.[6] The couple had five children (one died as a toddler) and lived long lives. Huldah died in November 1834 and Jared followed less than three months later.[7]

※ ※ ※

John Brown arrived on the Mohawk in late August 1780 and reported to Brigadier General Robert Van Rensselaer at Fort Rensselaer (also known as Fort Plain) near what is now the village of Fort Plain. The fort was about halfway between Albany and Fort Schuyler and was headquarters to a constellation of stockades and blockhouses. Van Rensselaer was a recent general who had been colonel of the 8th Albany County Regiment at Saratoga. In the spring of 1780, he had been part of an army of New Yorkers and Vermonters that nearly trapped Sir John Johnson at Crown Point after his destruction of Johnstown. *Nearly* is the key word. The Americans led by Governor George Clinton celebrated as if they had won a victory against the feared Sir John; Canadian historian Gavin Watt saw only a "failed pursuit" and "wishful thinking."[8]

On September 2, Van Rensselaer ordered Brown and two hundred men to escort a dozen boats of supplies west to Fort Schuyler. When Brown returned from that

Eighteen. "Ah! hapless friend, permit the tender tear"

assignment, he took command at Fort Paris, a blockhouse and stockade on high ground in Stone Arabia, a settlement about three or four miles north of the river, ten miles west of where his legal career began in Johnstown. Two companies from Brown's regiment were stationed at Fort Rensselaer; other men were sent to the forts along Schoharie Creek south of the Mohawk. The valleys bristled with "forts," a measure not of strength but of vulnerability. Terrified families crowded into these stockades and fortified houses, and men worked their fields with muskets ready.[9]

In late September, early October, Brown had the bitter satisfaction of learning of Arnold's betrayal. Likely he believed that the treason proved to the world that he had been right all along. But who did he see who might understand? On the Mohawk, he worked closely with Colonel Lewis Dubois, one of Arnold's supporters from the siege of Québec. In his letter to John Hancock accusing Brown of plundering, Arnold named Dubois as a witness. In May 1776, the Commissioners to Canada had recommended Dubois to the Congress for promotion at Arnold's request. What did Brown and Dubois say to each other when they spoke of Arnold?[10]

※ ※ ※

On October 16, after an exhausting march of nearly 150 miles from Oswego, Sir John Johnson's raiders reached Schoharie Creek about twenty-five miles south of where it joins the Mohawk. The Schoharie was defended by three forts. The raiders bypassed the upper fort (the Schoharie flows north, so "upper" is south), attempted to capture the middle fort, and then destroyed, plundered, and burned their way toward the Mohawk and Fort Hunter on the east bank of the creek. In Schenectady, General Van Rensselaer begged inhabitants for hundreds of horses and many wagons, but promises were made and not kept. He requisitioned beef cattle intended for Fort Schuyler and saw that his militiamen were fed. They left the town around noon, October 18, and marched through the day, paused in the evening at Fort Hunter, crossed Schoharie Creek in boats, and continued by moonlight until four in the morning. From Van Epps (today's Fultonville) after four a.m., his secretary, John Lansing, Jr., wrote Brown and Dubois. From Van Epps, Stone Arabia was across the river and ten miles away in a direct line. Johnson's raiders stood between Van Epps and Fort Rensselaer, so express rider William Wallace would have gone to Fort Rensselaer by way of Brown and Fort Paris.[11]

However strained their relationship had been at Québec, Brown and Dubois were in communication during the day. Like Brown, Dubois was a professional among part-timers, a retired Continental officer and former commander of the 5th New York returned to service. On October 18, he sent two companies of Brown's men to Fort Paris and at midnight, he wrote to Brown that he intended crossing the Mohawk "by break of Day." When John Johnson searched Brown's pockets after he was killed, he found Dubois's letter, which is now in the Frederick Haldimand Papers in the British Library. So when Van Rensselaer's letter arrived, Brown was already inclined to think he was participating in a coordinated attack.[12]

The letter from Lansing to Brown with Van Rensselaer's orders does not survive, although Johnson also found it in Brown's pocket and noted some of the contents. According to the letter, Van Rensselaer was already further west than Fort Hunter with six hundred militia and three field guns. Perhaps the letter to Brown was close to the one to Dubois. Lansing told Dubois that Van Rensselaer planned to attack "as soon as day appears" and advised him to march downstream "with all the men you have, with as much expedition as possible." Brown may have been read something similar: *March with all your men, and between General Van Rensselaer, Colonel Dubois, and you, we will crush Johnson.*[13]

But at sunrise in a thick fog, Johnson's raiders forded the Mohawk at Keator's Rift, near today's hamlet of Sprakers, and climbed from the valley toward Stone Arabia. They had escaped Van Rensselaer's trap, and Brown was facing them alone. Johnson believed that Brown was "induced to march" by two Loyalist deserters who told him that the raiders on the north side of the Mohawk were weak. Whatever the reason, on the morning of October 19—Brown's thirty-sixth birthday—he and more than three hundred men left Fort Paris. After Brown's death, it was believed in Pittsfield that Giles Parker dreamed of disaster and begged Brown to remain in the stockade. "What, are *you* afraid to march with me? Then stay behind," Brown said. Parker replied he was not afraid for himself, but for his colonel. Parker was among the first to die.[14]

In the Mohawk Valley and western Massachusetts, Van Rensselaer got the blame for the massacre that followed. In the Pittsfield account, Van Rensselaer—"an exceedingly sluggish and incompetent commander"—lingered over his breakfast, a version of events that misses the point. Van Rensselaer may be blamed for naively expecting a veteran enemy to stay put on the south side of the river while three separate forces converged and for not realizing how exhausted, frightened, and inexperienced his own men were, but he should not be blamed for a lack of initiative or for putting personal comfort first. Following a court of inquiry in March 1781, a brigadier and two colonels found that Van Rensselaer was "a good, active, faithful, prudent, and spirited officer" and that the "public clamor" against him was "without the least foundation." But the judges were not professional soldiers themselves, and the inquiry did not delve into the disaster at Stone Arabia. Had Van Rensselaer given unclear or overly optimistic orders? Or had Brown wrongly taken the initiative and suffered the consequences?[15]

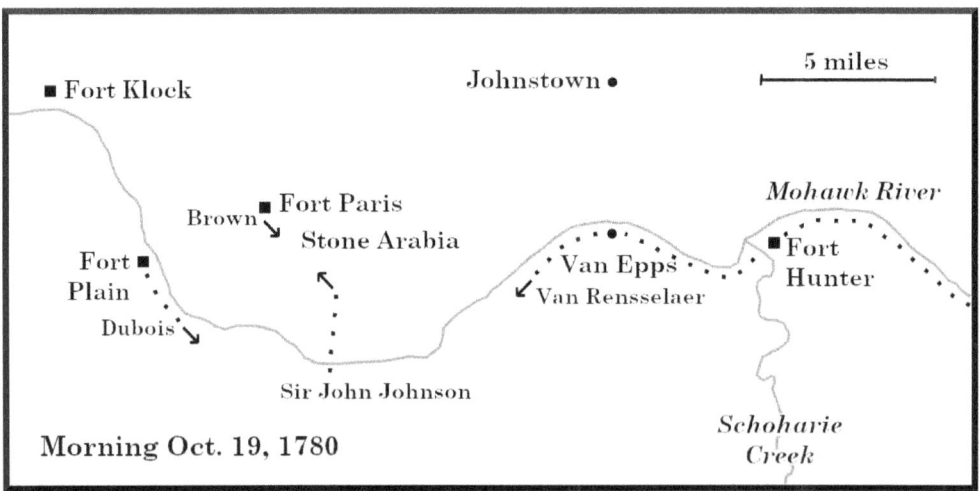

On the morning of October 19, 1780, Sir John Johnson and his raiders crossed the Mohawk River at Keator's Rift and moved toward Stone Arabia and John Brown, who faced him alone.

There are no totally reliable documents about the Battle of Stone Arabia. American narratives are based on early impressions and the recollections of old-timers filtered by nineteenth-century sensibilities. Sir John Johnson's report to Governor Frederick Haldimand, written less than two weeks after the battle, is detailed and seemingly convincing—and contradicts nearly everything found in Jeptha Simms's classic histories of the New York frontier and Smith's *History of Pittsfield*.[16]

In the Pittsfield account, Brown's men marched two miles before a stranger approached and said he had orders from Van Rensselaer for them to follow. With Brown and Major Oliver Root in the lead, the men from Fort Paris entered a clearing—"a treacherous *cul-de-sac*"—near the small Fort Keyser stockade. Suddenly a sergeant shouted, "See that damned Indian!" and a moment later the first volley tore through the column. "A thousand muskets, gleaming from behind sheltering trees, poured in a rapid and murderous crossfire upon the entrapped and bewildered troops." In the first volley, Brown was hit in the heart and "fell upon his face without word or struggle."[17]

In Johnson's report, after the first volleys, the raiders were in the clearing and Brown's men were behind trees. Rather than facing Brown with nearly a thousand men, Johnson sent forward Natives and "part of" three regiments. Canadian historian Watt estimated that the actual battle was between about 160 raiders and 170 of Brown's men, not 900 against 380. "It was not numbers that won, it was nerve, skill and decisive leadership," he wrote. But Johnson's report has an exaggeration that raises the question whether there might be even more storytelling. In patriot accounts, about forty Americans—"more than thirty" in Jeptha Simms's account—died at Stone Arabia, a believable catastrophe. But Johnson told Haldimand that "about one hundred Officers and Men were slain."[18]

Panic seized the Americans and they fled back toward Fort Paris or toward the Mohawk and the greater safety of Fort Rensselaer. Simms heard from old-timers that Brown was killed "contesting the ground inch by inch." Major Oliver Root, now in command, believed that many men escaped because the Indians stopped to kill and scalp. In Johnson's report, Brown was killed in the pursuit. His body was a special prize: he was completely scalped, not just the crown of his head, and he was stripped of clothes, except for a ruffled shirt.[19]

After the fighting had moved on, four men from Fort Keyser carried Brown's body into the stockade. At Fort Paris, Major Root organized the defense. The fort was so weak that the defenders had only three charges of powder and one ball for their four-pound cannon. A chain used to drag logs and a broken cooking pot were fired. Fortunately, the enemy was more interested in burning buildings and grain than in attacking the fort.[20]

Van Rensselaer's men started marching at dawn and around ten a.m. could hear musket fire across the river. At two o'clock in the afternoon, Dubois met Van Rensselaer below Fort Rensselaer and told him of Brown's defeat. Fording the Mohawk took time. Some men waded; others clambered across wagons that were dragged into the stream to form a bridge. With night coming on, an inconclusive battle was fought at Klock's Field on the north side of the river, but the raiders escaped as the American flanks fired upon each other and Van Rensselaer ordered a retreat. The next day Governor George Clinton took command, but by then the raiders had vanished.

Brown was memorialized in one of the first attempts at a major work of poetry by an American writer. In 1782, while part of the Continental Army encamped along the Hudson River, Lieutenant Colonel David Humphreys, an aide-de-camp to General Washington, wrote "Address to the Armies of the United States of America," a poem of 466 lines. His purpose, he explained, was "to inspire our countrymen, now in arms, or may hereafter be called into the field, with perseverance and fortitude, through every species of difficulty and danger, to continue their exertions for the defence of their country, and the preservation of its liberties."[21]

David Humphreys, an aide to General Washington, memorialized John Brown in one of the first attempts by an American to write a major work of poetry. This engraving is based on a portrait by Gilbert Stuart. The Miriam and Ira D. Wallach Division of Art, Prints and Photographs: Print Collection, The New York Public Library Digital Collections.

Like Alexander Hamilton, John Laurens, and Lafayette, Humphreys was one of the young officers who were part of Washington's military family and had a close bond with the general. You can imagine some alternative draft of the musical *Hamilton* in which Humphreys amuses the audience with clumsy rhymed couplets, a distant cousin of rap. Humphreys was with David Wooster when he was killed during the Danbury Raid: "Wooster was seen to stand—and like that oak, / I saw him fall beneath the fatal stroke."[22] Following the surrender at Yorktown, Humphreys carried the captured British colors and Washington's report to Congress. In peacetime, he served in Europe as a commissioner, diplomat, and secret agent; he was Washington's personal secretary at Mount Vernon and early in his presidency. As a writer, Humphreys was part of the literary group known as the Connecticut (or Hartford) Wits. An early-twentieth-century scholar put Humphreys's standing this way: "Of all the wooden poetry of the Connecticut bards, David Humphreys's seems to me the woodenest."[23] But no matter how contrived were his rhymes, his love of country and his admiration for Washington and his fellow soldiers cannot be mocked.

In "Address to the Armies," Humphreys shows the tragedy of war through the deaths of three men: Brown, Alexander Scammell, and John Laurens. *The Journal de Paris* commented that the recital of these deaths "will ever be read with sympathetic sorrow."[24] Scammell, who was a close friend of Washington, was killed at Yorktown less than three weeks before Cornwallis's surrender. Laurens fell during the

Eighteen. "Ah! hapless friend, permit the tender tear"

inconsequential Battle of the Combahee River, August 27, 1782, making him one of the last casualties of the war. Brown, who was introduced first in the poem and most sorrowfully, had been Humphreys's classmate at Yale.

> And scarce Columbia's arms the fight sustains,
> While her best blood gush'd from a thousand veins.
> Then thine, O Brown! that purpled wide the ground,
> Pursued the knife through many a ghastly wound.
> Ah! hapless friend! permit the tender tear
> To flow e'en now, for none flow'd on thy bier,
> Where cold and mangled, under northern skies,
> To famish'd wolves a prey thy body lies,
> Which erst so fair and tall in youthful grace,
> Strength in thy nerves, and beauty in thy face,
> Stood like a tow'r, till struck by the swift ball,
> Then what avail'd (to award th' untimely fall)
> The force of limbs, the mind so well inform'd,
> The taste refin'd, the breast with friendship warm'd
> (That friendship which our earliest years begun)
> Or what laurels that thy sword had won,
> When the dark bands from thee, expiring, tore
> Thy long hair mingled with the spouting gore?[25]

※ ※ ※

John Brown is buried in Stone Arabia near a magnificent stone church. His son, the sheriff of Berkshire County, erected the memorial in 1836. Author photograph.

The slain at Stone Arabia, including Brown, were buried in a mass grave, but a few days later, his body was exhumed and brought to a graveyard near the smoldering remains of the Dutch Reformed Church. In 1836 on the anniversary of the battle, a marble monument was dedicated at the site west of a magnificent limestone block church built after the war. An elderly pastor gave a discourse on Joshua 4:21–22: "When your children shall ask their fathers in time to come, saying, What *mean* these stones? Then ye shall let your children know, saying, Israel came over this Jordan on dry land." Henry C. Brown, sheriff of Berkshire County, who had been a-year-and-half old when his father died, purchased the monument and stood with the large crowd.[26]

Conclusion

"A few gentlemen became acquainted with his true character"

On the day John André was hanged as a spy, Nathanael Greene wrote to Rhode Island governor William Greene, his third cousin, "Since the fall of Lucifer, nothing has equaled the fall of Arnold. His Military reputation in Europe and America was flattering to the first Generals of the Age. He will now sink as low as he has been high before; and as the devil made war upon heaven after his fall, so I expect Arnold will upon America." Greene was recalling Milton's epic poem *Paradise Lost*, familiar to any literate person. Lucifer is the most favored of the angels, but declares, "Better to reign in Hell, than to serve in Heaven." Twenty-first-century Americans may recognize the archetype in Darth Vader, the greatest of the Jedi Knights before he goes over to the Dark Side. Like Lord Vader, Lucifer—"son of the morning" in the Book of Isaiah—is the most interesting character in the story.[1]

On the same day as Greene's letter, Anthony Wayne wrote to his friend Hugh Sheel, a Philadelphia doctor:

> I am confident that the perfidy of Genl. Arnold will astonish the multitude—the high rank he bore—the *eclat* he had Obtained (whether honestly or not) Justified the world in giving it him.
>
> But there were a few Gentlemen who at a very early period of this War became acquainted with his true Character!—when you asked my Opinion of that Officer I gave it freely—& believe you thought it rather strongly shaded—
>
> I think I informed you that I had the most despicable Idea of him both as a Gentleman & a Soldier—& that he had produced a conviction on me in 1776—that honor & true Virtue were Strangers to his Soul, and however Contradictory it might appear—that he never possessed either fortitude or personal bravery—he was naturally a Coward, and never went in the way of Danger but when Stimulated by Liquor even to Intoxication, consequently Incapacitated from Conducting any Command committed to his charge.[2]

Sheel replied that he remembered the conversation, which "made a strong impression on my mind." Arnold biographers keep a distance from Wayne's opinion and Sheel's confirmation that it predated Arnold's treason.[3]

Discussions of Arnold, his treason and his heroism, seldom stray far from the lines drawn by Greene and Wayne. Fallen angel or disreputable all along? In the beginning, people were willing to believe any story about Arnold's wickedness. His first biographer, Jared Sparks, wrote that as a boy he tortured baby birds so that he could hear the cries of the parents and that he scattered broken glass on the road where barefoot children walked to school. He was also so daring that he would cling to a mill wheel and ride it into the air and below the water.[4] When Isaac Arnold's biography was published in 1880, making the still shocking case that Benedict "was not so black as he has been painted," John Austin Stevens, a lifelong student of the Revolution, writing in the influential *Magazine of American History*, responded that Arnold was actually a "villain of a deeper dye than is commonly supposed.... Search thoroughly the character of Arnold, and the traits which culminated in the crowning treachery will be found characteristic of every part of his career and of each epoch of his life." The earliest writers were seldom troubled by the question of why Arnold betrayed the American cause. If he was reprehensible from childhood, you didn't need look much further for an explanation. In Sparks's biography, Arnold exhibited great heroism, but at Saratoga "all accounts agree, that his conduct was rash in the extreme, indicating rather the frenzy of a madman, than the considerate wisdom of an experienced general."[5]

Arnold's reputation first began to turn in 1847 with the publication of two books, both titled *Washington and his Generals*. The United States was at war with Mexico, and authors and readers were looking for military heroes. In George Lippard's Gothic romance—the source for Arnold's "Indian name" Dark Eagle and for the mysterious rider on a black horse—Arnold is a proud, troubled hero and patriot, roiled by the emotions of the Romantic Era. "The man who can read his life, in all its details, without tears, has a heart harder than the roadside flint," Lippard wrote.[6] The other *Washington and his Generals* was written by Joel T. Headley, a clergyman and editor, who was later New York secretary of state, elected as a member of the nativist American Party, formerly the Native American Party or the Know Nothings. Headley's history is nonfiction, but it is filled with melodramatic descriptions and patriotic sermonizing. Arnold's heroism was extraordinary. He was prudent and skillful; his mind worked quickly; and he was vigorous in attack and unyielding in retreat. On the Kennebec River, "Loud cheers received his frail canoe as it came and went in sight of those brave fellows who seemed suddenly to have caught his energy and determination." As the gunboats are torched at Ferris Bay, Arnold smiles with proud defiance "as he gazes off on the baffled enemy, and his brow knit like iron in stern resolve, he presents a picture on which it grieves us he should ever have cast such a dreadful shadow." Simply, "A *braver* man never led an army."[7]

And to further confuse the reading public and future researchers, a third book with a nearly identical title was published around the same time: *Washington and the Generals of the American Revolution* (1848) by Rufus W. Griswold, William Gilmore Simms, and Edward D. Ingraham. The authors and publishers of the three *Washington and his/the Generals* sparred about who had first claim to the concept and the powerful title. Carey & Hart, publishers of the Griswold-Simms-Ingraham effort, maintained that their book was underway before Headley began his. But in the chapter on Benedict Arnold, Griswold & Company appear to be reacting to Headley and Lippard. They denounced Arnold's "whimsical apologists," who excused his treason "by attributing it to some outward or irresistible pressure, or by the recapitulation of his earlier deeds of audacious bravery."[8]

The Civil War radically changed perceptions of warfare and of Arnold. If you are inspired by bold strategy, decisive battles with glorious charges, and casualties on an industrial scale, there is no comparing the Revolution to the Civil War. But Arnold can be made to fit the Civil War mold. You can imagine him in blue or a gray raiding behind enemy lines, holding a key road while others fled, or leading an unexpected charge across an open field against an entrenched enemy. An 1877 guide to Saratoga told visitors, "The genius of war thrilled Arnold's soul, as epic metres stir the poet, as rugged landscapes, shadowed under sunset lights, influence the artist's brain." John Watts de Peyster's nameless boot at Saratoga, Alfred Mahan's unqualified praise of Valcour Island, and Kenneth Roberts's novels all played a part in painting the portrait of a brilliant soldier. In 1954, historian Willard Wallace, who was a captain in World War II, compared Arnold the soldier to Stonewall Jackson, John Bell Hood, William Tecumseh Sherman, Douglas MacArthur, and George Patton.[9]

For people who pay little attention to history, *Benedict Arnold* is only a synonym for traitor, but for those who are interested in the American Revolution, he has become the early hero. Many writers have sympathized with the great, tragically flawed figure, hounded by lesser men. John Jay Chapman—a noted early-twentieth-century essayist, reformer, and descendant of John Jay—even wrote a play about Arnold, modeled on Greek tragedy and presided over by Father Hudson, the god of the river, and men's and women's choruses.[10] Today the notion that Arnold the patriotic soldier ranks next to Washington seems to delight scholarly and popular historians, novelists, filmmakers, and podcasters. Kevin Phillips, a savvy political commentator turned historian, in *1775: A Good Year for Revolution,* suggests Arnold was the "Indispensable Man of 1775" and writes, "It is jarring to read about an Arnold whose accomplishments were second only to Washington." Often the *next-to-Washington* phrase is perfunctory. Washington's strength was in the dull work of holding together a fragile army and a divided nation. A romanticized Arnold wins the glory.[11] If it were not for the weight of citations that support the many Arnold biographies, you might conclude you are reading a peculiar founding myth: *The greatest soldier from the birth of the republic was mistreated by politicians and fellow officers; he came to recognize the sordidness around him; and understandably (tragically or nobly, take your pick) he turned his coat.*

Arnold's own public explanation of his actions is that he did not betray the cause of liberty or that of his homeland, only an unjust rebellion. As he put it in a published address to the Inhabitants of America, October 7, 1780, written with the help of William Smith, Royal Chief Justice of New York, a tyranny of usurpers was "criminally protracting the War from Sinister Views, at the expense of the Public Interest." America's "worst enemies are in her own bosom." Leaders had accepted "the Insidious offers of France" while "I preferred those from Great Britain, thinking it infinitely wiser and safer to cast my Confidence upon her Justice and Generosity, than to trust a Monarchy ... [that] holds her Native Sons in Vassalage and Chains." Like many Arnold documents, the address seems sincere—unless you have studied his history of using the written word to deceive and manipulate.[12]

At times there is an undemocratic thread running through the praise of pre-treason Arnold. Know Nothing Joel Headley wrote, "The enemies of Arnold have a heavy account to render for their injustice, and our Congress would do well to take warning from their example."[13] In Kenneth Roberts's *Rabble in Arms*, fictional Peter Merrill comments that Arnold despised the "pettiness, timidity, inefficiency, futility and hesitation" of the Continental Congress. Roberts saw the same faults in the twentieth-century U.S. Congress. Writing in the *Saturday Evening Post* and republished in his 1924 book praising Italian fascism, Roberts termed the Democratic and Republican parties "two different brands of round, smelly, imported cheese." He wrote, "Of late years the nation's political flabbiness and lack of principle have been aggravated by organized and aggressive minorities who have discovered that when they scream loudly enough and long enough for certain things, their screams are mistaken by senators and representatives for nation-wide demands."[14]

As he was during the Revolution, John Brown is an inconvenient voice. If his allegations are true—or compelling enough to require serious investigation—then Washington and other leaders were mistaken, and the standard biographies and magisterial histories need rethinking. Not surprisingly, Arnold biographers are quick to dismiss Brown. They are like the Continental Congress's War Board, which sat down with Arnold on the evening of May 21, 1777, and, without hearing from Brown or anyone else, found in Arnold's favor. In his thirteen charges, Brown describes a man who has little in common with the Arnold found in biographies, histories, and novels. Arnold libels Brown in letters to authorities, slanders him in private before other officers, but will not back up his accusations in open court. He disobeys orders and avoids responsibility. He is cruel, devious, and a hypocrite; he is a heedless man who engages in a series of small betrayals before the ultimate disloyalty we have all heard about. Brown says nothing of his bravery on the battlefield, but is clear that Arnold lacks the true courage of an eighteenth-century gentleman.

Most of the American Revolution is forgotten today. In popular history, we are faced with books by a few bestselling authors focusing on a few celebrity founders, the great men who were (to use Thomas Carlyle's phrase again) the creators "of whatsoever the general mass of men contrived to do or attain."[15] For some, Benedict Arnold was such a person. Like Lucifer in *Paradise Lost*, he was the most compelling figure. We need not resolve the academic debate about Great Man Theory, history from below, and the cultural and economic conditions that shape events to recognize that exaggerations about Arnold are unjust to other leaders and to thousands of ordinary men and women. In the thin slice of the Revolution found in this narrative, Arnold's adversaries—Ethan Allen, James Easton, Roger Enos, Oliver Hanchet, Moses Hazen, John Philip de Haas, David Wooster, John Sullivan, Timothy Bedel, William Gilliland, Jacobus Wynkoop, David Waterbury, Horatio Gates, Joseph Reed, Timothy Matlack, etcetera—are given respectful hearings. With all their faults, they—and hundreds like them—are the foundation upon which the United States was built.

John Brown was confident, perhaps overconfident. It is easy to imagine that generals and political leaders found him annoying. Whistleblowers, to use the modern term, are troublesome because they insist on truths that others see but choose to ignore. Brown believed that he had done as much for the American cause as Arnold and once complained that Congress had allowed Arnold to "establish a character on the ruins of a man, who, to speak moderately, has rendered his country as essential service as that dangerous general."[16] This piece of eighteenth-century swagger may be a measure of Brown's conceit and arrogance, but it contains some truth. Brown contributed to bringing the Revolution to western Massachusetts and to creating the Massachusetts provincial government. He was an important messenger, spy, and express rider. He was a daring soldier. Alone among Continental officers, many of whom had doubts about Arnold, he was outspoken. Raising the issue of Arnold's conduct and never backing down was his most courageous act. Though he had reasons to be bitter, he remained loyal and died defending his country.

Appendix

John Brown's Thirteen Charges Against Benedict Arnold and Related Letters

American Archives, ser. 5, 3:1158–60; Papers of the Continental Congress, M247, r174, i154, v1, p125–28 and M247, r91, i78, v2, p117.

Potential Witnesses can be found in the margin of a copy sent from Brown to Theodore Sedgwick, December 6, 1776, Sedgwick Family Papers, Massachusetts Historical Society. In the list to Sedgwick, Brown reversed the order of two charges.

John Brown to John Hancock, President of the Continental Congress

Albany, 10th December, 1776. (Read in Congress, December 26, 1776.)

SIR: Enclosed is transmitted a copy of the second petition I preferred to Major-General Horatio Gates, praying a compliance with the order of Congress for a Court of Inquiry on myself, together with a complaint against, and petition for the trial of, General Arnold, for the crimes therein mentioned, as also a copy of the answer, which I obtained with difficulty, as will appear by the copies herewith transmitted; which puts me under the necessity of troubling you on a subject which ought to have been considered and determined by a different tribunal, agreeable to the rules of war. I must therefore once more request a peremptory rule of Congress for my own as well as General Arnold's trial, at such time and place as the honourable Congress shall think proper to appoint. I must nevertheless take the liberty of observing, that I think myself to have been treated in a most extraordinary and singular manner; and should my treatment be adopted as a precedent in the Continental Army, Congress would have nothing to do but hearing the trifling complaints of the officers in their service.

I must also request that proper provision be made for summoning, and compelling if need should be, such witnesses to attend the trial as shall be thought necessary.

I am, sir, with respect, your humble servant,
John Brown
To the Hon. John Hancock, Esq., President of the Continental Congress, at Philadelphia.

※ ※ ※

John Brown to Horatio Gates

December 1, 1776

To the Hon. Horatio Gates, Esq., Major-General in the Army of the United State of America, Commanding at Albany, humbly showeth:

That in the month of February last, Brigadier-General Arnold transmitted to the honourable Continental Congress an unjustifiable, false, wicked, and malicious accusation against me and my character, as an officer in their service; at the time when I was under his immediate command. That had there been the least ground for such accusation, the author thereof had it in his power, indeed it was his duty, to have brought me to a fair trial by a General Court-Martial in the country where the pretended crime is said to have originated. That I was left to the necessity of applying to Congress, not only for the charge given in against me, but an order for a Court of Inquiry on my own conduct with respect thereto. That in consequence of my application, I obtained a positive order of Congress to the then General commanding the Northern Department, for a Court of Inquiry, before whom I might justify my injured character. That the said order was transmitted to your Honour, at Ticonderoga, in the month of August last, and notwithstanding the most ardent solicitation on my part, the order of Congress has not yet been complied with. That upon my renewing my application to your Honour for a Court of Inquiry, you was pleased to refer me to the Board of War. Thus I have been led an expensive dance from Generals to Congress, and from Congress to Generals, and am now referred to a Board of War, who, I will venture to say, have never yet taken cognizance of any such matter, nor do I think it, with great submission to your Honour, any part of their duty. I therefore must conclude that this information, from the mode of its origin, as well as from the repeated evasions of a fair hearing, is now rested on the author's shoulders. I therefore beg your Honour will please to order Brigadier-General Arnold in arrest, for the following crimes, which I am ready to verify, viz:

> 1st. For endeavouring to asperse your petitioner's character, in the most infamous manner.
> Witnesses: Jeremy Duggan, Theodore Sedgwick
>
> 2d. For unwarrantably degrading and reducing the rank conferred on your petitioner by his (General Arnold's) superiour officer, and subjecting your petitioner to serve in an inferiour rank to that which he had been appointed.
> Witnesses: Frederick Weissenfels, Robert Cochran
>
> 3d. For ungentleman-like conduct in his letter to General Wooster, of the 25th of January last, charging your petitioner with a falsehood, and in a private manner, which is justly chargeable on himself.
> Witnesses and evidence: Robert Cochran, William Satterlee, the letter from Benedict Arnold to David Wooster, January 25, 1776
>
> 4th. For suffering the small-pox to spread in the camp before Quebeck, and promoting inoculations there in the Continental Army.
> Witnesses: Robert Cochran, Dr. Isaac Senter, Dr. John Coates, Frederick Weissenfels
>
> 5th. For depriving a part of the Army under his command of their usual allowance of provisions ordered by Congress.
> Witnesses: Seth Warner, Jeremiah Cady
>
> 6th. For interfering and countermanding the orders of his superiour officer.
> Witnesses: Moses Hazen, Samuel Brewer, Theodore Sedgwick
>
> 7th. For plundering the inhabitants of Montreal, in direct violation of a solemn capitulation agreement entered into with them by our late brave and worthy General Montgomery, to the eternal disgrace of the Continental arms.

Witnesses: Edward Antill, James Colwell, assistant quartermasters, Daniel Tucker, Orringh Stoddard, "Captain" John Patterson

8th. For giving unjustifiable, unwarrantable, cruel, and bloody orders, directing whole villages to be destroyed, and the inhabitants thereof put to death by fire and sword, without any distinctions to friend or foe, age or sex.
Evidence: "the Orders Themselves"

9th. For entering into an unwarrantable, unjustifiable, and partial agreement with Captain Foster for the exchange of prisoners taken at The Cedars, without the knowledge, advice, or consent of any officer than those present with him on the spot.
Witnesses and evidence: Moses Hazen, John Philip de Haas, the Resolves of Congress, July 10, 1776

10th. For ordering inoculation of the Continental Army at Sorel, without the knowledge of, and contrary to the intentions of, the General commanding that Northern Department, by which fatal consequences ensued.
Witnesses: Theodore Sedgwick, Samuel Brewer, Joshua Thomas

11th. [12th in the Sedgwick list] For great misconduct during his command, from the camp at Cambridge, in the year 1775, until he was superseded by General Montgomery, at Point-aux-Tremble, near Quebec.
Witnesses: Edward Antill, Roger Enos, William Goodrich

12th. [11th in the Sedgwick list] For great misconduct in his command of the Continental fleet in Lake Champlain, which occasioned the loss thereof.
Witnesses: David Waterbury, Edward Wigglesworth, Captain John-Baptiste Allin (?) "& Every Man of common Sense."

13th. For disobedience of the orders of his superiour officers, while acting by a commission from the Provincial Congress of the Province of the Massachusetts-Bay, and for disobedience of the orders of a Committee of the same Congress, sent from that State to inspect into his conduct; and also for insulting, abusing, and imprisoning the said Committee; as also for a treasonable attempt to make his escape with the navigators then at or near Ticonderoga, to the enemy at St. John's, which obliged the then commanding officer of Ticonderoga and its dependencies to issue a positive order to the officers commanding our batteries at Crown-Point to stop or sink the vessels attempting to pass that post, and by force of arms make a prisoner of the said General Arnold, (then a Colonel,) which was accordingly done.
Witnesses: Walter Spooner, James Sullivan, Jedediah Foster, William Duer, Robert Cochran, Benjamin Hinman, William Satterlee

Jno. Brown, Lieutenant-Colonel
Albany, 1st December, 1776.

※ ※ ※

John Brown to Horatio Gates

Albany, December 2nd, 1776

Sir: Having been put to the necessity to present your Honour with a petition yesterday, must beg your answer to the same.

I have the honour to be, with respect, your most obedient, humble servant,
Jno. Brown, Lieutenant-Colonel
To General Horatio Gates

※ ※ ※

John Brown to Horatio Gates

Albany, December 2nd, 1776

Sir: I am sorry that necessity once more obliges me to trouble your Honour on the present occasion. I really thought that the petition which I gave you yesterday contained matters of much importance, as either to entitle me to the prayer thereof, or an answer in writing, setting forth the reason why it was rejected; as the one would have been satisfactory, the other enabled me to lay the petition at large, and your answer, before Congress. Must therefore humbly request your Honour to give me your answer in writing.

I am, sir, with respect, your most obedient, humble servant,
Jno. Brown, Lieutenant-Colonel
To General Gates

※ ※ ※

Horatio Gates to Colonel Brown

Albany, 2nd December, 1776

Sir: Since you are so importunate for an answer in writing to your petition of yesterday, I think it proper to acquaint you that I shall lay your petition before Congress, who will, when they see fit, give such orders as they think necessary thereupon.

I am, sir, your humble servant,
Horatio Gates
To Lieutenant-Colonel Brown

Chapter Notes

Abbreviations

AA—Peter Force, ed., *American Archives,* 9 vols. Washington, D.C., 1837–1853.

BFTM—*Bulletin of the Fort Ticonderoga Museum*, especially vol. 13, no. 5 (1977), which brings together many sources on the May 10, 1775, conquest of Ticonderoga.

CCHS—*Collections of the Connecticut Historical Society*, vols. 1–2, 7, 10. Hartford: Connecticut Historical Society, 1860, 1870, 1899, 1905.

CMHS—*Collections of the Maine Historical Society*, vol. 1. Editor William Willis. Portland: Bailey & Noyes, 1865.

JCC—*Journals of the Continental Congress, 1774–1789*. Editors Worthington C. Ford, et al. Washington, D.C., 1904–37. Online at Library of Congress, American Memory.

LDC—*Letters of the Delegates to Congress, 1774–1789*. Editor Paul H. Smith; assistant editors Gerard W. Gawalt, Rosemary Fry Plakas, Eugene R. Sheridan. Washington: Library of Congress, 1976–2000.

MAH—*Magazine of American History.* New York: A.S. Barnes, 1877–1893.

NDAR—*Naval Documents of the American Revolution*, vols. 1–6. Editor William James Morgan. Washington: Naval History Division, Dept. of the Navy, 1964–1972.

NHSP—*New Hampshire Provincial and State Papers*, especially vols. 8 and 30.

NYPL—New York Public Library.

PCC—Papers of the Continental Congress. The citations refer to the microfilm: r, reel; i, item; v, volume; p, page. The papers can be found online at Fold3, the military genealogical research site, www.fold3.com.

VHS—Vermont Historical Society.

Founders Online, National Archives, https://founders.archives.gov/—This National Archives website brings together the correspondence and writings of George Washington, Benjamin Franklin, Alexander Hamilton, John Adams, Thomas Jefferson, and James Madison

People

BA—Benedict Arnold
BF—Benjamin Franklin
GW—George Washington
HG—Horatio Gates
JA—John Adams
JB—John Brown
JH—John Hancock
JS—John Sullivan
PS—Philip Schuyler
RM—Richard Montgomery

Introduction

1. *Massachusetts Soldiers and Sailors of the Revolutionary War* (Boston: Wright & Potter, 1896), 2:636–52; "American Participants at the Battles of Saratoga," Saratoga NYGenWeb Project, saratoganygenweb.com/sarapk.htm.

2. Joseph E. A. Smith, *History of Pittsfield* (Boston: Lee and Shepard, 1869), 181.
3. HG to PS, Sept. 11, 1776, *AA*, ser. 5, 2:294–5.
4. Clare Brandt, *The Man in the Mirror: A Life of Benedict Arnold* (New York: Random House, 1994), 114; Willard Wallace, *Traitorous Hero: The Life and Fortunes of Benedict Arnold* (New York: Harper & Brothers, 1954), 121; James Kirby Martin, *Benedict Arnold: Revolutionary Hero; An American Warrior Reconsidered* (New York: NYU Press, 1997), 299.
5. JB to Theodore Sedgwick, Dec. 6, 1776, Sedgwick Family Papers, Massachusetts Historical Society; JB to Congress, June 9, 1779, PCC, M247, r53, i42, v1, p181.
6. JB to HG, Dec. 1, 1776, *AA*, ser. 5, 3:1158; PCC, M247, r174, i154, v1, p125–28.
7. JB to HG, Dec. 1, 1776, *AA*, ser. 5, 3:1159.
8. HG to JB, Dec. 2, 1776, *AA*, ser. 5, 3:1160; PCC, M247, r91, i78, v2, p117.

Chapter One

1. Archibald M. Howe, "Colonel John Brown of Pittsfield, Massachusetts: The Brave Accuser of Benedict Arnold; An Address Delivered before the Fort Rensselaer Chapter of the D. A. R. at the Village of Palatine Bridge, New York September 29, 1908" (Boston: W.B. Clarke, 1908); Murray Nelson, "Colonel John Brown, 'A Prophet Hath No Honor in his own Country,'" Massachusetts Historical Society, Ms. S-24; Henry Cruger Van Schaack, "Col. John Brown: A Lecture Delivered before the Lyceum in Manlius New York, & at Fayetteville" (1857), Massachusetts Historical Society, Ms. S-24. Garret L. Roof, *Colonel John Brown: His Services in the Revolutionary War, Battle of Stone Arabia*; Oneida Historical Society (Utica: Ellis H. Roberts, 1884). Brown is a major topic in Smith, *History of Pittsfield*.
2. Wilkins Updike, "Oliver Arnold," *Memoirs of the Rhode-Island Bar* (Boston: Thomas H. Webb, 1842), 70–81. The internet has many Arnold genealogy sites, based on extensive research by the family.
3. JB to Gov. Trumbull, Aug. 14, 1775, *AA*, ser. 4, 3:135–136.
4. JB to Elizabeth Brown, April 7, 1771, *Massachusetts Historical Society Proceedings* 43 (Boston, 1910), 449–50.
5. Franklin Bowditch Dexter, *Biographical Sketches of the Graduates of Yale College with Annals of the College History*, vol. 3, *May 1763–July 1778* (New York: Henry Holt, 1903), 400–29.
6. John T. Morrison, *Tryon County and Sir William Johnson: Historical Sketch and Revolutionary Chronicles of "The Dark and Bloody Ground"* (c. 1922), www.fulton.nygenweb.net/history/150Anniv.html.
7. Smith, *History of Pittsfield*, 497–98.
8. Rollin Hillyer Cooke, ed., *Pittsfield, Mass. Church and other Records from Manuscripts Copied by Rollin Hillyer Cooke*. Internet Archive, 298; Payne Kenyon Kilbourn, *The Family Memorial: A History and Genealogy of the Kilbourn Family in the United States and Canada, from the Year 1635 to the Present Time* (Hartford: Brown & Parson, 1845), 79.
9. Berkshire County Probate File Papers, 1073:44, online at www.americanancestors.org.
10. Smith, *History of Pittsfield*, 184–86.
11. *Journals of Each Provincial Congress of Massachusetts in 1774 and 1775* (Boston: Dutton and Wentworth, 1838), 652–55; timeline at "Sedgwick Family Papers," Massachusetts Historical Society online.
12. JB to Committee of Correspondence, July 25, 1774, *Boston Committee of Correspondence 1772–1784*, NYPL, digitalcollections.nypl.org.
13. *Journals of Each Provincial Congress of Massachusetts*, 30, 45, 24, 27.
14. "Address to the Inhabitants of the Province of Quebec," *AA*, ser. 4, 1:930–934; *JCC*, 1:237–44.
15. *Journals of Each Provincial Congress of Massachusetts*, 59.
16. JB to Samuel Adams, Feb. 13, 1775, Samuel Adams Papers, NYPL, digitalcollections.nypl.org.
17. Samuel Adams; Harry Alonzo Cushing, ed., *The Writings of Samuel Adams* (New York: G. P. Putnam's Sons, 1907), 3:182.
18. JB to Committee of Correspondence, March 29, 1775, *AA*, ser. 4, 2:243–45.
19. William Slade, ed., *Vermont State Papers: 1779–1786* (Middlebury, VT: J.W. Copeland, 1823), 42–48.
20. E.B. O'Callaghan, ed., *Documentary History of the State of New York* (Albany: Charles Van Bethuysen, 1851), 4:891–97.
21. Thomas Jefferson to Martha Jefferson Randolph, May 31, 1791, Founders Online.
22. Douglas R. Cubbison, *The American Northern Theater Army in 1776: The Ruin and Reconstruction of the Continental Force* (Jefferson, NC: McFarland, 2010), 193; Allen French, *The Taking of Ticonderoga in 1775: The British Story* (Cambridge: Harvard University Press, 1928), 11–12, 55.
23. French, *Taking of Ticonderoga*, 7, 55.
24. Historical Section of the General Staff, *History of the Organization, Development and Services of the Military and Naval Forces of Canada* (1919) 1:135.
25. Historical Section of the General Staff, 1:135, 138; JB to Committee of Correspondence, March 29, 1775, *AA*, ser. 4, 2:243–45.
26. Historical Section of the General Staff, 1:138.

Chapter Two

1. Thomas Jones, *History of New York During the Revolutionary War, and of the Leading Events*

in the Other Colonies at that Period (New York: New-York Historical Society, 1879), 1:180; Martin, *Benedict Arnold*, 63.

2. BA to Massachusetts Committee of Safety, April 30, 1775, *NDAR*, William James Morgan, ed. (Washington: Naval History Division, Dept. of the Navy), 1:250; "Agreement of Captain Arnold and his Company," April 24, 1775, *AA*, ser. 4, 2:383–84.

3. Lucius Chittenden, *Capture of Ticonderoga* in *Proceedings of the Vermont Historical Society,* October 8, 1872 (Montpelier, Vt., 1872), 100–101; BA to the Massachusetts Committee of Safety, April 30, 1775, *NDAR* 1:250.

4. Edward Mott Journal, *CCHS* 1 (Hartford: Connecticut Historical Society, 1860), 168.

5. Smith, *History of Pittsfield*, 178.

6. Chittenden, *Capture of Ticonderoga*, 103; Epaphras Bull Journal, *BFTM* 13, no. 5 (1977), 315.

7. Benjamin Church to BA, May 3, 1775, *AA, ser.* 4, 2:751; Chittenden, *Capture of Ticonderoga*, 39.

8. Lincoln Diamant, *Bernard Romans: Forgotten Patriot of the American Revolution* (Harbor Hill Books, 1985), 36; Mott Journal, *CCHS* 1:169.

9. Edward Mott to the Massachusetts Provincial Congress, May 11, 1775, *BFTM* (1977), 336.

10. Bull Journal, *BFTM* (1977), 316.

11. Edward Mott to the Massachusetts Provincial Congress, May 11, 1775, *BFTM* (1977), 335; Doris Begor Morton, *Philip Skene of Skenesborough* (Granville, NY: Grastorf Press, 1959); James Hadden; Horatio Rogers, ed., *Hadden's Journal and Orderly Books: A Journal Kept in Canada and Upon Burgoyne's Campaign in 1776 and 1777* (Albany, NY: Joel Munsell's Sons, 1884), 505–17.

12. BA to Massachusetts Committee of Safety, May 14, 1775, *AA*, ser. 4, 2:584.

13. Bull Journal, *BFTM* (1977), 317; Mott Journal, *CCHS*, 1:171.

14. Mott to the Massachusetts Provincial Congress, *BFTM* (1977), 335.

15. "Veritas," June 25, 1775, *AA*, ser. 4, 2:1085–87; Ethan Allen, *The Narrative of Colonel Ethan Allen* (Bedford, MA: Applewood Books, n.d.; 1st edition, Philadelphia: Robert Bell, 1779), 6–7.

16. EA to Massachusetts Provincial Congress, May 11, 1775, Chittenden, *Capture of Ticonderoga*, 110.

17. EA, *Narrative*, 8.

18. French, *Taking of Ticonderoga*, 43–44.

19. EA, *Narrative*, 9–10; Bull Journal, *BFTM* (1977), 317; Committee to Massachusetts Congress, May 10, 1775, *BFTM* (1977), 332.

20. John Sparding to Congress of New York, June 1, 1775, *NDAR*, 1:588; *AA*, ser. 4, 2:588.

21. EA to Provincial Congress, May 11, 1775, *AA*, ser. 4, 2: 556; Edward Mott to Provincial Congress, May 11, 1775, *AA*, ser. 4, 2:557–60.

22. BA to Committee of Safety, May 11, 1775, *AA*, ser. 4, 2:557.

23. EA to the Albany Committee, May 11, 1775, *AA*, ser. 4, 2:605–6.

24. *Minutes of the Albany Committee of Correspondence* (Albany: University of the State of New York, 1923), 1:31–32.

25. *Albany Committee*, 1:31–32; Albany Committee to New York Committee, May 12, 1775 and EA to Albany Committee, May 11, 1775, *AA*, ser. 4, 2:605–6.

26. *Albany Committee*, 1:32, 977.

27. George Read to Mrs. Read, May 18, 1775, *LDC*, 1:360.

28. Martin, *Benedict Arnold,* 85.

29. *AA*, ser. 4, 2:623–24.

30. Minutes for May 18, 1775, *JCC* 2:56.

31. Journal of the Provincial Congress of New Hampshire, May 18, 1775, *NDAR*, 1:354.

Chapter Three

1. Walter Spooner to Gov. Trumbull, July 3, 1775, *NDAR*, 1:807–8.

2. *AA*, ser. 5, 3:1158–59.

3. Witnesses can be found in JB to Theodore Sedgwick, Dec. 6, 1776, Sedgwick Family Papers, Massachusetts Historical Society. The numbering of the charges is slightly different than in the list in the Papers of the Continental Congress.

4. Chittenden, *Capture of Ticonderoga*, 119; BA to Massachusetts Committee of Safety, May 19, 1775, *NDAR*, 1:364–67.

5. EA, *Narrative*, 10–11; BA to Massachusetts Committee of Safety, May 19, 1775, *NDAR*, 1:364–67.

6. BA to Massachusetts Committee of Safety, May 19, 1775, *NDAR*, 1:364–67; "Benedict Arnold's Regimental Memorandum Book," *Pennsylvania Magazine of History and Biography* 8 (1884), 368.

7. EA, *Narrative*, 10–11; "Arnold's Memorandum Book," 368.

8. Barnabas Deane to Silas Deane, June 1, 1775, *CCHS*, 2:246–49.

9. EA to Congress, May 29, 1775, *AA*, ser. 4, 2:732–34; BA to Congress, May 29, 1775, *AA*, ser. 4, 2:734–35.

10. Winslow C. Watson, *Pioneer History of the Champlain Valley Being an Account of the Settlement of the Town of Willsborough by William Gilliland* (Albany: J. Munsell, 1863), 175.

11. William Gilliland to Continental Congress, May 29, 1775, *AA*, ser. 4, 2:731–32.

12. Joseph Henshaw to BA, May 31, 1775, *AA*, ser. 4, 2:721.

13. "Arnold's Memorandum Book," 373.

14. EA and Others to Congress, June 10, 1775, *NDAR* 1:646–47.

15. "Arnold's Memorandum Book," 373.

16. "Veritas," June 23, 1775, *AA*, ser. 4, 2:1085–87.

17. BA to Congress, June 13, 1775, *AA*, ser. 4, 2:976–77.

18. Minutes for June 23, 1775, *JCC*, 2:105.

19. Martin, *Benedict Arnold,* 93.

20. *Journals of Each Provincial Congress of Massachusetts in 1774 and 1775*, 327–29.
21. Thomas Spooner, *Records of William Spooner, Plymouth, Mass., and His Descendants* (Cincinnati, 1883), 1:106–10.
22. *Journals of Each Provincial Congress of Massachusetts in 1774 and 1775*, 36.
23. Thomas C. Amory, *Life of James Sullivan with Selections from his Writings* (Boston: Phillips & Sampson, 1859), 2:369.
24. "Report of the Crown Point Committee to the Massachusetts Congress," July 6, 1775, *AA*, ser. 4, 2:1596–99.
25. Ibid.
26. F.B. Heitman, *Historical Register of Officers of the Continental Army during the War of the Revolution, April 1775 to December 1783* (Washington, DC: W.H. Lowdermilk, 1893), 221; *Journals of Each Provincial Congress of Massachusetts in 1774 and 1775*, 534; William Cothren, *History of Ancient Woodbury, Connecticut* (Waterbury, CT: Bronson Brothers, 1854), 1:371–73.
27. Edward Mott to Gov. Trumbull, July 6, 1775, *AA*, ser. 4, 2:1592.
28. Martin, *Benedict Arnold*, 96; Amory, *James Sullivan*, 1:53–54.
29. Suydam Hoffman, "Introduction," *Proceedings of a General Court Martial for the Trial of Major General Arnold* (Albany: Joel Munsell, 1865), xv–xvi.
30. Mott to Trumbull, *AA*, ser. 4, 2:1592–93; William Duer to PS, July 19, 1775, in Benson J. Lossing, *The Life and Times of Philip Schuyler* (New York: Sheldon, 1860), 1:384; Gordon S. Wood, *Empire of Liberty: A History of the Early Republic* (New York: Oxford University Press, 2009), 152–53.
31. "Arnold's Memorandum Book," 376.
32. "Veritas," June 23, 1775, *AA*, ser. 4, 2:1596; "Arnold's Memorandum Book," 375–76; William Delaplace, July 28, 1775, *AA*, ser. 4, 2:1087.
33. Silas Deane to Elizabeth Deane, June 18, 1775, *LDC*, 1:505.
34. "To Benedict Arnold from the Principal Inhabitants on Lake Champlain," July 3, 1775, *AA*, ser. 4, 2:1087–88; Watson, *Pioneer History*, 176; Chittenden, *Capture of Ticonderoga*, 73, was certain that Arnold "supervised, if he did not dictate," the letter.
35. BA to the Continental Congress, July 11, 1775, *AA*, ser. 4, 2:1646–47.
36. Benjamin Hinman to PS, July 7, 1775, *AA*, ser. 4, 2:1605–06.

Chapter Four

1. JH to GW, June 28, 1775, Founders Online; *JCC*, 2:109–10.
2. PS to GW, July 18, 1775, *AA*, ser. 4., 2:1685–86; PS to Congress, July 21, 1775, *AA*, ser. 4, 2:1702–03.
3. JB Certificate, July 22, 1776, *AA*, ser. 5, 1:498.

4. Ray Stannard Baker, "Remember Baker," *The New England Quarterly* 4 (October, 1931), 595–628.
5. Bayze Wells, "Journal of Bayze Wells of Farmington: May, 1775-February, 1777, at the Northward and in Canada," *CCHS* 7 (Hartford: Published by the Society, 1879), 241–96.
6. "Account of Remember Baker," July 26, 1775, *AA*, ser. 4, 2:1735.
7. Wells Journal, *CCHS*, 7:243–44.
8. JB to Gov. Trumbull, Aug. 14, 1775, *AA*, ser. 4, 3:135–36.
9. James Livingston, August 1775, *AA*, ser. 4, 3:468–69.
10. Wells Journal, *CCHS*, 7:245–47; JB to Gov. Trumbull, Aug. 14, 1775, *AA*, ser. 4, 3:136.
11. "James Stewart's Report," July 30–August 4, 1775, *AA*, ser. 4, 3:49; Ray Stannard Baker, 619; Ira Allen, *The Natural and Political History of the State of Vermont* (Rutland, VT: Charles E. Tuttle, 1969; 1st edition, London, 1798), 46.
12. JB to RM, Aug. 23, 1775, *AA*, ser. 4, 3:468.
13. RM to PS, Aug. 25, 1775, Lossing, *Schuyler*, 1:393.
14. Michael P. Gabriel, *Major General Richard Montgomery: The Making of an American Hero* (Cranbury, NJ: Associated University Presses, 2002), 39, 217.
15. Hal T. Shelton, *General Richard Montgomery and the American Revolution: from Redcoat to Rebel* (New York: NYU Press, 1994), 35, 117.
16. "To the Inhabitants of Canada," Sept. 5, 1775, *AA*, ser. 4, 3:671–72.
17. PS to JH, Sept. 8, 1775, *AA*, ser. 4, 3:669–672; "Benjamin Trumbull's Journal," *CCHS*, 7:141; "Journal of Col. Rudolphus Ritzema," *MAH* 1 (New York: A.S. Barnes, 1877), 99–100.
18. John Fassett, "Diary of Captain John Fassett, Jr.," *The Follett-Dewey Fassett-Safford Ancestry of Captain Martin Dewey Follett and his wife Persis Fassett* (1896), 217; RM to PS, Sept. 19, 1775, *AA*, ser. 4, 3:797–98.

Chapter Five

1. Louise Livingston Hunt, *Biographical Notes Concerning General Richard Montgomery* (Poughkeepsie, NY: News Printing House, 1876), 13; Shelton, *Richard Montgomery*, 106.
2. Fassett Diary, 221, 218.
3. EA, *Narrative*, 14; EA to RM, Sept. 20, 1775, *AA*, ser. 4, 3:754.
4. EA, *Narrative*, 14–15; Ira Allen, *History of Vermont*, 46–47.
5. PS to JH, Oct. 5, 1775, *NDAR*, 2:306.
6. EA to Connecticut Assembly, Aug. 8, 1776, *AA*, ser. 5, 1:860–61; for a description of crossing to Montréal, *Journal of Charles Carroll of Carrollton, During his Visit to Canada in 1776* (Baltimore: John Murray, 1876), 49.
7. Ira Allen, *History of Vermont*, 46–47.
8. Robert McConnell Hatch, *Thrust for*

Canada: The American Attempt on Quebec in 1775–1776 (Boston: Houghton Mifflin, 1979), 58; Mark R. Anderson, *The Battle for the Fourteenth Colony: America's War of Liberation in Canada, 1774–1776* (Hanover, NH: University Press of New England, 2013), 116–17; Harrison Bird, *March to Saratoga, General Burgoyne and the American Campaign: 1777* (New York, Oxford University Press, 1963), 135; Smith, *Our Struggle for the Fourteenth Colony: Canada and the American Revolution* (New York: G. P. Putnam's Sons, 1907), 1:388; Charles A. Jellison, *Ethan Allen, Frontier Rebel* (Syracuse University Press, 1969), 155; Michael A. Bellesiles, *Revolutionary Outlaws: Ethan Allen and the Struggle for Independence on the Early American Frontier* (Charlottesville: University Press of Virginia, 1993), 126–127; Willard Sterne Randall, *Benedict Arnold: Patriot and Traitor* (Barnes & Noble, 1999; first edition, William Marrow, 1990), 370–71.

9. Allen, *Narrative*, 24; Seth Warner to RM, Sept. 27, 1775, *AA*, ser. 4, 3:953–54.

10. RM to PS, Sept. 28, *AA*, ser. 4, 3:954–55; RM to PS, Oct. 6, *AA*, ser. 4, 3:1095–96.

11. Edward Mott to Gov. Trumbull, Oct. 6, 1775, *AA*, ser. 4, 3:973; RM to Janet Montgomery, Oct. 6, 1775, Hunt, *Biographical Notes*, 13; RM to PS, Oct. 9, 1775, *AA*, ser. 4, 3:1096.

12. Smith, *Struggle for the 14th Colony*, 1:446; RM to PS, Oct. 13, 1775, *AA*, ser. 4, 3:1097–98.

13. Most accounts omit Brown, but in a memorandum to Philip Schuyler, he stated that he passed by "*St. John's* myself in a boat, with cannon, &c." *AA*, ser. 5, 1:1218; for plunder see *AA*, ser. 4, 4:188–89 and *AA*, ser. 4, 3:1195–96.

14. Smith, *Struggle for the 14th Colony*, 1:426.

15. JB to Joseph Stopford, *AA*, ser. 4, 3:1133–34.

16. James Livingston to Congress, March 7, 1782, PCC M247 r50 i41 v5, p246–249; James Livingston to RM, Oct. 26, 1775, *AA*, ser. 4, 3:1195–96; Anderson, *Battle for the 14th Colony*, 260–61; Minutes for March 29, 1776, JCC, 4:239.

17. RM to PS, Oct. 20, 1775, *AA*, ser. 4, 3:1132–33.

18. JB to PS, Nov. 28, 1775, Schuyler Papers, NYPL; Anderson, *Battle for the 14th Colony*, 135–36.

19. JB to RM, Nov. 8, 1775, *AA*, Ser. 4, 3:1401; Smith, *Struggle for the 14th Colony*,1:469.

20. "Articles of Capitulation," *AA*, ser. 4, 3:1597.

21. Seth Warner, "Certificate," April 12, 1776, Hall Park McCollough Collection, Howe Library, University of Vermont; RM to PS, Dec. 5, 1775, *NDAR*, 2:1277–78.

22. Smith, *Struggle for the 14th Colony*, 1:487; Elisha Porter; Appleton Morgan, ed., "The Diary of Colonel Elisha Porter, of Hadley, Massachusetts," *MAH* 30 (New York, A.S. Barnes, 1893), 191.

23. Carroll Journal, 97.

24. Anderson, *Battle for the 14th Colony*, 387n; PS to JH, Feb. 23, 1776, *NDAR*, 4:52.

25. *Remembrancer 1776*, Part 2, 246–47.

26. BA to David Wooster, Jan. 25, 1776, Murray Nelson, "Colonel John Brown," 12–13; BA to JH, Feb. 1, 1776, *AA*, ser. 4, 4:907–8; Brown's 13 Charges, *AA*, ser. 5, 3:1159.

27. "Footguards' agreement," *AA*, ser. 4, 2:383–84; GW to JH, Sept. 25, 1776, Founders Online.

28. RM to PS, Nov. 13, 1775, *AA*, ser. 4, 3:1602–3.

29. RM to PS, Dec. 5, 1775, Sparks, *Correspondence,* 1:492–494; John Sullivan to New Hampshire Assembly, January 18, 1776, *AA*, ser. 4, 4: 768–69.

30. Smith, *Struggle for the 14th Colony*, 1:490; "Richard Smith's Diary," *LDC*, 3:378; *JCC*, 5:618.

31. PS to GW, August 29, 1776, Founders Online, 3n; Minutes for Aug. 17, 1776, *JCC*, 5:664.

32. RM to PS, Nov. 22, 1775, Philip Schuyler Papers, NYPL online.

Chapter Six

1. Roberts, *March to Quebec: Journals of the Members of Arnold's Expedition* (Garden City, NY: Doubleday, 1946). Stephen Darley, *Voices from a Wilderness Expedition: The Journals and Men of Benedict Arnold's Expedition to Quebec in 1775* (Bloomington, Ind.: AuthorHouse, 2011) adds previously unpublished material and questions the authenticity of some journals. The Arnold Expedition Historical Society of Pittston, Maine, has an informative website with many sources: www.arnoldmarch.com. For the most part, the following citations rely on the original publications, which can now be found online.

2. "Historians have a great advantage over a novelist in that they can state a supposed fact without explaining it" from Kenneth Roberts, *I Wanted to Write* (Garden City, N.Y.: Doubleday, 1949), 186; Roberts, *Black Magic* (New York: Bobbs-Merrill, 1924), 52.

3. Kenneth Roberts, *Arundel* (Camden, Maine: Down East Books, 1995; 1st edition, Doubleday, 1929–30), 476.

4. John Joseph Henry, *Accurate and Interesting Account of the Hardships and Sufferings of That Band of Heroes, Who Traversed the Wilderness in the Campaign against Quebec in 1775* (Lancaster, PA: William Greer, 1812), 16, 78.

5. *AA*, ser. 5, 3:1158–59.

6. JB to Theodore Sedgwick, Dec. 6, 1776, Sedgwick Family Papers, Massachusetts Historical Society.

7. Thomas Carlyle, Heroes, *Hero-Worship, and the Heroic in History: Six Lectures* (London: James Fraser, 1841), 1–2.

8. John Montresor & William Willis, ed., "Montresor's Journal," *CMHS* (Portland: Bailey & Noyes, 1865), 1:448–466.

9. Montresor Journal, *CMHS*, 1:462.

10. Arthur S. Lefkowitz, *Benedict Arnold's Army: The 1775 American Invasion of Canada*

during the Revolutionary War (New York: Savas Beatie, 2008), 25; John Montresor, "Journals of Capt. John Montresor," *Collections of the New-York Historical Society 1881* (New York: New-York Historical Society, 1882), 125.

11. GW's Orders to BA, September 14, 1775, *AA*, ser. 4, 3:765–67.

12. Simeon Thayer & Edwin Martin Stone, ed., *Journal of Captain Simeon Thayer Describing the Perils and Sufferings of the Army under Colonel Benedict Arnold* (Providence: Knowles, Anthony & Co., 1867), 3.

13. Thayer Journal, 3; Abner Stocking, *An Interesting Journal of Abner Stocking of Chatham, Connecticut...* (Tarrytown, NY: William Abbatt, 1921; 1st edition Catskill, NY: Eagle Office, 1810), 11.

14. Arthur S. Lefkowitz, *Benedict Arnold in the Company of Heroes* (California: Savas Beatie, 2012), 53–54.

15. BA to GW, Sept. 27. 1775, *CMHS*, 1:467; Stocking Journal, 11; Ephraim Squier, "Diary of Ephraim Squier: Sergeant in the Continental Line of the Continental Army," *MAH* 2 (New York: A.S. Barnes, 1878), 687. "Committing every enormity" comes from BA to Committee of Safety, May 11, 1775, *AA*, ser. 4, 2:557.

16. BA to GW, September 25, 1775, *AA*, ser. 4, 3:960–61; GW to Daniel Morgan, Oct. 4, 1775, Founders Online.

17. Stephen Clark, *Following in Their Footsteps: A Travel Guide & History of the 1775 Secret Expedition to Capture Quebec* (Shapleigh, ME: Clark Books, 2003), 25. Clark's travel guide is among the most thoughtful books on the trek. In addition to doing thorough research, he wrote as an outdoorsman and past president of the Maine Appalachian Trail Club. His understanding of wilderness travel gives him an edge over many other writers.

18. BA to GW, Sept. 25 [-27], 1775, Founders Online. Distances are taken from Arnold Expedition Historical Society, "Arnold's Wilderness March: Kennebec River, Maine to Lac Mégantic, Québec, Map and Guide" (Shapleigh, ME, 2009).

19. Clark, *Following in Their Footsteps*, 37, 49.

20. "How Many Calories Do You Burn Backpacking?" Appalachian Mountain Club, *www.outdoors.com*.

21. Clark, *Following in their Footsteps*, 49.

22. BA to GW, Oct. 13, 1775, Founders Online.

23. Roger Enos to GW, Nov. 9, 1775, Founders Online; *Remembrancer 1776*, Part 3, 77.

24. BA to GW, Oct. 13, 1775, *AA*, ser. 4, 3:1057–1058; Arnold was about 63 miles from Lake Megantic, which is nearly ten miles long. The Chaudière River is 115 miles long.

25. "Arnold's Journal," in Roberts, *March to Quebec*, 54–55.

26. "Arnold's Journal," 55; BA to GW, Oct. 27, 1775, *CMHS*, 1:477–478; "Return J. Meigs, Journal of the Expedition against Quebec (New York, 1864), 17–18; Martin, *Benedict Arnold*, 130–131; Randall, *Benedict Arnold*, 175–76.

27. *CCHS* 10, 1:169 & 2:6, 102, 238. Records for 1760 are incomplete, but it is likely Hanchet served.

28. BA to Roger Enos, October 24, 1775, *AA*, ser. 4, 3:1174–75.

29. Roberts, *Arundel*, 271–72.

30. George Morison, *An Interesting Journal of Occurrence During the Expedition to Quebec* (Tarrytown, NY: William Abbatt, 1916; 1st edition Hagerstown, MD: James Magee, 1803), 20–21.

31. Matthew L. Davis, *Memoirs of Aaron Burr with Miscellaneous Selections from his Correspondence* (New York: Harper & Brothers, 1855; 1st edition 1836–37), 1:iii, 78.

32. Isaac Senter, "The Journal of Isaac Senter, Physician and Surgeon," *Proceedings of the Historical Society of Pennsylvania* 1, no. 5 (March 1846), 17; Thayer Journal, 11.

33. Arthur Lefkowitz, *Benedict Arnold's Army*, 148; Justin Smith, *Arnold's March from Cambridge to Quebec: A Critical Study* (New York: G.P. Putnam's Sons, 1903), 388–89; Roger Enos to GW, Nov. 9, 1775, Founders Online; John Codman, *Arnold's Expedition to Quebec* (New York: Macmillan, 1902), 87.

34. *Remembrancer 1776*, Part 3, 78.

35. BA to GW, Oct. 27, 1775, *CMHS*, 1:476–77.

36. Martin accepts the story of Arnold publically criticizing Hanchet (*Benedict Arnold*, 135–36); "Arnold's Journal," 58–59; Smith, *Arnold's March*, 416–17.

37. BA to GW, Oct. 27, 1775, *CMHS*, 1:476–77.

38. Lefkowitz, *Arnold's Army*, 162.

39. BA to Field Officers and Captains, Oct. 27, 1775, *CMHS*, 1:477–78.

40. Smith, *Arnold's March*, 203; Henry Dearborn, *Journal of Captain Henry Dearborn in the Quebec Expedition, 1775* (Cambridge: University Press, 1886), 10; James Melvin & Andrew A. Melvin, ed., *The Journal of James Melvin, Private Soldier in Arnold's Expedition* (Portland, ME: Hubbard W. Bryant, 1902), 49–50.

41. Thayer Journal, 13.

42. Dearborn Journal 1775, 11; Senter Journal, 18, 22; Morison Journal, 32.

43. Martin, *Benedict Arnold*, 139; Lefkowitz, *Arnold's Army*, 317–318n; Morison Journal, 38; BA to GW, Nov. 8, 1775, *CMHS*, 1:482.

44. BA to (probably) PS, November 27, 1775, Roberts, 97–99; *CMHS*, 1:494–496; Senter Journal, 32.

Chapter Seven

1. BA to Oliver Hanchet, November 15, 1775, Roberts, 88; *CMHS* 1:485–86.

2. Henry, *Accurate and Interesting Account*, 85; Senter Journal, 27.

3. Henry, *Accurate and Interesting Account*, 87.

4. BA to Hector Cramahé, Nov. 14 & 15, 1775, *CMHS*, 1:486–87.
5. Henry, *Accurate and Interesting Account*, 89.
6. BA to GW, Nov. 20, 1775 & BA to PS, Nov. 27, 1775, *CMHS*, 1:490–91, 496.
7. Proclamation, Nov. 22, 1775, *AA*, ser. 4, 3:1639.
8. BA to Officers of the Continental Army, Nov. 30, 1775, *CMHS*, 1:497; John Pierce Journal in Roberts, *March to Quebec*, 684–86.
9. Thayer Journal, 23–24; Pierce Journal mentions snow fourteen inches deep on Nov. 29 in Roberts, *March to Quebec*, 686.
10. RM to PS, Dec. 5, 1775, *AA*, ser. 4, 4:188–90; RM to PS, Oct. 20, 1775, *AA*, ser. 4, 3:1132–33.
11. Thayer Journal, 25.
12. Thomas Ainslie & Sheldon Cohen, ed., *Canada Preserved: The Journal of Captain Thomas Ainslie* (New York: NYU Press, 1968), 27.
13. RM to PS, Dec. 18, 1775, *AA*, ser. 4, 4:310; PS to JH, Dec. 26, 1775, *AA*, ser. 4, 4:463–64; Roberts, *March to Quebec*, 701.
14. Roberts, *March to Quebec*, 589n; RM to PS, Dec. 26, 1775, *AA*, ser. 4, 4:464.
15. Smith, *Struggle for the 14th Colony*, 2:579–80.
16. JB to RM, Dec. 29, 1775, Murray Nelson, "Colonel John Brown," 11–12. The original document is in the Chicago History Museum Research Center.
17. Pierce Journal, 698–702.
18. Ritzema Journal, *MAH* 1, 104.
19. Joseph E.A. Smith, *History of Pittsfield*, 258; Justin Smith, *Struggle for the 14th Colony*, 2:579–80.
20. Ira Allen, "Autobiography," in James Benjamin Wilbur, *Ira Allen, Founder of Vermont 1751–1814* (Boston: Houghton Mifflin, 1928), 69–70.
21. Ainslie Journal, 31, 33–34.
22. Smith, *Struggle for the 14th Colony*, 2:132–33.
23. J. Hammond Trumbull, *Memorial History of Hartford County, Connecticut* (Boston: E.L. Osgood, 1886), 2:512; Roberts, *March to Quebec*, 27–40 for casualty lists by company. "Handchitt's Company" is on p. 39; "Alexander King Diary," 1776, page 11, online, Kent Memorial Library, Suffield, Connecticut, www.suffield-library.org; Lefkowitz, *Company of Heroes*, 206–7.

Chapter Eight

1. Senter Journal, 34–35.
2. BA to David Wooster, Jan. 2, 1776, *AA*, ser. 4, 4:670–71.
3. BA to unknown, Jan. 6, 1776, *Remembrancer 1776*, Part 1, 368–69; *AA*, ser. 4, 4:589–90; Anderson, *Battle for the 14th Colony*, 273.
4. Arnold to Congress, January 11, 1776, *AA*, ser. 4, 4:627–29.

5. Hunt, *Biographical Notes Concerning Montgomery*, 21–22.
6. BA to Wooster, Jan. 25, 1776 in Murray Nelson, "Colonel John Brown," 12–13.
7. *AA*, ser. 5, 3:1158–59; for witnesses: JB to Theodore Sedgwick, Dec. 6, 1776, Sedgwick Family Papers, Massachusetts Historical Society.
8. Jeremiah Dugan sworn before John Morton, August 1, 1776, Thomas Addis Emmet Collection, NYPL.
9. *AA*, ser. 5, 3:1158–59; for witnesses: JB to Theodore Sedgwick, Dec. 6, 1776, Sedgwick Family Papers, Massachusetts Historical Society.
10. *Ibid.*
11. BA to JH, Feb. 1, 1776, *AA*, ser. 4, 4:907–8.
12. JB to HG, Dec. 1, 1776, *AA*, ser. 4, 3:1158–59.
13. Brown to "Dear Wife," March 15, 1776, Van Schaack, "Col. John Brown," 14.
14. Nathan Peirce to James Barker, April 4, 1776, Crary Collection, Columbia University.
15. "Report on JB's Petition," Nov. 12, 1776, *AA*, ser. 5, 3:1567.
16. *AA*, ser. 4, 5:550.
17. *New York in the Revolution as Colony and State*, 2nd edition, James A. Roberts, comptroller (Albany: Brandow Printing, 1898), 61–62; John E. Goodrich, *Rolls of the Vermont Soldiers in the Revolutionary War* (Rutland, VT: Tuttle, 1904), 831–33; *NHSP*, 30:435–45.
18. Henry, *Accurate and Interesting Account*, 113.
19. Smith, *History of Pittsfield*, 260.
20. Dearborn Journal 1775, 25.
21. *American Archives*, ser. 5, 3:1158–59; for witnesses: JB to Theodore Sedgwick, Dec. 6, 1776, Sedgwick Family Papers, Massachusetts Historical Society.
22. Orders, Feb. 11, 1776 & March 15, 1776, *AA*, ser. 4, 5:550–51.
23. BA to Silas Deane, March 30, 1776, *AA*, ser. 4, 5:549–50.
24. Josiah Sabin Pension Application in John C. Dann, ed., *The Revolution Remembered: Eyewitness Account of the War for Independence* (Chicago: University of Chicago Press, 1980), 19–21; Porter Journal, 192–93.
25. Orders, Aug. 19, 1776, *AA*, ser. 5, 1:1128.
26. Seth Warner Certificate, April 12, 1776, Howe Library, University of Vermont; BA to PS, April 20, 1776, *AA*, ser. 4, 5:1098–99; Doyen Salsig, ed., *Parole: Quebec; Countersign: Ticonderoga: Second New Jersey Regimental Orderly Book 1776* (Cranbury, NJ: Associate University Presses, 1980), 79.
27. Ainslie Journal, 76; John Jay to Edward Rutledge, June 6, 1776, *AA*, ser. 5, 1:41–42.
28. Senter Journal, 37; John Thomas to GW, May 8, 1776, *AA*, ser. 4, 6:453.
29. Salsig, *2nd NJ Orderly Book*, 96–97; Ainslie Journal, 87–88.
30. Minutes for March 20, 1776, *JCC*, 4:215–16.
31. BF to JH, April 13, 1776, *AA*, ser. 4,

5:927–928; BF to Josiah Quincy, April 15, 1776 *AA*, ser. 4, 5:947; Carroll Journal, 56.

32. Samuel Chase to JA, April 28, 1776, Founders Online.

33. Carroll Journal, 92–93; Moses Hazen to PS, April 1, 1776, *AA*, ser. 4, 5:578; Note, *AA*, ser. 4, 5:1167.

34. Thomas O'Brien Hanley, *Revolutionary Statesman: Charles Carroll and the War* (Chicago: Loyola University Press, 1983), 125.

35. *LDC*, 3:611–12, 628–29, 639–40.

36. John Thomas to GW, May 8, 1776, *AA*, ser. 4, 6: 453–454; Salsig, *2nd NJ Orderly Book,* 97–99; John Thomas to Commissioners, May 7, 1776, *AA*, ser. 4, 6: 451.

37. Ainslie Journal, 88–89; Salsig, *2nd NJ Orderly Book,* 102.

38. Porter Journal, 192–93.

39. *Ibid.*, 191, 192–93.

40. Ralph Cross, "The Journal of Ralph Cross of Newburyport," *The Historical Magazine and Notes and Queries* 2, 2nd series (Morrisania, NY: Henry R. Dawson, 1870), 289–91.

41. RM to PS, December 5, 1775, *AA*, ser. 4, 4: 188–89; Council of War, May 7, 1776, *AA*, ser. 4, 6: 454–56.

42. Commissioners to JH, May 17, 1776, *AA*, ser. 4, 6:450, 588; Commissioners to PS, May 10, 1776, *AA*, ser. 4, 6:450.

43. BA to Commissioners, May 15, 1775, *AA*, ser. 4, 6:579–80; "Poor Richard Improved, 1750," Founders Online; Commissioners to Canada to John Thomas, May 15, 1776, *LDC*, 3:681.

44. BA to Commissioners, May 17, 1776, *AA*, ser. 4, 6:591–92.

45. Lewis Beebe & Frederic R. Kirkland, ed., "Journal of a Physician on the Expedition against Canada, 1776," *Pennsylvania Magazine of History and Biography* 59, no. 4 (Oct. 1936), 328.

46. *AA*, ser. 5, 3:1158–59; for witnesses: JB to Theodore Sedgwick, Dec. 6, 1776, Sedgwick Family Papers, Massachusetts Historical Society. For Samuel Brewer and Joshua Thomas, see Salsig, *2nd NJ Orderly Book,* 99.

47. John Thomas to Commissioners, May 20, 1776, *AA*, ser. 4, 6:592; Beebe Journal, 329–30.

Chapter Nine

1. Frye Bayley, "Colonel Frye Bayley's Reminiscences," *Proceedings of the Vermont Historical Society for the Years 1923, 1924 and 1925* (Bellows Falls, VT: P.H. Gobie Press, 1926), 32–33.

2. Commissioners to JH, May 17, 1776, *AA*, ser. 4, 6: 588; "Colonel Bedel's Defence" in Aldrich, 214; Frye Bayley Reminiscences, 38; Elizabeth A. Fenn, *Pox Americana: The Great Smallpox Epidemic of 1775–82* (New York: Hill & Wang, 2002), 73, 297.

3. Commissioners to PS, May 16, 1776 *AA*, ser. 4, 6:578–79.

4. British figures from *An Authentic Narrative of Facts Relating to the Exchange of Prisoners Taken at the Cedars* (London: T. Cadell, 1777), 21–22; six hundred from "Report on the Committee on the Capitulation," June 17, 1776, *AA*, ser. 5, 1:159–60.

5. Congressional documents on the Cedars, *AA*, ser. 5, 1:166; *An Authentic Narrative*, 26; JA to Abigail Adams, June 26, 1776, Founders Online.

6. Henry Sherburne to a Gentleman, June 18, 1776, *AA*, ser. 4, 6:598–600.

7. PS to GW, May 24, 1776, *AA*, ser. 4, 6:564; commissioners to JH, May 17, 1775, *AA*, ser. 4, 6:587–88.

8. James Wilkinson, *Memoirs of My Own Times* (Philadelphia: Abraham Small, 1816), 1:42. Wilkinson recalled that the second man was Philip Williams (second in command in Porter's Regiment), but a contemporary report put Williams in Montréal. See Joseph Vose & Henry Winchester Cunningham, ed., *Journal of Lieutenant-Colonel Joseph Vose, April-July, 1776* (Cambridge: John Wilson and Son, 1905), 13.

9. Wilkinson Memoir, 1:42.

10. BA to Commissioners, May 27, 1776, *AA*, ser. 4, 6:595–96.

11. Allen Everest, *Moses Hazen and the Canadian Refugees in the American Revolution* (Syracuse University Press, 1976), 1–45, quote on 13; Abram Hess, "The Life and Services of General John Philip de Haas 1735–1786," *Lebanon County Historical Society County Historical Society* 15, no. 1 (1976, originally published 1916), 9–11.

12. Wilkinson Memoir, 1:46.

13. BA to Commissioners, *AA*, ser. 4, 6:595–96.

14. Commissioners to JH, May 27, 1776, *AA*, ser. 4, 6:589–90; William Thompson to GW, *AA*, ser. 4, 6:628.

15. *American Archives*, ser. 5, 3:1158–59; for witnesses: JB to Theodore Sedgwick, Dec. 6, 1776, Sedgwick Family Papers, Massachusetts Historical Society.

16. Resolution of Congress, July 10, 1776, *AA*, ser. 5, 1:162.

17. BA to Commissioners, June 2, 1776, *AA*, ser. 5, 1:165.

18. *AA*, ser. 5, 3:1158–59; for evidence: JB to Theodore Sedgwick, Dec. 6, 1776, Sedgwick Family Papers, Massachusetts Historical Society.

19. Wilkinson Memoir, 1:47–48.

20. BA to Commissioners, June 2, 1776, *AA*, ser. 5, 1:165.

21. John F. Ross, *War on the Run: The Epic Story of Robert Rogers and the Conquest of America's First Frontier* (New York: Bantam Books, 2009), 251.

22. Frederick Cook, ed., *Journals of the Military Expedition of Major General John Sullivan against the Six Nations of Indians in 1779* (Auburn, NY: Knapp, Peck & Thomson, 1887), 296–305, 101; Franklin B. Hough, *The Northern invasion of October 1780: a series of papers relating to the expeditions from Canada under Sir John Johnson* (New York, 1866), 210.

23. BA to Henry Clinton, Sept. 8, 1781, in Isaac Arnold, *Life of Arnold*, 348–352; Eric D. Lehman, *Homegrown Terror: Benedict Arnold and the Burning of New London* (Middletown, CT: Wesleyan University Press, 2014), 140–61.
24. Chase to PS, May 31, 1776, *LDC*, 4:105.
25. Beebe Journal, 332.
26. John Sullivan to GW, June 5, 1776, *AA*, ser. 4, 6:921–23.
27. Proceedings of a General Court-Martial, Dec. 1, 1775, *AA*, ser. 4, 3:1709–10.
28. *American Archives*, ser. 5, 3:1158–59; for witnesses: JB to Theodore Sedgwick, Dec. 6, 1776, Sedgwick Family Papers, Massachusetts Historical Society.
29. William Thompson to GW, June 2, 1776, *AA*, ser. 4, 6:684–685; BA to JS, June 5, 1776, *AA*, ser. 4, 6:924.
30. BA to PS, June 6, 1776, *AA*, ser. 4, 6:926.
31. John Sullivan to GW, June 5–6, 1776, *AA*, ser. 4, 6:921–923; JS to GW, June 8 -12, *AA*, ser. 4, 6:1036–38.
32. John Sullivan to GW, June 8 & 12, 1776, *AA*, ser. 4, 6:1037.
33. June 12, 1776, *AA*, ser. 4, 6: 826–828; Hatch, *Thrust for Canada*, 217; Wilkinson Memoir, 1:55.
34. Commissioners to Congress, May 27, 1776, *AA*, ser. 4, 6:590.
35. Wilkinson Memoir, 1:48.
36. BA to PS, June 13, 1776, *AA*, ser. 4, 6:1038; BA to JS; Moses Hazen to John Sullivan, June 13, 1776, *AA*, ser. 4, 6:1105.
37. PCC, M247, r71 i58, p385–86, 397.
38. Sparks, *Life and Treason*, 68–69; Isaac Arnold, *Life of Arnold*, 97; Wallace, *Traitorous Hero*, 104; Edward Dean Sullivan, *Benedict Arnold: Military Racketeer* (New York: Vanguard Press, 1932).
39. *AA*, ser. 5, 3:1158–59; for witnesses: JB to Theodore Sedgwick, Dec. 6, 1776, Sedgwick Family Papers, Massachusetts Historical Society.
40. BA to John Sullivan, June 13, 1776, *AA, ser.* 4, 6:1104–5; Salsig, *2nd NJ Orderly Book*, 63.
41. *AA*, ser. 4, 6:796; Beebe Journal, 334; Moses Hazen to JS, June 13, 1776, *AA*, ser. 4, 6:1105–6.
42. *American Archives*, ser. 5, 3:1158–59; for witnesses: JB to Theodore Sedgwick, Dec. 6, 1776, Sedgwick Family Papers, Massachusetts Historical Society.
43. Samuel Williams, "Historical Memoirs of Colonel Seth Warner," *The Natural and Civil History of Vermont*, 2nd edition (Burlington, VT: Samuel Mills, 1809), 2:445–50.
44. BA, Moses Hazen, Edward Antill, separately, to John Sullivan, June 13, 1776, *AA*, ser. 4, 6:1104–6.
45. John Greenwood & Isaac J. Greenwood, ed., *Revolutionary Services of John Greenwood of Boston and New York 1775–1783* (New York: Joseph R. Greenwood, 1922), 34–36.
46. Charles Cushing to his Brother, July 8, 1776, *AA*, ser. 5, 1:128–132; Porter Journal, 197; Everest, *Moses Hazen*, 43; Wilkinson Memoir, 1:55.
47. Jeduthan Baldwin & Thomas Williams Baldwin, ed., *The Revolutionary Journal of Col. Jeduthan Baldwin 1775–1778* (Bangor, Maine: 1906), 56; Porter Journal, 197; Howard Parker Moore, *A Life of General John Stark* (New York, 1949), 231.
48. BA to GW, June 25, 1776, Founders Online.
49. Beebe Journal, 336.
50. JS to GW, June 24 & June 25, 1776, Founders Online; Vose Journal, 17–18.
51. Vose Journal, 18; Greenwood Memoir, 36–37.

Chapter Ten

1. JA to Abigail Adams, July 7, 1776, Founders Online; Vose Journal, 19.
2. Sullivan to GW, July 2, 1776, *AA*, ser. 4, 6:1219.
3. Max M. Mintz, *The Generals of Saratoga: John Burgoyne & Horatio Gates* (New Haven: Yale University Press, 1990), 12–16.
4. Paul David Nelson, *General Horatio Gates: A Biography* (Baton Rouge: Louisiana State University Press, 1976), 1–6; Martin, *Benedict Arnold*, 390; Helga Doblin, trans.; Mary C. Lynn, ed., *The Specht Journal: A Military Journal of the Burgoyne Campaign* (Westport, CT: Greenwood Press, 1995), 102.
5. JA to JS, June 23, 1776, *LDC*, 4:296.
6. JA to Abigail, June 26, 1776, *LDC*, 4:323.
7. Minutes for April 26, 1776, *JCC*, 4:312–14.
8. JB's petition, June 26, 1776, *AA*, ser 5, 1:1219–20; Minutes for June 27, 1776, *JCC*, 5:485; JB to Committee of War, June 29, 1776, PCC, M247, r91, i78, v2, p11.
9. Minutes for August 17, 1776, *JCC*, 5:665; JA Diary, August 17, 1776, online at Massachusetts Historical Society; William Williams to Joseph Trumbull, August 10, 1776, *LDC*, 4:651.
10. Minutes for July 30 & August 1, 1776, *JCC*, 5:617–19, 626.
11. PS to GW, July 12, 1776, *AA*, ser. 5, 1:232–33; "Minutes of a Council of War," July 7, 1776, *AA*, ser. 5, 1:233; "Minutes of a Council of General Officers," July 8, 1776, *AA*, ser. 5, 1:236.
12. Beebe Journal, 341–42.
13. "Colonel Bedel's Defence," in Edgar Aldrich, "The Affair of the Cedars and the Service of Colonel Timothy Bedel in the War of the Revolution," *Proceedings of the New Hampshire Historical Society* 3 (Dec. 1891), 213–14.
14. Timothy Bedel to HG, July 12, 1776, *AA*, ser. 5, 1:239; General Orders, August 1, 1776, *AA*, ser. 5, 1:801.
15. Timothy Bedel to HG, August 3, 1776, *AA*, ser. 5, 1:747–748; Edgar Aldrich, "Affair of the Cedars," 217.
16. Horatio Gates to Arnold, July 15, 1776, *AA*, ser. 5, 1:358.

17. PS to Hermanus Schuyler, June 7 & June 22, 1776, *NDAR*, 5:410–411, 680.
18. HG to JH, July 16, 1776, *AA*, ser. 5, 1:375–376.
19. Russell P. Bellico, *Sails and Steam in the Mountains: A Maritime and Military History of Lake George and Lake Champlain* (Fleischmanns, NY: Purple Mountain Press, 1992), 140; BA to HG, July 24, 1776, *AA*, ser. 5, 1:563–64.
20. Cornelius Wynkoop to HG, July 23 and July 25, 1776, *AA*, ser. 5, 1:547, 582.
21. Wynkoop to HG, July 25, 1776, *AA*, ser. 5, 1:582; Wynkoop to HG, July 30, 1776, *AA*, ser. 5, 1:678.
22. HG to JH, July 29, 1776, *AA*, ser. 5, 1: 649.
23. Beebe Journal, 344; Porter Journal, 202.
24. Ennis Duling, "Arnold, Hazen, and the Mysterious Major Scott," *Journal of the American Revolution: Annual Volume 2017* (Yardley, PA: Westholme, 2017), 141–153; online at JAR (Feb. 23, 2016), allthingsliberty.com.
25. Field Officers to JH, Aug. 19, 1776, *AA*, ser. 5, 1:1072.
26. Enoch Poor to HG, Aug. 6, 1776, *AA*, ser. 5, 1:1273.
27. Arnold's Protest, *AA*, ser. 5, 1:1272.
28. Enoch Poor to BA, Aug. 1, 1776, ser. 5, 1:1272; Porter Journal, 203; Court to HG, Aug. 6, 1776, *AA*, ser. 5, 1:1273–74.
29. BA to Court, Aug. 1, 1776, *AA*, ser. 5, 1:1273; Minutes for June 30, 1775, *JCC*, 2:114.
30. HG to JH, Sept. 2, 1776, *AA*, ser. 5, 1:1268.

Chapter Eleven

1. Jacobus Wynkoop to New York Congress, Aug. 15, 1775, *AA*, ser. 4, 3:140.
2. HG to Arnold, July 17, 1776, *AA*, ser. 5, 1:397; Wells Journal, *CCHS*, 7:268.
3. HG to BA, July 17, 1776, *AA*, ser. 5, 1:397; HG to JH, July 29, 1776, *AA*, ser. 5, 1:649; Matthias Ogden to Aaron Burr, Aug. 11, 1776, *AA*, ser. 5, 1:901. As early as July 26, Ogden was aware that Arnold would "command the water craft on the Lake in person." Ogden to Burr, July 26, 1776, *AA*, ser. 5, 1:604.
4. Gates's Orders to Arnold, Aug. 7, 1776, *NDAR*, 6:95–96.
5. Petition of Jacobus Wynkoop to Congress, Aug. 27, 1776, *AA*, ser. 5, 1:1186; Jacobus Wynkoop to BA, Aug. 17, 1776, *AA*, ser. 5, 1:1275.
6. BA to Jacobus Wynkoop, Aug. 17, 1776, *AA*, ser. 5, 1:1275–76.
7. *Ibid.*
8. BA to HG, Aug. 17, 1776, *AA*, ser. 5, 1:1275–76.
9. Jacobus Wynkoop to HG, Aug. 17, 1776, *AA*, ser. 5, 1:1276.
10. HG to BA, Aug. 18, 1776, *AA*, ser. 5, 1:1277.
11. BA to Jacobus Wynkoop, Aug. 18, 1776; BA to HG Aug. 18, 1776; HG to PS, Aug. 20, 1776, *AA*, ser. 5, 1:1275–77; PS to JH, Aug. 29, 1776, *AA*, ser. 5, 1:1217.
12. HG to Hancock, Sept. 2, 1776, *AA*, ser. 5, 1:1268.
13. Ennis Duling, "Did Benedict Arnold's Fleet Plunder an American Settlement?" *Journal of the American Revolution* (Aug. 29, 2017), online at allthingsliberty.com.
14. Wells Journal, *CCHS*, 7:270–85.
15. William Gilliland to Continental Congress, likely 1777, in Watson, *Pioneer History*, 176–77.
16. Thomas Hartley to HG, July 24, 1776, *AA*, ser. 5, 1:564.
17. Salsig, *2nd NJ Orderly Book*, 214.
18. BA to HG, Aug. 31, 1776, *NDAR*, 6:371; Wells Journal, *CCHS*, 7:272.
19. *Ibid.*, 272–73.
20. William Gilliland to BA, Sept. 1, 1776, *AA*, ser. 5, 2:112–13.
21. BA to HG, Sept. 28, 1776, *AA*, ser. 5, 2:591–92.
22. Thomas Hartley to HG, Oct. 2, 1776, *AA*, ser. 5, 2:834.
23. Baldwin Journal, 79; William Gilliland to Continental Congress, likely 1777, in Watson, *Pioneer History*, 180.
24. JB to PS, Aug. 27, 1776, *AA*, ser. 5, 1:1218–19; "Colonel Brown's Complaint against General Arnold," Sept. 3, 1776, *AA*, ser. 5, 2:143.
25. PS to HG, Sept. 8, 1776, *AA*, ser. 5, 2:249; HG to PS, Sept. 11, 1776, *AA*, ser. 5, 2:294–95.
26. Andrew Brown found in *AA*, ser. 5, 2:1193; Doyen Salsig, *2nd NJ Orderly Book*, 235–38; *AA*, ser. 5, 2:475–78.
27. *Connecticut Military Record, 1775–1848: Record of Connecticut Men in the Military and Naval Service during the War of the Revolution 1775–1783* (Hartford: The Case, Lockwood & Brainard, 1889), 113.
28. *AA*, ser. 5, 2:476.
29. Beebe Journal, 346; Ammi Robbins, *Journal of the Rev. Ammi R. Robbins, A Chaplain in the American Army* (New Haven: B.L. Hamlen, 1850), 37.
30. Donald H. Wickman & Mount Independence Coalition, *Strong Ground: Mount Independence and the American Revolution* (Orwell, VT: Mount Independence Coalition, 2017).
31. James Easton to Continental Congress, Oct. 5, 1776, *AA*, ser. 5, 2:911.
32. Officers' Certificate, Oct. 11, 1776, *AA*, ser. 5, 1:1219; PCC, M 274, r173, i153, v2, p323; JB to PS, Aug. 27, 1776, *AA*, ser. 5 1:1218–19; PS to Congress, Aug. 16, 1776, *AA*, ser. 5, 1:984; "Report on JB's Petition," Nov. 12, 1776, *AA*, ser. 5, 3:1567.
33. Salsig, *2nd NJ Orderly Book*, 255; Baldwin Journal, 80.

Chapter Twelve

1. Press release, April 29, 2019, National Museum of American History.

2. Kenneth Roberts, *Rabble in Arms* (Garden City: Doubleday, 1933).

3. Gates's Orders to BA, August 7, 1776, *NDAR*, 6:95; HG to BA, Sept. 12, 1776, *NDAR*, 6:791.

4. Wells Journal, *CCHS*, 7:277–280; BA to HG, Sept. 18, 1776, *NDAR*, 6:884; BA to HG, Sept. 21, 1776, *NDAR*, 6:926.

5. BA to HG, Sept. 15, 1776; HG to BA Sept. 12, 1776; BA to HG, Sept. 28, 1776, *NDAR*, 6:837, 791, 1032.

6. Wells Journal, *CCHS*, 7:280–283.

7. *NDAR*, 6:1343–44; HG to PS, Aug. 18, 1776, *NDAR*, 6: 223; David Waterbury to JH, October 24, 1776, *AA*, ser. 5, 2:1224.

8. *NDAR*, 6:1343.

9. BA to HG, October 12, 1776, *NDAR*, 6:1235.

10. *NDAR*, 6:1235, 1259; Wells Journal, *CCHS*, 7:283–84.

11. BA to HG, Oct. 12, 1776, *NDAR*, 6:1235; Thomas Pringle to Philip Stephens, Oct. 15, 1776, *NDAR*, 6:1274; "Three British Naval Lieutenants to Thomas Pringle," June 8, 1777, *NDAR*, 9:49–51.

12. BA to HG, Oct. 12, 1776, *NDAR*., 6:1235.

13. Wells Journal, *CCHS*, 7:284.

14. David Waterbury to JH, Oct. 24, 1776, *AA*, ser. 5, 2:1224; Waterbury to HG, Feb. 26, 1777, in Stephen Darley, *The Battle of Valcour Island: The Participants and Vessels of Benedict Arnold's 1776 Defense of Lake Champlain* (Self-published, 2013), 147–50.

15. BA to PS, Oct. 15, 1776, *NDAR*, 6:1276.

16. Thomas Hartley to HG, Oct. 13, *AA*, Oct. 13, 1028; Baldwin Journal, 81.

17. Salsig, *2nd NJ Orderly Book*, 265. Spelling has been standardized.

18. James Maxwell to William Livingston, Oct. 20, 1776, *AA*, ser. 5, 2:1143.

19. David Hackett Fischer, *Washington's Crossing* (New York: Oxford University Press, 2004), 348–49.

20. Maxwell to Livingston, Oct. 20, 1776, *AA*, ser. 5, 2:1143.

21. Richard Henry Lee to Thomas Jefferson, Nov. 3, 1776, *LDC*, 5:431.

22. *AA*, ser. 5, 3:1158–59; for witnesses: JB to Theodore Sedgwick, Dec. 6, 1776, Sedgwick Family Papers, Massachusetts Historical Society.

23. David Waterbury to HG, Feb. 26, 1777, Darley, *Battle of Valcour Island*, 147–50.

24. "Colonel John Brown's Expedition," *New England Historical and Genealogical Register* 18 (Albany: J. Munsell, 1864), 288.

25. William Gordon, *The History of the Rise, Progress, and Establishment, of the Independence of the United States of America* (London: Charles Dilly & James Buckland, 1788), 2:384–85; David Ramsay, *The History of the American Revolution* (Philadelphia: R. Aitken & Son, 1789), 1:278–79; Mercy Otis Warren, *History of the Rise, Progress and Termination of the American Revolution* (Boston: Manning & Loring for E. Larkin, 1805), 1:343–45.

26. Wilkinson Memoir, 1:92–93.

27. Arnold, *Life of Arnold*, 118; Sparks, *Life and Treason*, 81–82.

28. Alfred Mahan, "The Naval Campaign of 1776 on Lake Champlain," *Scribner's Magazine* 23, no. 2 (Feb. 1898), 147, 158–59; Mahan, *The Major Operations of the Navies in the War of American Independence* (Boston: Little, Brown, 1913), 8–28.

29. Guy Carleton to John Burgoyne, Oct. 12–15, *NDAR*, 6:1272–74; Carleton to George Germain, Oct. 14, 1776, *NDAR*, 6:1257–58.

30. Beebe Journal, 355.

31. Salsig, *2nd NJ Orderly Book*, 274.

32. John Trumbull, *Autobiography, Reminiscences and Letters of John Trumbull from 1756 to 1841* (New York: Wiley and Putnam, 1841), 36.

33. Nov. 13, 1776, *Orderly Book of the Northern Army, at Ticonderoga and Mt. Independence* (Albany: J. Munsell, 1859), 75; Council of War, Nov. 21, 1776, *AA*, ser. 5, 3:797.

Chapter Thirteen

1. *Minutes of the Albany Committee of Correspondence 1775–1778*, 1:614–25.

2. Minutes for Sept. 20, 1776, *JCC*, 5:795; JB to HG, Dec. 1, 1776, *AA*, ser. 5, 3:1158–59.

3. HG to JB, Dec. 2, 1776, *AA*, ser. 5, 3:1160.

4. Sparks, *Life and Treason*, 71–72; Arnold, *Life of Arnold*, 104; Carl Van Doren, *Secret History of the American Revolution* (New York: Viking Press, 1941), 156; Wallace, *Traitorous Hero*, 121–122; Brandt, *The Man in the Mirror*, 114; James Martin, *Benedict Arnold*, 299, 314; Stephen Brumwell, *Turncoat: Benedict Arnold and the Crisis of American Liberty* (New Haven: Yale University Press, 2018), 84.

5. Court of Inquiry, Dec. 2, 1776, *AA*, ser. 5, 3:1044–45.

6. William Leete Stone, *Life of Joseph Brant (Thayendanegea)* (Albany: J. Munsell, 1865, original 1838), 2:116–18.

7. Letter of Gen. William Chamberlain, March 2, 1827, *Proceedings of the Massachusetts Historical Society*, ser. 2, 10:500.

8. Wilkinson Memoir, 1:108–12.

9. GW to HG, Dec. 14, 1776, Founders Online; GW to HG, Dec. 23, 1776, Founders Online; Wilkinson Memoir, 1:127–28.

10. Thomas Smart Hughes, *History of England by Hume and Smollett with a Continuation by the Rev. T.S. Hughes, B.D.* (London: A.J. Valpy, 1835),15:271; Randall, *Benedict Arnold*, 323; Brian Richard Boylan, *Benedict Arnold: The Dark Eagle* (New York: W.W. Norton, 1973), 87.

11. Wilkinson Memoir, 1:127–28.

12. Greenwood Memoir, 38–40.

13. Wilkinson Memoir, 1:129–30.

14. Greenwood Memoir, 41.

15. Greenwood Memoir, 41–42.

16. JS to Meschech Weare, Feb 13, 1777, *NHSP*, 8:491–92.

17. JB to Theodore Sedgwick, Dec. 6, 1776, Sedgwick Family Papers, Massachusetts Historical Society. Although the wording is the same, the order of charges is slightly different in the list Brown sent to Sedgwick.
18. PCC, M247, r174, i154, v1, p125–28; labeled as a copy on page 128.
19. JB to JH, Dec. 10, 1776, *AA*, ser. 5, 3:1158–60; Minutes for Dec. 26, 1776, *JCC*, 6:1040.
20. PS to GW, Feb. 4–5, 1777, Founders Online.
21. GW to William Shippen, Jr., Feb. 6, 1777, Founders Online.
22. GW to PS, Feb. 19, 1777, Founders Online.
23. JB to JH, Feb. 22, 1777, PCC, M247, i78, v2, p137.
24. Van Schaack, "Col. John Brown," 24; Minutes for March 15, 1777, *JCC*, 7:181.
25. Smith, *History of Pittsfield*, v, 273. Some of Van Schaack's *Autographic History of the American Revolution* can be found in the collections of the New-York Historical Society and the Chicago History Museum, but no Brown handbill.
26. Stone, *Life of Joseph Brant*, 2:116. Van Schaack, who presumably had a copy of the April handbill, includes the "Money is this man's God" quote, but he seems to cite Stone for the quote. See Van Schaack, "Col. John Brown," 23.
27. BA to GW, Jan. 31, 1777, 8:197–98; Martin, *Benedict Arnold*, 301–3.
28. Thomas Burke's Notes, *LDC*, 6:263–64; Benjamin Rush's Notes, *LDC*, 6:324–25.
29. Minutes for February 21, 1777, *JCC*, 7: 141; John Stark to New Hampshire Council and House, undated but likely March 22, 1777, *NHSP*, 8:518.
30. GW to BA, March 3, 1777, Founders Online; BA to GW, March 11, 1777, Founders Online; Martin, *Benedict Arnold*, 314; BA to HG, March 25, 1777, New-York Historical Society.
31. GW to BA, April 3, 1777, Founders Online.
32. James Montgomery Bailey, *History of Danbury, Conn., 1684–1896* (New York: Burr Printing House, 1896), 60–87; William Hanford Burr, "The Invasion of Connecticut by the British," *The Connecticut Magazine*, 139–52; Martin, *Benedict Arnold*, 316–21.
33. Thomas Burke to Richard Caswell, May 2, 1777, *LDC*, 7:13–14; Howard H. Peckham, *Toll of Independence*, 33.
34. JA to Abigail Adams, May 2, 1777, *LDC*, 7:12; JA to Nathanael Greene, May 9, 1777, *LDC*, 7:49.
35. GW to JH, May 12, 1777, Founders Online.
36. JA to Nathanael Greene, May 9, 1777, *LDC*, 7:49; Isaac Arnold, *Life of Arnold*, 135; Minutes for May 20, 1777, *JCC*, 7:372–73.
37. Richard Henry Lee to Thomas Jefferson, May 20, 1777, *LDC*, 7:94–95.
38. Minutes for May 23, 1777, *JCC*, 8:382; JA to Abigail Adams, May 22, 1777, *LDC*, 7:103.

Chapter Fourteen

1. *Orderly Book of the Northern Army*, 162–65; Wickman, *Strong Ground*, 41–44.
2. Arthur St. Clair & William Henry Smith, ed., *The St. Clair Papers: The Life and Public Services of Arthur St. Clair* (Cincinnati: Robert Clarke, 1882), 387.
3. GW to Massachusetts Council, March 13, 1777, Founders Online; *Proceedings of a General Court Martial ... For the Trial of Major General St. Clair; Collections of the New-York Historical Society for the Year 1880* (New York: New-York Historical Society, 1881), 135–36.
4. Arthur St. Clair to PS, June 13, 1777, *St. Clair Papers*, 1:396–400; GW to PS, June 20, 1777, Founders Online.
5. Arthur St. Clair & U.S. House of Representatives, *Narrative of the Manner in which the Campaign against the Indians, in the Year 1790 Was Conducted* (Philadelphia: Jane Aitken, 1812), 244–45.
6. PS to GW, July 7, 1777, Founders Online.
7. Samuel Adams to Samuel Cooper, July 15, 1777, Samuel Adams, *Writing of Samuel Adams*, 3:389.
8. *Journals of the Provincial Congress of Massachusetts in 1774 and 1775*, 15, 22.
9. Thomas Allen, *Connecticut Courant* (Sept. 1, 1777); Patrick Cogan to John Stark, July 17, 1777, *NHSP*, 8:640–641; GW to PS, July 15, 1777, Founders Online.
10. Ebenezer Elmer, "Journal of Ebenezer Elmer," *Proceedings of the New Jersey Historical Society* 3, no.1 (1848), 39–40 (Newark, NJ: Daily Advertiser, 1849).
11. *Massachusetts Acts and Resolves 1779–1780*, 21:615.
12. John Burgoyne to Earl Hervey, July 11, 1777, Edward De Fonblanque, *Political and Military Episodes ... from the Life and Correspondence of the Right Hon. John Burgoyne* (London: MacMillan, 1876), 248; Roger Lamb, *An Original and Authentic Journal* (Dublin: Wilkinson and Courtney, 1809), 144; John Burgoyne, *A State of the Expedition from Canada*, 2nd edition (London: J. Almon, 1780), 53–54.
13. John Fellows to GW, July 24, 1777, Founders Online.
14. PS to GW, July 23, 1777 and John Fellows to GW, July 24, 1777, Founders Online.
15. JB to PS, July 27, 1777, *GW Papers*, 10:483–84.
16. PS to GW, Aug. 1, 1777, Founders Online.
17. Minutes for July 7, 1777, *JCC*, 8:537; JA to Nathanael Greene July 7, 1777, *LDC*, 7:305–7; John Adams Diary, Sept. 18, 1777, Founders Online.
18. BA to Congress, July 11, 1777, PCC, M247, r179, i162, v1, p106–7; GW to JH, July 10, 1777, Founders Online.
19. *JCC*, 8:545; BA to JH, July 12, 1777, PCC, M247, r179, i162, v1, p108; GW to PS, July 18, 1777, Founders Online.

20. Baldwin Journal, 112; PS to GW, July 26–27, 1777, Founders Online.
21. BA to GW, July 27, 1777, Founders Online; Arthur St. Clair to GW, July 25, 1777, Founders Online.
22. *Proceedings of a General Court Martial for the Trial of Major General St. Clair; Collections of the New-York Historical Society for the 1880* (New York: New-York Historical Society, 1881), 171.
23. PS to JH, August 4, 1777, PCC, M247, r189, i170, v2, p210–12.
24. Smith, *History of Pittsfield*, 479, 483, 490; Persifor Frazer to Molly Frazer, July 25 & Sept. 21, 1776 in Persifor Frazer & grandson Persifor Frazer, ed., *General Persifor Frazer: A Memoir* (Philadelphia, 1907), 99, 119. Jacob Down does not appear in *Massachusetts Soldiers and Sailors*.
25. GW to John Sullivan, August 1, 1777, Founders Online; GW to Jonathan Trumbull, August 4, 1777, Founders Online.
26. Peter Deygart to PS, Aug. 6, 1777, George Clinton, J. Austin Holden & Hugh Hastings, ed., *Public papers of George Clinton* (New York and Albany: State of New York, 1899–1914), 2:191–92; Gavin Watt, *Rebellion in the Mohawk Valley: The St. Leger Expedition of 1777* (Toronto: Dundurn Press, 2002), 317–18.
27. PS to JH, Aug. 8 & 10, 1777, PCC, M247, r189, i170, v2, p217–19.
28. William H. Sumner, "Colonel Brooks and Captain Bancroft," *Proceedings of the Massachusetts Historical Society 1855–1858* (Feb. 1858), 3:279; Wilkinson Memoir, 1:272.
29. Lossing, *Schuyler*, 1:286–288; Arnold, *Life of Arnold*, 153–54. For more recent versions, Wallace, *Traitorous Hero*, 141; Martin, *Benedict Arnold*, 363; Joyce Lee Malcolm, *The Tragedy of Benedict Arnold: An American Life* (New York: Pegasus Books, 2018), 200.
30. PS to Nicholas Herkimer, Aug. 12, 1777, PS Letter Book, Schuyler Papers, NYPL; Peter Nelson, "Learned's Expedition to the Relief of Fort Stanwix," *Quarterly Journal of the New York State Historical Association* 9, No. 4 (Oct. 1928), 380–85.
31. BA to HG, Aug. 21, Sparks, *Correspondence*, 2:518–519; Watt, *Rebellion in the Mohawk Valley*, 242–43.
32. James Thomas Flexner, "How A Madman Helped Save The Colonies," *American Heritage* 7, no. 2 (Feb. 1956) at www.americanheritage.com/how-madman-helped-save-colonies.
33. Joseph Jackson, "George Lippard: Misunderstood Man of Letters," *Pennsylvania Magazine of History and Biography* 59, no. 4 (Oct. 1935), 376.
34. Chauncey Burr, "Introduction," George Lippard, *Washington and his Generals: or, Legends of the Revolution* (Philadelphia: G. B. Zieber, 1847), xvi.
35. Lippard, *Washington and His Generals*, 161.
36. Boylan, *Benedict Arnold: The Dark Eagle*; John Ensor Harr, *Dark Eagle: A Novel of Benedict Arnold and the American Revolution* (New York: Viking, 1999); Randall, *Benedict Arnold*, 348; Wallace, *Traitorous Hero*, 143; Martin, *Benedict Arnold*, drops "dark eagle" in quotes into his account of the relief of Fort Schuyler, 365; Nathaniel Philbrick, who reveals he knows better in an endnote, titled chapter five "The Dark Eagle" in *Valiant Ambition: George Washington, Benedict Arnold, and the Fate of the American Revolution* (New York: Viking, 2016), 108–140, 349. Steve Darley, "The Dark Eagle: How Fiction Became Historical Fact" online at Archiving Early America\ www.varsitytutors.com/earlyamerica/early-america-review/volume-10/dark-eagle-fiction-became-historical-fact. Troops as numerous as "leaves on the trees" see William Leete Stone, *The Campaign of Lieut. Gen. John Burgoyne, and the Expedition of Lieut. Col. Barry St. Leger* (Albany: Joel Munsell, 1877), 215; also Stimson, *My Story*, 283; Randall, *Benedict Arnold*, 348; Brandt, *Man in the Mirror*, 128; Malcolm, *Tragedy of Benedict Arnold*, 201.
37. "Heap Fighting Chief" see Charles Burr Todd, *The Real Benedict Arnold* (New York: A.S. Barnes, 1903), 142; Frederic Jesup Stimson's novel *My Story: Being the Memoirs of Benedict Arnold . . .* (New York: Charles Scribner's Sons, 1917), 283; James Thomas Flexner, *The Traitor and the Spy: Benedict Arnold and John André* (Syracuse University Press, 1991; 1st edition, Harcourt, Brace, 1953), 166.
38. Watt, *Rebellion in the Mohawk Valley*, 246.
39. Wilkinson Memoir, 1:222; PS to GW, April 15, 1777, Founders Online.
40. Henry Dearborn, *Journals of Henry Dearborn, 1776–1783* (Cambridge: John Wilson & Son, 1887), 5; Mintz, *Generals of Saratoga*, 181.
41. Baldwin Journal, 118–19; Richard M. Ketchum, *Saratoga: Turning Point of America's Revolutionary War* (New York: Henry Holt, 1997), 347; Randall, *Benedict Arnold*, 351–52; Miecislaus Haiman, *Kosciuszko in the American Revolution* (New York: Kosciuszko Foundation and the Polish Institute of Arts and Sciences, 1976), 25; Wilkinson Memoir, 1:232; John Armstrong to Jared Sparks, August 1837, bMS Sparks 49.1 (9), Houghton Library, Harvard University.

Chapter Fifteen

1. *Massachusetts Acts and Resolves* 20, 1777–1778, 622; Smith, *History of Pittsfield*, 297.
2. Edward A. Hoyt & Ronald F. Kingsley, "The Pawlet Expedition, September 1777," *Vermont History* 25, no. 2 (Summer/Fall 2007), 69–100; "Thermopylae" in Benjamin Lincoln to John Laurens, Feb. 5, 1781, Massachusetts Historical Society; Richard Varick to PS, Sept. 18, 1777, in John A. Luzader, *Saratoga: A Military History of the Decisive Campaign of the American Revolution*

(New York & California: Savas Beatie, 2008), 212–13.
 3. Lincoln to the Council of Massachusetts, September 23, Sparks, *Correspondence*, 2:529.
 4. Lemuel Roberts, *Memoirs of Captain Lemuel Roberts* (Bennington: Anthony Haswell, 1809), 53–54; Thomas Wood Pension Application in Dann, *Revolution Remembered*, 93.
 5. Richard Wallace Pension Application in Dann, *Revolution Remembered*, 97–98.
 6. Roberts Memoir, 54.
 7. Allen, *History of Vermont*, 70.
 8. JB to HG (?), Oct. 4, 1777, "Colonel John Brown's Expedition against Ticonderoga and Diamond Island, 1777," *New England Historical and Genealogical Register* 74 (Oct. 1920), 292.
 9. JB surrender demand, Sept. 18, 1777 & Henry Watson Powell's response, "John Brown and the Dash for Ticonderoga," *BFTM* 2, no. 1 (Jan. 1930), 36–37.
 10. JB to Benjamin Lincoln, Sept. 18 & Sept. 19, 1777, "Colonel John Brown's Expedition against Ticonderoga and Diamond Island, 1777," 285–87.
 11. Benjamin Lincoln to Samuel Johnson, Sept. 13, 1777 & Benjamin Lincoln to HG, Sept. 14, 1777, "Col. John Brown's Attack of September, 1777, on Fort Ticonderoga," *BFTM* 11, no. 4 (July 1964), 212–13.
 12. Cross Journal, 9; John Starke, "Col. John Brown's Attack of September, 1777, on Fort Ticonderoga," 209–210; JB to Jonathan Warner, Sept. 19, 1777, "Colonel John Brown's Expedition against Ticonderoga and Diamond Island, 1777," 287.
 13. Bellico, *Sails and Steam in the Mountains*, 184.
 14. Paul David Nelson, "The Gates-Arnold Quarrel, September 1777," *New-York Historical Society Quarterly* 55, no. 3 (July 1971), 235–252; "Chapter 11: Between Battles: Fortifying and Squabbling," Luzader, *Saratoga*, 245–73.
 15. Wilkinson Memoir, 1:241; Richard Varick to PS, Sept. 22, 1777, in Henry Steele Commager & Richard B. Morris, *The Spirit of 'Seventy-Six: The Story of the American Revolution as Told by Participants* (New York: Harper & Row, 1975), 584.
 16. *St. Clair Papers*, 1:443; Isaac Arnold, "Benedict Arnold at Saratoga: Reply to John Henry Stevens, and New Evidence of Mr. Bancroft's Error," *The United Service: A Monthly Review of Military and Naval Affairs* (Philadelphia: L.R. Hamersly, 1880), 3:299–314; Luzader, *Saratoga*, 380–93; Arnold, *Life of Benedict Arnold*, 174; Wayne Lynch, "Debating Arnold's Role at Freeman's Farm" *Journal of the American Revolution* (Sept. 12, 2013; allthingsliberty.com); Reuben Aldridge Guild, *Chaplain Smith and the Baptists* (Philadelphia: American Baptists Publication Society, 1885), 213.
 17. Wilkinson Memoir, 1:245–46.
 18. Baldwin Journal, 121–22.
 19. HG to JH, Sept. 22, 1777, PCC, M247, r190, i171, p114–16; Dean Snow, *1777: Tipping Point at Saratoga* (Oxford University Press, 2016), 163.
 20. General Orders, Sept. 28, 1777, GW Papers, Founders Online.
 21. The Committee for Foreign Affairs to the American Commissioners, 6[–9] October 1777, Founders Online.
 22. Wilkinson Memoir, 1:254.
 23. Wilkinson Memoir, 1:254–255; Henry Brockholst Livingston to PS, Sept. 23, 1777, in Arnold, *Life of Benedict Arnold*, 180–181; BA to JH, July 12, 1777, PCC, M247, r179, i162, v1, p108.
 24. BA to HG, Sept. 22, 1777, Commager & Morris, *Spirit of 'Seventy-Six*, 581–83.
 25. Henry Brockholst Livingston to PS, Sept. 23, 1777, Commager & Morris, *Spirit of 'Seventy-Six*, 583.
 26. Luzader, *Saratoga*, 271; Baldwin Journal, 120–122; Dearborn Journals 1776–1783, 7–8.
 27. Henry Brockholst Livingston to PS, Sept. 23, 1777, Commager & Morris, *Spirit of 'Seventy-Six*, 584.

Chapter Sixteen

 1. Sumner, "Colonel Brooks and Captain Bancroft," 3:273.
 2. Mattoon to PS, Oct. 7, 1835, in Stone, *Campaign of John Burgoyne*, 368–81.
 3. Wilkinson Memoir, 1:267–68.
 4. Nathaniel Bacheller to wife, Oct. 9, 1777, transcription courtesy of Eric Schnitzer, Saratoga National Historical Park; Stephen Williams, "Letters change view of Benedict Arnold, Gen. Gates," *Daily Gazette* (March 26, 2016), Online.
 5. Wilkinson Memoir, 1:269.
 6. Luzader, *Saratoga*, 278, 282, 374.
 7. Arnold, *Life of Benedict Arnold*, 198; Wilkinson Memoir, 1:27; Elliott C. Cogswell, *History of Nottingham, Deerfield, and Northwood* (Manchester, NH: John B. Clarke, 1878), 346; *MAH* 3 (1879), 310–11; Martin, *Benedict Arnold*, 398.
 8. Arnold, *Life of Benedict Arnold*, has a lengthy discussion of the horse, 205–6.
 9. Arnold, *Life of Benedict Arnold*, 204.
 10. Samuel Woodruff in William Leete Stone, *Visits to the Saratoga Battle-grounds* (Albany: Joel Munsell's Sons, 1895), 226; Stone, *Life of Joseph Brant*, lvi; Jeptha Root Simms, *History of Schoharie County and Border Warfare* (Albany: Munsell & Tanner, 1845), 259; Stone, *Campaign of John Burgoyne*, 373.
 11. Philip Van Cortlandt & Pierre C. Van Wyck, ed., "Autobiography of Philip Van Cortlandt: Brigadier-General in the Continental Army," *MAH* 2 (New York: A.S. Barnes, 1878), 287.
 12. Gordon, *History of the Rise, Progress, and Establishment of the Independence of the United States*, 2:563.
 13. Wilkinson Memoir, 1:273; Hoffman

Nickerson, *The Turning Point of the Revolution or Burgoyne in America* (Boston: Houghton Mifflin, 1928), 366; Randall, *Benedict Arnold*, 368.

14. Lippard, *Washington and his Generals*, 179, 180, 182. To name a few of many textbooks on public speaking that included "The Black Horse and his Rider": *The Golden Treasury of Poetry and Prose* (1883); *School and College Speaker* (1901); *The Speaker's Garland and Literary Bouquet* (1915). The advice on delivery comes from Harlan H. Ballard, *Pieces to Speak: A Collection of Declamations and Dialogues for Home and School with Helpful Notes as to Delivery* (Syracuse: C.W. Bardeen, 1897), 29.

15. Stone, *Campaign of John Burgoyne*, 375; Sumner, "Colonel Brooks and Captain Bancroft," 273.

16. Stone, *Campaign of John Burgoyne*, 66–67; Dearborn, "Narrative of the Saratoga Campaign," *BFTM* 1, no. 5 (Jan. 1929), 9; Dearborn Journals 1776–1783, 8.

17. Sumner, "Colonel Brooks and Captain Bancroft," 274.

18. John Fellows to HG, Oct. 8, 1777, & Fellows to Benjamin Lincoln, Oct. 8, 1777, New-York Historical Society; Wilkinson Memoir, 1:280.

19. Luzader, *Saratoga*, 298–99; Wilkinson Memoir, 1:281; Bayley Reminiscences, 51–53.

20. *Collections of the VHS*, 1:237, 239; Charles Neilson, *An Original, Compiled, and Corrected Account of Burgoyne's Campaign* (Albany: J. Munsell, 1844), 198.

21. William Leete Stone & Max von Eelking, *Memoirs and Letters and Journals of Major General Riedesel* (Albany: J. Munsell, 1868), 173; Gordon, *History of the Rise, Progress, and Establishment of the Independence of the United States* 2:567, 571–572; John Burgoyne to George Germain, Oct. 20, 1777, Burgoyne, *State of the Expedition*, 2nd edition, appendix, xcii; Specht Journal, 95.

22. Neilson, *Burgoyne's Campaign*, 198; *Collections of the VHS*, 1:243; Watt, *Rebellion in the Mohawk Valley*, 295.

23. Wilkinson Memoir, 1:285–89; Sumner, "Colonel Brooks and Captain Bancroft," 279.

24. Stone, *Riedesel Memoir*, 1:175–78; William Digby & James Phinney Baxter, *The British Invasion from the North with the Journal Lieut. William Digby* (Albany, NY: Joel Munsell's Sons, 1887), 304.

25. John Henry Brandow, *The Story of Old Saratoga*, 2nd edition (Albany, NY: Brandow Printing, 1919), 172; Stone, *Riedesel Memoir*, 179; Moore, *Life of Stark*, 384.

26. Wilkinson Memoir, 1:312; Stone, *Riedesel Memoir*, 179.

27. Wilkinson Memoir, 1:321.

28. Chastellux in Stone, *Visits to the Saratoga Battle-Grounds*, 81; Wilkinson Memoir, 1:321–22; Specht Journal, 57.

29. Enos Hitchcock & William B Weeden, ed., "Diary of Enos Hitchcock, D.D., a Chaplain in the Revolutionary War," *Rhode Island Historical Society Publications* 7 (Providence: 1899), 159; Specht Journal, 101.

30. Minutes for January 8, 1778, *JCC*, 10: 29–35.

31. Cross Journal, 10–11; Dearborn Journals 1776–1783, 10.

32. "The American Commissioners: A Public Announcement, 4 December 1777," Founders Online.

33. "American Commissioners to [the Comte de Vergennes], 4 December 1777," Founders Online.

Chapter Seventeen

1. JB to John Jay, June 6, 1779, PCC, M247, r53, i42, v1, p179–81.

2. *Acts and Resolves Public and Private of the Province of Massachusetts Bay* 20 (Boston: Wright & Potter, 1918), 279; *Journals of the House of Representatives of Massachusetts 1778–1779* (Boston: Massachusetts Historical Society, 1989), 129; Robert J. Taylor, *Western Massachusetts in the Revolution* (Providence: Brown University Press, 1954), 84; Smith, *History of Pittsfield*, 346.

3. *Acts and Resolves Public and Private of the Province of Massachusetts Bay* 5 (Boston: Wright & Potter, 1886), 1028–32.

4. *Acts and Resolves* 5, 1032–33.

5. Smith, *History of Pittsfield*, 363–64; Taylor, *Western Massachusetts in the Revolution*, 98.

6. "Inventory of the Estate of John Brown," Berkshire County Probate Records, 1073–50, online at americanancestors.org.

7. *Massachusetts Soldiers & Sailors*, 2:695; Arthur Zilversmit, "Quok Walker, Mumbet, and the Abolition of Slavery in Massachusetts," *The William and Mary Quarterly* 25, no. 4 (Oct. 1968), 614–624.

8. Patricia Lynch, *The Impact of the Revolution on Local Government: Concord, Gloucester, and Pittsfield 1763–1789* (Louisiana State University Historical Dissertation, 1978), 442; Berkshire County Probate Records, 1073:44, americanancestors.org.

9. Minutes for Nov. 29, 1777, *JCC*, 9:981.

10. GW to BA, June 19, 1778, Founders Online.

11. George Bancroft, *Joseph Reed: A Historical Essay* (New York: W. J. Widdleton, 1867), 6; John F. Roche, *Joseph Reed: A Moderate in the American Revolution* (New York: Columbia University Press, 1957), vii, 221; Philbrick, *Valiant Ambition*, 234.

12. Minutes for August 11, 1778, JCC, 11:772.

13. Hoffman, *Proceedings of a General Court Martial*, 4–8.

14. Van Doren, *Secret History*, 188; William Reed, *Life and Correspondence of Joseph Reed* (Philadelphia: Lindsay & Blakiston, 1847), 2:49.

15. Brandt, *Man in the Mirror*, 144, 156–157; BA to Peggy Shippen, Sept. 25, 1778 in Lewis Burd

Walker, "Life of Margaret Shippen, Wife of Benedict Arnold," *Pennsylvania Magazine of History & Biography* 25, no. 1 (1901), 20–46; BA to Betsy Deblois, April 8, 1778, Massachusetts Historical Society.

16. Davis, *Memoirs of Aaron Burr*, 1:220; Arnold, *Life of Benedict Arnold*, 316–321; Malcolm, *Tragedy of Benedict Arnold*, xv; Flexner, *Traitor and the Spy*, 279.

17. Flexner, *The Traitor and the Spy*, 227: Reed "could have been one of the Jacobins who, during the French Revolution, gleefully counted the heads that rolled from the guillotine"; Joseph Reed to Nathanael Greene, Nov. 5, 1778, in William Reed, *Life and Correspondence of Joseph Reed*, 2:38. Peter C. Messer, "'A Species of Treason & Not the Least Dangerous Kind': The Treason Trials of Abraham Carlisle and John Roberts," *Pennsylvania Magazine of History and Biography* 123, no. 4 (Oct. 1999), 318.

18. *Pennsylvania Packet*, Feb. 9, 1779.

19. Chris Coelho, *Timothy Matlack: Scribe of the Declaration of Independence* (Jefferson, NC: McFarland, 2013); Asa Matlack Stackhouse, "Col. Timothy Matlack, Patriot and Soldier: A Paper Read before the Gloucester County Historical Society, April 14, 1908," (Printed privately, 1910).

20. *Pennsylvania Packet*, Feb. 27, 1779.

21. *Pennsylvania Packet*, March 4, 1779.

22. JB to Joseph Reed, March 7, 1779, in Hoffman, "Introduction," *Proceedings of a Court Martial*, xv–xvi.

23. Timothy Matlack to JB, March 29, 1779, *Ibid.*, xvi.

24. *Pennsylvania Packet*, March 6, 1779.

25. JB to Samuel Adams, April 20, 1779, PCC, M247, r91, i78, v3, p309; James Easton to Congress, Oct. 5, 1776, *AA*, ser. 5, 2:911; Minutes for July 16, 1779, *JCC*, 14:843; James Easton Memorial to Congress, Aug. 22, 1786, PCC, M247, r49, i41, v3, p131–136; Minutes for Aug. 22, 1786, *JCC*, 31:553; Minutes for Jan. 12, 1791, Feb. 16, 1791, *Journal of the House of Representatives*, 1:352, 1:380 online at American Memory.

26. The original is in the Papers of the Continental Congress, but is badly degraded: JB to John Jay, June 6, 1779, PCC, M247, r53, i42, v1, p179–81. The transcription in Smith, *History of Pittsfield*, 275–77, based presumably on Brown's copy, appears to be mostly identical, although the PCC copy has too many blotches and bleed-throughs to be certain. Unaccountably, Smith has Brown visiting Charles Thomson in York in March 1777, two months *before* the War Board meeting they discussed. The poor PCC copy is legible on this point: "Nov. 1777"; Charles Thomson to JB, May 5, 1780, *LDC*, 15:89.

27. John André to BA, mid-June, 1779; BA to John André, June 18, 1779; Joseph Stansbury to John André, July 11, 1779, in Van Doren, *Secret History*, 448–49.

28. C. Page Smith, "The Attack on Fort Wilson," *Pennsylvania Magazine of History and Biography* 78, no. 2 (Apr., 1954), 185; Van Doren, *Secret History*, 455.

29. Arnold to André, June 18, 1779, Van Doren, *Secret History*, 448–49.

30. Hoffman, *Proceedings of a General Court Martial*, 106–7.

31. *Ibid.*, 21–22; 107, 112–13.

32. *Ibid.*, 133.

33. *Ibid.*, 144.

34. *Ibid.*, 144–45.

35. François Barbé-Marbois, *Complot d'Arnold et de Sir Henry Clinton contre les États-Unis d'Amérique et contre le général Washington: septembre 1780* (Paris : Chez P. Didot, 1816), 33–34; "Conspiracy of Arnold," *The American Register*, 2:25; Arnold, *Life of Benedict Arnold*, 237; Sparks, *Life and Treason*, 144–45; Van Doren, *Secret History*, 250.

36. General Orders, April 6, 1780, Founders Online.

37. George Frederick Houghton, "The Life and Services of Col. Seth Warner," *Addresses on the Battle of Bennington and the Life and Services of Col. Seth Warner Delivered before the Legislature of Vermont in Montpelier, October 20, 1848* (Burlington, VT, Free Press, 1849), 66; James Thacher, *A Military Journal during the American Revolutionary War from 1775 to 1783 Describing Interesting Events and Transactions of the Period*, 2nd edition (Boston: Cotton & Bernard, 1827), 418–419.

38. Van Buren, *Secret History*, 258, 459; BA to PS, May 25, 1780, Schuyler Papers, NYPL.

39. Arnold to Greene, Sept. 12, 1780 in Van Doren, *Secret History*, 310; "Arnold's Memorandum Book," 368.

40. Lesser, *Sinews of Independence*, 181.

Chapter Eighteen

1. GW to George Clinton, October 16, 1780, Founders Online; Franklin B. Hough, *The Northern Invasion of October 1780* (New York, 1866), 63–64; Watt, 67, 274.

2. Gavin K. Watt, *The Burning of the Valleys: Daring Raids from Canada against the New York Frontier in the Fall of 1780* (Toronto: Dundurn Press, 1997), 164.

3. Gary B. Nash, *The Unknown American Revolution: The Unruly Birth of Democracy and the Struggle to Create America* (New York: Viking, 2005), 290–305; Smith, *History of Pittsfield*, 311, 480; *Journal of the Convention for Framing a Constitution of Government for the State of Massachusetts Bay* (Boston: Dutton and Wentworth, 1832), 238.

4. Smith, *History of Pittsfield*, 311; Thomas Cushing, *History of Berkshire County, Massachusetts* (New York: J.B. Beers, 1885), 2:550–551; Berkshire County Probate File Papers, 1073:44, www.americanancestors.org.

5. Edward Deming Andrews, *The People

Called Shakers: A Search for the Perfect Society (New York: Dover Publications, 1963), 28; Lossing, *Pictorial Field-Book*, 1:281.

6. Berkshire County Probate File Papers, 1073:44, www.americanancestors.org.

7. Cooke, *Pittsfield Church Records* (Internet Archive), 1:379; Massachusetts Soldiers and Sailors, 8:625; Smith, *History of Pittsfield*, 416.

8. *George Clinton Papers*, 5:919–20; Watt, *Burning of the Valleys*, 80.

9. Van Rensselaer to George Clinton, Sept. 4, 1780, in Hough, *Northern Invasion of October 1780*, 76–77.

10. Although there is no document that proves Brown knew of Arnold's treason, the news traveled as fast any during the Revolution and certainly reached the Mohawk before his death. BA to JH, Feb. 1, 1776, *AA*, ser. 4, 4: 907–8; "Petition and Memorial of John Brown," June 26, 1777, *AA*, ser. 5, 1:1220; Commissioners to Canada to JH, May 16, 1776, *AA*, ser. 4, 6:482.

11. Simms, *History of Schoharie County*, 425; "Van Rensselaer Court of Inquiry," in Hough, *Northern invasion of October 1780*, 187–88.

12. John Johnson to Frederick Haldimand, Oct. 31, 1780, Haldimand Papers, H-1652, 170–77, online at heritage.canadiana.ca.

13. Hough, *Northern Invasion of October 1780*, 165–66; Simms, *History of Schoharie County*, 425.

14. Smith, *History of Pittsfield*, 313.

15. Smith, *History of Pittsfield*, 312; Hough, *Northern invasion of October 1780*, 208.

16. Watt, *Burning of the Valleys*, 306.

17. Smith, *History of Pittsfield*, 314.

18. Watt, *Burning of the Valleys*, 207; Haldimand Papers, H-1652, 170–77, heritage.canadiana.ca.

19. Simms, *History of Schoharie County*, 426; Haldimand Papers, H-1652, 170–77, heritage.canadiana.ca.

20. Smith, *History of Pittsfield*, 315.

21. David Humphreys, "Address to the Armies of the United States of America," *Miscellaneous Works of David Humphreys* (New York: T. & J. Swords, 1804), 3.

22. Humphreys, "A Poem on the Love of Country," *Miscellaneous Works*, 144.

23. Henry A. Beers, *The Connecticut Wits and Other Essays* (New Haven: Yale University Press, 1920), 23.

24. Humphreys, "Recommendatory Extracts," *Miscellaneous Works*, xii.

25. Humphreys, "Address to the Armies of the United States of America," *Miscellaneous Works*, 9–10.

26. Van Schaack, "Col. John Brown," 14–15.

Conclusion

1. Nathanael Greene to Gov. William Greene, Oct. 2, 1780, in Gerald M. Carbone, *Nathanael Greene: A Biography of the American Revolution* (New York: Palgrave Macmillan, 2008), 140; Isaiah 14:12.

2. Wayne to Hugh Sheel, Oct. 2, 1780, in Charles J. Stillé, *Major-General Anthony Wayne and the Pennsylvania Line in the Continental Army* (Philadelphia: J.B. Lippincott, 1893), 235–36.

3. Hugh Sheel to Wayne, Oct. 22, 1780, in Stillé, *Anthony Wayne*, 237–38.

4. Sparks, *Life and Treason*, 5–6.

5. Isaac Arnold, *Life of Arnold*, 3; John Austin Stevens, "Benedict Arnold and His Apologist," *MAH* 4 (New York: A.S. Barnes, 1880), 181–82; Sparks, *Life and Treason*, 118.

6. Lippard, *Washington and His Generals*, 154.

7. Joel Tyler Headley, *Washington and His Generals* (New York: Baker and Scribner, 1847), 1:155, 172, 195.

8. Rufus W. Griswold, William Gilmore Simms, Edward Duncan Ingraham, *Washington and the Generals of the American Revolution* (Philadelphia: Carey & Hart, 1848), "Notice," 243.

9. Guild, *Chaplain Smith and the Baptists*, 213; Ellen Hardin Walworth, *Saratoga: The Battle—Battleground—Visitor's Guide with Maps* (New York: American News, 1877), 27; Wallace, *Traitorous Hero*, 315.

10. John Jay Chapman, *Treason & Death of Benedict Arnold: A Play for Greek Theatre* (New York: Moffat & Yard, 1910).

11. Kevin Phillips, *1775: A Good Year for Revolution* (New York: Penguin Books, 2012), 471–74.

12. Arnold to the Inhabitants of America, Oct. 7, 1780, Isaac Arnold, 330–332.

13. Headley, *Washington and his Generals*, 1:194.

14. Roberts, *Rabble in Arms*, 578; Roberts, *Black Magic*, 166, 167–68.

15. Carlyle, *Heroes*, 1–2.

16. JB to John Jay, June 6, 1779, PCC, M247, r53, i42, v1, p181; Smith, *History of Pittsfield*, 277.

Bibliography

The Acts and Laws of the Commonwealth of Massachusetts: Acts and Resolves of Massachusetts, 1780–81. Boston: Wright & Potter, 1890.

The Acts and Resolves Public and Private of the Province of the Massachusetts Bay: To Which Are Prefixed the Charters of the Province with Historical and explanatory Notes, and an Appendix, vol. 5, 1769–1780; vol. 19, 1775–1776; vol. 20, 1777–1778; vol. 21, 1779–1780. Boston: Wright and Potter, 1886, 1918.

Adams, Samuel. Samuel Adams Papers, New York Public Library, archives.nypl.org.

_____. *The Writing of Samuel Adams.* Editor Harry Alonzo Cushing. New York: G. P. Putnam's Sons, 1907.

Ainslie, Thomas. *Canada Preserved: The Journal of Captain Thomas Ainslie.* Editor Sheldon Cohen. New York: New York University Press, 1968.

Aldrich, Edgar. "The Affair of the Cedars and the Service of Colonel Timothy Bedel in the War of the Revolution." *Proceedings of the New Hampshire Historical Society* 3 (Dec. 1891), 194–231.

Allen, Ethan. *The Narrative of Colonel Ethan Allen.* Bedford, MA: Applewood Books, n.d. (1st edition, Philadelphia: Robert Bell, 1779).

Allen, Ira. *The Natural and Political History of the State of Vermont.* Rutland, VT: Charles E. Tuttle, 1969 (1st edition, London: J.W. Myers, 1798).

Amory, Thomas C. *Life of James Sullivan with Selections from his Writings.* Boston: Phillips, Sampson, 1859.

Anderson, Mark R. *The Battle for the Fourteenth Colony: America's War of Liberation in Canada, 1774–1776.* Hanover, NH: University Press of New England, 2013.

Arnold, Benedict. "Benedict Arnold's Regimental Memorandum Book, Ticonderoga and Crown Point, 1775." *Pennsylvania Magazine of History and Biography* 8 (1884), 363–76.

Arnold, Isaac N. "Benedict Arnold at Saratoga: Reply to John Henry Stevens, and New Evidence of Mr. Bancroft's Error," *The United Service: A Monthly Review of Military and Naval Affairs,* 3: 299–314. Philadelphia: L.R. Hamersly, 1880.

_____. *The Life of Benedict Arnold: His Patriotism and his Treason.* Chicago: Jansen & McClurg, 1880.

Arnold Expedition Historical Society. "Arnold's Wilderness March: Kennebec River, Maine to Lac Mégantic, Québec, Map and Guide." Shapleigh, Maine, 2009.

An Authentic Narrative of Facts Relating to the Exchange of Prisoners Taken at the Cedars. London: T. Cadell, 1777.

Bachman, Ryan. "Popular Rage: The Background to the Closing of the Berkshire County Courthouse." *Clio* (2012). Copy from author.

Bailey, James Montgomery. *History of Danbury, Conn., 1684–1896.* New York: Burr Printing House, 1896.

Baker, Ray Stannard. "Remember Baker." *The New England Quarterly* 4 (October 1931), 595–628.

Baldwin, Jeduthan, and Thomas Williams Baldwin, ed. *The Revolutionary Journal of Col. Jeduthan Baldwin 1775–1778.* Bangor, ME: 1906.

Bales, Jack. *Kenneth Roberts: The Man and His Work.* Metuchen, NJ: The Scarecrow Press, 1989.

Bancroft, George. *Joseph Reed: A Historical Essay.* New York: W. J. Widdleton, 1867.

Barbé-Marbois, François. *Complot d'Arnold et de Sir Henry Clinton contre les États-Unis d'Amérique et contre le général Washington: septembre 1780.* Paris: Chez P. Didot, 1816.

_____. "Conspiracy of Arnold, and Sir Henry Clinton, against the United States, and against General Washington." *The American Register; or Summary Review of History, Politics, and Literature* 2, pp. 3–63. Philadelphia: Thomas Dobson and Son, 1817.

Bayley, Frye. "Colonel Frye Bayley's Reminiscences." *Proceedings of the Vermont Historical Society for the Years 1923, 1924 and 1925,* pp. 22–86. Bellows Falls, VT: P.H. Gobie Press, 1926.

Beebe, Lewis, and Frederic R. Kirkland, ed. "Journal of a Physician on the Expedition against Canada, 1776." *Pennsylvania Magazine of History and Biography* 59, no. 4 (Oct. 1936), 321–61.

Beers, Henry A. *The Connecticut Wits and Other Essays.* New Haven: Yale University Press, 1920.

Bellesiles, Michael A. *Revolutionary Outlaws: Ethan Allen and the Struggle for Independence on the Early American Frontier.* Charlottesville: University Press of Virginia, 1993.

Bellico, Russell P. *Sails and Steam in the Mountains: A Maritime and Military History of Lake George and Lake Champlain.* Fleischmanns, NY: Purple Mountain Press, 1992.

Bird, Harrison. *Attack on Quebec: The American Invasion of Canada 1775–1776.* New York: Oxford University Press, 1968.

_____. *March to Saratoga: General Burgoyne and the American Campaign, 1777.* New York, Oxford University Press, 1963.

Bland, Humphrey. *A Treatise of Military Discipline; in which is laid down and explained the duty of the officer and soldier.* 6th edition. London: J. & P. Knapton, 1746.

Boston Committee of Correspondence Records 1772–1784, New York Public Library, digitalcollections.nypl.org

Boylan, Brian Richard. *Benedict Arnold: The Dark Eagle.* New York: W.W. Norton, 1973.

Brandow, John Henry. *The Story of Old Saratoga.* 2nd edition. Albany, NY: Brandow Printing, 1919.

Brandt, Clare. *The Man in the Mirror: A Life of Benedict Arnold.* New York: Random House, 1994.

Bratten, John R. *The Gondola Philadelphia & the Battle of Lake Champlain.* College Station: Texas A & M University Press, 2002.

Brumwell, Stephen. *Turncoat: Benedict Arnold and the Crisis of American Liberty.* New Haven: Yale University Press, 2018.

Bulletin of the Fort Ticonderoga Museum 13, no. 5 (1977). An issue devoted to the capture of Fort Ticonderoga.

Burgoyne, John. *A State of the Expedition from Canada as Laid Before the House of Commons by Lieutenant-General Burgoyne, and Verified by Evidence: with a Collection of Authentic Documents,* 2nd edition. London: J. Almon, 1780.

Burr, William Hanford. "The Invasion of Connecticut by the British." *The Connecticut Magazine* (1906), 139–52.

Butterfield, Charles H. "Major Isaac Butterfield of Westmoreland and his Surrender at the Cedars, 1776." *Historical New Hampshire* 52, no. 1–2 (1997), 28–44.

Campbell, William W. *Annals of Tryon County; or, the Border Warfare of New-York During the Revolution.* New York: J. & J. Harper, 1831.

Carbone, Gerald M. *Nathanael Greene: A Biography of the American Revolution.* New York: Palgrave Macmillan, 2008.

Carlyle, Thomas. *Heroes, Hero-Worship, and the Heroic in History: Six Lectures.* London: James Fraser, 1841.

Carroll, Charles. *Journal of Charles Carroll of Carrollton, During His Visit to Canada in 1776, as One of the Commissioners from Congress.* Baltimore: John Murray for the Maryland Historical Society, 1876.

Chapman, John Jay. *The Treason & Death of Benedict Arnold: A Play for Greek Theatre.* New York: Moffat & Yard, 1910.

Chipman, Daniel. *Memoir of Colonel Seth Warner.* Middlebury, VT: L.W. Clark, 1848.

Chittenden, Lucius E. *The Capture of Ticonderoga; Proceedings of the Vermont Historical Society* (October 8, 1872). Montpelier, 1872.

Clark, Stephen. *Following Their Footsteps: A Travel Guide & History of the 1775 Secret Expedition to Capture Quebec with Canoeing & Hiking Guides & Maps of the Entire Route.* Shapleigh, ME: Clark Books, 2003.

Clinton, George. *Public papers of George Clinton, First Governor of New York, 1777–1795, 1801–1804.* J. Austin Holden and Hugh Hastings. Vols. 1–6. New York: State of New York, 1899–1914.

Codman, John. *Arnold's Expedition to Quebec.* New York: Macmillan, 1902.

Coelho, Chris. *Timothy Matlack: Scribe of the Declaration of Independence.* Jefferson, NC: McFarland, 2013.

Coffin, Charles. *The Life and Services of Major General John Thomas, Colonel Thomas Knowlton, Colonel Alexander Scammell, Major General Henry Dearborn.* New York: Egbert, Hovey & King, 1845.

Cogswell, Elliott C. *History of Nottingham, Deerfield, and Northwood Comprised within the Original Limits of Nottingham, Rockingham County, N.H., and Genealogical Sketches.* Manchester: John B. Clarke, 1878.

"Col. John Brown's Attack of September, 1777, on Fort Ticonderoga." *Bulletin of the Fort Ticonderoga Museum* 11, no. 4 (July 1964), 207–13.

Collections of the Connecticut Historical Society 1–2, 7, 10. Hartford: Connecticut Historical Society, 1860, 1870, 1899, 1905.

Collections of the Maine Historical Society 1. Editor William Willis. Portland: Bailey & Noyes, 1865.

Collections of the Vermont Historical Society 1. Montpelier, VT.: Vermont Historical Society, 1870.

"Colonel John Brown's Expedition against Ticonderoga and Diamond Island, 1777." *New England Historical and Genealogical Register* 74 (Oct. 1920), 284–93.

Commager, Henry Steele, and Richard B. Morris. *The Spirit of 'Seventy-Six: The Story of the American Revolution as Told by Participants.* New York: Harper & Row, 1975.

Connecticut Military Record, 1775–1848: The Record of Connecticut Men in the Military and Naval Service During the War of the Revolution 1775–1783. Editor Henry P. Johnson. Hartford: Case, Lockwood & Brainard, 1889.

Cook, Frederick, ed. *Journals of the Military Expedition of Major General John Sullivan Against* the Six Nations of Indians in 1779 with Records of Celebrations. Auburn, NY: Knapp, Peck & Thomson, 1887.

Cooke, Rollin Hillyer. *Pittsfield, Mass. Church and other Records from Manuscripts Copied by Rollin Hillyer Cooke*. Internet Archive.

Coyle, Lee. "Kenneth Roberts and the American Historical Novel." *Popular Literature in America: A Symposium in Honor of Lyon N. Richardson*. Editors James C. Austin & Donald A. Koch. Bowling Green, Ohio: Bowling Green Popular Press, 1972.

Crary, Catherine S. Collection. Columbia University Libraries.

Cross, Ralph. "The Journal of Ralph Cross of Newburyport, Who Commanded the Essex Regiment, at the Surrender of Burgoyne, in 1777." *Historical Magazine and Notes and Queries Concerning the Antiquities, History and Biography of America* 2, 2nd series, pp. 8–11. Morrisania, NY: Henry R. Dawson, 1870.

Cubbison, Douglas R. *The American Northern Theater Army in 1776: The Ruin and Reconstruction of the Continental Force*. Jefferson, NC: McFarland, 2010.

Cushing, Thomas, ed., and Joseph Edward Adams Smith. *History of Berkshire County, Massachusetts, with Biographical Sketches of its Prominent Men*. New York: J.B. Beers, 1885.

Daniels, George F. *History of the Town of Oxford, Massachusetts, with Genealogies and Notes on Person and Estates*. Oxford, MA: author and town, 1892.

Dann, John C. *The Revolution Remembered: Eyewitness Account of the War for Independence*. Chicago: University of Chicago Press, 1980.

Darley, Stephen. *The Battle of Valcour Island: The Participants and Vessels of Benedict Arnold's 1776 Defense of Lake Champlain*. Self-published, 2013.

_____. "The Dark Eagle: How Fiction Became Historical Fact." varsitytutors.com/earlyamerica/early-america-review/volume-10/dark-eagle-fiction-became-historical-fact

_____. *Voices from a Wilderness Expedition: The Journals and Men of Benedict Arnold's Expedition to Quebec in 1775*. Bloomington, IN: AuthorHouse, 2011.

Davis, Matthew L. *Memoirs of Aaron Burr with Miscellaneous Selections from his Correspondence*. New York: Harper & Brothers, 1855 (1st edition 1836–37).

Dearborn, Henry. *Journal of Captain Henry Dearborn in the Quebec Expedition, 1775*. Cambridge: University Press, 1886.

_____. *Journals of Henry Dearborn, 1776–1783*. Cambridge: John Wilson & Son, 1887.

_____. "A Narrative of the Saratoga Campaign." *Bulletin of the Fort Ticonderoga Museum* 1, no. 5 (January 1929), 2–12.

DeCosta, Benjamin Franklin. *Notes on the History of Fort George during the Colonial and Revolutionary Periods, With Contemporaneous Documents and an Appendix*. New York: J. Sabin and Sons, 1871.

De Fonblanque, Edward. *Political and Military Episodes in the Latter Half of the Eighteenth Century Derived from the Life and Correspondence of the Right Hon. John Burgoyne, General, Statesman, Dramatist*. London: Macmillan, 1876.

Desjardin, Thomas A. *Through a Howling Wilderness: Benedict Arnold's March to Quebec 1775*. New York: St. Martin's Press, 2006.

Dexter, Franklin Bowditch. *Biographical Sketches of the Graduates of Yale College with Annals of the College History* 3, May 1763-July1778. New York: Henry Holt, 1903.

Diamant, Lincoln. *Bernard Romans: Forgotten Patriot of the American Revolution*. Harbor Hill Books, 1985.

Diestelow, Kevin. "The Fort Wilson Riot and Pennsylvania's Republican Formation." *Journal of the American Revolution* (Feb. 28, 2019). Online at JAR, allthingsliberty.com.

Digby, William, and James Phinney Baxter. *The British Invasion from the North. The Campaigns of Generals Carleton and Burgoyne from Canada, 1776–1777, with the Journal of Lieut. William Digby of the 53d, or Shropshire Regiment of Foot*. Albany, NY: Joel Munsell's Sons, 1887.

Duffy, John J., ed., with Ralph H. Orth, J. Kevin Graffagnino, Michael A. Bellesiles. *Ethan Allen and his Kin: Correspondence, 1772–1819*. Hanover, NH: University Press of New England, 1998.

_____, and H. Nicholas Muller III. *Inventing Ethan Allen*. Hanover, NH: University Press of New England, 2014.

_____, H. Nicholas Muller III, and Gary G. Shattuck. *The Rebel and the Tory: Ethan Allen Philip Skene, and the Dawn of Vermont*. Barre and Montpelier: Vermont Historical Society, 2020.

Duling, Ennis. "Arnold, Hazen, and the Mysterious Major Scott." *Journal of the American Revolution: Annual Volume 2017*, pp. 141–153. Yardley, PA: Westholme, 2017. Online at JAR (Feb. 23, 2016), allthingsliberty.com.

_____. "Did Benedict Arnold's Fleet Plunder an American Settlement?" *Journal of the American Revolution*. Online at JAR (Aug. 29, 2017), allthingsliberty.com.

_____. "Ethan Allen and *The Fall of British Tyranny*: A Question of What Came First." *Vermont History* 75, no. 2 (Summer/ Fall 2007), 134–40.

Elmer, Ebenezer. "Journal of Ebenezer Elmer," *Proceedings of the New Jersey Historical Society* 3, no. 1 (1848), 21–90. Newark, J.J.: Daily Advertiser, 1849.

Everest, Allan. *Moses Hazen and the Canadian Refugees in the American Revolution*. Syracuse University Press, 1976.

Fassett, John, and Harry Parker Ward, ed. "Diary of Captain John Fassett, Jr. (1743–1803) When a First Lieutenant of the 'Green Mountain Boys.'"

The Follett-Dewey Fassett-Safford Ancestry of Captain Martin Dewey Follett and his wife Persis Fassett. Columbus, OH: Champlin Printing, 1896.

Fenn, Elizabeth A. *Pox Americana: The Great Smallpox Epidemic of 1775–82*. New York: Hill & Wang, 2002.

Fenton, Walter S. "Seth Warner," *Proceedings of the Vermont Historical Society* 8, no. 4 (December 1940), 325–50.

Fischer, David Hackett. *Washington's Crossing*. New York: Oxford University Press, 2004.

Flexner, James Thomas, "How A Madman Helped Save The Colonies," *American Heritage* 7, no. 2 (Feb. 1956) at www.americanheritage.com/how-madman-helped-save-colonies

_____. *The Traitor and the Spy: Benedict Arnold and John André*. Syracuse University Press, 1991 (1st edition Harcourt Brace, 1953).

Force, Peter, ed. *American Archives, consisting of a collection of authentick records, state papers, debates, and letters and other notices of publick affairs, the whole forming a documentary history of the origin and progress of the North American colonies; of the causes and accomplishment of the American revolution*. 9 vols. Washington, D.C., 1837–1853. Also online at Northern Illinois University, digital.lib.niu.edu/amarch.

Founders Online, National Archives, founders.archives.gov.

Frazer, Persifor, and grandson Persifor Frazer, ed. *General Persifor Frazer: A Memoir Compiled Principally from his Own Papers*. Philadelphia, 1907.

French, Allen. *The Taking of Ticonderoga in 1775: The British Story*. Cambridge: Harvard University Press, 1928.

Furneaux, Rupert. *The Battle of Saratoga*. New York: Stein and Day, 1971.

Gabriel, Michael P. *The Battle of Bennington: Soldiers & Civilians*. Charleston: The History Press, 2012.

_____. *Major General Richard Montgomery: The Making of an American Hero*. Cranbury, NJ: Associated University Press, 2002.

_____, S. Pascale Vergereau-Dewey, trans. *Quebec during the American Invasion, 1775–1776: The Journal of François Baby, Gabriel Taschereau, and Jenkin Williams*. East Lansing: Michigan State University, 2005.

Gansevoort, Peter, David A. Ranzan, and Matthew J. Hollis, eds. *Hero of Fort Schuyler: Selected Revolutionary War Correspondence of Brigadier General Peter Gansevoort, Jr*. Jefferson, NC: McFarland, 2014.

Gerlach, Don R. *Proud Patriot: Philip Schuyler and the War of Independence, 1775–1783*. Syracuse University Press: 1987.

Goodhue, Josiah Fletcher. *History of the Town of Shoreham, Vermont*. Middlebury, VT: A.H. Copeland, 1861.

Goodrich, John E., ed. *Rolls of the Vermont Soldiers in the Revolutionary War*. Rutland, VT: Tuttle, 1904.

Gordon, William. *The History of the Rise, Progress, and Establishment, of the Independence of the United States of America*. 3 vols. London: Charles Dilly & James Buckland, 1788.

Graham, James. *The Life of General Daniel Morgan, or the Virginia Line of the Army of the United States*. New York: Derby & Jackson, 1856.

Greenwood, John, and Isaac J. Greenwood, ed. *The Revolutionary Services of John Greenwood of Boston and New York 1775–1783*. New York: Joseph R. Greenwood, 1922.

Griswold, Rufus Wilmot, William Gilmore Simms, and Edward Duncan Ingraham. *Washington and the Generals of the American Revolution*. 2 vols. Philadelphia: Carey & Hart, 1848.

Guild, Reuben Aldridge. *Chaplain Smith and the Baptists or, Life, Journals, Letters and Addresses of the Rev. Hezekiah Smith, D.D., of Haverhill, Massachusetts, 1737–1805*. Philadelphia: American Baptists Publication Society, 1885.

Hadden, James M., and Horatio Rogers, ed. *Hadden's Journal and Orderly Books: A Journal Kept in Canada and Upon Burgoyne's Campaign in 1776 and 1777 by Lieut. James M. Hadden*. Albany, NY: Joel Munsell's Sons, 1884.

Haiman, Miecislaus. *Kosciuszko in the American Revolution*. New York: Kosciuszko Foundation and the Polish Institute of Arts and Sciences, 1976 (1st edition, 1943).

Hanley, Thomas O'Brien. *Revolutionary Statesman: Charles Carroll and the War*. Chicago: Loyola University Press, 1983.

Harr, John Ensor. *Dark Eagle*. A novel. New York: Viking, 1999.

Haskell, Caleb, and Lothrop Withington, ed. *Caleb Haskell's Diary May 5, 1775-May 30 1776: A Revolutionary Soldier's Record before Boston and with Arnold's Quebec Expedition*. Tarrytown, NY: William Abbatt, 1922 (1st edition, Newburyport, MA: William H. Huse, 1881).

Hatch, Robert McConnell. *Thrust for Canada: The American Attempt on Quebec in 1775–1776*. Boston: Houghton Mifflin, 1979.

Hazard, Samuel, ed. *Pennsylvania Archives, Commencing 1779*, vol. 8. Philadelphia: Joseph Severns, 1853.

Headley, Joel Tyler. *Washington and His Generals*. 2 vols. New York: Baker & Scribner's, 1847.

Heitman, F. B. *Historical Register of Officers of the Continental Army during the War of the Revolution, April 1775 to December 1783*. Washington, D.C.: W.H. Lowdermilk, 1893.

Henry, John Joseph. *Accurate and Interesting Account of the Hardships and Sufferings of That Band of Heroes, Who Traversed the Wilderness in the Campaign against Quebec in 1775*. Lancaster, PA: William Greer, 1812.

Hess, Abram. "The Life and Services of General John Philip de Haas 1735–1786." *Lebanon*

County Historical Society *County Historical Society* 15, no. 1 (1976, originally published 1916).

Higginbotham, Don. *Daniel Morgan: Revolutionary Rifleman*. Chapel Hill: University of North Carolina Press, 1961.

Hill, William. *Old Fort Edward before 1800*. Fort Edward, NY: Printed privately, 1929.

Historical Section of the General Staff, *A History of the Organization, Development and Services of the Military and Naval Forces of Canada from the Peace of Paris in 1763, to the Present Time 1: The Local Forces of New France, The Militia of the Province of Quebec, 1763–1775*. Canadian Government Printer, 1919.

Hitchcock, Enos, and William B Weeden, ed. "Diary of Enos Hitchcock, D.D., a Chaplain in the Revolutionary War," *Rhode Island Historical Society Publications* 7 (Providence: 1899), 86–231.

Hoffman, Francis Suydam. *Proceedings of a General Court Martial for the Trial of Major General Arnold: With an Introduction, Notes, and Index*. New York: J. Munsell, 1865.

Hough, Franklin B. *The Northern Invasion of October 1780: a series of papers relating to the expeditions from Canada under Sir John Johnson and others against the frontiers of New York which were supposed to have connection with Arnold's treason*. New York: Bradford Club, 1866.

Houghton, George Frederick. "The Life and Services of Col. Seth Warner." *Addresses on the Battle of Bennington and the Life and Services of Col. Seth Warner Delivered before the Legislature of Vermont in Montpelier, October 20, 1848*. Burlington, VT: Free Press, 1849.

Howe, Archibald M. "Colonel John Brown of Pittsfield, Massachusetts: The Brave Accuser of Benedict Arnold; An Address Delivered before the Fort Rensselaer Chapter of the D.A.R. at the Village of Palatine Bridge, New York September 29, 1908." Boston: W.B. Clarke, 1908.

Hoyt, Edward A. and Ronald F. Kingsley. "The Pawlet Expedition, September 1777." *Vermont History* 25, no. 2 (Summer/Fall 2007), 69–100.

Hughes, Thomas Smart. *History of England by Hume and Smollett with a Continuation by the Rev. T.S. Hughes, B.D.* London: A.J. Valpy, 1835.

Humphreys, David. *The Miscellaneous Works of David Humphreys*. New York: T. and J. Swords, 1804.

Hunt, Louise Livingston. *Biographical Notes Concerning General Richard Montgomery Together with Hitherto Unpublished Letters*. Poughkeepsie, NY: News Printing House, 1876.

Jackson, Joseph. "George Lippard: Misunderstood Man of Letters." *Pennsylvania Magazine of History and Biography* 59, no. 4 (Oct., 1935), 376–91.

Jellison, Charles A. *Ethan Allen, Frontier Rebel*. Syracuse: Syracuse University Press, 1969.

"John Brown and the Dash for Ticonderoga." *Bulletin of the Fort Ticonderoga Museum* 2, no. 1 (Jan. 1930), 23–40.

Jones, Charles Henry. *History of the Campaign for the Conquest of Canada in 1776 from the Death of Montgomery to the Retreat of the British Army under Guy Carleton*. New York: Research Reprints, 1970 (1st edition, Philadelphia: Porter & Coates, 1882).

Jones, Thomas, and Edward Floyd de Lancey, ed. *History of New York During the Revolutionary War, and of the Leading Events in the Other Colonies at that Period*. New York: New-York Historical Society, 1879.

Journal of the Convention for Framing a Constitution of Government for the State of Massachusetts Bay: from the Commencement of their First Session, September 1, 1779, to the Close of their Last Session, June 16, 1780. Boston: Dutton and Wentworth, 1832.

Journals of Each Provincial Congress of Massachusetts in 1774 and 1775 and the Committee of Safety, with an Appendix Containing the Proceeding of the County Conventions—Narratives of the Events of the nineteenth of April, 1775—Papers Relating to Ticonderoga and Crown Point, and Other Documents Illustrative of the Early History of the American Revolution. Boston: Dutton and Wentworth, 1838.

Journals of the Continental Congress, 1774–1789. Editors Worthington C. Ford et al. Washington, D.C., 1904–37. Online at Library of Congress, American Memory.

Journals of the House of Representatives of Massachusetts 1773–1774 & 1778–1779. Boston: Massachusetts Historical Society, 1981, 1989. Online at HathiTrust Digital Library.

Kenny, Kevin. *Peaceable Kingdom Lost: The Paxton Boys and the Destruction of William Penn's Holy Experiment*. New York: Oxford University Press, 2009.

Ketchum, Richard M. *Saratoga: Turning Point of America's Revolutionary War*. New York: Henry Holt, 1997.

Kilbourn, Payne Kenyon. *The Family Memorial: A History and Genealogy of the Kilbourn Family in the United States and Canada, from the Year 1635 to the Present Time*. Hartford: Brown & Parson, 1845.

King, Alexander. "Alexander King Diary." Online, Kent Memorial Library, Suffield, Connecticut, www.suffield-library.org.

Lamb, Roger. *An Original and Authentic Journal of Occurrences During the Late American War from its Commencement Until 1783*. Dublin: Wilkinson and Courtney, 1809.

Langston, Paul David. "'A Fickle, and Confused Multitude': War and Politics in Revolutionary Philadelphia, 1750–1783." Ph.D. Dissertation, University of Colorado, 2013.

Leake, Isaac Q. *Memoir of the Life and Times of General John Lamb*. Albany: Joel Munsell, 1850.

Lefkowitz, Arthur S. *Benedict Arnold in the Company of Heroes: The Lives of the Extraordinary*

Patriots Who Followed Arnold to Canada at the Start of the American Revolution. California: Savas Beatie, 2012.

_____. *Benedict Arnold's Army: The 1775 American Invasion of Canada during the Revolutionary War.* New York: Savas Beatie, 2008.

Lehman, Eric D. *Homegrown Terror: Benedict Arnold and the Burning of New London.* Middletown, CT: Wesleyan University Press, 2014.

Lesser, Charles H. *The Sinews of Independence: Monthly Strength Reports of the Continental Army.* Chicago: University of Chicago Press, 1976.

Letters of Delegates to Congress, 1774–1789. Paul H. Smith, editor; Gerard W. Gawalt, Rosemary Fry Plakas, Eugene R. Sheridan, assistant editors. Washington: Library of Congress, 1976–2000. Online at Library of Congress, American Memory.

Lincoln, Benjamin Papers. ProQuest, Reel #2.

Linklater, Andro. *An Artist in Treason: Extraordinary Double Life of General James Wilkinson.* New York: Walker, 2009.

Linn, John Blair, and William H. Egle, eds. *Pennsylvania in the War of the Revolution, Battalion and Line 1775–1783.* 2 vols. Harrisburg: Lane S. Hart, 1880.

Lippard, George. *Washington and His Generals: or, Legends of the Revolution.* Philadelphia: G. B. Zieber, 1847. Also published as *The Legends of the American Revolution "1776." or Washington and his Generals.* Philadelphia: T.B. Peterson & Brothers, 1876.

Lossing, Benson J. *The Life and Times of Philip Schuyler.* 2 vols. New York: Sheldon, 1873 (1st edition, 1860).

_____. *The Pictorial Field-Book of the Revolution.* 2 vols. New York: Harper & Brothers, 1860 (1st edition, 1850–52).

Luzader, John F. *Saratoga: A Military History of the Decisive Campaign of the American Revolution.* New York and California: Savas Beatie, 2008.

Lynch, Patricia. *The Impact of the Revolution on Local Government: Concord, Gloucester, and Pittsfield 1763–1789.* Louisiana State University Historical Dissertation, 1978.

Lynch, Wayne. "Debating Arnold's Role at Freeman's Farm." *Journal of the American Revolution.* Sept. 12, 2013. Online at allthingsliberty.com.

MacDonald, Mary Lee. "Seth Warner: A True Hero from the New Hampshire Grants." *Vermont History* 86, no. 2 (Summer/Fall 2018), 67–94.

Mahan, Alfred T. *The Major Operations of the Navies in the War of American Independence.* Boston: Little, Brown, 1913.

_____. "The Naval Campaign of 1776 on Lake Champlain." *Scribner's Magazine* 23, no. 2 (Feb., 1898), 147–60.

Malcolm, Joyce Lee. *The Tragedy of Benedict Arnold: An American Life.* New York: Pegasus Books, 2018.

Marshall, Christopher, and William Duane, ed. *Extracts from the Diary of Christopher Marshall Kept in Philadelphia and Lancaster during the American Revolution, 1774–1781.* Albany: Joel Munsell, 1877.

Martin, James Kirby, *Benedict Arnold: Revolutionary Hero; An American Warrior Reconsidered.* New York: NYU Press, 1997.

Massachusetts Soldiers and Sailors of the Revolutionary War. 17 vols. Boston: Wright & Potter Printing, 1896–1908.

Maxey, David W. *Treason on Trial in Revolutionary Pennsylvania: The Case of John Roberts, Miller.* Philadelphia: American Philosophical Society, 2011.

Meigs, Return Jonathan, and Charles I. Bushnell, ed. *Journal of the Expedition against Quebec, Under Command of Col. Benedict Arnold, In the Year 1775.* New York: Privately printed, 1864.

Melvin, James, and Andrew A. Melvin, ed. *The Journal of James Melvin, Private Soldier in Arnold's Expedition against Quebec in the Year 1775.* Portland, ME: Hubbard W. Bryant, 1902.

Messer, Peter C. "'A Species of Treason & Not the Least Dangerous Kind': The Treason Trials of Abraham Carlisle and John Roberts." *Pennsylvania Magazine of History and Biography* 123, no. 4 (Oct. 1999), 303–332.

Mintz, Max M. *The Generals of Saratoga: John Burgoyne & Horatio Gates.* New Haven: Yale University Press, 1990.

Minutes of the Albany Committee of Correspondence 1775–1778, 1. James Sullivan, director and state historian. 2 vols. Albany: University of the State of New York, 1923.

Minutes of the Supreme Executive Council of Pennsylvania from Its Organization to the Termination of the Revolution, 1776 to 1779, vol. 11; 1779 to 1781, vol. 12. Harrisburg: Theo. Penn, 1852–1853.

Montresor, John, and G. D. Scull, ed. "Journals of Capt. John Montresor 1757–1778." *Collections of the New York Historical Society for the Year 1881.* New York: New-York Historical Society, 1882.

Moore, Howard Parker. *A Life of General John Stark of New Hampshire.* New York: Privately printed, 1949.

Morgan, Daniel. "General Daniel Morgan. An Autobiography." *The Historical Magazine, and Notes and Queries* 9, 2nd ser. (June 1871). Morrisania, NY: Henry B. Dawson, 1871.

Morison, George. *An Interesting Journal of Occurrences during the Expedition to Quebec Conducted by the Celebrated Arnold at the Commencement of the American Revolution.* Tarrytown, NY: William Abbatt, 1916 (1st edition, Hagerstown, MD: James Magee, 1803).

Morrison, John T. *Tryon County and Sir William Johnson: Historical Sketch and Revolutionary Chronicles of "The Dark and Bloody*

Ground" (c. 1922). www.fulton.nygenweb.net/history/150Anniv.html

Morton, Doris Begor. *Philip Skene of Skenesborough*. Granville, NY: Grastorf Press, 1959.

Murdoch, Richard K. "Benedict Arnold and the Owners of the Charming Nancy." *Pennsylvania Magazine of History and Biography* 84, no. 1 (Jan. 1960), 22–55.

Nash, Gary B. *The Unknown American Revolution: The Unruly Birth of Democracy and the Struggle to Create America*. New York: Viking, 2005.

Naval Documents of the American Revolution 1–6. William James Morgan, ed. Washington: Naval History Division, Dept. of the Navy, 1964–1972.

Neilson, Charles. *An Original, Compiled, and Corrected Account of Burgoyne's Campaign: And the Memorable Battles of Bemis's Heights, Sept. 19, and Oct. 7, 1777*. Albany: J. Munsell, 1844.

Nelson, James L. *Benedict Arnold's Navy: The Ragtag Fleet that Lost the Battle of Lake Champlain but Won the American Revolution*. Camden, ME: McGraw-Hill, 2006.

Nelson, Murray. "Colonel John Brown, 'A Prophet Hath No Honor in his own Country.'" Massachusetts Historical Society, Ms. S-24.

Nelson, Paul David. "The Gates-Arnold Quarrel, September 1777." *The New-York Historical Society Quarterly* 55, no. 3 (July 1971), 235–52.

_____. *General Horatio Gates: A Biography*. Louisiana State University Press, Baton Rouge, 1976.

Nelson, Peter. "Learned's Expedition to the Relief of Fort Stanwix." *Quarterly Journal of the New York State Historical Association* 9, no. 4 (Oct., 1928), 380–85.

New England Historical and Genealogical Register 18. Albany: J. Munsell, 1864.

New Hampshire Provincial and State Papers 8; *Documents and Record Relating to the State of New-Hampshire during the Period of the American Revolution from 1776 to 1783*. Nathaniel Bouton, ed. Concord, NH: Edward A, Jenks, 1874.

New Hampshire Provincial and State Papers 30; *Miscellaneous Revolutionary Documents of New Hampshire*. Albert Stillman Batchellor, ed. Manchester, NH: John B. Clarke, 1910.

New York in the Revolution as Colony and State. 2nd edition. James A. Roberts, comptroller. Albany: Press of Brandow Printing, 1898.

Nickerson, Hoffman. *The Turning Point of the Revolution, Or Burgoyne in America*. Boston: Houghton Mifflin, 1928.

O'Callaghan, E.B., ed. *Documentary History of the State of New York* 4. Albany: Charles Van Bethuysen, 1851.

Orderly Book of the Northern Army, at Ticonderoga and Mt. Independence from October 17th, 1776, to January 8th, 1777, with Biographical and Explanatory Notes and an Appendix. Albany: J. Munsell, 1859.

Papers of the Continental Congress, Fold 3, www.fold3.com.

Peckham, Howard H. *The Toll of Independence: Engagements & Battle Casualties of the American Revolution*. Chicago: University of Chicago Press, 1974.

Pell, John. *Ethan Allen*. Boston: Houghton Mifflin, 1929.

Philbrick, Nathaniel. *Valiant Ambition: George Washington, Benedict Arnold, and the Fate of the American Revolution*. New York: Viking, 2016.

Phillips, Kevin. *1775: A Good Year for Revolution*. New York: Penguin Books, 2012.

Porter, Elisha, and Appleton Morgan, ed. "The Diary of Colonel Elisha Porter, of Hadley, Massachusetts." *Magazine of American History* 30, pp. 187–205. New York, A.S. Barnes, 1893.

Proceedings of a General Court Martial for the Trial of Major General St. Clair; Collections of the New-York Historical Society for the Year 1880. New York: New-York Historical Society, 1881.

Quarles, Benjamin. *The Negro in the American Revolution*. Chapel Hill: University of North Carolina Press, 1961.

Ramsay, David. *The History of the American Revolution*. 2 vols. Philadelphia: R. Aitken & Son, 1789.

Randall, Willard Sterne. *Benedict Arnold: Patriot and Traitor*. Barnes & Noble, 1999 (1st edition, William Marrow, 1990).

_____. *Ethan Allen: His Life and Times*. New York: W.W. Norton, 2011.

Raphael, Ray. *The First American Revolution: Before Lexington and Concord*. New York: New Press, 2002.

Reed, William B. *Life and Correspondence of Joseph Reed*. 2 vols. Philadelphia: Lindsay and Blakiston, 1847.

_____. *President Reed of Pennsylvania: A Reply to Mr. George Bancroft and Others*. Philadelphia: Howard Challen, John Campbell, 1867.

The Remembrancer or, Impartial Repository of Public Events For the year 1776. London: J. Almon, 1777.

Ritzema, Rudolphus. "Journal of Col. Rudolphus Ritzema." *Magazine of American History* 1, pp. 98–107. New York: A.S. Barnes, 1877.

Robbins, Ammi. *Journal of the Rev. Ammi R. Robbins, A Chaplain in the American Army in the Northern Campaign of 1776*. New Haven: B.L. Hamlen, 1850.

Roberts, Kenneth. *Arundel*. Camden, ME: Down East Books, 1995 (1st edition, Doubleday, 1929–30).

_____. *Black Magic*. New York: Bobbs-Merrill, 1924.

_____. *I Wanted to Write*. Garden City, NY: Doubleday, 1949.

_____. *March to Quebec: Journals of the Members of Arnold's Expedition*. Garden City, NY: Doubleday, 1946.

_____. *Rabble in Arms*. Garden City, NY: Doubleday, 1957 (1st edition, 1933).

_____. *Why Europe Leaves Home*. Indianapolis: Bobbs-Merrill, 1922.

Roberts, Lemuel. *Memoirs of Captain Lemuel Roberts*. Bennington: Anthony Haswell, 1809.

Roche, John F. *Joseph Reed: A Moderate in the American Revolution*. New York: Columbia University Press, 1957.

Roof, Garret L. *Colonel John Brown: His Services in the Revolutionary War, Battle of Stone Arabia; Oneida Historical Society*. Utica: Ellis H. Roberts, 1884.

Rowland, Kate Mason. *The Life of Charles Carroll of Carrollton, 1737–1832 with his Correspondence and Public Papers*. New York: G.P. Putnam's Son, 1898.

St. Clair, Arthur, U.S. House of Representatives. *Narrative of the Manner in which the Campaign against the Indians, in the Year 1790 Was Conducted, Under the Command of Major General St. Clair*. Philadelphia: Jane Aitken, 1812.

_____, William Henry Smith, ed. *The St. Clair Papers: The Life and Public Services of Arthur St. Clair*. Cincinnati: Robert Clarke, 1882.

Salsig, Doyen. *Parole: Quebec; Countersign: Ticonderoga: Second New Jersey Regimental Orderly Book 1776*. Cranbury, NJ: Associate University Presses, 1980.

Sanguinet, Simon. *L'Invasion du Canada par les Bastonnois: Journal de M. Sanguinet*. Ministère des Affaires culturelles, 1975.

Schuyler, Philip. *Philp Schuyler Papers*. New York Public Library, digitalcollections.nypl.org.

Sedgwick Family Papers, Massachusetts Historical Society.

Sellers, Charles Coleman. *Benedict Arnold: The Proud Warrior*. New York: Minton, Balch, 1930.

Senter, Isaac. "The Journal of Isaac Senter, Physician and Surgeon to the Troops Detached from the American Army Encamped at Cambridge, Mass., On a Secret Expedition against Quebec." *Proceedings of the Historical Society of Pennsylvania* 1, no. 5 (March 1846).

Sheinkin, Steve. *The Notorious Benedict Arnold: A True Story of Adventure, Heroism & Treachery*. Nonfiction for young adults. New York: Roaring Brook Press, 2010.

Shelton, Hal T. *General Richard Montgomery and the American Revolution: from Redcoat to Rebel*. New York: NYU Press, 1994.

Simms, Jeptha Root. *The Frontiersmen of New York: Showing Customs of the Indians, Vicissitudes of the Pioneer White Settlers, and Border Strife in Two Wars*. Albany: Geo. C. Riggs, 1883.

_____. *The History of Schoharie County and Border Warfare*. Albany: Munsell & Tanner, 1845.

Slade, William, ed. *Vermont State Papers: 1779–1786*. Middlebury: J.W. Copeland, 1823.

Smith, C. Page. "The Attack on Fort Wilson." *Pennsylvania Magazine of History and Biography* 78, no. 2 (Apr., 1954), 177–88.

Smith, Joseph E. A. *The History of Pittsfield (Berkshire County,) Massachusetts, from the Year 1734 to the Year 1800*. Boston: Lee and Shepard, 1869.

Smith, Justin H. *Arnold's March from Cambridge to Quebec: A Critical Study*. New York: G.P. Putnam's Sons, 1903.

_____. *Our Struggle for the Fourteenth Colony: Canada and the American Revolution*. 2 vols. New York: G. P. Putnam's Sons, 1907.

Snow, Dean. *1777: Tipping Point at Saratoga*. Oxford University Press, 2016.

Sparks, Jared, ed. *Correspondence of the American Revolution; Being Letters of Eminent Men to George Washington, from the Time of His Taking Command of the Army to the End of his Presidency*. Boston: Little, Brown, 1853.

_____. *The Life and Treason of Benedict Arnold*. Boston: Hilliard, Gray, 1835.

Specht, Johann Friedrich; Helga Doblin, trans.; Mary C. Lynn, ed.; and Donald M. Londahl-Smidt, military notes. *The Specht Journal: A Military Journal of the Burgoyne Campaign*. Westport, CT: Greenwood Press, 1995.

Spooner, Thomas. *Records of William Spooner, Plymouth, Mass., and His Descendants*. Cincinnati, 1883.

Stackhouse, Asa Matlack. "Col. Timothy Matlack, Patriot and Soldier: A Paper Read Before the Gloucester County Historical Society at the Old Tavern House, Haddonfield, N. J. April 14, 1908." Printed privately, 1910.

Stark, Caleb. "The Life and Services of Maj. Gen. John Stark." *Reminiscences of the French War*. Concord, NH: Luther Roby, 1831.

_____. *Memoir and Official Correspondence of Gen. John Stark*. Concord, NH: G.P. Lyon, 1860.

Stevens, John Austin. "Benedict Arnold and His Apologist." *Magazine of American History with Notes and Queries* 4, p. 181–91. New York: A.S. Barnes, 1880.

Stillé, Charles J. *Major-General Anthony Wayne and the Pennsylvania Line in the Continental Army*. Philadelphia: J.B. Lippincott, 1893.

Stimson, Frederic Jesup. *My Story: Being the Memoirs of Benedict Arnold; Late Major General in the Continental Army and Brigadier-General in that of His Britannic Majesty*. A novel. New York: Charles Scribner's Sons, 1917.

Stocking, Abner. *An Interesting Journal of Abner Stocking of Chatham, Connecticut, Detailing the Distressing Events of the Expedition Against Quebec Under the Command of Col. Arnold in the Year 1775*. Tarrytown, NY: William Abbatt, 1921 (1st edition, Catskill, NY: Eagle Office, 1810).

Stone, William Leete. *The Campaign of Lieut. Gen. John Burgoyne, and the Expedition of Lieut. Col. Barry St. Leger*. Albany: Joel Munsell, 1877.

_____. *Life of Joseph Brant (Thayendanegea)*. 2 vols. Albany: J. Munsell, 1865 (1st edition, 1838).

_____, Max von Eelking. *Memoirs and Letters and*

Journals of Major General Riedesel. Albany: J. Munsell, 1868.

_____. *Visits to the Saratoga Battle-Grounds 1780–1880 with Introduction and Notes.* Albany: Joel Munsell's Sons, 1895.

Sullivan, Edward Dean. *Benedict Arnold: Military Racketeer.* New York: Vanguard Press, 1932.

Sumner, William H. "Colonel Brooks and Captain Bancroft." *Proceedings of the Massachusetts Historical Society 1855–1858,* vol. 3 (Feb. 1858), 265–77.

Taylor, Robert J. *Western Massachusetts in the Revolution.* Providence: Brown University Press, 1954.

Thacher, James. *A Military Journal during the American Revolutionary War from 1775 to 1783 Describing Interesting Events and Transactions of this Period,* 2nd edition. Boston: Cotton & Bernard, 1827.

Thayer, Simeon, and Edwin Martin Stone, ed. *Journal of Captain Simeon Thayer Describing the Perils and Sufferings of the Army under Colonel Benedict Arnold, in Its March through the Wilderness to Quebec.* Providence: Knowles, Anthony, 1867.

Todd, Charles Burr. *The Real Benedict Arnold.* New York: A.S. Barnes, 1903.

Topham, John. "The Journal of Captain John Topham, 1775–76." Arnold Expedition Historical Society, www.arnoldsmarch.com/research

Trumbull, Benjamin. "Benjamin Trumbull's Journal of the Expedition against Canada, 1775." *Collections of the Connecticut Historical Society* 7, pp. 175–218. Hartford, 1899.

Trumbull, J. Hammond. *Memorial History of Hartford County, Connecticut.* Boston: E.L. Osgood, 1886.

Trumbull, John. *Autobiography, Reminiscences and Letters of John Trumbull from 1756 to 1841.* New York: Wiley & Putnam, 1841.

Updike, Wilkins. *Memoirs of the Rhode-Island Bar.* Boston: Thomas H. Webb, 1842.

Van Cortlandt, Philip, and Pierre C. Van Wyck, ed. "Autobiography of Philip Van Cortlandt: Brigadier-General in the Continental Army." *Magazine of American History with Notes and Queries* 2, pp. 278–98. New York: A.S. Barnes, 1878.

Van Doren, Carl. *Secret History of the American Revolution.* New York: Viking Press, 1941.

Van Schaack, Henry Cruger. "Col. John Brown: A Lecture Delivered before the Lyceum in Manlius New York, & at Fayetteville" (1857). Massachusetts Historical Society Ms. S-24.

Vose, Joseph, and Henry Winchester Cunningham, ed. *Journal of Lieutenant-Colonel Joseph Vose, April-July, 1776.* Cambridge: John Wilson & Son, 1905.

Walker, Lewis Burd. "Life of Margaret Shippen, Wife of Benedict Arnold." *Pennsylvania Magazine of History & Biography* 25, no. 1 (1901), 20–46.

Wallace, Willard M. *Traitorous Hero: The Life and Fortunes of Benedict Arnold.* New York: Harper & Brothers, 1954.

Walworth, Ellen Hardin. *Saratoga: The Battle—Battleground—Visitor's Guide with Maps.* New York: American News, 1877.

Ward, Harry M. *General William Maxwell and the New Jersey Continentals.* Westport, CT: Greenwood Press, 1997.

Warren, Mercy Otis. *History of the Rise, Progress and Termination of the American Revolution: Interspersed with Biographical, Political and Moral Observations.* 3 vols. Boston: Manning & Loring, 1805.

Watson, Winslow C. *Pioneer History of the Champlain Valley Being an Account of the Settlement of the Town of Willsborough by William Gilliland.* Albany: J. Munsell, 1863.

Watt, Gavin K., and James Morrison, research assistance. *The Burning of the Valleys: Daring Raids from Canada against the New York Frontier in the Fall of 1780.* Toronto: Dundurn Press, 1997.

_____. *Rebellion in the Mohawk Valley: The St. Leger Expedition of 1777.* Toronto: Dundurn Press, 2002.

Wells, Bayze. "Journal of Bayze Wells of Farmington: May, 1775-February,1777, at the Northward and in Canada." *Collections of the Connecticut Historical Society* 7, pp. 241–296. Hartford: Published by the Society, 1879.

Wickman, Donald H., and Mount Independence Coalition. *Strong Ground: Mount Independence and the American Revolution.* Orwell, VT: Mount Independence Coalition, 2017.

Wilbur, James Benjamin. *Ira Allen, Founder of Vermont 1751–1814.* 2 vols. Boston: Houghton Mifflin, 1928.

Wilkinson, James. *Memoirs of My Own Times.* 3 vols. Philadelphia: Abraham Small, 1816.

Williams, Samuel. "Historical Memoirs of Colonel Seth Warner." *The Natural and Civil History of Vermont,* 2nd edition, vol. 2, pp. 445–50. Burlington, VT: Samuel Mills, 1809.

Zeoli, Stephen. *Mount Independence: The Enduring Legacy of a Unique Historic Place.* Hubbardton, VT: Stephen Zeoli, 2011.

Index

Numbers in ***bold italics*** indicate pages with illustrations

abatis 156
Abenaki 92
abolition of slavery 177; *see also* slavery
Adams, John: on appointment of officers 135; on Arnold 137, 138; on Cedars surrender 88, 101; and Massachusetts constitution 185; on retreat from Canada 100; on smallpox 101
Adams, Samuel ***11***; and Brown 12, 15–16; and Fort Ticonderoga 18; and Massachusetts Provincial Congress 11–12; on Schuyler, Philip 142
"Address to the Armies of the United States of America" (Humphreys) 190–91
African Americans *see* Blacks
ague 119
Ainslie, Thomas 70, 72–73, 81, 84
Albany (NY) 128; Arnold/Brown conflict 131, 135; and British strategy 139, 185; headquarters of Northern Army 127–28; Schuyler home 36, 37
Albany Committee of Correspondence 12, 25, 26
Albany Committee of Safety 128
Albany County militia 162
Alexander, William 136
Allen, Ebenezer 125, 155
Allen, Ethan ***23***; and Arnold 21–22, 25, 29, 30, 32, 183–84; attack on Montréal 45–47; background 22; Brown on 38–39; captured at Montréal 47; and Continental Congress 33; Fort Ticonderoga 19, 20, 22–23, 24; French and Indian War 22; Gilliland, William on 31; historians on 22, 46; and Hough, Benjamin 13; inclusion on muster roll 79; and Montgomery, Richard 38; New Hampshire Grants 12; personality 22; recruits troops in Canada 45; St. John (Canada), capture of 29–30, 45; and Schuyler, Philip 38, 42; and Young, Thomas 12

Allen, Hemen 18, 19
Allen, Ira 40, 46, 72
Allen, Lucy 85
Allen, Thomas 142, 152, ***172***, 172–73, 185
Allin, John-Baptiste 125
American Heritage 149
American Party 194
Anderson, John 22
André, John 49, 180, 184, 193
Andros, Edmund 7
Anstruther, William 52
Antill, Edward 54, 68–69, 96, 97–98
Appalachian Mountain Club 58
Armstrong, John 151, 163
Arnold, Benedict ***21***, ***164***; Adams, John on 137, 138; aggressiveness 7, 9; and Allen, Ethan 21–22, 25, 29, 30, 32, 183–84; on alliance with France 195; and André, John 180; Arnold, Isaac on 96, 125–26, 148, 162, 176, 182, 194; attack on Canassadaga 90–92; attack on Québec 67–69; Bacheller, Nathaniel on 162; background 22; Battle of Bemis Heights (Second Saratoga) 151, 161–67; Battle of Freeman's Farm (First Saratoga) 158–59; Beebe, Lewis on 92–93, 97, 103; British general 184; Brooks, John on 161, 164, 165; and Brown 51, 77, 78–79, 91, 114, 131, 196 (*see also* thirteen charges against Benedict Arnold); Burr, Aaron on 62; calls for invasion of Canada 33; on Canadian campaign 94; Carroll, Charles on 83; on casualties 74; charged with profiteering 175–76; claims for reimbursement 182; command at West Point 183–84; and Commissioners to Canada 83, 93; and Connecticut Footguards 17; on Connecticut Militia 137; and Continental Congress 135, 137–38, 174; council at Camp Disaster 61; council in Chambly 90–91; court-martial of 179–81; Crown Point 29, 37; Danbury Raid 136–37; and de Haas, Philip 91, 103; death of wife 37; destruction of New London (CT) 92; Duer, William on 35; early career 7, 9, 22; and Easton, James 27, 32, 36, 117; and Enos, Roger 61; epistolary warfare 32; fake Indian names for 149, 150, 212*nn*36–37; finances 182; on Fort George 37; Fort Schuyler rescue expedition 148–49; on Fort Ticonderoga 24–25, 37; Fort Wilson Riot 180; Foster, Lafayette on 163; and Franks, David 176; and Fraser, Simon 163–64; French and Indian War 22; Gates, Horatio on 4, 105, 108, 115; and Gates, Horatio 103, 109, 118–19, 120, 129–30, 157–58, 160; on Gates, Horatio 101, 183; and Gilliland, William 31, 37, 114;

231

Gordon, William on 125, 164; greed 182, 183; and Green Mountain Boys 30, 33; and Hanchet, Oliver 63, 67, 69, 70; and Hancock, John 78; and Hazen, Moses 90, 95, 97, 103, 106–8, 129, 130–31, 180; and Hendricks, William 68; Henry, John Joseph on 54, 67; and Hinman, Benjamin 33, 35; historians on 4, 22, 28, 34, 57, 62, 70, 91, 96, 107, 125; honorable discharge ordered 31; hospitalized 174; and inoculation 85; Lachine (Canada) 88–89; leadership 54, 57, 61–62, 64, 71, 132, 157–58; Lee, Richard Henry on 124, 138; Lewis, Morgan on 131, 135; lifestyle 176, 179; Lippard, George on 165; Livingston, Henry Brockholst on 160; and Loyalists 176, 183; Mahan, Alfred Thayer on 126, 195; marriage 22, 176; and Massachusetts Provincial Congress 33, 34; Matlack, Timothy on 179; Mattoon, Ebenezer on 161, 165; Maxwell, William on 124; and McCormick, James 57; memorandum book 32, 34, 35; military governor of Philadelphia 174–77; Mohawk Valley 148–49; and Montgomery, Richard 69, 76; monument to 166, *166*, *195*; and Morgan, Daniel 57–58, 68, 159–60; Morison, George on 62; Mott, Edward on 34, 35; and Mount Independence 102, 103, 104; and naval fleet 104–5, 119; negotiations with British 180; Ogden, Mathias on 109; and Pennsylvania Supreme Executive Council 174–82; and Philadelphia turmoil 180; Philbrick, Nathaniel on 175; on plan to capture Newport 135, 136; plan to capture Skenesborough 20; plundering 51, 96–97, 113; Poor, Enoch on 108; and Porter/Trumbull dispute 105–6; prisoner exchange 90, 91; profiteering 175–76; promotion 136, 137; and quartering of soldiers 85; Ramsay, David on 125; on Reed, Joseph 180, 181; Reed, William on 176; reputation 4, 69–70, 91, 125–26, 135, 136, 137, 193–96; resignation 34, 146; retreat from Canada 97, 98; on return of prisoners 89; Roberts, Kenneth on 54, 195–96; and St. Clair, Arthur 146; St. John (Canada), capture of 29–30; and Schuyler, Philip 37, 74, 111, 115; seizure of supplies in Montréal 95–97, 107–8, 179; Senter, Isaac on 74; service as private citizen 146, 160; and Shippen, Peggy 176; and siege of Québec 67–73; and smallpox 80–81, 85–86; Smith, Justin on 70; and Smith, Matthew 68; Sparks, Jared on 194; and Sullivan, John 93, 94, 98; treason 4, 182, 184, 195; treatment of the sick 97; on Tryon County militia 149; Valcour Island, Battle of 118–23; Van Cortlandt, Philip on 164; Van Doren, Carl on 176; Varick, Richard on 158; and War Board 137–38, 179, 196; and Warner, Seth 81; Warren, Mercy Otis on 125; and Washington, George 54–55, 132, 137, 146, 174, 181; Wayne, Anthony on 193; Wilkinson, James on 90, 91, 125, 158, 160, 163, 165; Woodruff, Samuel on 163; and Wooster, David 17, 51, 74, 77–78, 81; wounded 73, 74–75, 165; Wynkoop, Cornelius on 105; and Wynkoop, Jacobus 109–11; *see also* Québec, Arnold expedition to; thirteen charges against Benedict Arnold; "Veritas"

Arnold, Benedict (governor of Rhode Island) 7

Arnold, Isaac: on Arnold 96, 125–26, 148, 162, 176, 182, 194; on Battle of Bemis Heights (Second Saratoga) 162; on Battle of Freeman's Farm (First Saratoga) 158; on Brown 130; on Shippen, Peggy 176; on Washington, George 182

Arnold, Margaret "Peggy" 176–77

Arnold, Oliver 7, 9, 174

Arnold, Richard 7

Arnold Bay 123

Arnold Expedition Historical Society 58, 207*n*1

Arnold Pond 65

Arnold River 63

Arthur, Mr. 145
Articles of War 51, 129
Arundel (Roberts) 53–54, 118
Ashley, John 10
Ashley, John, Jr. 186
Augusta (ME) 56
Austin, Jonathan Loring 171

Bacheller, Nathaniel 162
Bacon, Mathew 174
Baie de Vaudreuil 89
Baker, Remember 32, 39–40
Balcarres Redoubt 164
Baldwin, Jeduthan: Battle of Freeman's Farm 160; bridge across Hudson River 151; on Brown's Raid 159; Fort Ticonderoga 127; and Gilliland, William 114; Mount Independence 117, 124; retreat from Canada 98
Ball, Josiah 143
Bancroft, George 175
Bancroft, James 165
Barbé-Marbois, François 182
Barber Farm 162
Barker, Joseph 9
Basking Ridge (NJ) 131
battles. *see* specific battle locations
Bayley, Frye 87, 167
Beaumarchais, Pierre-Augustin Caron de 171
Beautiful Meadow 65
Bedel, Timothy: on Brown 117; Canadian campaign 44, 50; cashiered 52, 103, 117; Cedars 87, 88; court-martial 87, 103; military career 103
Beebe, Lewis: on Arnold 92–92, 97, 103; Fort Ticonderoga/Mount Independence 127; on illness at forts 116; on retreat from Canada 99; on smallpox inoculation 85; on Thomas, John 86, 92–93; Yale 9
Bemis Heights (Second Saratoga), Battle of 161–71, *164*; Arnold, Isaac on 162; Brooks, John 165; Burgoyne, John 151, 161–71; and Continental Congress 159; Dearborn, Henry 161, 165, 171; Gates, Horatio 161–70; historians on 162, 163; Learned, Ebenezer 162, 163, 165; Lincoln, Benjamin 161; location 151; Morgan, Daniel 151, 159, 161, 162, 163; Poor, Enoch 162; significance 162; Wilkinson, James on 151, 161–62, 163, 165

Benedict Arnold: Military Racketeer (Sullivan) 96
Bennington (VT) 12–13, 19, 20, 148
Bennington, Battle of 152, 159, 167
Berkshire Constitutionalists 173
Berkshire County, politics 10–11, 172–73
Berkshire County Court 10–11, 173
Berkshire County militia: and Brown 141–42, 143, 166, 172; and Burgoyne retreat 166; and Burgoyne's advance 141–42, 143, 152; in Mohawk Valley 185–89
Berkshire levies 186
Berthier (Canada) 49
Bethlehem (PA) 132
Bigelow, Timothy 60
Birmingham (NJ) 133
Bishop, Reuben 57
"Black Horse and His Rider" (Lippard) 165
Black Magic (Roberts) 54
Blacks 22, 76, 147, 174; *see also* abolition of slavery; slavery
Bland, Humphrey 106
Board of Treasury 182
Board of War *see* War Board
Bond, William 107, 128
Boot Monument **166**
Boquet River 112
Boston Committee of Correspondence 12
Boston Tea Party 10
Brandt, Clare 130, 176
Brant, Joseph 185
Braunschweigers 141; *see also* Germans
Brewer, Samuel 85, 93, 115
Breymann Redoubt 165
Brickett, James 115, 127
British Army, retreat from Saratoga 167–69
British Army, strength: Battle of Stone Arabia 189; Chambly 48; Crown Point 14, 26, 170; Fort Ticonderoga 14, 24, 139; St. John 29–30, 31, 39, 42; Saratoga surrender 170–71; Trois-Riviéres 95
British Library 187
Brooks, John: on Arnold 161, 164, 165; Battle of Bemis Heights (Second Saratoga) 165; and Burgoyne's retreat 169; on Gates, Horatio 161; on Learned, Ebenezer 148; Mohawk Valley 149
Brown, Abijah 115

Brown, Andrew 115
Brown, Benjamin 115
Brown, Daniel 7
Brown, Elizabeth 7, 9
Brown, Henry Clinton 9, 192
Brown, Huldah Kilbourne 9–10, 173, 174, 186
Brown, Jacob 71, 75
Brown, John: and Adams, Samuel 12, 15–16; and Albany Committee of Correspondence 25; on Allen, Ethan 38–39; Allen, Ira on 46; appointed judge 173; appointed major 35; and Arnold 4, 51, 77–79, 91, 114, 129, 131, 178, 196; Arnold, Isaac on 130; and Arnold's treason 187, 219*ch*18*n*10; and Arthur, Mr. 145; attack on Montréal 45–46; attack on Québec 72; attack on the *Fell* (snow) 49–50; background 3, 7, 9; Battle of Stone Arabia 187–89; and Bayley, Frye 167; Bedel, Timothy on 117; and Berkshire County Court 10; and Berkshire County militia 41–42, 143, 166, 172; and Berkshire County politics 172–73; Brandt, Clare on 130; Brumwell, Stephen on 130; and Burgoyne's advance 152; Canada, emissary to 12–16; Canada, retreat from 97; Cochran, Robert on 117; Committee for Foreign Affairs on 171; and Continental Congress 3, 5, 24–26, 78, 134, 159, 172, 179, 196, 218*n*26; council in Chambly 90–91; death 3, 92, 188–91; demands surrender of British fleet 50; and Dubois, Lewis 76, 78, 187; Duggan, Jeremiah on 78; and Easton, James 101–2, 179; estate of 174, 186; eyesight 79, 117, 153; finances 182; Fort Chambly 3, 47–49; Fort Paris 187; Fort Schuyler 115; Fort Ticonderoga 3, 13, 16, 18–19, 22, 23, 24, 115, 141, 142; on French Canadians 14–15; and Gates, Horatio 4, 5, 133–34, 201–2; and Hancock, John 5, 134; historians on 4, 130, 196; *History of Pittsfield* (Smith) on 3, 135; Humphreys, David on 190–91; on invasion of Canada 40; on Kahnawake Indians 15; King's

attorney 9; and La Corne, Luc de 47; Lachine (Canada) 88–89; and Lee, Ann 186; Lewis, Morgan on 131, 135; and Livingston, James 40, 48, 117; Martin, James Kirby on 130; and Massachusetts House of Representatives 172; and Massachusetts Provincial Congress 11–12; and Matlack, Timothy 178–79; memorialized 190–92, **191**; Montgomery, Richard 44, 47, 49, 69, 71; Mott, Edward on 20; Mott, Gershom on 117; Mount Independence 115; plundering, accusations of 3, 51, 52, 71, 77, 96, 114; Prescott surrenders to 50–51; promotion 50, 71, 81, 102, 185; property inventory 173–74; and Reed, Joseph 178; report on British fleet 41; reputation 70; requests trials 4, 134; resignation 134, 172; Satterlee, William on 117; and Schuyler, Philip 4, 42, 117, 145; and Sedgwick, Theodore 4; seizure of British vessels 3; siege of Quebec 3, 70–73, 76, 83; skirmish north of St. John 43–44; and smallpox inoculation 81; Smith, Justin on 72; Sparks, Jared on 130; spying mission 39–40; Stockbridge convention 10; Trois-Riviéres 101; Van Doren, Carl on 130; on War Board 179; on Warner, Jonathan 156; and Washington, George 5, 134; whistleblower 4; and Wooster, David 71, 81; Yale 9; *see also* Berkshire County militia; Brown's Raid; thirteen charges against Benedict Arnold
Brown, John (of Providence) 3
Brown, John (Private) 115
Brown, John Henry 173
Brown, Jonathan 31
Brown, Mehitable Sanford 7
Brown, Thomas 174
Brown University 7
Brown's Raid 152–57, **154**; Baldwin, Jeduthan on 159; and Burgoyne's retreat 168, 169; Committee for Foreign Affairs on 159; and Lincoln, Benjamin 152, 153; spoils of 155–56, 159; and Warner, Seth 153; Washington, George on 159

Brumwell, Stephen 130
Bull, Epaphras 19, 20, 21, 22
Bunker Hill, Battle of 33
Burgoyne, John: advance to south 139, 141–43; Battle of Bemis Heights (Second Saratoga) 151, 161–71; Battle of Freeman's Farm (First Saratoga) 158–59; on road building 143; surrender 169–71; Wilkinson, James on 167
Burke, Thomas 135
Burr, Aaron 62, 69, 76, 176
Burr, C. Chauncey 149–50
Butler, Richard 179–80
Butler's Loyalist Rangers 185
Butterfield, Isaac 87, 103
Button (Buttonmould) Bay 112, 113

Cady, Jeremiah 79, 97
Caghnawaga Mohawks *see* Kahnawake Mohawks
Cambridge (MA) 54, 55
Cambridge (NY) 152
Camden (SC) 183
Camp Disaster 61
Campbell, Donald 76, 78
Canada, French *see* French Canadians
Canassadaga Mohawks *see* Kanesatake Mohawks
Cape Diamond **68**, 71
Caratunk Falls 58
Carey & Hart (publisher) 193
Carleton (schooner) 121, 123, 156
Carleton, Christopher 185
Carleton, Guy **76**; Battle of Quebec 69, 71; on Battle of Trois-Riviére 95; on Battle of Valcour Island 126–27; escape 50; and fireship 82; and Montgomery, Richard 47; and St. John relief 49
Carlyle, Thomas 54, 196
Carroll, Charles: on Arnold 83; Cedars 87; Commissioner to Canada 50, 82, 83; and inoculation 85; and seizure of supplies in Montréal 95; and War Board 138
Carroll, John 82
cartel (prisoner exchange agreement) 90–91
Cartwright's Inn 128
Castleton (VT) 20
Catamount Tavern 19
Catholicism *see* Roman Catholicism
Caughnawaga (Canada) 15
Caughnawaga Mohawks *see* Kahnawake Mohawks

Cedars, The **88**; Adams, John on 88, 101; American surrender 87–88; and Bedel, Timothy 87–88; Hancock, John on 91
Chadwick, Edmund 163
Chambly (Canada): location 39–40; Porter, Elisha on 84; and seized goods 95–96, 103–4, 129, 130; war council 90–91; *see also* Fort Chambly
Chapman, John Jay 195
Charlan, Pierre 39, 40
Charming Nancy (schooner) 181
Chase, Samuel: Cedars 87; Commissioner to Canada 82, 83; and inoculation 85; and seizure of supplies in Montréal 95; on Thomas, John 92
Chaudiere Pond *see* Lac-Mégantic
Chaudiére River 55, 60, 64–65
Cheeseman, Jacob 73
Cheshire's Mill 105
Chester, Leonard 163
Chimney Point 14
Church, Benjamin 12, 37
Civil War 3, 194–95
Clark, Stephen 208n17
Clerke, Francis 162
Clinton, George 186, 189
Clinton, Henry 169, 170, 180
Clinton, James 76–77
Coates, John 80
Cochran, Robert: attack on Québec 72; on Brown 117; and Burgoyne's retreat 168; finances 183; Fort Edward 167; Fort Schuyler 150; grave 183; Green Mountain Boys 13, 20, 28; spying mission 39–40; witness in thirteen charges 78, 80
Coercive Acts 10, 85
Cogan, Patrick 142
Colburn, Reuben 56
Combahee River, Battle of the 191
Commissioners to Canada: and Arnold 83, 93; and The Cedars 87; on discharged soldiers 88; instructions from Continental Congress 82–83; on provisions 85; and seizure of supplies in Montréal 95, 96; on smallpox inoculation 85; and Thomas, John 92; on Wooster, David 91
Committee for Foreign Affairs 159, 171
Common Sense (Paine) 173
Conestoga Indians 92

Congress (row-galley) 120, 121, 123
Connecticut Courant 142
Connecticut Footguards 17
Connecticut Military Record 1775–1848 115
Connecticut Militia 137
Connecticut Wits 190
Constitutionalists 173, 185
Continental Congress: and Allen, Ethan 33; appointment of new officers 135–36; and Arnold 135, 137–38, 174; Articles of War 129; and Battle of Freeman's Farm (First Saratoga) 159, 171; and Brown 3, 5, 24–26, 78, 134, 159, 172, 179, 196, 218n26; and Burgoyne's surrender 170; and French Canada 11; hearing into Causes of the Miscarriages in Canada 96, 102; journal of 175; orders invasion of Canada 38; papers of 134; payment of officers 182; prisoner exchange agreement 91; and retreat from Canada 101–2; and Warner, Seth 33, 102; and Wooster, David 102, 135; *see also* Board of Treasury; Commissioners to Canada; Committee for Foreign Affairs; War Board
Convention Army *see* British Army
Copley, John Singleton **11**
Cornplanter (Seneca chief) 185
Cornwallis, Charles 183
Coudray, Philippe Charles Tronson du 145–46
court-martials: Arnold 179–81; Bedel, Timothy 103; Enos, Roger 62–63, 93; Hazen, Moses 95–96, 104, 106–8; St. Clair, Arthur 146–47
Cramahé, Hector T. 68
Crisis, The (Paine) 129
Cross, Ralph 170–71
Cross, Uriah 84
Crown Point: and Arnold 29, 37; burned 123; capture by Warner, Seth 25; and retreat from Canada 100; Schuyler, Philip on 38; strength 14, 29
Crown Point-Chimney Point narrows 14
Cumberland Head 120
Cuyler, Abraham 25

Danbury Raid 136–38, 190
"Dark Eagle" 149, 150, 194, 215n36

Darley, Stephen 207*n*1
Darth Vader 193
Davis, Matthew L. 62
Day, Thomas 114
Dead River 60
Deane, Barnabas 30, 31
Deane, Silas 30, 36, 80, 171, 181
Dearborn, Henry: Arnold expedition to Québec 65; Battle of Bemis Heights (Second Saratoga) 161, 165, 171; on Battle of Freeman's Farm (First Saratoga) 160; captive in Québec 80; on Gates, Horatio 150–51; later career 165
Death of General Montgomery in the Attack on Quebec, December 31, 1775 (Trumbull) **72**
Deblois, Elizabeth "Betsy" 135, 136, 176
Declaration of Independence 85, 104, 178
de Haas, Philip 89, 90; Arnold on 91; declines promotion 107, 136; and French and Indian War 90; and Hazen, Moses court-martial 107; Lachine (Canada) 89; possible arrest 103; witness in thirteen charges 91
Delaplace, William 23–24, 36
Delaware River 131, 132–33
de Peyster, John Watts 166, 195
Deschambault (Canada) 84, 94
deserters 75
de Woedtke, Frederick William 94, 99
Diamond Island (Lake George) 156–57
Dominion of New England 7
Dovecote (NY) 167
Down, Jacob 147
Dresden (NY) 153
Dubois, Lewis 76, 78, 187–88, 189
Duer, William 28, 35
Duggan, Jeremiah 47–49, 77–78, 114
Dunlap's Pennsylvania Packet 26, 177, 178, 179
Du Roi, Anton Adolph Heinrich 170
Du Simitière, Pierre Eugène **175**

Easton (NJ) 132
Easton, James: and Arnold 27, 32, 36, 117; and Berkshire County politics 173; and Brown 101–2, 179; finances 182; Fort Ticonderoga 18–19, 20, 22, 27; *History of Pittsfield* (Smith) on 19; imprisoned 101–2; and Massachusetts Congress 24, 26–27; Montgomery, Richard on 52; and plundering 51, 52, 78; promoted 35, 49; reputation 36; tavern keeper 18; trial called for 179
Easton, James, Jr. 185
Elmore, Samuel 28
Elmore's Connecticut State Regiment 115
Emerson, William 13–14
Enos, Roger: and Arnold 61; court-martial 62–63, 93; and provisions 60, 61, 62; role in Arnold's expedition to Quebec 54, 58; and Stark, John 63; and Sullivan, John 63, 93; witness in thirteen charges 54
Enterprise (sloop) 31, 32, 34, 35, 39, 104
epistolary warfare 32

Faden, William **75, 122**
Fairfield (CT) 136
Falconer, William 174
Falls of Richelieu 84
Fassett, John 44, 45
Fay, Jonas 52
Febiger, Christian 67
Fell (snow) 50
Fellows, John 142, 145, 166–67
Feltham, Jocelyn 23–24
Ferris Bay 123
fireship 81–82
Fischer, David Hackett 124
Fishkill (Fish Creek) 166, 168, 170
Flexner, James 218*n*17
Following in Their Footsteps (Clark) 208*n*17
Forster, George 87, 90
Fort Albany 128
Fort Ann 105, 143, 145
Fort Ann, Battle of 143, **144**
Fort Chambly **48**; *see also* Chambly (Canada); and Brown 3, 39–40, 47–49; burned 98; Smith, Justin on 48
Fort Dayton 148
Fort Edward 142–45, 146, 167–68
Fort Frederick 128
Fort George 13, 25, 37
Fort Griswold 92
Fort Halifax 55

Fort Hardy 169, 170
Fort Hunter 187
Fort Keyser 189
Fort Lennox National Historic Site 98
Fort Montgomery 169
Fort Paris 187, 188, 189
Fort Plain 186
Fort Plain (NY) 186
Fort Rensselaer 186, 187, 189
Fort Schuyler 115, 145, 147–50, 159, 186
Fort Stanwix *see* Fort Schuyler
Fort Ticonderoga **110, 116**; and Allen, Ethan 19, 20, 22–23, 24; Allen, Thomas on retreat from 142; American capture of 17–19, 21–24, **23**; American command at 24, 25; American retreat from 141–43, **144**; and Arnold 17–18, 22, 37; British retreat from 127; and Brown 3, 13, 16, 18–19, 22, 23, 24, 115, 141, 142; and Brown's Raid 153–56; Cogan, Patrick on retreat from 142; Emerson, William on 13–14; French Lines 104, 127, 141, 155; and Herrick, Samuel 31, 33, 34, 168; and Hinman, Benjamin 31, 37; illness 139; and Mott, Edward 18, 19, 20, 21, 24; and retreat of American fleet 123; St. Clair, Arthur command 139–43; Schuyler, Philip on 38; strength 14, 29, 116, 127, 139, 141; Trumbull, John on 127; Washington, George on 141
Fort Western 56
Fort William Henry 13
Fort Wilson Riot 180
Foster, Jedediah 28, 33–34
Foster, Lafayette 163
Fox, Ansel 119
France 171, 195
Franklin, Benjamin 77, 82–83, 85, 171, 178
Franks, David 176, 183
Fraser, Simon 95, 158, 163–64
Frazer, Persifor 147
Frederick Haldimand Papers 187
Free Quakers 177; *see also* Quakers
Freeman, Elizabeth 174
Freeman, John 158
Freeman's Farm (First Saratoga), Battle of 158–59, 160
French and Indian War: Allen, Ethan 22; Arnold 22; de Haas, Philip 90; geography

13; Hanchet, Oliver 61; Hazen, Moses 90; Montgomery, Richard 41; Morgan, Daniel 57; Schuyler, Philip 36; Wynkoop, Jacobus 109
French Canadians: Brown on 14–15, 40; colonial attitudes toward 11; Smith, Justin on 75; Wells, Bayze on 39–40
French Lines 104, 127, 141, 155
Friends of Order 173
Fultonville (NY) 187

Gage, Thomas 11, 109
Gardinerstown (ME) 56
Gaspé (schooner) 47, 49, 50
Gates (row-galley) 127
Gates, Horatio: ambitions 128–29; and Arnold 4, 101, 103, 105, 108, 109, 115, 118–19, 120, 129–30, 157–58, 160, 183; Bacheller, Nathaniel on 162; background 100–101, *101*; Battle of Bemis Heights (Second Saratoga) 161–70; Battle of Freeman's Farm (First Saratoga) 158–59; on Battle of Valcour Island 124; Brooks, John on 161; and Brown 4, 5, 133–34, 201–2; and Brown's Raid 159; and Burgoyne's surrender 170; command of Northern Army 100; Committee for Foreign Affairs on 171; Dearborn, Henry on 150–51; and Fort Ticonderoga/Mount Independence 117, 127; illness 132; leadership 157–58; Mattoon, Ebenezer on 161; and Mount Independence 102; on plundering 113; and Schuyler, Philip 100, 139, 147, 148; on Skenesborough ship construction 104; and smallpox inoculation 81; and Stark, John 167; Varick, Richard on 158; and Washington, George 131–32; on Waterbury, David 120–21; and Wilkinson, James 131–32, 150, 158, 160, 162; and Wynkoop, Jacobus 109, 111
Germain, George 127
Germans: Battle of Bemis Heights (Second Saratoga) 165, 167, 171; Battle of Bennington 152; Battle of Freeman's Farm (First Saratoga) 158; Battle of Trenton 132–33; Bennington (VT) 148; Fort Ticonderoga 141; and Johnson, John 185; Mount Independence 156; New London (CT) 92; *see also* Braunschweigers; Hessians; Jaegers
Gilliland, William *112*; on Allen, Ethan 31; and Arnold 31, 37, 114; and Arnold/Allen dispute 30–31; arrested 114; and Baldwin, Jeduthan 114; and British army 141; and plundering 113–14; slaves 31; support for troops 14, 112–13
Glover, John 168, 169, 170
Gnadenhutten Massacre 92
gondolas 104
Goodrich, William 54, 57, 65
Gordon, William 125, 164
Grand Isle (VT) 117
Grand River 88, 89
Great Barrington (MA) 173
Great Carrying Place 60
Great Man Theory 196
Great Swamp 134
Greaton, John 128
Green Mountain Boys 30, 33, 37, 38
Greene, Christopher 57–58, 62, 63, 73
Greene, Nathanael 63, 133, 145, 193
Greene, William 193
Greenwood, John 98, 99, 132–33
Griswold, Rufus W. 194
gunboats 104

Haldimand, Frederick 14, 187, 189
Half Moon (NY) 145
Hall, Isaac 65
Hamilton (musical) 190
Hamilton, Alexander 190
Hamilton, James Inglis 158
Hanchet, Oliver: and Arnold 63, 67, 69, 70; Arnold's expedition to Québec 61, 63; and French and Indian War 61; leadership in Québec 73; military career 73; Montgomery, Richard on 70; and siege of Québec 67; Thayer, Simeon on 69
Hancock (MA) 173
Hancock, John: and Arnold 78; on British threat 139; and Brown 5, 134; on The Cedars 91; and Massachusetts Provincial Congress 11–12
Harmar, Josiah 179–80
Hartford Wits 190
Hartley, Thomas 113, 114, 123
Haverstraw Bay 184
Hawley, Joseph 11

Hazen, Moses: and Arnold 90, 95, 97, 103, 106–8, 129, 130–31, 180; arrest 103; on Canadians 42, 83; council in Chambly 90–91; court-martial 95–96, 104, 106–8; and French and Indian War 90; house burned 98; on Loyalists 92; prisoner 51; and retreat from Canada 97–98; witness in thirteen charges 91, 93
Headley, Joel T. 194, 195
"Heap Fighting Chief" 149, 150, 212*n*37
Hendricks, William 57, 68
Henry, John Joseph 54, 67, 68, 79
Henshaw, Joseph 31
Herkimer (NY) 148
Herkimer, Nicholas 147–48
Heroes, Hero-Worship, and the Heroic in History (Carlyle) 54
Herrick, Samuel: Brown's Raid 153, 155; Fort Ticonderoga 31, 33, 34, 168; sent to Skenesborough 20
Hessians 128, 132, 133; *see also* Germans
Hinman, Benjamin: and Arnold 33, 35; command at Crown Point 33, 34; Fort Ticonderoga 31, 37; invasion of Canada 44; witness in thirteen charges 28
historians: on Allen, Ethan 22, 46; on Arnold 4, 22, 28, 34, 57, 62, 70, 91, 96, 107, 125; on Battle of Bemis Heights (Second Saratoga) 162, 163; on Battle of Valcour Island 118, 125; on Brown 4, 130, 196; on defeat in Canada 102; on Fort Wilson Riot 180; on Pennsylvania turmoil 177; on Reed, Joseph 175, 177; on retreat from Fort Ticonderoga/Mount Independence 143; on thirteen charges 130, 178
History of Pittsfield (Smith); on Allen, Thomas 172–73; on Ashley, John, Jr. 186; on Battle of Québec 72; on Battle of Stone Arabia 188–89; on Brown 3, 135; on Easton, James 19
Holland House 74, 76, 83, 84
Hough, Benjamin 13
House, Lieutenant 52
"How a Madman Helped Save the Colonies" 149

Howe, Robert 179, 180
Howe, William 139, 145, 147, 176
Hoyt, Winthrop 13, 15
Hubbard, Jonas 70
Hubbardton, Battle of 143, *144*, 155
Hudson Falls (NY) 183
Hudson River *140*; and Gates, Horatio 170; navigability 142; as travel route 12, 13, 25; and Washington, George 180; West Point 183, 184
Humphreys, David 9, ***190***, 190–91

Île d'Orléans (Canada) 81, 84
Île-aux-Noix (Canada) 42, 98, 99, 185
Île-aux-Têtes 119
illness 115–16, 119, 139; *see also* ague; malaria; measles; smallpox
Independent Company of New York Artillery 51
Indians 149–50, 189; *see also* Abenaki; Conestoga Indians; Iroquois; Kahnawake Mohawks; Kanesatake Mohawks; Lenni Lenape; Mohawks; Mohicans; St. Francis Abenaki; Senecas; Stockbridge Mohicans
Inflexible (square rigged ship) 121, 123
Influence of Sea Power upon History 1660–1783 (Mahan) 126
Ingersoll, Huldah 186; *see also* Brown, Huldah Kilbourne
Ingersoll, Jared 9, 186
Ingraham, Edward D. 194
Intolerable Acts 10, 85
Iroquois 92, 149, 180, 185
Irvine, William 95, 179–80
Isaac Van Campen's Inn 131
Isis (frigate) 84
Isle la Motte (VT) 42, 99

Jaegers 185; *see also* Germans
Jaffry (black soldier) 147
Jefferson, Thomas 13, 102
John Trumbull, Autobiography (Trumbull) ***106***
Johnson, John 92, 185–89
Johnson, Martin 52
Johnson, Samuel 153, 154
Johnson, William 9
Johnstown (NY) 9
Jones's Tavern 106
Journal de Paris 190
Journal of the Continental Congress 175

Kahnawake (Canada) 15, 39
Kahnawake Mohawks 13, 15, 87
Kanesatake Mohawks 90–92
Katherine (schooner) 20, 29; *see also Liberty* (schooner)
Keator's Rift 188
Kennebec River 53–60, ***59***
Kilbourne, Huldah *see* Brown, Huldah Kilbourne
King's Arms Tavern 128
Kingston (NY) 131
Kittatinny Ridge 131
Klock's Field, Battle of 189
Know Nothings 194
Knox, Henry 29, 135, 145
Knox, Lucy 135
Kosciuszko, Thaddeus 151

La Prairie (Canada) 15, 46
Lac aux Araignées 65–66
Lac des Deux Montagnes 90, 92
Lac des Joncs 65
Lachine (Canada) 88–89
Lac-Mégantic 55, 63, ***64***, 65, 66
La Corne, Luc de 47, 51
Lady's Magazine or Entertaining Companion for the Fair Sex 27
Lafayette, Marquis de 190
Lake Champlain ***29***; American strategy 20, 26, 30, 41, 98, 100, 102, 126; British strategy 139, 141, 168, 185; travel on 12–14
Lake Flagstaff 60
Lake George Landing 38, 141, 153–56
Lake Megantic *see* Lac-Mégantic
Lake of Two Mountains 90, 92
Lamb, John 73, 183, 184
Lamb, Roger 143
Lansing, John 187
Laurens, John 190–91
Learned, Ebenezer: Battle of Bemis Heights (Second Saratoga) 162, 163, 165; Brooks, John on 148; and Burgoyne's retreat 168, 169; relief of Fort Schuyler 148, 150; retreat from Fort Ticonderoga/Mount Independence 142; Wilkinson, John on 148
Lee, Ann 186
Lee, Arthur 171
Lee, Charles 33, 63, 129, 131–32
Lee, Richard Henry 124, 138
Legger, John 39–40
L'Enfant, Pierre Charles ***183***

Lenni Lenape 92
Les Cédres *see* Cedars, The
Lévis (Canada) 67
Lewis, Morgan: and American vessels 128; on Arnold 131, 135; Battle of Freeman's Farm (First Saratoga) 163; on Brown 131, 135; and Burgoyne's surrender 170
Lexington and Concord (MA) 17
Liberty (schooner) 29, 31, 34, 41, 104, 110; *see also Katherine* (schooner)
Life and Times of Philip Schuyler (Lossing) 148
Lincoln, Benjamin: Battle of Bemis Heights (Second Saratoga) 161; Brown's Raid 152, 153; promotion 136, 159; and Schuyler, Philip 148; and Washington, George 174; wounded 167
Lippard, George ***149***, 149–50, 165, 194, 217*ch*16*n*14
Livingston, Henry Brockholst 157–58, 160
Livingston, James: and Arnold treason 184; Battle of Québec 71, 76; and Brown 40, 48, 117; colonel of Canadian regiment 49; Fort Chambly 47–49; and Montgomery, Richard 48–49; and Schuyler, Philip 42
Long Island, Battle of 133
Longueuil 46, 49, 85, 98
Longueuil, Battle of 66
Lossing, Benson 148
Loyal Convert (gondola) 123
Loyalists: and Arnold 176, 183; Hazen, Moses on 92; in Mohawk Valley 185; and Reed, Joseph 174; Schuyler, Philip on 147; and Sullivan, John 92; Willsboro (NY) 113
Lucifer 193, 196
Lyman, Phineas 61

MacLean, Allan 49, 68
Macpherson, John 73
Magazine of American History 194
Mahan, Alfred Thayer 126, ***126***, 195
Major Operations of the Navies in the War of American Independence (Mahan) 126
malaria 119
Malcolm, Joyce Lee 176–77
Malmedy, Francis Marquis de 170
Man in the Mirror (Brandt) 130

Index

Maria (schooner) 121, 123, 126, 156
Martin (sloop) 84
Martin, James Kirby 130
Massachusetts Committee of Safety 18, 19
Massachusetts constitution 185
Massachusetts House of Representatives 172, 173
Massachusetts Provincial Congress 11, 26–27, 33, 182
Massachusetts Spy or, American Oracle of Liberty 27
Matlack, Timothy 176, *177*, 177–79, 181
Mattoon, Ebenezer 161, 163, 165
Maxwell, William 95, 107, 124, 180
McCormick, James 57
measles 152
Meigs, Return Jonathan 58, 61, 74
Memoirs of My Own Times (Wilkinson) 89, 125
Mènard, Joseph 39, 40
Metcalf, Simon 40
Mettowee River 152
Middlebrook (NJ) 179
Middlebury (VT) 141
Mifflin, Thomas 136
military officers, election of 20, 185
Milton, John 193
Mohawk River Valley *140*; and Arnold 148–49; Battle of Oriskany 147; and British strategy 139; and Brown 9, 185–89; diversity in 9; and Johnson, John 185–89; and Schuyler, Philip 148
Mohawks 15, 90, 185
Mohicans 9, 115
Money, John 143, 145
Montgomery, Richard *41*; and Allen, Ethan 38; on Arnold 69; on Arnold's expedition to Québec 47; attack on Québec 70–71; background 41–42; brings provisions to Québec 69; and Brown 44, 47, 49, 69, 71; and Carleton, Guy 47; death *72*, 73; on Easton, James 52; Fort Ticonderoga 40; French and Indian War 41; on Hanchet, Oliver 70; invasion of Canada 41–44; inventory of effects 76; on La Corne, Luc de 47 ; and Livingston, James 48–49; on New England soldiers 45; and plundering 51–52, 96; on Prescott, Richard 52; siege of St. John 45; signs Montréal capitulation 50
Montréal *15*; Allen, Ethan attack 45–47; Arnold seizure of supplies 51, 95–97, 179; Brown mission to 14–16; and Commissioners to Canada 83; retreat from 98; surrender to Montgomery 50
Montresor, John 14, 55, *64*
Morgan, Daniel: and Arnold 57–58, 68, 159–60; Arnold expedition to Québec 61, 65; background 57; Battle of Québec 73; Battles of Saratoga 151, 159, 161, 162, 163; and Burgoyne's retreat 168; Camp Disaster 61; command of riflemen 55; French and Indian War 57; siege of Québec 67, 70
Morison, George 62, 66
Morristown (NJ) 131, 134, 181
Morton, John 77–78
Motel Arnold 65
Mott, Edward: on Arnold 34, 35; on Brown 20; Fort Ticonderoga 18, 19, 20, 21, 24
Mott, Gershom 117
Mott, Samuel 47
Mount Bigelow 60
Mount Defiance 141, 155
Mount Hope 141
Mount Independence *106*, *110*, *116*, *157*; Allen, Thomas on American retreat from 142; American retreat from 141–43, *144*; and Arnold 102, 103, 104; British retreat from 127; and Brown 115, 155–56; and Brown's Raid 153–57; and Germans 156; illness 139; named 103–4; Patrick Cogan on American retreat from 142; and St. Clair, Arthur 139–43; strength 116–17, 127, 139, 141; Trumbull, John on 127
Mount Pleasant 176
Mumbet (freed slave) 174
Murphy, Tim 163
Murray, James 90
Mussolini 54

Narrative of Colonel Ethan Allen (Allen) 22–23, 30, 45, 46
Nason, Stephen (fictional character) 54
Natanis (as fictional character) 150
Native American Party 194
Natives *see* Indians
"Naval Campaign of 1776 on Lake Champlain" (Mahan) 126
naval fleet, American 104–5, 111–12, *120*
naval fleet, British 121, 123, 127
Neilson, John 151
Neilson House 161
Neuville (Canada) 69
New Abridgment of the Law (Bacon) 174
New England Chronicle 26–27
New Englanders 45, 145, 147; *see also* military officers, election of
New Hampshire Grants 12–13; *see also* Vermont
New Hampshire Provincial Congress 27
New London (CT) 92, 132
New York Committee of Correspondence 25
New York Provincial Congress 38
Newburyport (MA) 55
Newport (RI) 132, 135, 136
newspaper accounts, invented details 27
New-York Journal 32
Nixon, John 168, 169
Norridgewock Falls 58
Norris's Tavern 180
North Hero (VT) 117
North River 147
Northern Army, conflict over command 82, 100, 139, 148, 150–51
Northern Army, strength 75, 79, 80, 82, 85, 162, 169
Northwest Passage (Roberts) 92

Ogden, Mathias 76, 109, 184, 212*n*3
Oka (Canada) 92
Oriskany, Battle of 147, 150
Ottawa River 88, 89
Otter River 141

Packet see Dunlap's Pennsylvania Packet
Paine, Robert Treat 173
Paine, Thomas 129, 172–73
Paradise Lost (Milton) 193, 196
Parker, Giles 188
Parsons, Samuel 17–18
Passy (France) 171
Paterson, John 87, 107
Patten, Thomas *15*

Pawlet (VT) 152, 153
Paxton Boys 57–58, 92
Peale, Charles Willson *41*, 101
Peale, James *101*
Peale, Rembrandt *177*
Peggy (brigantine) 81–82
Peirce, Nathan 79
Penn Mansion 176
Pennsylvania Constitution 177, 178
Pennsylvania Packet see Dunlap's Pennsylvania Packet
Pennsylvania Supreme Executive Council 58, 174–82
Philadelphia (gondola) 105, 118, *119*, *120*, 121
Philadelphia (PA); and Allen, Ethan 33; and Arnold 174–77; and Brown 26, 101–2; turmoil in 177, 180
Philbrick, Nathaniel 175
Phillips, Kevin 195
Pittsfield (MA): and Allen, Thomas 152, 172–73; Black soldiers 147; and Boston Tea Party 10; and Brown 12, 134, 135; population 9; smallpox inoculation 80; *see also* Berkshire County militia; *History of Pittsfield* (Smith)
plundering: Arnold accused of 51, 96–97; and Articles of War 51–52; Brown accused of 3, 51, 71, 77, 114; Easton, James accused of 78; Gates, Horatio on 113; Gilliland, William complains of 113–14; and Montgomery, Richard 51–52, 96; Washington, George on 55; Wells, Bayze on 113
Poe, Edgar Allen 149
Pointe Lévy (Canada) 67
Pointe-aux-Tremble (Canada) 69
Pomeroy, Seth 11–12
Poor, Enoch 106–8, 136, 160, 162
Popham (ME) 55
portages *see* Arnold expedition to Québec: portages
Porter, Elisha: and Hazen, Moses court-martial 107; illness 128; retreat from Canada 50, 84, 98, 99; and Trumbull, John 105–6
Potts, Jonathan 158
Powell, Henry Watson 155
Prescott, Richard 47, 50, 52, 133
Preston, Charles 42
Price of Freedom (exhibit) 118
Primer, Leonard 110

Prince (black soldier) 147
Pringle, Thomas 121, 123
prisoner exchange 90, 91
Proceedings of a General Court Martial for the Trial of Major General Arnold 181
profiteering 175–76
prostitutes 79
Providence (gondola) 112, 113
Putnam, Israel 15

Quakers 174, 177, 178
Quartering Act 85
quartering of soldiers 85
Québec, Arnold expedition to 53–66, *56*, *59*; Arnold on 60, 61, 63, 64, 66; bateaux 56, 58, *59*, 64, 65; Camp Disaster 61; casualties 57, 65, 66; Clark, Stephen on 208n17; Dead River 60; duration 60; Fort Western 56–57; illness 58, 61, 62; launch 55; Montgomery, Richard on 47; Montresor map 55; ordered by Washington, George 54–55; portages 58, *59*, 60, 63; provisions 58, 60, 61–63, 64, 65, 66; rations 58, 60, 61, 68; route 55, 58; Smith, Justin on 62–63, 65; weather 58, 60, 62
Québec, Battle of *72*; and Arnold 68 and Brown 72; *History of Pittsfield* (Smith) on 72; and Livingston, James 71, 76; and Montgomery, Richard 70–71; *see also* Québec, siege of
Québec, city 68, *75*, 79–80
Québec, province 10, 26
Québec, siege of 67–73; American surrender 73; and Brown 3, 70–73, 76, 83; ended 83–84; and Morgan, Daniel 67, 70; smallpox 79–80, 101; *see also* Québec, Battle of
Quebec Act 10, 11
Quebec Gazette 75
Quincy, Josiah 83

Rabble in Arms (Roberts) 118, 195–96
Ramsay, David 125
Randolph, Peyton 26
Rattlesnake Hill 102; *see also* Mount Independence
rattlesnakes 155
Read, George 26
Redding (CT) 136
Reed, Joseph *175*; Arnold on 180, 181; and Brown 35, 178;

Flexner, James on 218n17; historians on 175, 177, 218n17; and Loyalists 174; and Pennsylvania Supreme Executive Council 174; and Philadelphia turmoil 180; Philbrick, Nathaniel on 175
Reed, William 176
Remembrancer 27, 75
Remington, Zadock 20
Republican Society 180
Resolves of Congress 91, 97
return (inventory) 68, 85
Revenge (schooner) 104, 110
Revere, Paul 11
Rhode Island College 7
Richelieu River 14, 42, *43*, *88*, 98; *see also* Chambly (Canada); Île-aux-Noix (Canada); St. John (Canada)
Ridgefield, Battle of *see* Danbury Raid
Robbins, Ami 116
Roberts, Kenneth *53*, 53–54; on Abenaki 92; on Arnold 54, 62, 118, 195–96; on historical fiction 207n2
Roberts, Lemuel 153
Roche, John F. 175
Rogers, Robert 92
Roman Catholicism 11, 40, 45, 55
Romans, Bernard 19
Rome (NY) 115
Root, Oliver 189
Ross, Betsy 177–78
Rossiter, David 152
row-galleys 104–5
Royal Highland Emigrants 42, 49, 73, 84
Royal Savage (schooner) 47, 104, 109, 110, *120*, 121
Ruggles, Benjamin 153
Rupert (VT) 20
Rush, Benjamin 151
Rush Lake 65
Rutland (VT) 13

Sabin, Josiah 80–81
Sacramento River 92
Safford, Samuel 79
Saint-Augustin-de-Woburn (Canada) 65
St. Clair, Arthur *141*; approach of British fleet 127; and Arnold 146; Battle of Trenton 133; court-martial 146–47; Fort Ticonderoga/Mount Independence 139–43; invasion of Canada 94; late career 147; promoted 136
St. Clair Papers 141
St. Francis (Canada) 39, 92

St. Francis Abenaki 13
Saint-Georges (Canada) 64
Saint-Jean *see* St. John (Canada)
St. John (Canada); abandoned by Americans 98; and Allen, Ethan 29–30, 45; location 14; refortified 31, 39, 42; shipyard 41; siege of 45–49; surrender of 49, 51–52
St. John Gate 67, 71, 73
St. Lawrence River **15**, **43**, **68**, **88**
St. Leger, Barry 150, 168
St. Roch (Canada) 70, 74, 77
Sainte-Anne (Canada) 89
Sainte-Anne-de-Bellevue (Canada) 89
Salem (NY) 152
Sand Creek 92
Sandisfield (MA) 7
Sandy Hill (NY) 183
Saratoga (NY) 166, 167
Saratoga, First Battle of *see* Freeman's Farm, Battle of
Saratoga, Second Battle of *see* Bemis Heights, Battle of
Saratoga National Historical Park 166, 195
Sartigan (Canada) 64, 65, 66
Satterlee, William 28, 34, 117
Saturday Evening Post 53–54, 196
Saturday Night Live 131
Scammell, Alexander 190
Schoharie Creek 187
Schuyler, Hermanus 104
Schuyler, Hon Yost 149, 150
Schuyler, Philip **36**; Adams, Samuel on 142; and Allen, Ethan 38; and Arnold 37, 74, 111, 115; background 36; Battles of Saratoga 151, 170; and Blacks 147; and British threat 141, 142; and Brown 4, 117, 145; command of Northern Army 100; command on Lake Champlain 142; on Crown Point 38; Deane, Silas on 36; on Fort Edward 146; on Fort Ticonderoga 38; French and Indian War 36; and Gates, Horatio 100, 139, 147, 148; and Green Mountain Boys 37, 38; headquarters 128; health 36, 42, 54; home 128, 168, 170; invasion of Canada 42–43; on Lake George Landing 38; letter to Canadians 42; and Lincoln, Benjamin 148; and Livingston, James 42; on Loyalists 147; Mohawk Valley 148;

Mount Independence 102; and New Englanders 145, 147; relieved of command 148; and siege of Québec 70; on Skenesborough ship construction 104; slaves 36; and Stark, John 148; and Warner, Seth 148; Wilkinson, James on 150; on Wynkoop, Jacobus 111
Schuyler's Island 123
Schuylerville (NY) 166
Scots Magazine 27
Scott, John Budd 95, 107
Scribner's 126
Second Battle of Saratoga *see* Bemis Heights (Second Saratoga), Battle of
Secret History of the America Revolution (Van Doren) 130
Sedgwick, John 107
Sedgwick, Theodore **93**; background 10; and Brown 4; and Friends of Order 173; and slavery 174; witness in thirteen charges 77, 85, 93, 133
Seneca Indians 178, 185
Senter, Isaac: on Arnold 74; Arnold's expedition to Québec 62, 66; Battle of Québec 67, 73; on Thomas, John 82; witness in thirteen charges 80
Seven Mile Stream 63, 65
1775: A Good Year for Revolution (Phillips) 195
Shakers 186
Sheel, Hugh 193
Sherburne, Henry 87, 88, 90, 133
Shippen, Edward 176
Shippen, Margaret "Peggy" 176–77
Shipwreck (Falconer) 174
Shoreham (VT) 21
Sillery (Canada) 69, 82
Silliman, Gold 136–37
Simitière, Eugène Du **21**
Simms, Jeptha 189
Simms, William Gilmore 194
Simonds, Isaiah 113, 119
Skene, Andrew 20
Skene, Philip 20, 22
Skenesborough (NY) 20, 21, 104–5, 143
Skowhegan Falls 58, **59**
slaves: and Frazer, Persifor 147; and Gilliland, William 31; Johnstown (NY) 9; and Matlack, Timothy 178; Pittsfield (MA) 9; and Schuyler, Philip 36; and Sedgwick, Theodore 174; and Skene,

Philip 22; soldiers 147; *see also* abolition of slavery
smallpox: abates 115; Adams, John on 101; and Brown 75; and defeat in Canada 102; inoculation 79–81, 82, 85, 134; and new troops 85; and retreat from Canada 98, 99; siege of Québec 70; and Washington's troops 134
Smith, Joseph E. A. *see History of Pittsfield* (Smith)
Smith, Justin: on Arnold 62–63, 68, 70; on Arnold expedition to Québec 62–63, 65; on Brown 72; on Fort Chambly 48; on French Canadians 75; on strength of Northern Army 75
Smith, Matthew 57–58, 68, 92
Smith, William 195
Smith's Tavern 20
Smithsonian Museum of American History 118
Snook Kill 168
Socialborough 13
Society of Friends *see* Quakers
Sorel (Canada); American retreat from 97–100; Arnold 94; and Bedel, Timothy 103; and Brown 49, 50, 51, 71, 77–78, 101; and Easton, James 49, 50, 102; Porter, Elisha on 50; smallpox 85; and Sullivan, John 93
Sorel River *see* Richelieu River
South Mountain 155
Sparding, John 24
Sparks, Jared 96, 130, 194
Spencer, Joseph 132, 135
Spider Lake 65–66
Split Rock 112, 119, 123
Spooner, Walter 28, 33–35, 173, 178
Sprakers (NY) 188
Stansbury, Joseph 183
Stark, John: Battle of Bennington 152, 167; Battle of Trenton 133; and Burgoyne's retreat 169; and Enos, Roger 63; and Gates, Horatio 167; illness 152; resignation 136; retreat from Canada 98; and Schuyler, Philip 148; Wilkinson, James on 133
Starke, John 156
Stark's Knob 169
Stephen, Adam 136
Stevens, John Austin 194
Stewart, James 40, 41
Stillwater (NY) 148, 151
Stirling, Lord 136

Stockbridge (MA) 9, 10
Stockbridge Mohicans 9, 115
Stocking, Abner 57
Stone Arabia (NY) 187, 188
Stone Arabia, Battle of 187–89, *188*
Stopford, Joseph 48
Stuart, Gilbert **190**
Suffolk Resolves 11
Sugar Hill 141
Sugar Loaf 141
Sullivan, Edward Dean 96
Sullivan, James: and Arnold 34–35; background 33–34; and Berkshire County politics 173; witness in thirteen charges 28, 33, 178
Sullivan, John: and Arnold 93, 94, 98; arrival in Canada 93; Battle of Trenton 133; Crown Point 100; and Enos, Roger 63, 93; and Iroquois 92, 180, 185; and Loyalists 92; retreat from Canada 98–99; on Thompson, William 94; threatens resignation 145; Trois-Riviére 94
Sunderland, Peleg 13, 15
Surprise (frigate) 84
Sutherland, Nicholas 167–68

Tappan Zee 184
taverns 19; *see also* names of specific taverns
Tekakwitha, Kateri 15
Teller's Point 184
Ten Broeck, Abraham 162
Ten Eyck, Barent 25
Terrible Carrying Place 63
Thayer, Simeon: on cannon fire 70; Fort Western incident 56–57; on Hanchet, Oliver 69; prison escape plot 73; and provisions 62; on swamp crossing 65
thirteen charges against Benedict Arnold; 1st 77; 2nd 78; 3rd 78; 4th 80–81; 5th 97; 6th 93–94; 7th 50, 51, 96; 8th 91; 9th 91; 10th 85; 11th 54; 12th 124–25; 13th 35, 178; core accusations 135; historians on 130, 178; Matlack, Timothy on 178–79; printed as handbill 135; published in *Dunlap's Pennsylvania Packet* 178; sent to Reed, Joseph 178; summary of 5; text 199–201; timing of 129; and War Board 129, 137–38
Thomas, John: Chase, Samuel on 92; command of Northern Army 82; and Commissioners to Canada 92; death 86, 92; retreat from Québec 84; Senter, Isaac on 82; siege of Québec 82–84; and smallpox inoculation 81, 82, 85
Thomas, Joshua 85
Thompson, William 91, 94–95
Thomson, Benjamin 96
Thomson, Charles 172, 178
Three-Mile Point 141
Thunderer (radeau) 121
Ticonic Falls 58
Titus (black soldier) 147
Topham, John 56–57, 69, 70
Tories *see* Loyalists
Town and Country Magazine 27
Traitor and the Spy (Flexner) 218*n*17
Treatise of Military Disciple (Bland) 106
Trenton (NJ) 132
Trenton, Battle of 133
Trois-Riviére (Canada) 84
Trois-Riviére, Battle of 94–95, 101, 180
Trumbull (row-galley) 120, 121, 127
Trumbull, John **36**, *72*, **93**, *106*, *141*; artist of the Revolution 106; on Fort Ticonderoga 127; on Mount Independence 127; and Porter, Elisha 105–6
Trumbull, Jonathan 18, 28
Tryon, William 136
Tryon County militia 149, 150
Twitter 32

United States, use of term 103

Vader, Darth 193
Valcour Island, Battle of 118–27, **120**, **122**; Arnold on 119–20, 123; Carleton, Guy on 126–27; Gates, Horatio on 124; historians on 118, 125; Wells, Bayze on 120, 121, 123; Wilkinson, James on 125
Valiant Ambition (Philbrick) 175
Valley Forge (PA) 174
Van Cortlandt, Philip 130, 164
Van Doren, Carl 130, 176
Van Epps (NY) 187
Van Rensselaer, Robert 186, 187–88, 189
Van Schaack, Henry Cruger 134–35
Van Schaick Island 148, 150
Varick, Richard 152, 157–58, 183
Vergennes, Comte de 171
"Veritas" 22–23, 32, 36
Vermont 141, 148; *see also* New Hampshire Grants
Voices from a Wilderness Expedition (Darley) 207*n*1
Von Steuben, Baron 183
Vose, Joseph 99, 100, 128
Vulture (sloop-of-war) 184

Walker, Thomas 14, 40, 51
Wallace, Richard 154–55
Wallace, Willard 96, 130, 195
Walloomsac River 152
Walpack Ridge 131
War Board: and Arnold 137–38, 178, 196; Brown on 179; and thirteen charges 129, 137–38
Ward, Samuel 65
Warner, Jonathan 153, 156
Warner, Seth: Allen, Ira on 46; and Arnold 81; and Arnold/Allen rivalry 32; attack on Montréal 46; Battle of Bennington 152; Battle of Hubbardton 143; Brown's Raid 153; and Burgoyne's retreat 169; and Burgoyne's surrender 170; on capture of Ethan Allen 47; commander 38, 79, 102; and Continental Congress 33, 102; Crown Point 25; finances 182–83; Fort Ticonderoga 20, 22, 24; frostbite 79; invasion of Canada 44; Longueuil 49; and Montgomery's effects 76; recruits 79; regiment returns home 50; retreat from Canada 97; and Schuyler, Philip 148; and smallpox inoculation 80; witness in thirteen charges 97
Warner, Seth (row-galley captain) 120, 121
Warren, Joseph 11–12, 15–16, 37
Warren, Mercy Otis 125
Washington (row-galley) 120, **120**, 121, 123, 125
Washington, George: and Arnold 54–55, 58, 132, 137, 146, 174, 181–82; Arnold, Isaac on 182; on Battle of Freeman's Farm 159; begins war 33; on British strategy 147; and British threat 141; and Brown 5, 134; on Brown's Raid 159; Committee for Foreign Affairs on 171; crossing the Delaware River 132–33; on Fort

Ticonderoga 141; and Gates, Horatio 131–32; and Humphreys, David 190; Lee, Charles on 131–32; and Lincoln, Benjamin 174; orders for expedition to Québec 58; on plundering 51; on retreat from Fort Ticonderoga/Mount Independence 142–43
Washington and His Generals (Headley) 194
Washington and His Generals (Lippard) 149–50, 165, 194
Washington and the Generals of the American Revolution (Griswold, Simms, Ingraham) 194
Washington's Crossing (Fischer) 124
Watchung Mountains 134
Waterbury, David 120–21, 123, 124–25
Watson, Edward 113
Watson, John 114
Watt, Gavin 186, 189
Watt, Isaac 174
Wayne, Anthony 95, 136, 139, 193
Weare, Meschech 133
Webb, Charles 30
Webster, Samuel 154–55
Weissenfels, Frederick 76, 78, 80, 170, 180
Wells, Bayze: aboard *Providence* (gondola) 112; on Battle of Valcour Island 120, 121, 123; on French Canadians 39–40; illness 119; on plundering 113; spy mission 39–40
West Point *183*, 183–84
West Trenton (NJ) 133
Whigs 177, 180
Whipple, William 167
whistleblowers 4, 196
White, William 174
White Creek (NY) 152
Whitehall (NY) 20
Why Europe Leaves Home (Roberts) 54
Wigglesworth, Edward 121, 124, 130
Wilkinson, James **89**; on Arnold 90, 91, 125, 158, 160, 163, 165; background 89–90; on Battle of Valcour Island 125; on Battles of Saratoga 151, 158, 161–62, 163, 165; and Burgoyne's retreat 167, 168; Burgoyne's surrender 169–70; and Gates, Horatio 131–32, 150, 158, 160, 162; and Gates/Arnold conflict 157–58; later career 165; on Learned, Ebenezer 148; *Memoirs of My Own Times* 89, 125; on retreat from Canada 98; on Schuyler, Philip 150; on seizure of supplies in Montréal 95; on Stark, John 133
Williams, Thomas 60
Williams, William 102
Willsboro (NY) 14, 112, 113, 141
Wilson, James 180
Winslow (ME) 55
Wintersmith, Charles **116**
witch hunt 175
witnesses to thirteen charges against Benedict Arnold: Allin, John-Baptiste 124–25; Antill, Edward 54, 96; Brewer, Samuel 85, 93; Cady, Jeremiah 97; Coates, John 80; Cochran, Robert 28, 78, 80; Colwell, James 96; de Haas, Philip 91; Dubois, Lewis 187; Duer, William 28; Duggan, Jeremiah 77–78; Enos, Roger 54; Foster, Jedediah 28, 33; Goodrich, William 54; Hazen, Moses 91, 93; Hinman, Benjamin 28; Patterson, John 96; Satterlee, William 28, 78; Sedgwick, Theodore 77, 85, 93, 133; Senter, Isaac 80; Spooner, Walter 28, 33, 178; Stoddard, Orringh 96; Sullivan, James 28, 33–34, 178; Thomas, Joshua 85; Tucker, Daniel 96; Warner, Seth 97; Waterbury, David 121, 124–25; Weissenfels, Frederick 78, 80; Wigglesworth, Edward 121, 124; *see also* individual names
Wood Creek 105, 143
Woodruff, Samuel 163
Wooster, David: and Arnold 17, 51, 74, 77–78, 81; background 17; and Brown 71, 81; and Continental Congress 102, 135; council in Chambly 90–91; Danbury Raid 136–37; death 137, 190; and fireship 82; Humphreys, David on 190; removed by Commissioners to Canada 91; Williams, William on 102
Wounded Knee 92
Wynkoop, Cornelius 105, 109
Wynkoop, Jacobus 109–11, 126

Yale 7, 9, 22, 85, 191
Yankees *see* New Englanders
Yates, Abraham 25
York (PA) 172
Young, Joseph 12
Young, Thomas 12

Zadock Remington's tavern 20
Zedwitz, Herman 76

www.ingramcontent.com/pod-product-compliance
Lightning Source LLC
Chambersburg PA
CBHW080803300426
44114CB00020B/2810